LEARNING Microsoft® Office Publisher 2003

Faithe Wempen

PEARSON
Prentice Hall
DDC

Vice President and Publisher: Natalie E. Anderson
Executive Acquisitions Editor: Jodi McPherson
Executive Editor: Jennifer Frew
Manufacturing Buyer: Natacha St. Hill Moore
Technical Editor: Lisa A. Bucki
Cover Designer: Amy Capuano
Composition: Shu Chen
Associate Director, Multimedia Production: Karen Goldsmith
Manager, Print Production: Christy Mahon
Printer/Binder: Quebecor World Book Services/Dubuque
Cover Printer: Phoenix Color Corporation

Credits and acknowledgements borrowed from other sources and reproduced, with permission, in this textbook are as follows:

PEARSON
Prentice Hall
DDC

10 9 8 7 6 5
ISBN 0-13-147642-4

Contents

Lesson 5: Creating Various Publications

Lesson 6: Creating Web and E-mail Content

Introduction

How We've Organized the Book

Each lesson in **Learning Microsoft® Office Publisher 2003** is made up of several exercises designed for using Publisher 2003 in real-life business settings. Every application exercise (except for the Critical Thinking exercises) is made up of seven key elements:

- **On the Job**. Each exercise starts with a brief description of how you would use the features of that exercise in the workplace.
- **Exercise Scenario**. The Publisher tools are then put into context by setting a scenario.
- **Terms**. Key terms are included and defined at the start of each exercise, so you can quickly refer back to them. The terms are then bolded in the text.
- **Notes**. Concise notes describe and outline the computer concepts.
- **Procedures**. Hands-on mouse and keyboard procedures teach all necessary skills.
- **Application Exercise**. Step-by-step instructions put your skills to work.
- **On Your Own**. Each exercise concludes with a critical thinking activity that you can work through on your own. You are challenged to come up with data and then additionally challenged to use the data in a presentation. The *On Your Own* sections can be used as additional reinforcement, for practice, or to test skill proficiency.
- In addition, each lesson ends with **Critical Thinking Exercises**. As with the *On Your Owns*, you need to rely on your own skills to complete the task.

Working with Data and Solution Files

As you work through the exercises in this book, you'll be creating, opening, and saving files. You should keep the following instructions in mind:

- Many exercises instruct you to open a file from the CD-ROM that comes with this book. The data files are used so that you can focus on the skills being introduced. The files are located in the **Datafiles** folder on the CD-ROM.
- The Directory of Data Files on CD-ROM lists the data files you can use to complete each exercise.
- Unless the book instructs otherwise, use the default settings when creating a document. If someone has changed the default software settings for the computer you're using, your exercise files may not look the same as those shown in this book. In addition, the appearance of your files may look different if the system is set to a screen resolution other than 800 x 600.

To Access the Files Included with This Book

1. Insert the *Learning Microsoft Office Publisher 2003* CD in the CD-ROM drive.
2. Navigate to your CD-ROM drive; right-click start and choose Explore from the shortcut menu.
3. Navigate to your CD-ROM drive.
4. Right-click the **datafiles** folder.
5. Navigate to the location where you wish to place the folder.
6. Right-click and choose Paste from the Shortcut menu.

Support Material

A complete instructor support package is available with all the tools teachers need:

- **Annotated Teacher's Guide** includes entire student book with teacher notes, course curriculum guide, and lesson plans. Solution files included on CD-ROM. (ISBN: 0-13-147685-8)
- **Solutions Manual** includes printouts of exercise solutions with solution file CD-ROM. (ISBN: 0-13-147694-7)
- **Solution Files** on CD-ROM. (ISBN: 0-13-147691-2)
- **Visual Aids**, 25-slide PowerPoint presentation correlated to the book. (ISBN: 0-13-147688-2)

Directory of Data Files on CD-ROM

Exercise #	File Name	Page #
1	None	7
2	PUB02	12
3	PUB03	16
4	PUB04	22
5	PUB05	27
6	None	31
7	PUB07, PUB07Import1.doc, PUB07Import2.doc	36
8	PUB08.doc	38
9	None	40
10	PUB10	48
11	None	54
12	PUB12, PUB12Import.doc	58
13	PUB13	62
14	PUB14	66
15	PUB15	70
16	None	72
17	None	75
18	PUB18	84
19	PUB19	91
20	PUB20	97
21	PUB21	101
22	PUB22	107
23	PUB23A, PUB23B	111
24	PUB24	117
25	PUB25	121
26	PUB26	126
27	PUB27	128
28	PUB28	130
29	PUB29	138
30	PUB30, 30heron.jpg	143
31	PUB31	148

Exercise #	File Name	Page #
32	PUB32	152
33	PUB33	158
34	PUB34	162
35	PUB35	166
36	PUB36, 36DATA.xls	171
37	PUB37, 37dog.jpg	173
38	PUB38, 38garden.jpg	175
39	PUB39	181
40	None	188
41	40PIC.emf	192
42	PUB42Import.doc, 42pastel.jpg, 42loom.jpg	198
43	None	207
44	44DATA.xls	212
45	PUB45	221
46	46Story1.doc, 46BEN.jpg, 46Story2.doc, 46ADDRESS.doc	223
47	None	225
48	None	231
49	PUB49	237
50	PUB50	241
51	None	248
52	PUB52	253
53	PUB53	257
54	54TEXT.doc, 54GOLDHOSTA.jpg, 54BLACKEYESUSANS.jpg, 54GREENHOSTA.jpg, 54IMPATIENS.jpg, 54SNAPDRAGONS.jpg, 54MARIGOLDS.jpg	259

Lesson 1

Getting Started with Publisher

Exercise 1
- Start Publisher
- Create a Quick Publication
- Use the Task Pane
- View Additional Toolbar Buttons
- Save Your Work
- Close a Publication
- Exit Publisher

Exercise 2
- Open a Saved Publication
- Zoom In and Out
- Edit Text Placeholders
- Print Your Work
- Save Your Changes

Exercise 3
- Select an Object
- Resize an Object
- Move an Object
- Delete an Object

Exercise 4
- Place a New Text Box
- Type in a Text Box
- Turn on AutoFit
- Insert a Symbol
- Check Spelling
- Set Spelling Options

Exercise 5
- Select Text
- Move or Copy Text
- Delete Text
- Use Undo and Redo

Exercise 6
- Update Personal Information
- Insert Personal Information
- Insert the Current Date and Time
- Use AutoCorrect

Exercise 7
- Open a File from Another Program
- Open a Word Document
- Insert Text from Other Programs
- Edit a Story in Word

Exercise 8
- Critical Thinking

Exercise 9
- Critical Thinking

Exercise 1

Skills Covered:

◆ **Start Publisher** ◆ **Create a Quick Publication** ◆ **Use the Task Pane**
◆ **View Additional Toolbar Buttons** ◆ **Save Your Work**
◆ **Close a Publication** ◆ **Exit Publisher**

On the Job

Microsoft Office Publisher 2003 is a desktop publishing program (DTP) you can use to create professional publications with all kinds of design elements. It comes with a catalog of project templates to help you get a quick start on your publications. These templates also provide design ideas that you may not have thought of on your own. In most cases you will want to start with one of these templates rather than create a new publication from scratch.

The Geology Club at Cutler College is having an informational meeting to recruit new members. In this exercise, you will start the flyer. You will add text to it and edit it in upcoming exercises.

Terms

Task pane A section of the screen containing a list of common tasks you can perform. The content of the task pane varies depending on the context.

Publication A document created in Publisher. A publication can be a newsletter, a flyer, a brochure, or any of dozens of types of print materials.

Template A file that provides basic design elements, such as styles, page layout settings, and graphics.

Quick Publication A design category of publications consisting of a single-page flyer with placeholders for a picture and a few simple text blocks.

Color Scheme A collection of colors designed to work well together.

Font Scheme A collection of fonts that work well together.

Extension The code (usually 3 letters) that follows the period in a file's name (such as .pub for a Publisher file). The extension helps Windows determine what type of file it is and launch the correct application to open it.

Notes

Start Publisher

- There are several ways to start Publisher, but one of the easiest is to choose it from the Start button's menu system, just as you would any other Windows-based program.
- Since Publisher is a Microsoft Office component, it is located on the Microsoft Office menu.

Start Publisher from the Start menu

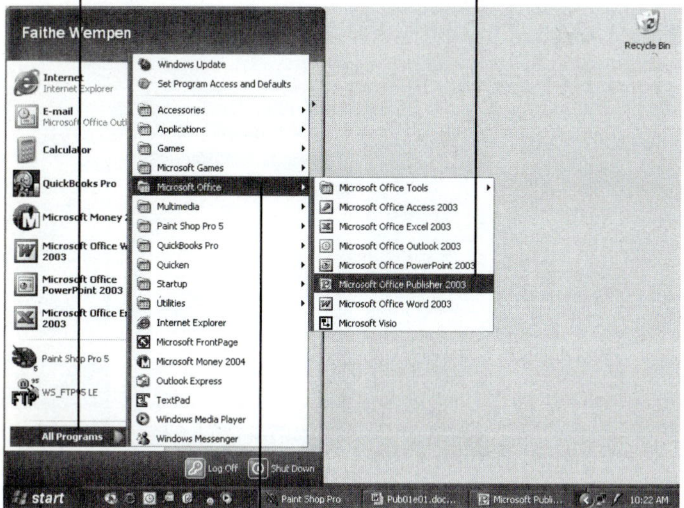

✓ *If you use Publisher frequently, consider pinning it to the Start menu so it will appear on the list directly above the Start button, as Word, Excel, and PowerPoint do in the above figure. To do so, right-click its entry in the menu system and choose Pin to Start Menu.*

- The New Publication **task pane** appears listing various categories of publication designs.

The task pane lists categories of publications, with designs for the chosen publication to the right

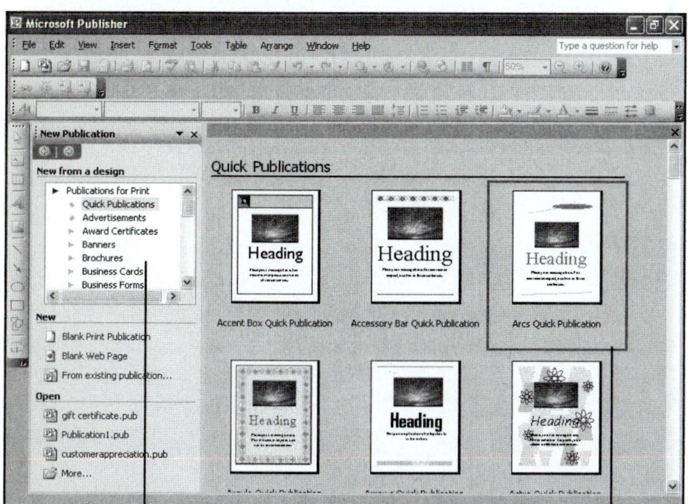

- You can select a design on which to base a new **publication**; you can start a new blank publication; you can base a new publication on a saved **template**; or you can open an existing publication.
- First you choose a broad category, such as Publications for Print, and then you choose something more specific, such as a flyer or newsletter.
- You can redisplay the task pane and its list of publication categories any time you want to start a new publication by opening the File menu and choosing New or clicking the New button on the toolbar.

Create a Quick Publication

- The New Publication task pane offers many categories of publications for you to start with.
- One of these categories, **Quick Publications**, offers single-sheet generic pages that can be used as posters, advertisements, and so on.
- To start a Quick Publication, double-click one of the designs in the right pane when Quick Publication is selected in the task pane (as shown at bottom left).

  ✓ *The first time you start a new publication after installing Publisher, you will be prompted to enter personal information. You can skip this by clicking OK. You will learn about personal information sets later in this lesson.*

- After you select a Quick Publication, the task pane changes to Quick Publication Options and these hyperlinks become available: Quick Publication Options, Publication Designs, Color Schemes, and Font Schemes.
- Quick Publication Options comes first. Its controls enable you to select a layout (that is, an arrangement of placeholders).

The first decision for a Quick Publication is the layout

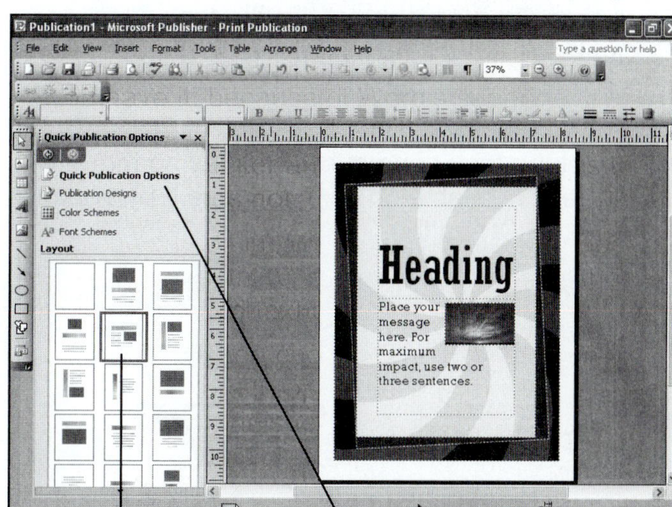

- After choosing a layout, click the next formatting item in the task pane: Publication Designs. You chose a design when you double-clicked originally, but you can change your mind here.
- After choosing a design, click the next formatting item: **Color Schemes**. Then choose a color scheme. Then do the same for **Font Scheme**.

Choose a color scheme from the task pane

Click Color Schemes

Then choose a color scheme

- When you are finished making choices for your publication, you will probably want to replace the sample text with your own words, and you may want to make other changes as well.

Use the Task Pane

- After making your choices in the task pane, you can leave the task pane open and continue working on your publication. You can return to it at any time.
- To get the task pane out of the way so more space is available on-screen, close it by clicking its Close (X) button.

Close the task pane when you don't need it to save space

Click here to close the task pane

- To redisplay the task pane later, open the View menu and choose Task Pane.
- The task pane is not just for creating new publications; it has many other uses as well. Its tools change automatically depending on what you are doing.
- You can also switch manually to a different task pane view, to access different features in the task pane. To do so, click the down arrow in the task pane's top-right corner and select from the menu.
- You will work with other task pane views in upcoming exercises, but you can experiment with them at any time on your own as well.

Choose a different task pane view

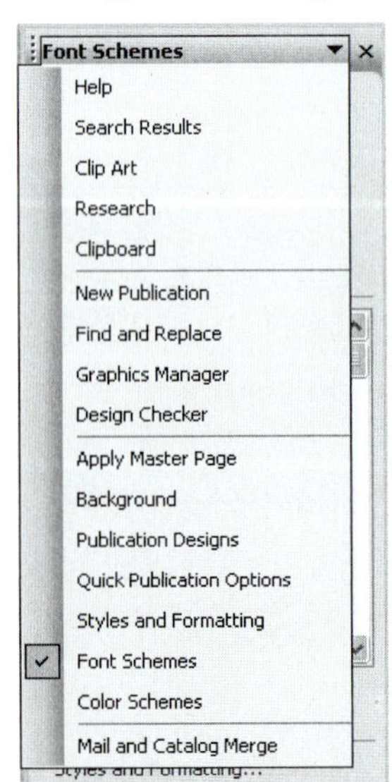

View Additional Toolbar Buttons

- If your screen resolution does not permit all toolbar buttons to appear on-screen at once, a double-arrow button will appear at the right end of the toolbar. You can click this button (Toolbar Options) to reveal the extra toolbar buttons.

Toolbar buttons that don't fit on-screen are on the Toolbar Options button's list

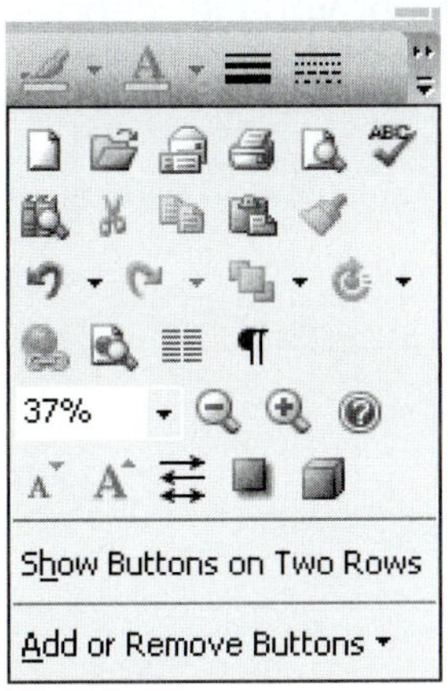

- The toolbar is usage-sensitive. If you do not use a certain toolbar button, Publisher notices this fact, and if you use one of the hidden toolbar buttons, Publisher displays the button you used and hides one of the buttons you have not used.
- If a toolbar button appears to be missing, click the >> button; Publisher has probably hidden it because you haven't used it recently.

  ✓ *You can avoid most toolbar jam-ups completely by simply placing each toolbar on a separate row. From the menu shown above, choose Show Buttons on Two Rows; this will place the Standard and Formatting toolbars on separate rows so that there is room on-screen for all the buttons from each toolbar to display at once.*

Save Your Work

- It is important to save your work so that it is retained when you exit Publisher and turn off your PC. You can open saved files and view, edit, or print them any time you want.

  ✓ *You will learn how to open a saved presentation in Exercise 2.*

- The first time you save a publication, you provide a name. When you save the file subsequent times, Publisher uses the same name automatically.
- Publisher automatically adds a .pub **extension** to a saved publication file's name.

Use the Save As dialog box to specify a file name

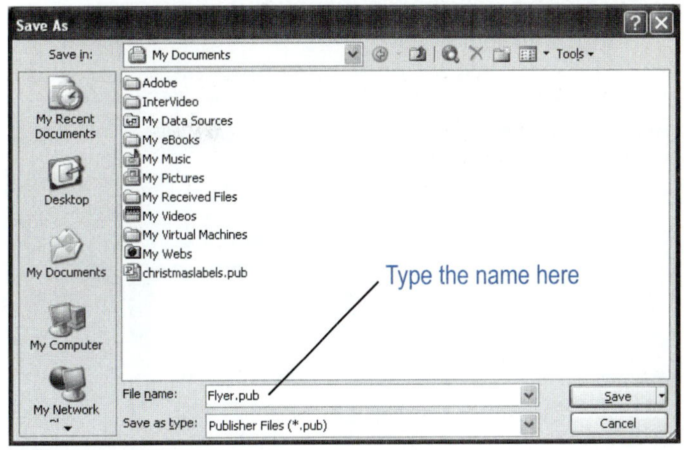

✓ *Windows may be set up to hide file extensions for known file types; if that's the case on your PC, you will not see the .pub extension or *.pub in the Save As dialog box as shown above.*

- To change the file's save location, open the Save in drop-down list and select the disk on which you want to save. Then navigate through the folders that appear for that disk (by double-clicking on one to move to it) until you reach the folder where you want to save.

  ✓ *The File name text box also has a drop-down list, from which you can choose a previously used file name. Choosing a previously used file name will overwrite the existing file.*

- You can save a copy of the file later with a different name, or in a different location, with the Save As command on the File menu. This command reopens the Save As dialog box for an already saved file. (In contrast, the Save command merely saves changes made to the file using the same name and location originally specified.) If this is your first time saving this file, the Save As dialog box will appear. Type the name of your publication and choose a drive and folder to save it.

Close a Publication

- You can have many publications open at once. However, unless there is a reason to leave a publication open, you should close it when you are finished working on it to ensure changes have been saved correctly and to free up your PC's memory for other tasks.
- To close a publication, use the Close command on the File menu. If you have made any changes, you will be prompted to save them.

- When you exit Publisher with the File, Exit command, all open publications are closed automatically.

The Close command closes the open presentation

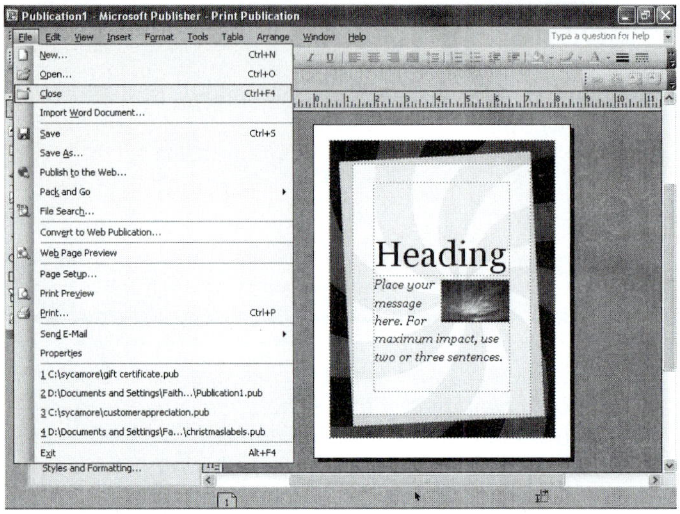

Exit Publisher

- Exit Publisher when you are finished working with the program.
- Exiting ensures that all publication data has been saved, and no data will be lost if the computer is shut down or loses power temporarily.
- There are several ways to exit Publisher: you can use the menu system (File, Exit) or shortcut keys (Alt+F4), or you can choose the Close button on the Publisher window.

Procedures

✓ *If you are using Windows XP and do not see the underlined selection letters in the names of dialog box controls, press the Alt key to make them appear.*

Start Publisher

1. Click **Start** button start .... Win
2. Point to **All Programs** .... P
3. Point to **Microsoft Office**.
4. Click **Microsoft Office Publisher 2003**.

Pin Publisher to the Start Menu

1. Follow steps 1-3 from "Start Publisher."
2. Right-click **Microsoft Office Publisher 2003**.
3. Click **Pin to Start Menu** I

Start a Quick Publication

1. Click **Publications for Print** in the New Publication task pane.
2. Click **Quick Publications**.
3. Click the publication design you want.
4. Click the layout you want.
5. Click **Publication Designs**.
6. Click the design you want (if not already selected).
7. Click **Color Schemes**.
8. Click the color scheme you want.
9. Click **Font Schemes**.
10. Click the font scheme you want.

Close the Task Pane

- Click the **Close** button on the task pane.

OR

- Press **Ctrl+F1** .... Ctrl+F1

OR

1. Click **View**.................... Alt+V
2. Click **Task Pane** .... K

Display the Task Pane

1. Click **View**.................... Alt+V
2. Click **Task Pane** .... K

Change the Task Pane View

1. Click the **down arrow** on the task pane.
2. Click the view to switch to.

Save Your Work

1. Click **File** .... Alt+F
2. Click **Save** .... S

   OR

   Click the **Save** button.

   OR

   Press **Ctrl+S** .... Ctrl+S

   ✓ *If you have saved this file before, this is all you need to do. The changes are saved. If this is the first time for saving this file, the Save As dialog box appears. Continue with the following steps.*

3. In the **File name** text box, type the name of the publication .... Alt+N
4. (Optional) To change the file location, choose a disk from the **Save in** list, and then double-click the folder you want to save in on that disk.
5. Click the **Save** button Save .... Enter

Close the Publication

1. Click **File** .... Alt+F
2. Click **Close** C
3. If prompted to save your changes, choose **Yes** or **No** .... Y or N

   ✓ *If the file has not yet been saved and you choose **Yes** in step 3, the Save As dialog box appears. Refer to the procedure "Save Your Work."*

Exit Publisher

1. Click **File** .... Alt+F
2. Click **Exit** X

   OR

   Press **Alt+F4** .... Alt+F4

   OR

   Click the **Close** button ✕ in the top-right corner of the Publisher window.
3. If prompted to save your changes, choose **Yes** or **No** .... Y or N

   ✓ *If you choose to save your changes (Yes) and you have not saved the open publication before, the Save As dialog box will appear. Refer to "Save Your Work."*

Exercise Directions

1. Start Publisher, if necessary.
2. Start a new Quick Publication using the following directions:
   - Use the Wavy Frame Quick Presentation design.

     ✓ *You will need to scroll down to access this design. It is near the bottom of the list.*
   - For the layout, choose No Picture. (It's the middle one in the fourth row.)
   - For the color scheme, choose Parrot.
   - For the Font Scheme, choose Punch.
3. Save the publication as **01GEO.pub**.
4. Close the publication and exit Publisher.

On Your Own

1. Start Publisher, if necessary.
2. Start creating a flyer to publicize a fundraiser car wash.

   ✓ *Rather than using a Quick Publication, explore the Flyer category under Publications for Print. There are several there specifically for car washes.*
3. Choose a color scheme that you think would attract attention and be appropriate for a car wash.
4. Save the publication as **01WASH.pub**.
5. Save your work and exit Publisher.

Exercise 2

Skills Covered:

◆ **Open a Saved Publication** ◆ **Zoom In and Out**
◆ **Edit Text Placeholders** ◆ **Print Your Work** ◆ **Save Your Changes**

On the Job

You may not always have time to complete a project in a single sitting. That's why it's important to save your work, as you learned in Exercise 1. You then can reopen a saved presentation any time you need it. Once it is open, you can edit it, print it, and save the changes you have made.

You will continue to work on the flyer for the Geology Club meeting in this exercise. The club president has given you the date, time, and location, and you will enter that information on the flyer. Then you will print a hard copy for her to look at, and save the changes you have made.

Terms

Zoom The magnification at which the publication appears on-screen.

Placeholder Sample text or graphics to help guide you in placing your own text or graphics.

Print range In a multipage document, the pages that you specify should be printed.

Notes

Open a Saved Publication

- Open a saved publication whenever you want to view, edit, and/or print it.
- The Open section the bottom of the New Publication task pane shows shortcuts to recently opened files.
- These same recently opened publications also appear at the bottom of the File menu, so you can easily access them even if the task pane is not displayed.

Choose a recently opened publication from the New Publication task pane

- To open some other publication, open the File menu and choose Open or click the Open button  on the Standard toolbar to display the Open Publication dialog box.

Open Publication dialog box

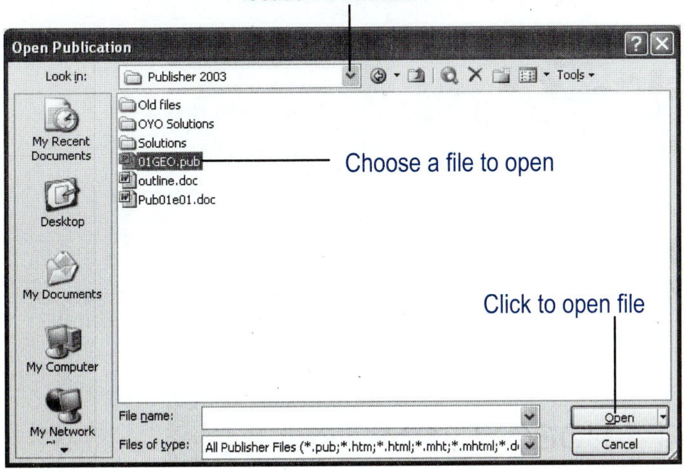

- Once in the Open Publication dialog box, navigate to the disk and folder where the file is stored, choose it from the file list, and then click Open.
  - ✓ *By default, the Files of type setting (at the bottom of the Save As dialog box) is set to All Publisher Files. This shows files of all types that Publisher can open, not just Publisher files. This includes Word documents and Web documents. If you want to show only Publisher files (those files with a .pub extension), open the Files of type drop-down list and choose Publisher Files. Depending on your Windows setting, the valid extensions for publisher files may or may not appear. They do show in the figure above.*

Zoom In and Out

- The **Zoom** feature lets you change your view of the publication on-screen by enlarging or reducing it.
- Zooming does not affect the printout; it is for on-screen viewing purposes only.
- The larger the zoom number, the larger (closer) the publication appears. For example, a zoom of 200% focuses closely on one area of the publication.

Zoom in to work closely with a part of the page

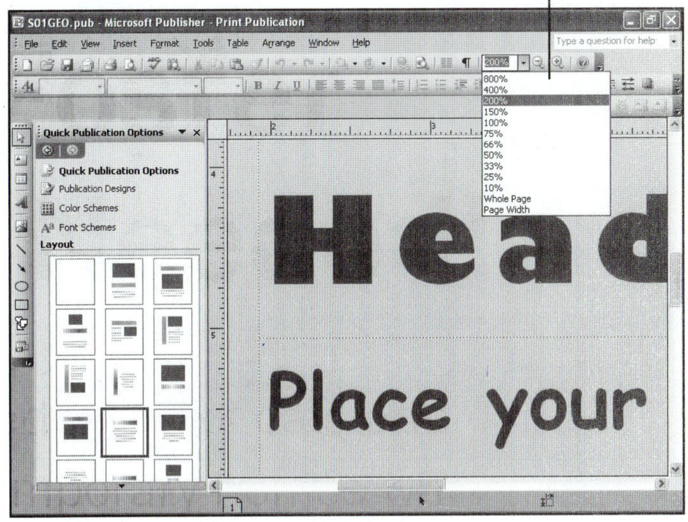

- A smaller zoom percentage gives you a better overall view of the publication, with fewer readable details.
  - ✓ *A Zoom to Selected Objects option is available when an object is selected. It zooms in on whatever object is selected (text box, graphic, etc.) so that it is the maximum size it can be and still fit entirely on-screen at once.*

Zoom out to see a bird's-eye view of your publication

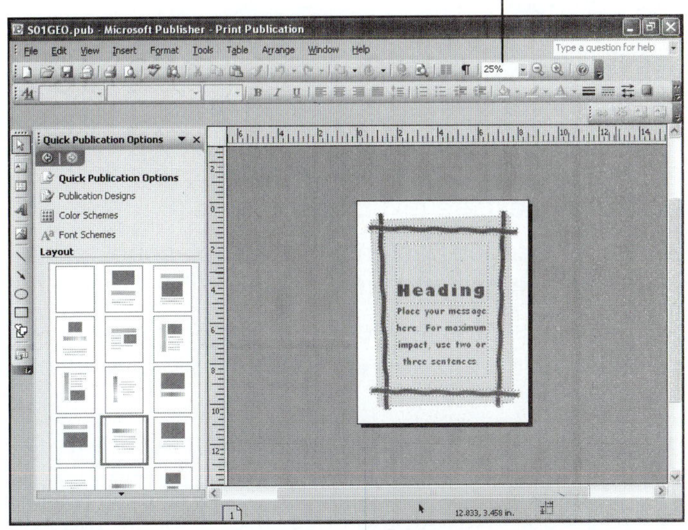

- You can set the zoom either from the Zoom drop-down list on the Standard toolbar or from the Zoom submenu of the View menu.

You can zoom from the View menu instead of the Standard toolbar if you prefer

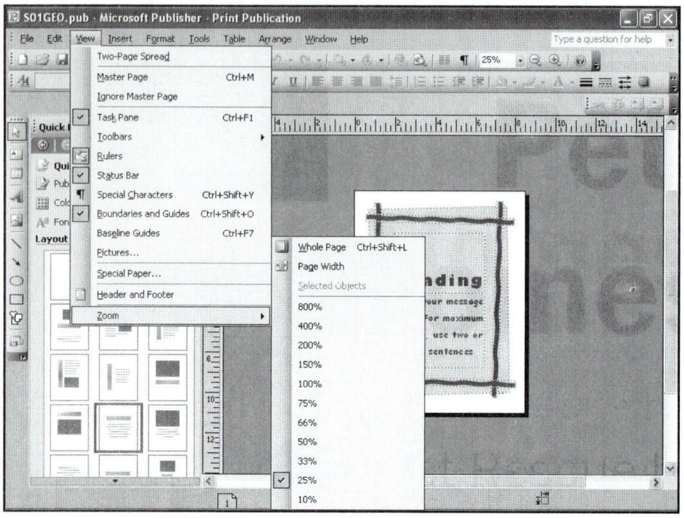

- The exact zoom percentage needed to show the entire page or the page's entire width varies depending on the resolution at which your video display is running. To allow for this, there are two special Zoom options: Whole Page and Page Width.
  - The Whole Page zoom option sets the zoom to the largest number possible while still showing the entire page.
  - The Page Width zoom option sets the zoom to the largest number possible while still showing the entire width of the page from left to right.

Edit Text Placeholders

- When you create a publication (except for a blank one), sample text appears, showing where you should type your own text. These bits of sample text are text **placeholders**.
- To replace the contents of a text placeholder, select the text and then type over it.
- With most placeholder text boxes, you can simply click anywhere on the text block to select the entire block.
- To select text with the mouse, drag across it while holding down the left mouse button.
- To select text with the keyboard, position the insertion point at the beginning and hold down the Shift key as you press the arrow keys to expand the selection.
- Selected text appears in reverse colors (for example, white on black instead of black on white).

Select text in a text placeholder and type to replace it

Text placeholder selected

Print Your Work

- When you click the Print button on the Standard toolbar, one copy of the publication prints immediately, using the default print settings.
- For more control, you must open the Print dialog box (from the File menu). There you will find controls for specifying the number of copies, the **print range**, and more.

The Print dialog box provides basic printing options

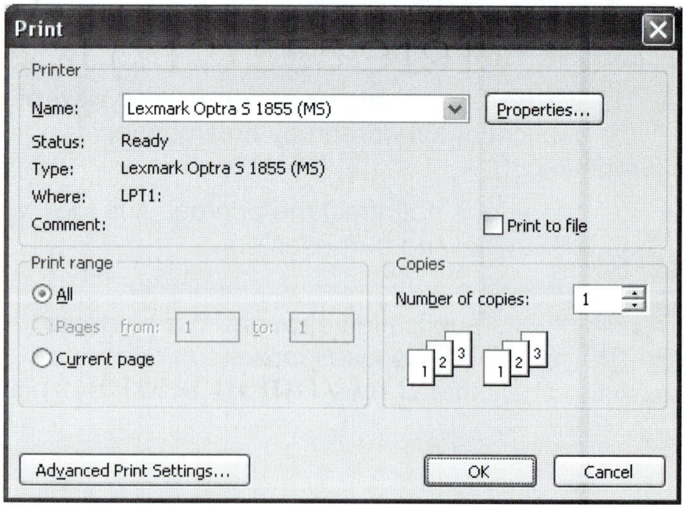

- The Advanced Print Settings button in the Print dialog box opens a Print Settings dialog box with additional printing controls. They are different for different models of printers.

Save Your Changes

- In Exercise 1, you learned how to save a publication for the first time.
- When you save the same document subsequent times, Publisher does not prompt for a file name or location; it saves using the same one you originally specified.
- You can save a copy of the file with a different name, or in a different location, with the Save As command on the File menu. This command reopens the Save As dialog box for an already saved file.

Procedures

Open a Saved Publication

1. From the New Publication task pane, click **More**.

   OR

   Click the **Open** button on the Standard toolbar.

   OR

   Press **Ctrl+O** .... Ctrl+O

   OR

   a. Click **File**................ Alt+F

   b. Click **Open**.................... O
2. (Optional) To change the location, open the **Look in** drop-down list and choose a different disk .... Alt+I
3. (Optional) If needed, double-click on a different folder.
4. Click the file you want to open.
5. Click the **Open** button Open .... Alt+O

Zoom In and Out

1. Click the **down arrow** next to the **Zoom** box on the Standard toolbar.

   ✓ *The drop-down list opens.*
2. Click the zoom setting you want.

OR

1. Click **View**.................... Alt+V
2. Click **Zoom** .... Z
3. Click the zoom setting you want.

   ✓ *To zoom quickly to 100%, click anywhere on the publication and press F9.*

Edit Text in Placeholders

1. Select the text you want to replace.
2. Type the new text.

   ✓ *To select all the text in the current text box,*
   press ***Ctrl + A*** .... Ctrl+A

Print Using the Default Settings

- Click the **Print** button on the Standard toolbar.

Print Using the Print Dialog Box

1. Click **File** .... Alt+F
2. Click **Print** .... P

   OR

   Press **Ctrl + P** .... Ctrl+P
3. (Optional) Set the print range if you don't want to print the entire publication:
   - Click **Pages** and then enter a page range in the **from** and **to** boxes.

   OR

   - Click **Current page**.
4. (Optional) Type the number of copies in the **Number of copies** box if you want more than one.
5. (Optional) Set advanced print options:
   - Choose **Advanced Print Settings**........ Alt+V
   - Make any changes needed in the Print Settings dialog box.
   - Click **OK**.
6. Click **OK** to begin printing........................... Enter

Save Changes to an Existing File

1. Click **File**.................... Alt+F
2. Click **Save**.......................... S

OR

- On the Standard toolbar, click the **Save** button.

OR

- Press **Ctrl + S** .... Ctrl+S

Save an Existing File with a New Name or Location

1. Click **File**.................... Alt+F
2. Click **Save As** .... A
3. In the **File name** text box, type the name of the publication............ Alt+N
4. (Optional) To change the file location, choose a disk from the **Save in** list, and then double-click the folder in which you want to save on that disk.
5. Click the **Save** button Save .... Alt+S

   ✓ *If you chose the name of an existing publication in step 3, a warning appears asking whether you want to overwrite the original. Choose* ***Yes*** *or* ***No***.

Exercise Directions

1. Start Publisher, if necessary.
2. Open the file PUB02. Save it as 02GEO.
3. Hide the task pane.
4. Zoom in to 75%.
5. Replace the Heading text placeholder with **Geology Club Meeting**.
6. Replace the Message text placeholder with the text as shown in Illustration A.
7. Set the zoom to Whole Page.
8. Print the flyer using the Print dialog box.
9. Save your work and exit Publisher.

Illustration A

On Your Own

1. Start Publisher, if necessary.
2. Open the file OPUB02. Save it as 02WASH.
3. Customize the text on the flyer to describe a car wash:
    - Held by the Women's Rugby Club at Cutler College
    - To be held on May 22 of this year from 10:00 a.m. to 3:00 p.m.
    - The location will be 3722 Winford Way, in the Stanley Crafts parking lot, in Indianapolis, Indiana, 46240.
    - The phone number to call for more information is 317-555-9281.
    - The proceeds will go toward new team uniforms.
4. If you do not need all the text placeholder boxes, delete the sample text from them, leaving them blank.
5. Print the flyer.
6. Save your work and exit Publisher.

Exercise 3

Skills Covered:

- **Select an Object** ◆ **Resize an Object**
- **Move an Object** ◆ **Delete an Object**

On the Job

Everything in a publication is an object. There are objects that hold text, graphic objects, and so on. Not only can you change the object content, as you saw when you edited text in Exercise 2, but you can resize, move, and even delete the objects themselves.

The Geology Club president likes the flyer that you made and printed for her in Exercise 2, but she would like you to reposition some of the text and make a few other small changes. You will accomplish those changes by working with the text box objects.

Terms

Object Any free-floating content on a publication layout, usually bounded by a rectangular border. A text box is one type of object; there are others as well.

Selection handles Round white circles on the border of a selected object. You can drag one of these to resize the object.

Rotation handle The green circle at the top of a selected object, used to rotate the object.

Aspect ratio The ratio of width to height for an object. If you change the aspect ratio for a picture, it becomes distorted.

Notes

Select an Object

- There are many types of **objects**: text boxes, graphics, WordArt, drawn lines or shapes, and so on.
- Each object holds a single type of content, and in most cases a single item. The exception is a text box. A text box may hold any amount of text.

  ✓ *Objects can overlap. By default, the most recently placed object is "on top" and the contents of the object beneath it wrap around the top one. You will learn how to change the stacking order of overlapping objects later in this book.*

- To select an object, click on it. You see **selection handles** around the border of a selected object; these are white circles that help you resize the object.
- To select more than one object at once, hold down the Ctrl key as you click on each one. You can then move, copy, or delete them as a group.

This publication has several types of objects in it

- To deselect an object, click on some other object, or click away from all objects.
- If an object contains a graphic or other nontext item, you can select it by clicking anywhere on (or in) the object.
- When an object is selected or when the insertion point lies inside it, you see a border around it. This border does not print.
- An additional circle (green) appears at the top of a selected object. This is a **rotation handle**, used to rotate the object. You will learn more about it later.

Click inside a text box to move the insertion point into it, or click on the border to select the object itself

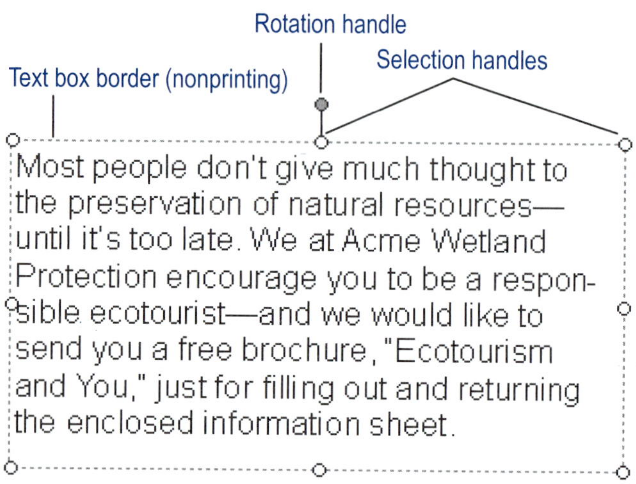

- To select a text box (for example, if you need to format or delete the text box), you must click on the outside border to select the box itself.
- If you click *inside* the text box, you move the insertion point inside it. The text box is selected in an indirect way, but your actions will apply to the text at the insertion point rather than the text box as a whole.

Resize an Object

- Drag a round white selection handle to change the object's size.
- The ratio of width to height for an object is called its **aspect ratio**.
- Be careful when resizing graphic objects so that you do not distort the image by changing its aspect ratio.
- To maintain the aspect ratio for an object as you resize it, hold down the Shift key as you drag a corner selection handle.

Resize an object by dragging a selection handle

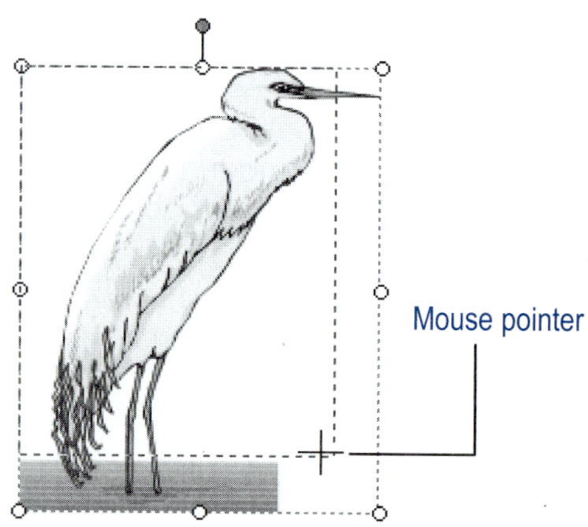

Move an Object

- Position the mouse pointer over the object so that it turns into a Move pointer then drag the object to a new location.

The mouse pointer turns into a MOVE pointer when it is positioned correctly for moving

✓ *In previous versions of Publisher the mouse pointers looked different when moving, resizing, and so on. These were called "helpful mouse pointers" and you can turn them back on if you prefer them. Open the Tools menu and choose Options, and on the User Assistance tab, mark the Use Helpful Mouse Pointers check box.*

- With a text box, the mouse pointer turns into a Move pointer when pointing to a border of the object but not to a selection handle.
- With a nontext object, the mouse pointer turns into a Move pointer when positioned *anywhere* over the object except over a selection handle.

Delete an Object

- To delete an object, select it and then press the Delete key, or right-click it and choose Delete from the shortcut menu.
- To delete a text box, make sure you have selected the text box itself and not moved the insertion point into the box; otherwise, pressing Delete removes a single character at the insertion point instead of deleting the whole text box.
- Other ways to delete a text box are to choose Edit, Delete Object or to right-click the text box and choose Delete Object from the shortcut menu.
- These menu methods always work, whether the object itself is selected or the insertion point is merely inside it.

  ✓ *A shortcut menu appears when you right-click on an object. The shortcut menu contains commands you can select to act upon that object; the commands vary depending on the object chosen.*

You can delete any object by right-clicking it and choosing Delete Object

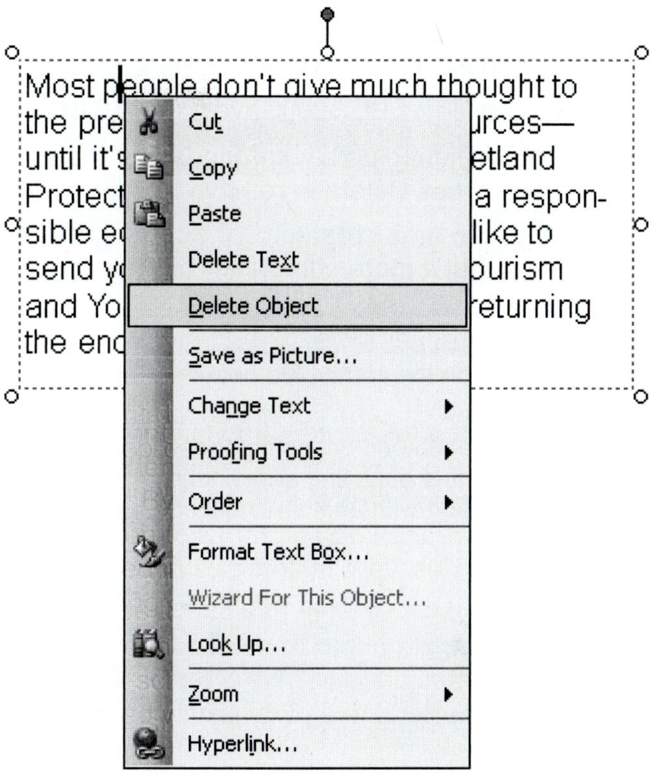

Procedures

Select a Single Object

- Click on the object's border.

Select Multiple Objects

1. Click on the first objects.
2. Hold down the **Ctrl** key .... Ctrl
3. Click on other objects you also want to select.
4. Release the **Ctrl** key .... Ctrl

Resize an Object

1. Select the object.
2. Drag one of the selection handles on the object.

Resize a Graphic Object While Maintaining the Aspect Ratio

1. Select the object.
2. Hold down the **Shift** key .... Shift
3. Drag one of the corner selection handles.
4. Release the **Shift** key .... Shift

Move an Object

1. Position the mouse pointer over the object so that the Move pointer appears.
2. Drag the object to a new location.

Delete a Nontext Object

1. Select the object.
2. Press the **Delete** key .... Del

Delete a Text Box

1. Select the text box.
2. Click **Edit** .... Alt+E
3. Click **Delete Object** .... D

OR

1. Right-click the text box.
2. Click **Delete Object** .... D

Exercise Directions

1. Start Publisher, if necessary.
2. Open the file PUB03. Save it as **03GEO**.
3. Select the light blue background behind the text and press Delete to remove it.
4. Enlarge the area created by the wavy graphic lines so that it more completely fills the available space:
   a. Move each of the wavy graphic lines so that each is on top of the blue dotted margin guides on the page.
   b. Stretch each end of each of the wavy graphic lines so that each line sticks out past the intersection with another line by about ½".
5. Use the rotation handles on each wavy graphic line to make it more exactly vertical or horizontal (little or no tilt).
6. Delete the Geology Club Meeting text box, and resize/reposition the remaining text box as shown in Illustration A.

   ✓ *Don't worry that there is no longer a title on the flyer; you'll add one in Exercise 4.*
7. Print the publication.
8. Save your work and exit Publisher.

Illustration A

On Your Own

1. Start Publisher, if necessary.
2. Open the file OPUB03. Save it as 03WASH.
3. Move, resize, and/or delete the various elements on the flyer as desired. Here are some ideas of things you could do:
   a. Delete the text box.
   b. Make the starburst graphics larger and move them around.
   c. Make the Car Wash text box at the top a little bit smaller so it is less overwhelming.
   d. Make the white oval larger, and make the text box that sits on top of it larger too.
4. Save your work and exit Publisher.

Exercise 4

Skills Covered:

◆ **Place a New Text Box** ◆ **Type in a Text Box** ◆ **Turn on AutoFit** ◆ **Insert a Symbol** ◆ **Check Spelling** ◆ **Set Spelling Options**

On the Job

You can do a lot with the text boxes provided by Publisher's templates, but you may sometimes want to create your own text boxes to type in. You should always check your spelling to make sure you haven't made any mistakes. At times you may want to insert special typographical symbols that do not appear on your keyboard.

You will continue to work with the Geology Club's flyer. The club president has asked you to replace the Geology Club Meeting text box that you removed in Exercise 3 and has suggested that you add some more explanation about the club's purpose and activities.

Terms

Symbol Any character that is not a letter or number (such as # or @). You can type some symbols directly with the keyboard; others must be inserted with a command in Publisher.

Story The text in a text box plus any text boxes that are linked to it. A single story can span several text boxes on several pages, as in a newspaper or magazine.

Notes

Place a New Text Box

- Create a new text box whenever you want to place a block of text in a spot where there is not already a text box.
- A text box can hold as much text as you want, so there is no need to create a separate text box for each paragraph; create a new box only when you want to separate one block of text from another.
- Use the Text Box tool on the Objects toolbar (the toolbar on the left side of the screen) to create a new text box.

This document contains several different text blocks, each in its own box

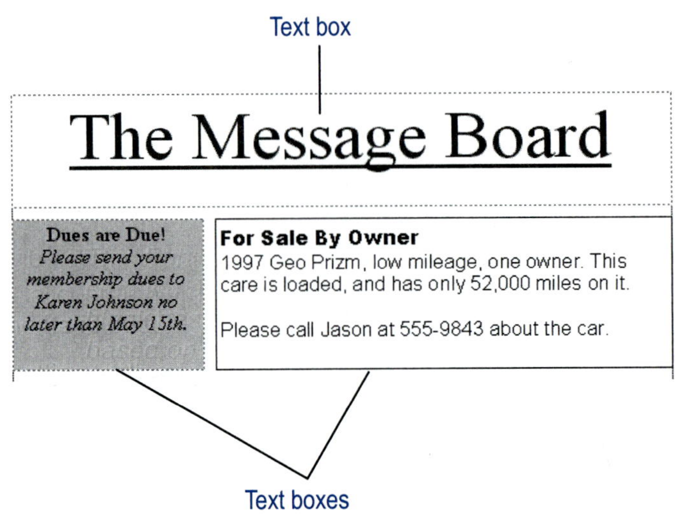

Type in a Text Box

- When you click anywhere within a text box, the insertion point moves into that box.
- As you type, the insertion point moves, showing where the next character you type will appear.

The insertion point shows where the next character will be

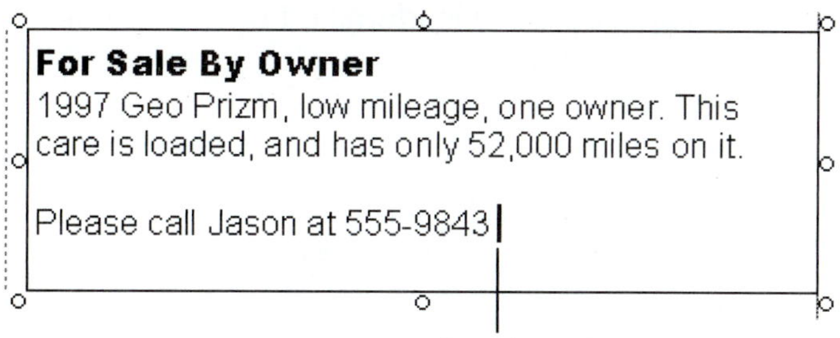

Insertion point

- You can move the insertion point by clicking where you want it, or by pressing the arrow keys on your keyboard.

Turn on AutoFit

- You will learn in a later exercise how to set a specific size for text, but in the meantime you may want to set the text in the text boxes you create to AutoFit.
- By default, text in placeholder boxes is already set to AutoFit. You may have noticed this when you resized a text box and the text size changed.
- To set text to AutoFit, right-click it and point to Change Text, point to AutoFit Text, and then click Best Fit. You can also choose Format, AutoFit Text, Best Fit.

AutoFit the text in a text box you created

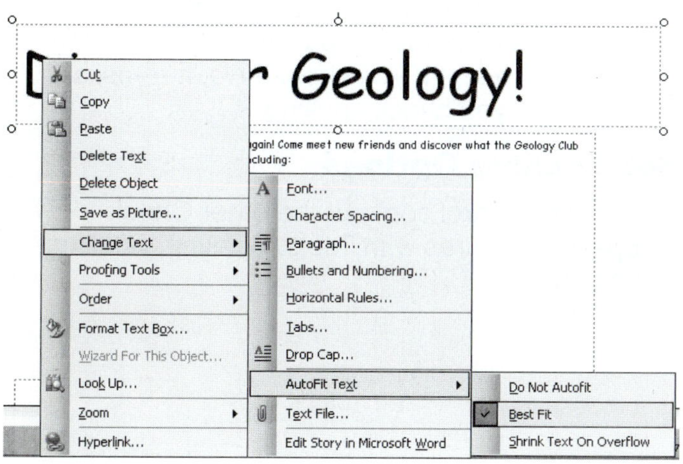

Insert a Symbol

- Your keyboard contains many **symbols** (mostly above the numbers); hold down Shift as you press the key to enter them.
- There are many other symbols that do not appear on your keyboard, however. You can insert these with the Insert, Symbol command.

  ✓ *Commonly used symbols include the em dash (—), the copyright symbol (©), and the trademark symbol (™).*

- When you open the Insert menu and choose Symbol, the Symbol dialog box appears, from which you can select a symbol.
- You are not limited to the symbols available in the current font; you may choose any font from the Symbol dialog box.
- Some fonts consist of nothing but graphic symbols; Wingdings is one such font.

Use the Symbol dialog box to select a symbol to insert

Recently used symbols appear here

Scroll down to see more characters

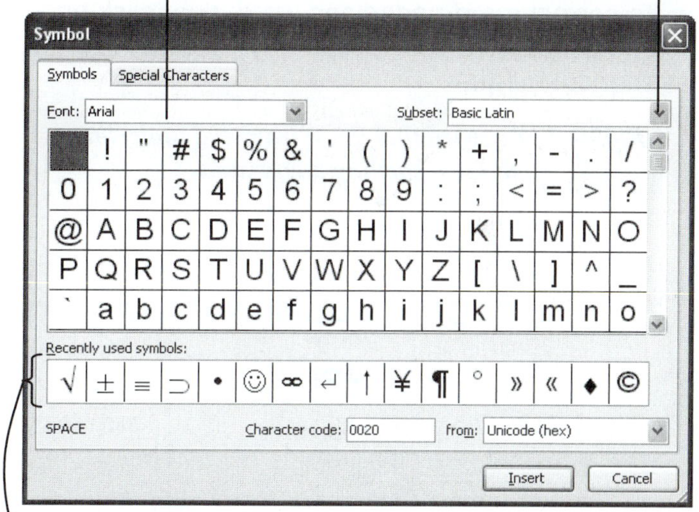

Recently used symbols appear here

- The fonts available depend on which are installed on your PC.
- The Special Characters tab in the Symbol dialog box lists common typographical symbols you can insert. If you are looking for a common symbol but do not know which font to look in, try this tab's list.

The Special Characters tab provides quick access to many common typographical symbols

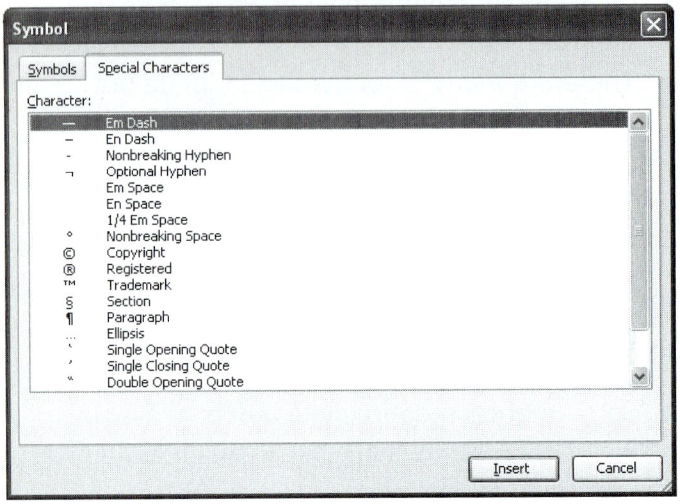

Check Spelling

- Publisher automatically checks your spelling as you type and marks any words that are not in its dictionary with a wavy red underline.
- To correct a red-underlined word, right-click on it and choose the correct spelling from the shortcut menu.

Right-click a word that has a wavy red underline to see a spelling suggestion

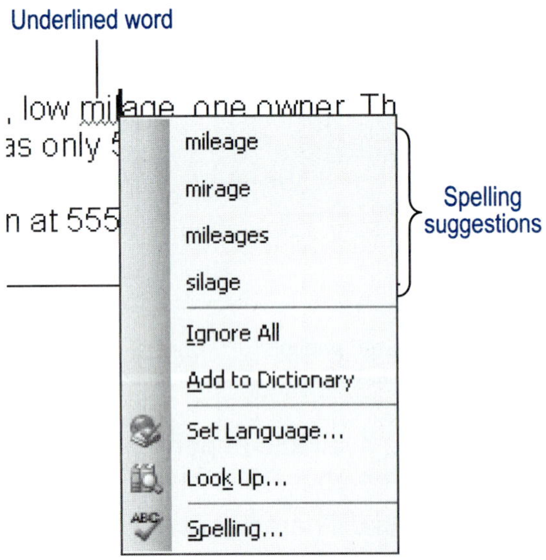

- Not all red-underlined words are necessarily misspelled. Many proper names and brand names are erroneously marked as errors because they are not in Publisher's dictionary.
- If the correct spelling does not appear, you can correct the spelling manually, as you would edit any other text.
- You can also run a complete spelling check with the Check Spelling utility in Publisher.
- To run a full spelling check, select a text box and choose Tools, Spelling, Spelling or press F7, opening the Check Spelling dialog box.
- If a misspelled word is identified by the Check Spelling dialog box, you may choose to add it to the dictionary, ignore it, or correct it.

Use the Check Spelling dialog box to correct spelling errors

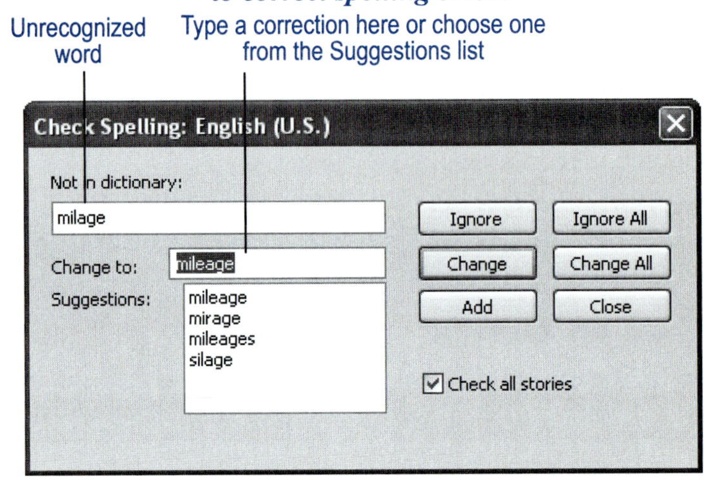

- A full spelling check looks for misspellings in the current **story**. You can check all stories in the entire publication by marking the Check all stories check box.
- If you have not marked the Check all stories check box, Publisher asks after checking the current story whether you want to check the rest of the publication.
- If you choose *Yes*, Publisher remembers your answer and does not ask again unless you clear the Check all stories check box when running the spell check. If you choose *No*, it re-asks each time you check spelling.

Set Spelling Options

- You can control some of the other Check Spelling features with Tools, Spelling, Spelling Options.

Set spelling options here

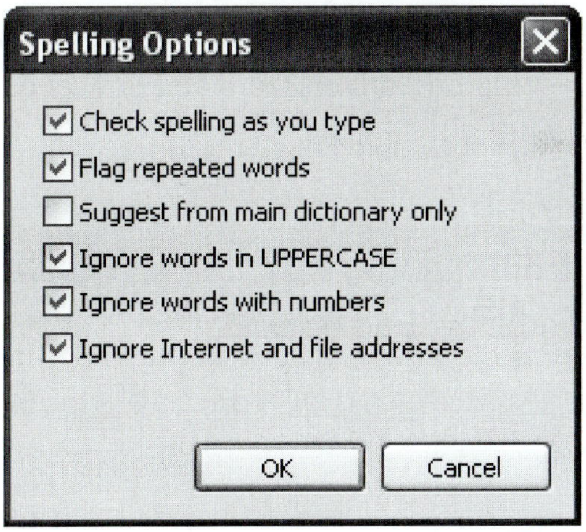

- You may choose whether or not to check spelling as you type. If you turn this option off, no words will be red underlined on-screen.

  ✓ *To hide the wavy red underlines temporarily, choose Tools, Spelling, Hide Spelling Errors as a quick alternative to the above. Choose Tools, Spelling, Show Spelling Errors later to turn them back on.*

- You may choose whether or not to flag repeated words. A repeated word is a word that appears twice in a row, as in "the the."
- You may choose to limit the spell check to the main dictionary only. This re-marks as misspelled any words that you have added to your custom dictionary with the Add button.
- You may choose whether or not to ignore words that appear in uppercase letters, *LIKE THIS.*
- You may choose whether or not to ignore words that contain numbers. For example, computer user names such as *Joe98471* would not be checked.
- You may choose whether or not to ignore Internet and file addresses. For example, Web addresses such as *http://www.mysite.com* would not be checked, nor would e-mail addresses such as *Joe@mysite.com*.

Procedures

Place a New Text Box

1. Click the **Text Box** button on the Objects toolbar.
2. Drag across the page, holding down the left mouse button, to create the text box.
3. Release the mouse button.

Type in a Text Box

1. Click inside the text box in which you want to type.
2. Type the text.

Set a Text Box to AutoFit Best Fit

1. Right-click text in the text box.
2. Point to **Change Text** .... N
3. Point to **AutoFit Text** X
4. Click **Best Fit** .... B

Insert a Symbol

1. Click **Insert** .... Alt+I
2. Click **Symbol** .... S
3. Click the **Font** drop-down list's arrow .... Alt+F
4. Click the font from which you want to select a symbol.
5. Click the symbol you want.
6. Click **Insert** .... Alt+I

Check Spelling of an Individual Word

1. Right-click a word that has a wavy red underline.
2. Click the correct spelling on the shortcut menu, if it appears.

Start the Check Spelling Feature

1. Click **Tools** .... Alt+T
2. Click **Spelling** .... S
3. Click **Spelling** .... S

   ✓ *You can press* ***F7*** .... F7 *instead of doing steps 1 through 3 if you prefer.*

   ✓ *You can click the Check Spelling button on the Standard toolbar instead of doing steps 1 through 3 if you prefer.*

4. Use one of the following procedures to deal with the found word(s).

Add or Ignore a Possible Misspelling

- Click **Add** .... Alt+A
  to add it to the dictionary.

OR

- Click **Ignore** .... Alt+I
  to ignore this instance of it.

OR

- Click **Ignore All**........... Alt+G
  to ignore all instances of it in this publication.

Correct a Possible Misspelling

Do one of the following to specify the correct spelling:

- Choose the correction from the **Suggestions** list.......... Alt+S
- Type a correction in the **Change to** box .... Alt+T

Do one of the following to correct the spelling:

- Click **Change**.............. Alt+C
  to change that instance.
- Click **Change All** .... Alt+N
  to change all instances in this publication.

Set Spelling Options

1. Click **Tools** .... Alt+T
2. Click **Spelling** .... S
3. Click **Spelling Options** .... O
4. Select or deselect any of the option check boxes.
5. Click **OK**.

Exercise Directions

1. Start Publisher, if necessary.
2. Open the file PUB04. Save it as **04GEO**.
3. Add a text box at the top of the flyer (immediately beneath the top red line), and make it 1" tall.
4. In the new text box, type **Discover Geology!**
   ✓ *If the text you are typing is too small to read, press the F9 key to zoom in.*
5. Set the new text box's text to Best Fit for its AutoFit setting.
6. Add another text box between the two existing text boxes, and type the text in it as shown in Illustration A.
   ✓ *Make the same spelling errors shown in Illustration A, so you will have mistakes to correct with the Check Spelling feature.*
7. Insert a registered trademark symbol (®) after the phrase Cool Rockz.
   ✓ *The registered trademark symbol (®) can also be inserted by just typing (r) and pressing the spacebar after the word* Rockz.
8. Correct the spelling of **Geoloogy** with the right-click method.
9. Right-click Rockz and choose Ignore All to allow this spelling in this document only.
10. Turn off the display of spelling errors on-screen.
11. Correct the rest of the misspellings in the publication using the Check Spelling dialog box.
12. Set this text box for Best Fit for its AutoFit setting.
13. Print the publication.
14. Save your work and exit Publisher.

Illustration A

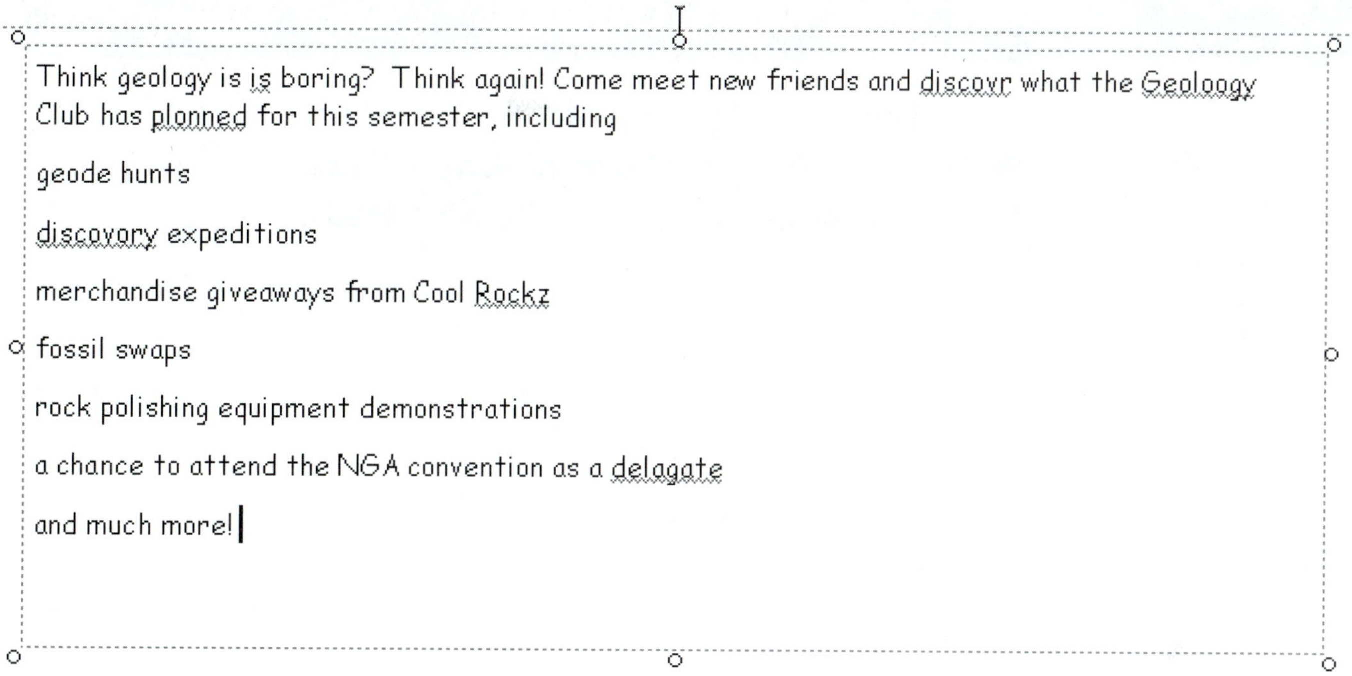

On Your Own

1. Start Publisher, if necessary.
2. Open the file **OPUB04**. Save it as **04WASH**.
3. Place a new text box on the flyer in the blank space, and type **A Benefit for the Cutler College Women's Rugby Team**.
   ✓ *Don't worry that the text appears in black lettering. You will learn how to fix this in a later exercise.*
4. Set the text in the new box to Best Fit for its AutoFit setting.
5. Correct all the spelling errors in all text boxes. Practice both the dialog box and the right-click methods.
   ✓ *If you turned off the display of spelling errors on-screen in the preceding steps, you will need to turn it back on.*
6. Add a trademark ™ symbol after Stanley Crafts.
7. Save your work and exit Publisher.

Exercise 5

Skills Covered:

- Select Text
- Move or Copy Text
- Delete Text
- Use Undo and Redo

On the Job

Publisher allows you to select any amount of text you wish and work with it as a whole. For example, you can move, copy, or delete a selected text block.

You will rearrange and edit the list of events on the Geology Club flyer in this exercise, adding some new items, deleting some existing ones, and placing the list items in a different order.

Terms

Select To highlight something (usually text or a frame) so that whatever command you issue applies to it.

Clipboard A temporary holding area used by Windows programs to move or copy text.

Undo To reverse an action or command.

Redo To reverse an Undo action.

Notes

Select Text

- **Selecting** text marks it so that whatever command you issue next affects it. For example, you might select a block of text and then issue the Copy command.
- You can select any amount of text, from a single character to the entire contents of a frame. (You can also select frames, as you learned in Exercise 3.)
- You can select text with either the mouse or the keyboard. To select with the mouse, drag across the text with the left mouse button held down. To select with the keyboard, position the insertion point at the start point and then hold down Shift as you press arrow keys to extend the selection.
- Selected text appears in reverse colors. For example, if the text is normally black on white, it appears white on black when selected.

Selected text appears in reverse colors

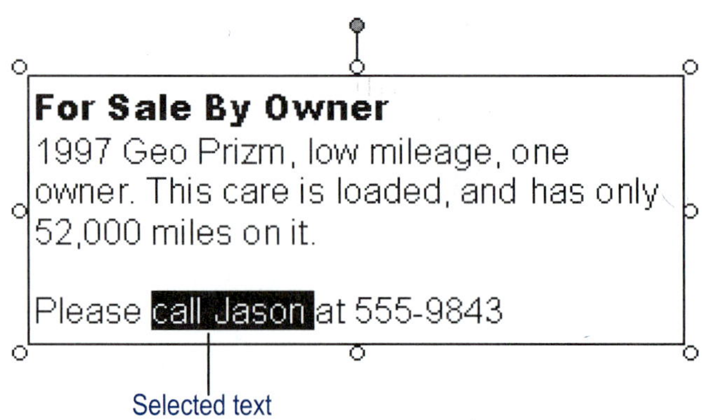

- You can select a single word by double-clicking on it, or a single paragraph by triple-clicking on it.

- To select all the text in the entire story (that is, the current frame and all frames linked to it), choose Edit, Select All or press Ctrl+A. Either command will work equally well in a text frame that is not linked to any other. Linking text frames is covered in Exercise 42.

Move or Copy Text

- Drag selected text to move it. To copy text instead of moving it, hold down Ctrl as you drag the selection to a new spot.
- When you cut or copy a selection, Windows places it on the **Clipboard**, a holding area. Then, when you paste, whatever is on the Clipboard is placed at the insertion point.
- There are many ways to cut, copy, and paste; choose the method you prefer. You can use the Cut, Copy, and Paste buttons on the Formatting toolbar; use the commands on the Edit menu; right-click and choose Cut, Copy, or Paste; or use shortcut key combinations: Ctrl+X for Cut, Ctrl+C for Copy, and Ctrl+V for Paste.
- You are not limited to moving and copying within a single frame; you can move or copy among frames and even among publications.
- When you paste a selection, a Paste Options button appears in the lower-right corner of the pasted selection. You can click it to see a menu of paste options, as shown below.

The Paste Options button helps you specify how you want a selection to be pasted

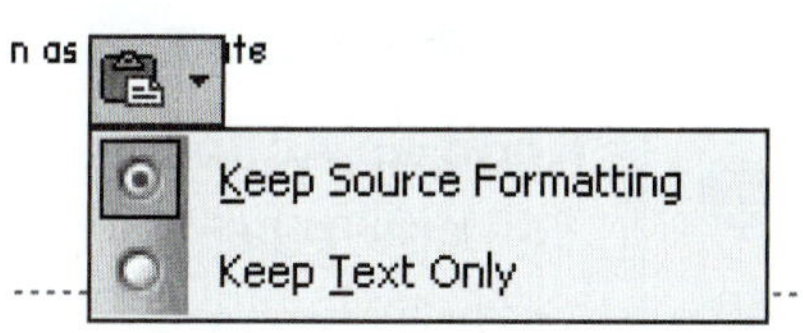

Delete Text

- You can delete individual text characters by placing the insertion point and then using Backspace or Delete to remove characters to the left or right of the insertion point, respectively.
- To delete more than one character at a time, select the text you want to delete, and then press the Delete key or choose Edit, Delete Text.
- The difference between Delete and Cut: Cut moves the selection to the Clipboard, while Delete does not.

Use Undo and Redo

- **Undo** allows you to reverse the last action you took. To undo, click the Undo button on the Standard toolbar or choose Edit, Undo {*action*}.
- The {*action*} part will be replaced by whatever your last action was; for example, if your last action was to resize a text box, the command will be Undo Resize.

The Undo command, at the top of the Edit menu, changes to show what will be undone

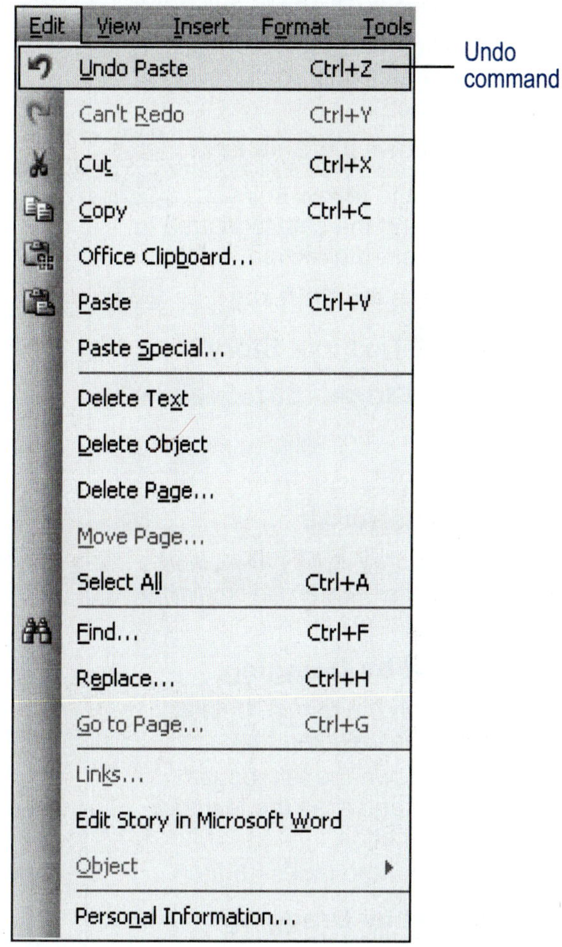

- The **Redo** command reverses an Undo action. You can redo as many actions as you have undone, as long as you have not done anything else in the interim. It is not available if you have not undone anything.
- You can also use the Undo and Redo buttons on the Standard toolbar instead of the menu, or press Ctrl+Z for Undo or Ctrl+Y for Redo.

Procedures

Select Text with the Mouse

1. Position the mouse pointer at the beginning of the text to select.
2. Hold down the left mouse button and drag across the text.
3. Release the mouse button.

Select Text with the Keyboard

1. Position the insertion point at the beginning of the text to select.
2. Hold down the **Shift** key..... Shift
3. Press the **arrow keys** .... (arrow keys) to extend the selection area in the desired direction.
4. Release the **Shift** key .... Shift

Select All Text in a Story

- Press **Ctrl+A**................ Ctrl+A

OR

1. Click **Edit** .... Alt+E
2. Click **Select All** L

   ✓ *The Edit, Select All method also selects text in any linked text boxes as well.*

Move Text by Dragging

1. Position the mouse pointer over the selected text.
2. Hold down the left mouse button and drag the text to a new location.
3. Release the mouse button.

Copy Text by Dragging

1. Position the mouse pointer over the selected text.
2. Hold down the **Ctrl** key .... Ctrl
3. Hold down the left mouse button and drag the copy to a new location.
4. Release the mouse button.
5. Release the **Ctrl** key .... Ctrl

Move Text with Cut and Paste

1. Select the text to be moved.
2. Do any of the following to cut the selection to the Clipboard:
   - Click the **Cut** button.
   - Press **Ctrl+X**........... Ctrl+X
   - Click **Edit**................ Alt+E

     Then click **Cut** .... T
   - Right-click the text.

     Then click **Cut** .... T
3. Position the insertion point where you want to move the text.
4. Do any of the following:
   - Click the **Paste** button.
   - Press **Ctrl+V**........... Ctrl+V
   - Click **Edit**................ Alt+E

     Then click **Paste**............ P
5. (Optional) Specify how you want the selection pasted:

   a. Click the **Paste Options** button next to the pasted text.

   b. Choose how you want the text pasted:
      - **Keep Source Formatting**................ K
      - **Keep Text Only** .... T

Copy Text with Copy and Paste

1. Select the text to be copied.
2. Do any of the following to copy the selection to the Clipboard:
   - Click the **Copy** button.
   - Press **Ctrl+C** .... Ctrl+C
   - Click **Edit**................ Alt+E

     Then click **Copy** C
   - Right-click the text.

     Then click **Copy** C
3. Position the insertion point where you want to place a copy of the text.
4. Do any of the following:
   - Click the **Paste** button.
   - Press **Ctrl+V** .... Ctrl+V
   - Click **Edit** .... Alt+E

     Then click **Paste** .... P
5. (Optional) Specify how you want the selection pasted:

   a. Click the **Paste Options** button next to the pasted text.

   b. Choose how you want the text pasted:
      - **Keep Source Formatting** .... K
      - **Keep Text Only** .... T

Delete Text

1. Select the text to be deleted.
2. Press the **Delete** key.......... Del

Undo an Action

1. Click **Edit**..................... Alt+E
2. Click **Undo** .... U

OR

- Click the **Undo** button.

OR

- Press **Ctrl+Z** .... Ctrl+Z

Redo an Action

1. Click **Edit**..................... Alt+E
2. Click **Redo** .... R

OR

- Click the **Redo** button.

OR

- Press **Ctrl+Y** .... Ctrl+Y

Exercise Directions

1. Start Publisher, if necessary.
2. Open the file PUB05. Save it as 05GEO.
3. Zoom in so you can see the list of items clearly.
4. Select and delete **discovery expeditions**, and then type **camping trips** in its place.
5. Copy the line **fossil swaps** and paste a copy beneath the original.
6. Edit the second instance to read **jewelry-making workshops**.
7. Undo the last two actions, removing the editing and then removing the copy.
8. Redo the two actions, restoring the copy and then restoring the editing.
9. Rearrange the list items using cut and paste so that they are in alphabetical order (except leave “and much more” at the bottom).
10. Print the publication.
11. Save your work and exit Publisher.

On Your Own

1. Start Publisher, if necessary.
2. Open OPUB05A and print it for reference.
3. Open OPUB05B and save it as 05WASH.
4. Use a combination of retyping and copy-and-paste to make it contain the same information as in OPUB05A.
5. Delete the Organization logo.
6. Save your work and exit Publisher.

Exercise 6

Skills Covered:

◆ **Update Personal Information** ◆ **Insert Personal Information** ◆ **Insert the Current Date and Time** ◆ **Use AutoCorrect**

On the Job

You may find yourself typing the same information, such as your name and address, the current date, or your company's name or motto, over and over in different publications. In this exercise, you will learn how to save time by inserting such boilerplate text automatically. You will also learn how to save time correcting typing mistakes with the AutoCorrect feature.

The Geology Club at Cutler College has asked you to be their official publication designer. To prepare for this responsibility, you will create a personal information set for the club and modify Publisher's AutoCorrect settings. You will also start a new flyer that will be handed out at the club's first meeting and insert some of the data from the personal information set on it, along with the current date and time.

Terms

Personal information set Stored information about yourself, your job, your company, and how to contact you.

Date code A code placed in the publication that automatically pulls the current date from your computer's clock whenever the publication is saved or printed.

Time code Same as date code, except it shows the current time.

AutoCorrect A program feature that attempts to "guess" your intentions for typing and formatting and applies a change automatically.

Notes

Update Personal Information

- Publisher maintains up to four separate **personal information sets**. You may use these as their names suggest (Primary Business, Secondary Business, Other Organization, and Home/Family), or you may use them for four separate people who share the same PC.
- The first time you start a new publication in Publisher, you may be prompted to enter personal information.
- To update personal information, choose Edit, Personal Information, and then select a set from the top list. Then make your changes to the set's information in each of the other boxes.

Enter or edit the contact information here

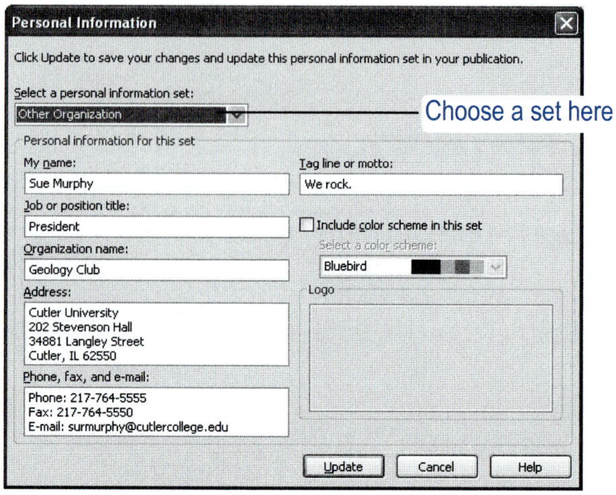

✓ *When inserting personal information, you cannot interactively choose which set to pull from; it pulls from whatever set was displayed in the Personal Information dialog box when you clicked Update to close it. Therefore, make sure that the set you want to use at the moment is displayed when you close the dialog box.*

Insert Personal Information

- Some wizards insert personal information automatically for you in certain spots in the publication. You can insert personal information yourself, too.
- To insert a certain item from the personal information, choose Insert, Personal Information and then choose from the list of common fields that appears.

  ✓ *The inserted information appears in its own text box. Each bit of information you insert has its own box. For example, if you insert the Business Name and the Address, they appear separately. You can perform a cut-and-paste operation to place them in a common text box if you like.*

Choose an item of information to insert

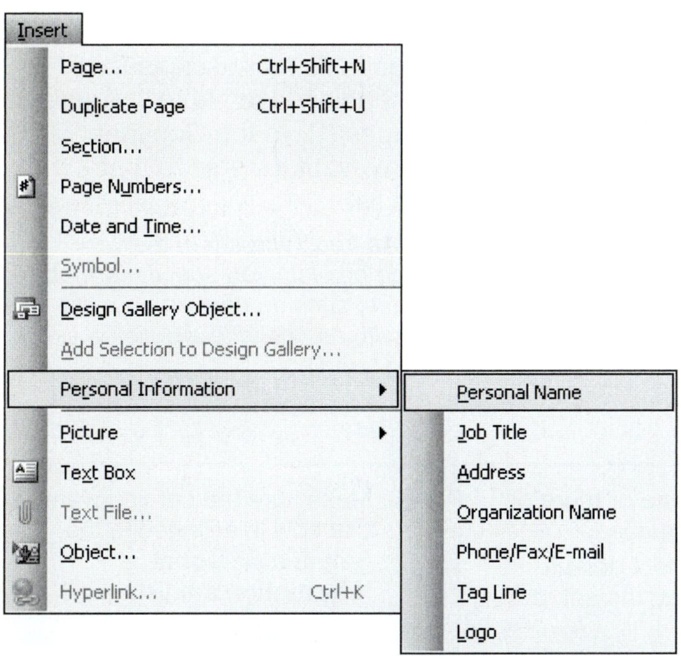

Insert the Current Date and Time

- Choose Insert, Date and Time to open a dialog box from which you can choose a date or time to place in your publication.
- The date or time you insert is current as of the computer's clock at the moment you insert it. If you want the date to be updated each time the publication is saved or printed, make sure you mark the Update automatically check box in the Date and Time dialog box. When this box is checked, Publisher places a **date code** or **time code** in the document.
- You can choose from among many date/time formats from many countries. The default is English (United States), but you can select any language.
- Publisher makes no distinction between date formats and time formats. If you want a date, simply choose a format that includes the date. If you want a time, choose a format that includes the time.

Choose a date/time format and whether to update it automatically

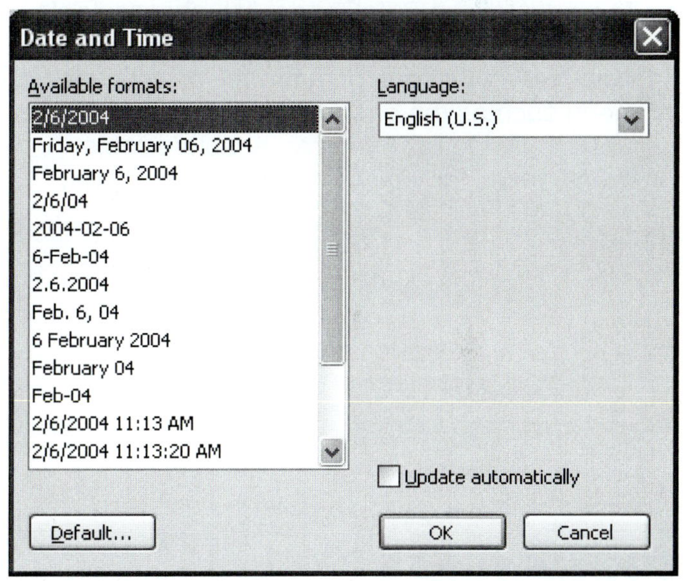

Use AutoCorrect

- **AutoCorrect** is a popular feature from Word that has been included in Publisher. It maintains a list of commonly misspelled words; whenever you make one of the misspellings, it automatically fixes the error.
- AutoCorrect works automatically; you do not need to do anything special to enable it.
- When you make a misspelling, Publisher corrects it, and a small blue minus sign appears below the corrected text when your mouse pointer is over it, like this:

about

- When you point to that minus sign, an AutoCorrect Options button appears. You can click on that button to open a menu, from which you can choose how you want this and other similar situations to be handled.

AutoCorrect options for a correction that Publisher has made

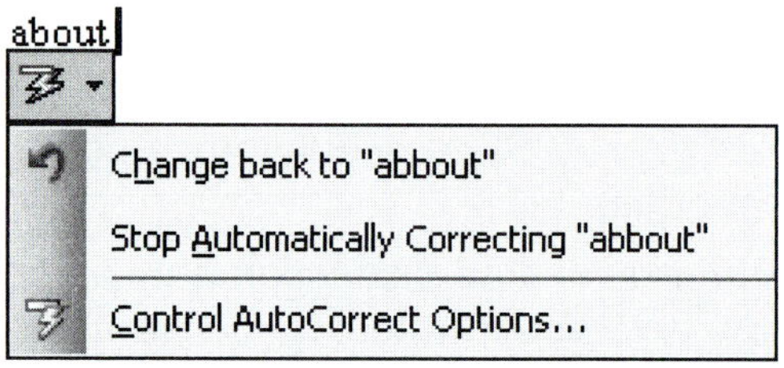

- You can fine-tune AutoCorrect over time by using the menus for individual corrections, as shown above, or you can work directly with the AutoCorrect list.
- To work with the AutoCorrect list, choose Tools, AutoCorrect Options, or click Control AutoCorrect Options on an AutoCorrect button's menu such as the one above. In the AutoCorrect Options dialog box, you can enable/disable check boxes for various types of corrections.

Fine-tune how AutoCorrect works

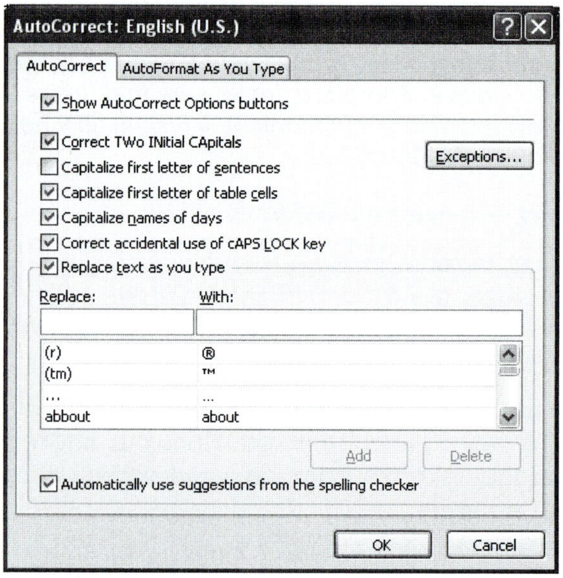

- You can also add or remove entries from the AutoCorrect list. To add an entry, type the misspelling in the Replace box and the replacement in the With box. Then click Add.
- To delete an entry, select it and click Delete.
- For example, suppose you work for a company that uses a (C) code in its manuscripts to indicate a certain heading level. AutoCorrect automatically changes (C) to the Copyright symbol ©. You might want to remove that correction from the list.

  ✓ *The AutoFormat As You Type tab in the AutoCorrect dialog box lets you specify formatting corrections to make, such as converting a list of items that begin with asterisks to a bulleted list.*

Procedures

Display the Personal Information Dialog Box

1. Click **Edit** .... Alt+E
2. Click **Personal Information** .... N

Edit Personal Information

1. Start in the Personal Information dialog box (see the preceding steps).
2. Choose the personal information set you want to edit.
3. Edit the text in one or more of the text fields provided.
4. (Optional) To select default color schemes for the set, do the following:
   a. Click the **Include color** scheme in this set check box .... Alt+C
   b. Click the arrow to open the drop-down list.
   c. Select a color scheme.
5. If you want to change any of the other sets, repeat steps 2–4.
6. Make sure the set you want to use now is selected in the **Select a personal information set** list.
7. Click **Update** .... Enter

Insert Personal Information with the Insert Menu

1. Make sure you have chosen the desired information set in the Personal Information dialog box (see the preceding procedure).
2. Display the publication page where you want the personal information to appear.

3. Click **Insert** .... Alt+I
4. Click **Personal Information** .... R
5. Click the information you want to insert. The text appears in its own text box.
6. Drag the text box where you want it, or move the text into an existing box and then delete the empty box.

Insert the Date and/or Time

1. Position the insertion point inside the text box where you want to insert the date or time.
2. Click **Insert** .... Alt+I
3. Click **Date and Time** .... T
4. (Optional) Select a language from the **Language** drop-down list .... Alt+L if you want a language other than English (United States).
5. Click a format from the **Available formats** list ... Alt+A
6. (Optional) To update the date or time code each time you open or print the publication, click the **Update automatically** check box .... Alt+U
7. Click **OK** .... Enter

Control an Individual AutoCorrect Action

✓ *Do the following when you see a blue minus sign under some text, indicating that an AutoCorrect action has occurred.*

1. Point to the blue minus sign ▭.
2. Click the **AutoCorrect** button.
3. Click an AutoCorrect option.

Change AutoCorrect Settings

1. Click **Tools** .... Alt+T
2. Click **AutoCorrect Options** .... A
3. Click check box for option to turn on or off.

   ✓ *You can click the Exceptions button to set up exceptions to any of the check box rules.*

4. To add an AutoCorrect entry:
   a. Type an error in the **Replace** box. .... Alt+R
   b. Type a correction in the **With** box .... Alt+W
   c. Click **Add** .... Alt+A
5. To remove an AutoCorrect entry:
   a. Click an AutoCorrect entry on the list.
   b. Click **Delete** .... Alt+D
6. To change an AutoCorrect entry:
   a. Click an AutoCorrect entry on the list.
   b. Change the error in the **Replace** box .... Alt+R
   c. Change the correction in the **With** box .... Alt+W
   d. Click **Replace** .... Alt+A
7. Click **OK** .... Enter

Exercise Directions

1. Start Publisher, if necessary.
2. Update the Other Organization personal information set with the data shown in Illustration A.
3. Start a new publication based on the Axis Informational Flyer template. Do not include a graphic.

   ✓ *To do this, from the New Publication task pane, click Publications for Print, then click Flyers, and then click Axis Informational Flyer. In the Flyer Options task pane, click None and then close the task pane.*

4. Reopen the Personal Information dialog box (Edit, Personal Information), select Other Organization, and click Update. The information box in the bottom-left corner of the flyer should now contain the data you entered in step 2, as shown in Illustration B.

   ✓ *Step 4 is necessary because the new publication defaults to the Primary Business information set.*

5. Delete the Organization logo graphic from the flyer.
6. Add a text box at the bottom-right corner of the flyer, and in it type **Last update:** and then insert an automatically-updated date code.
7. Change the vertical Geology Club text near the top to read **Cutler College**.
8. Change the text in the Product/Service Information box to read **Geology Club**. The top of the flyer should resemble Illustration C at this point.
9. Go into the AutoCorrect settings and set up an AutoCorrect entry that changes **gelogy** to **geology**.

   ✓ *If another student has done this already on this computer, you may not need to do step 7; check to see if the entry already exists.*

10. Print the flyer.

    ✓ *Don't worry that it isn't complete yet; you will finish it up in the next exercise.*

11. Save your work as **06GEO** and exit Publisher.

Illustration A

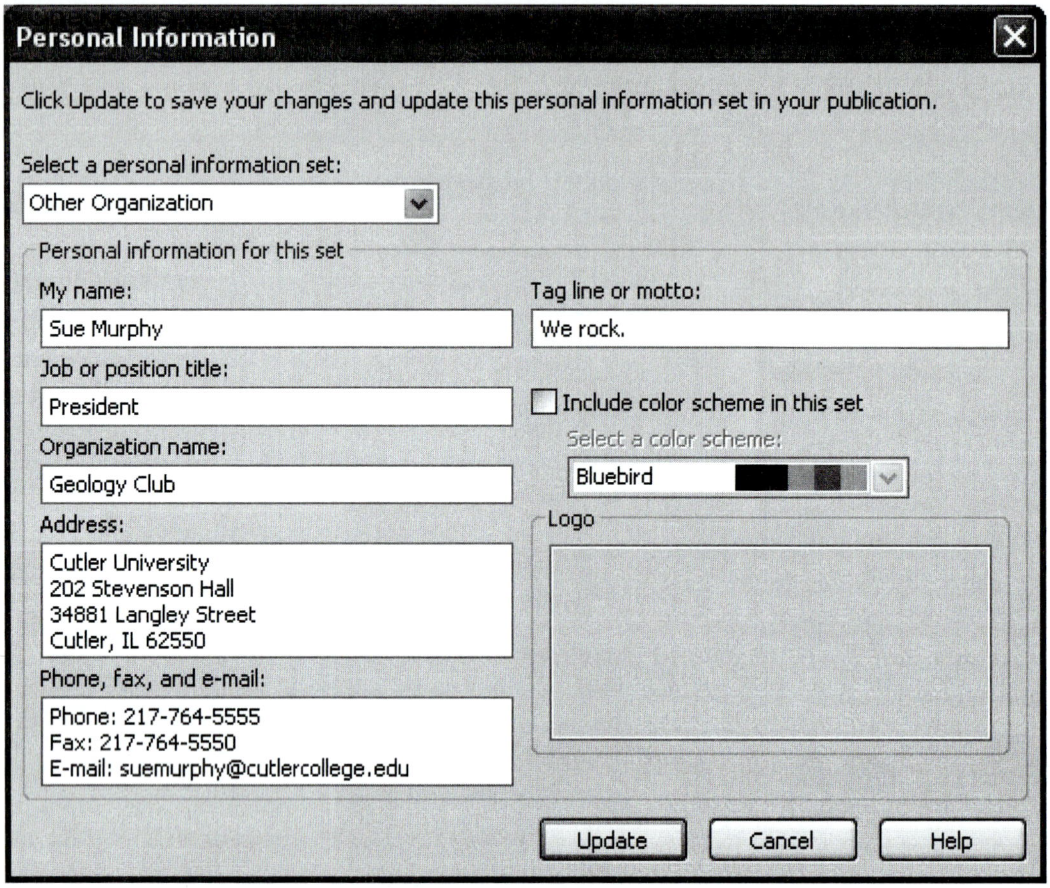

Illustration B

Illustration C

On Your Own

1. Start Publisher, if necessary.
2. Begin a new publication based on any of the Quick Publication Wizards. Choose any color scheme. For the layout, choose *Personal information with picture*.
   ✓ *To determine the name of a layout, point the mouse at it to see a ScreenTip.*
3. Open the Personal Information dialog box, choose the Home/Family set, and enter your own information (or make up information if you do not want to store your personal information on a shared computer).
4. Click Update. Notice that the information in the publication changes.
5. Edit the personal information again to add a tag line **Hang together or hang separatly** (including the typo **separatly**).
6. Add the tag line to the publication, and enlarge its text box so the entire tag line is visible.
7. Add an AutoCorrect entry that changes **separatly** to **separately**.
8. Position the insertion point at the end of **separatly** in the publication and press the spacebar. Publisher corrects it.
9. Save your work as **06PERSON** and exit Publisher.

Exercise 7

Skills Covered:

◆ **Open a File from Another Program** ◆ **Open a Word Document**
◆ **Insert Text from Other Programs** ◆ **Edit a Story in Word**

On the Job

Sometimes you may want to include text in a publication that has already been typed in another program. You can either open a file created in another program (and save it as a new publication), or insert a text file from another program as a story in your existing publication. In addition, Publisher comes with a template designed especially for importing Word documents.

Sue Murphy, president of the Geology Club, has typed up some text she wants you to put on the flyer you began in the preceding exercise, and has provided it to you in Microsoft Word format. You will import that file into the publication. You will also use the Word template to publish a letter to current club members that Sue has prepared.

Terms

Import To bring something in (e.g., text or a graphic) from another program or format.

Autoflow A feature that allows a story to continue into linked text boxes when the original text box is too small to hold it.

Story The text in a single text box or in a series of linked text boxes.

Notes

Open a File from Another Program

- Publisher can open files of several types. Besides its native format (.pub), it can also open Microsoft Word files (.doc), Web files (.htm), and plain text (.txt), among others.
- By default, the Files of type setting in the Open Publication dialog box is set to All Publisher Files, which means that several of these types appear on the list automatically. Simply choose the file to open, and if it is not a .pub file, Publisher converts it as it opens.
- If you want to see files of every type that Publisher can possibly open, open the Files of type list and choose All Text Formats.

You may choose from a variety of formats to open

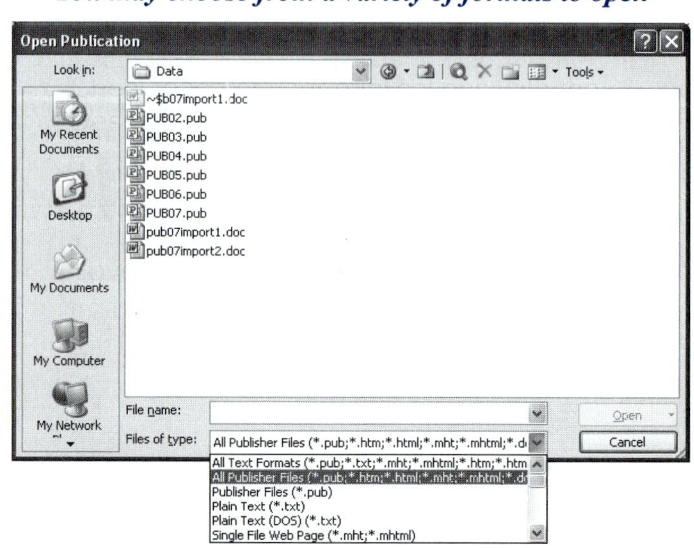

- If you want to see only files of a certain type on the list, open the Files of type list and choose that type.

  ✓ *You may see a message that Publisher needs to install the converter needed for that particular format; if so, click Yes to install it. You will need the Publisher or Office 2003 CD.*

- If the document is too long to fit on a single page, multiple pages are created, each with a single text box, and the document text flows automatically (using **autoflow**) from box to box via text box links.

  ✓ *Exercise 42 covers text box linking in more detail.*

A long document occupies multiple pages in a publication.

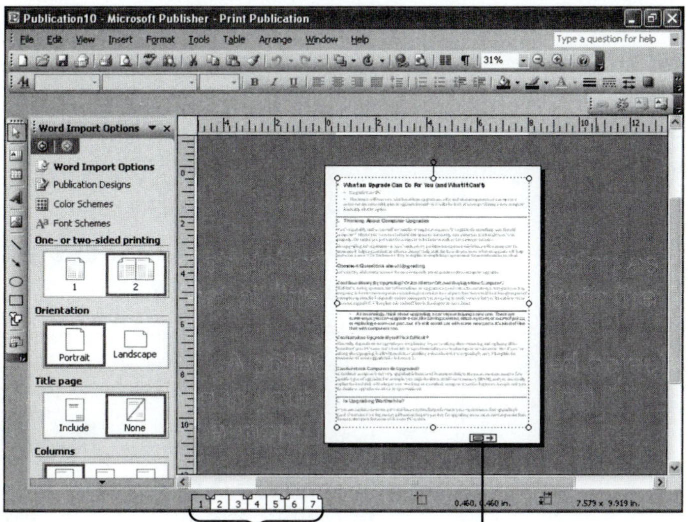

Multiple pages

This indicates the text boxes are linked

- The imported document will likely need some formatting work to resemble the original; you will learn about text formatting in Lesson 3.

Open a Word Document

- If the document to open is a Word file, you can use the File, Import Word Document command. This is almost the same as opening a Word file normally in Publisher except that the dialog box has a different title and the Files of Type setting is preset to show only Word documents (.doc and .rtf extensions).
- Word Import Options task pane appears automatically when the imported file is a Word document. Import options include page layout, color scheme, and design, the same as with other types of Publisher publications.

Insert Text from Other Programs

- You may prefer to insert the contents of a text file as a **story** within an existing publication rather than placing it in its own new publication.
- To insert text, first create a text box to hold it and position the insertion point inside that text box. Then choose Insert, Text File.
- If the file type you are inserting is something other than regular text (for example, if it is a Word table or an Excel spreadsheet), it appears as its own separate object, regardless of the insertion point's position.
- If the imported text is too lengthy to fit in the text box, a message appears asking whether you want to use autoflow. If you choose Yes, Publisher automatically flows the text throughout your publication, asking for confirmation before it flows into existing text boxes. If you choose No, you will need to create more text boxes and flow the text into them manually. (Exercise 42 covers that.)
- If you answer Yes to the autoflow question, Publisher asks whether you want it to create the needed text boxes automatically or not. If you choose Yes, it creates both text boxes and pages as needed.
- For the purposes of this exercise, answer Yes to both of the above questions.

Edit a Story in Word

- You may prefer to edit text in Microsoft Word, if you have it, because of Word's superior editing capabilities. For example, Word includes a grammar checker and many other features that Publisher does not.
- When you edit in Word, the entire story appears there (that is, the current text box and all the text from any linked text boxes).
- Within Publisher, choose Edit, Edit Story in Microsoft Word to open the story in Word. Then when you are finished in Word, choose File, Close & Return to {*publication name*}.

Procedures

Open a File from Another Program

1. Click **File** .... Alt+I
2. Click **Open** .... O

   ✓ *You can click the **Open** button on the Standard toolbar or press Ctrl+O instead of doing steps 1–2.*

3. Click the arrow on the **Files of type** drop-down list............. Alt+T
4. Click the file format desired.
5. Navigate to the folder and disk containing the file you want.
6. Click the file to select it.
7. Click the **Open** button [Open] .... Alt+O

Use a Word Template to Import a Word Document

1. Click **File**..................... Alt+F
2. Click **New** .... N
3. Click **Publications to Print**.
4. Click **Import Word Documents**.
5. Click a design.
6. Navigate to the folder and disk containing the file you want.
7. Click the file to select it.
8. Click layout options in the task pane as needed.
9. (Optional) Change the color scheme:
   a. Click **Color Schemes.**
   b. Click a scheme.
10. (Optional) Change the font scheme:
    a. Click **Font Schemes**.
    b. Click a font scheme.

Insert Text from Other Programs into an Existing Publication

1. Position the insertion point in the text box where you want to begin the imported story.
2. Click **Insert**................. Alt+I
3. Click **Text File**..................... E
4. Navigate to the folder and disk containing the file you want.
5. Click the file to select it.
6. Click **OK** .... Enter

Edit a Story in Microsoft Word

1. Click the text box containing the story you want to edit.

   ✓ *If the story is in multiple linked text boxes, select any of the boxes in which it resides.*

2. Click **Edit**.................... Alt+E
3. Click **Edit Story in Microsoft Word** .... W
4. Edit the story in Word as desired.
5. In Word, click **File** .... Alt+F
6. Click **Close & Return to {*publication*}** C

Exercise Directions

1. Start Publisher, if necessary.
2. Open the file **PUB07**. Save it as **07GEO**.
3. Replace all text in the middle text box with the text from the file **PUB07Import1.doc** (a Word document).

   ✓ *Notice that the imported text retains its formatting from Word and uses a different font and size.*

4. Edit the story in Word, changing **April 21** to **April 23**. Then return to Publisher.
5. Save your work and close the file.
6. Open the file **PUB07Import2.doc** in Publisher.
7. Resize the text box containing the letter so the text box's right and left sides are 1" from the edge of the paper and the top and bottom are 2" from the edge.
8. Edit the story in Word, changing **April 21** to **April 23**. Then return to Publisher.
9. Print the letter, and save it as **07GEOLET**.
10. Save your work and exit Publisher.

On Your Own

1. Start Publisher, if necessary.
2. Open the file **OPUB07A.doc** (a Word document) as a new publication in Publisher. You can either use a Word template, opening it directly from the Open dialog box, or use the File, Import Word Document command.
3. Save it in Publisher format as **07ESSAY**.
4. Resize the text box on the first page to make 1" of extra space at the top, and then place the contents of **OPUB07B.doc** in a text box above the main article.
5. Go through the article looking for red-underlined, words, and change their spellings to American spellings of those words. You may use the spell checker (as in Exercise 4) to change all instances of each word, or do this manually.
6. Return to Publisher, save your work, and exit Publisher.

Exercise 8

◆ **Critical Thinking**

The local elementary school is having a science fair, and a friend who is a teacher wants you to make some signs for her. She needs a sign to help parents find their way from the entry to the classroom where the science exhibits are displayed and also a sign that lists the evening's schedule of award presentations. In this exercise, you will make the signs she needs.

Exercise Directions

1. Start Publisher, if necessary.
2. Create a new publication from the Catalog based on the Bubbles Quick Publication.
3. Choose a colorful, bright color scheme.
4. For the Layout, choose Heading only.
5. Edit the text to read **Science Fair Room 121**, as shown in Illustration A.
6. Save the publication as **08SIGN1**.
7. Save the publication as **08SIGN2**.
8. Switch the publication layout to Message Only.
9. Replace the sample text with the text from **PUB08.doc**.
10. Open the schedule for editing in Word. Rearrange the events so they are in chronological order.
11. Resize the text box so there is 2" of space above it, and place a new text box in that space.
12. Cut-and-paste the title text (**Science Fair Schedule of Events**) from its original location into the new text box.
13. Set the new text box for AutoFit Text Best Fit. It should look like Illustration B at this point.
14. Print the schedule using the default print settings.
15. Close **08SIGN2**, and reopen **08SIGN1**. Then print it, too.
16. Save your work and exit Publisher.

Illustration A

Illustration B

Exercise 9

◆ Critical Thinking

Pet Rescue, a local charity, is looking for volunteers to provide foster homes for dogs and cats while they await permanent homes. You have been asked to create a flyer that explains the responsibilities and rewards of the job, to be handed out at events where animal-lovers are likely to attend. In the following exercise, you will develop the flyer they need.

Exercise Directions

1. Start Publisher, if necessary.
2. Begin a new Quick Publication based on the Straight Edge design. Use any color scheme you like. For the Layout, choose No Picture.
3. Replace the Heading placeholder with **Pet Foster Homes Needed!**.
   - ✓ *AutoFit Best Fit will be enabled for the Heading text box; if it does not seem to be working, resize the text box slightly and it will kick in.*
4. Resize the heading frame to make it wider and shorter, so that the text occupies only two lines, and move it higher up on the flyer as shown in Illustration A.
5. Resize the message frame as shown in Illustration A and type the text shown there.
6. Edit the Personal Information (the Secondary Business set) to show the following contact information:

   Name: **Ray James**

   Job or position title: **Volunteer Coordinator**

   Organization name: **Pet Rescue**

   Address: **2077 W. 166th St., Indianapolis, IN 46240**

   Phone/fax/e-mail: Phone: **212-555-9191**, fax: **212-555-9089**, e-mail: **rjames@petrescueindy.org**

   Tag line or motto: **Loving and Caring for Companion Animals**
7. Insert the organization name, address, and phone/fax/e-mail information from the Personal Information you entered in step 6.
8. Delete the fax line.
9. Using cut-and-paste, move all the inserted personal information into a single text box and delete the empty text boxes left over.
10. Set the text box's AutoFit setting to Best Fit. Then resize the text box so that the text is a readable size.
    - ✓ *Illustration B shows the finished flyer.*
11. Check the spelling for the entire publication.
12. Zoom out to Whole Page view and examine your work. Make any changes if needed for a more attractive layout.
13. Save your work as **09FOSTER**.
14. Print the flyer.
15. Save your work and exit Publisher.

Illustration A

Illustration B

Lesson 2

Changing the Design and Layout

Exercise 10
- Change the Design
- Change the Color Scheme
- Create New Color Schemes
- Change the Layout
- Change the Font Scheme

Exercise 11
- Change the Paper and Fold Type
- Work with Special Papers
- Show/Hide Layout Guides
- Change the Layout Guides
- Place Ruler Guides

Exercise 12
- Insert Pages
- Delete Pages
- Go to a Specific Page
- Work with Headers and Footers
- Use Page Numbering

Exercise 13
- Work with Master Pages
- Name Pages
- Move Pages

Exercise 14
- Work with Master Sets
- Use the Design Checker

Exercise 15
- Insert a Design Gallery Object
- Customize a Design Gallery Object
- Create Your Own Design Gallery Objects

Exercise 16
- Critical Thinking

Exercise 17
- Critical Thinking

Exercise 10

Skills Covered:

- **Change the Design**
- **Change the Color Scheme**
- **Create New Color Schemes**
- **Change the Layout**
- **Change the Font Scheme**

On the Job

As you work on a publication, you may decide that it would look better with a different design, a different layout, or a different color scheme. Fortunately, each of these aspects is easy to change.

You have shown your draft publication from Exercise 7 to the Geology Club members. They like it, but they would like to see some other designs, layouts, and color schemes. In this exercise, you will change those parts of the publication in several ways to provide them with some choices.

Terms

Design The appearance theme of the publication. Publisher offers dozens of designs from which to choose.

Color scheme A set of preselected colors that work well together in a publication.

Layout The arrangement of placeholder elements on the page (such as Heading, Picture, and Message).

Notes

Change the Design

- Even blank publications have a **design**. (They have a design called Blank.) There are dozens of designs available to choose from in Publisher.
- You can apply any design to a publication, at any time. Changing the design does not change any text in the publication; it merely arranges items differently and places different background graphics.
- To apply a different design, choose Format, Publication Designs. The task pane appears (if it was not on-screen already) displaying various publication design choices. Click the one you want.
  - ✓ *After changing the publication design, some of your content might have shifted; rearrange objects if needed.*

Click the Publication Designs hyperlink and then click the design you want

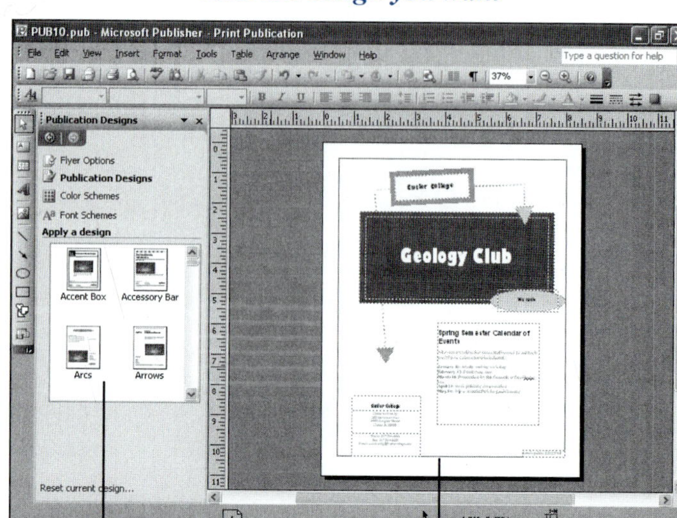

Click a design

The publication updates immediately (some objects might need resizing or repositioning)

✓ *Instead of using the commands on the Format menu to change the design, color scheme, and layout in this exercise, you can simply keep the task pane on-screen and click the hyperlink for the needed feature to display its controls.*

- If you apply a design and then make changes to it, you can return to the original design by clicking Reset current design (at the bottom of the task pane). This opens the Reset Design dialog box, in which you can specify which elements you want to reset.

Reset some or all elements of the chosen design

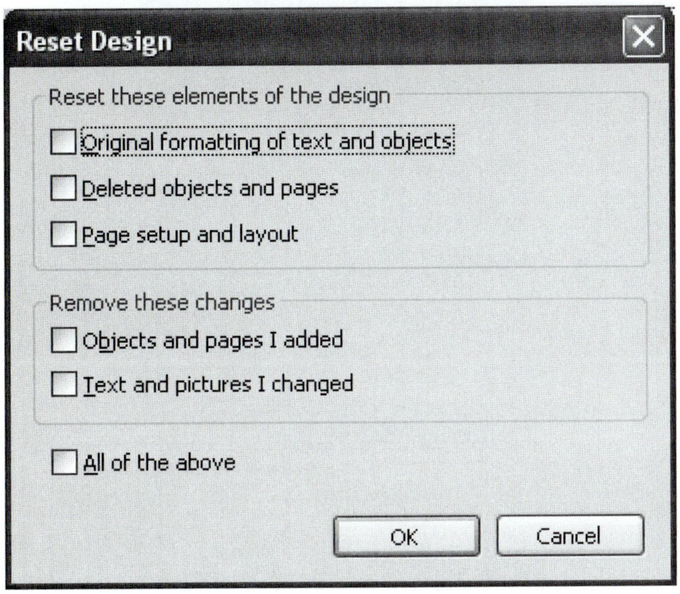

✓ *When you reset a design element, any customization you have done to it reverts to the default. That means that any text you have typed is wiped out and replaced by the original placeholder text. Don't reset elements for which you want to keep any text or graphics you have placed.*

Change the Color Scheme

- The colors used for various objects on the page come from the chosen **color scheme**. By applying a different color scheme, you recolor everything formatted with one of these placeholder colors. (You will learn how to manually recolor objects in Lesson 3.)

- You can change the color scheme from the task pane, just as you can for the design. Choose Format, Color Schemes. Then click your choice on the list of color schemes that appears in the task pane.

Select a different color scheme from the schemes provided

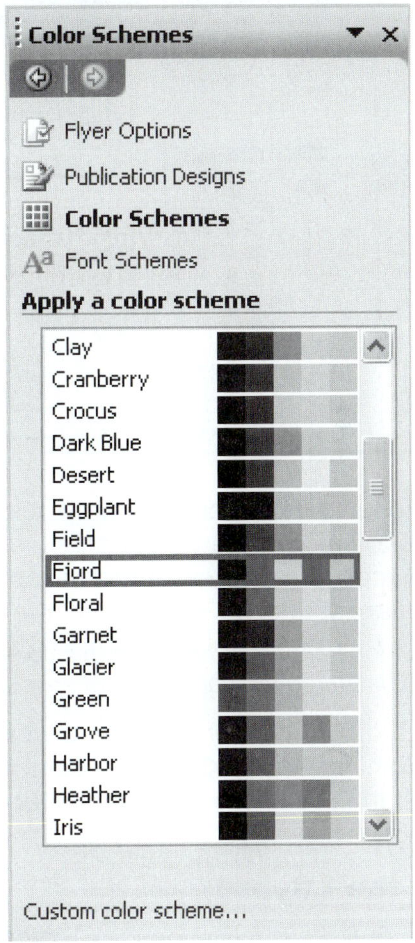

Create New Color Schemes

- You can also create your own color schemes by modifying existing ones. To do so, click the Custom color scheme hyperlink at the bottom of the task pane. This opens the Color Schemes dialog box with the Custom tab displayed.
- The colors for the currently applied scheme appear. Open the New drop-down list for one of the scheme placeholders and choose a different color if desired.

Create a custom color scheme

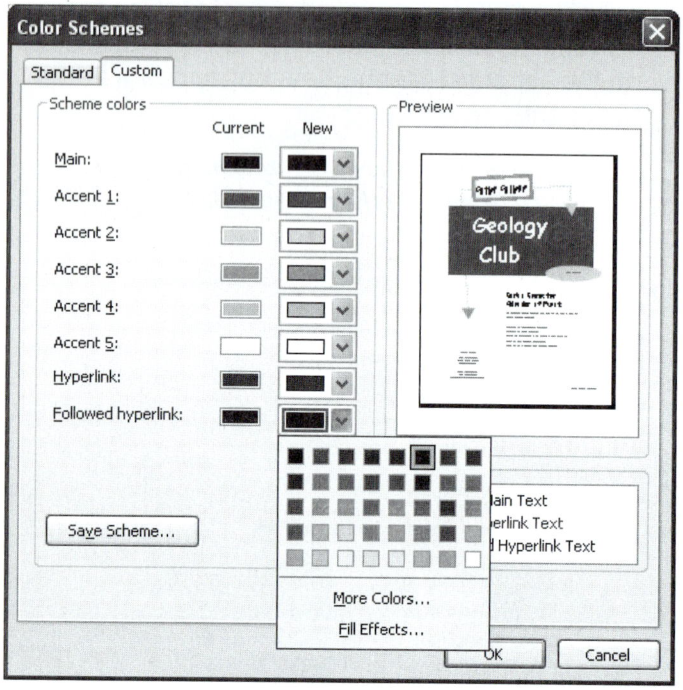

- After choosing the colors you want, click Save Scheme to create a new color scheme based on your choices. This new scheme will appear on the regular list of color schemes in the future.

  ✓ *If you don't expect ever to use this color combination again, you need not save it.*

✓ To pick a different color scheme to work with, go to the Standard tab and select a standard scheme; then return to the Custom tab to change it.

Change the Layout

- You can make a publication look radically different just by changing its **layout**. The layout specifies which placeholder elements will appear (picture, heading, sidebar heading, message, and so forth) and where each will be placed.
- Different publication types have different layout options.
- To change the layout, choose Format, {publication type} Options. The exact name depends on the template you used to create the publication; for a Flyer, the command is Flyer Options.

✓ *If you have moved objects around or resized objects in the publication, be prepared to resize and reposition them again after changing the layout. The new layout will reset all sizes and positions to the default. In addition, if you have any text or graphics in a placeholder box that is not a part of the newly chosen layout, it will disappear. (Publisher will store it, however, and restore it to the publication if you switch back to a layout that includes it.)*

Select a different layout for your publication from the Layout controls on the task pane

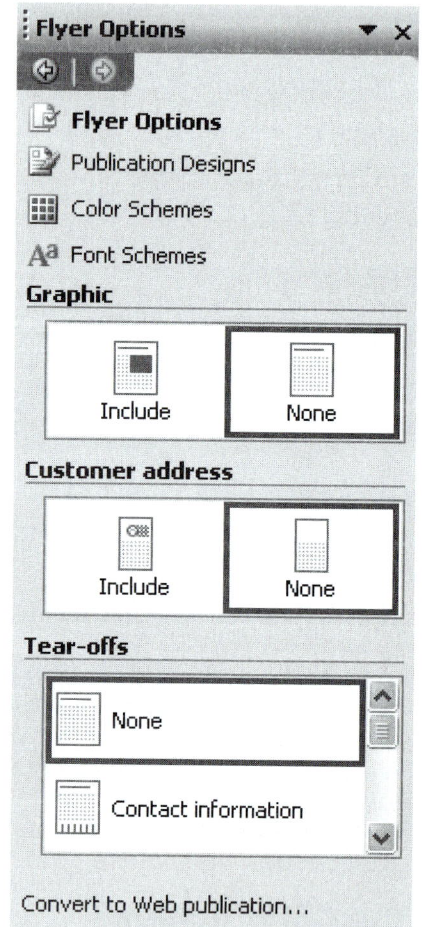

Change the Font Scheme

- Like the other schemes, a font scheme applies a predefined set of formatting. In this case, they apply a set of fonts that are chosen to look good together.
- You apply font schemes from the task pane, just like other schemes. Choose Format, Font Schemes to display the font scheme controls on the task pane.

Select a different font scheme

- To fine-tune how the font scheme works, click the Font Scheme Options hyperlink at the bottom of the task pane. This opens the Font Scheme Options dialog box, shown below.

Control how the font scheme will be applied

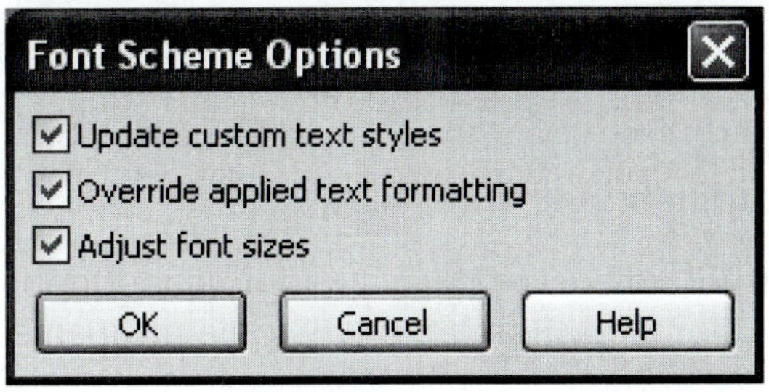

- These font scheme options let you specify how comprehensively the font scheme will be applied. By default, it applies the new fonts to all text, even text that has been specifically formatted in some other way, such as with text formatting or a style.
- Clearing the check boxes in the dialog box tells the font scheme to allow certain text to remain formatted with its own font choices.

Procedures

Change the Design

1. Click **Format** .... Alt+O
2. Click **Publication Designs** .... U

   ✓ *If the task pane already appears on-screen, you can simply click the Publication Designs hyperlink in it instead of doing steps 1–2.*

3. Click the design you want to apply.

Reset the Design

1. If the Publication Designs task pane does not already appear:
   a. Click **Format** .... Alt+O
   b. Click **Publication Designs** .... U
2. Click **Reset current design**.
3. Click the check boxes for the elements you want to reset.

   OR

   Click **All of the above** to choose all elements. .... Alt+A

   ✓ *Warning: If you choose **Text and pictures I changed**, you will lose any text you have entered in the publication's placeholders. If you choose **Objects and pages I added**, you will lose any text or other elements you have inserted as new objects*

4. Click **OK** .... Enter

   ✓ *A warning box appears.*

5. Click **OK** .... Enter

Choose a Color Scheme

1. Click **Format** .... Alt+O
2. Click **Color Schemes** C

   ✓ *If the task pane already appears on-screen, you can simply click the Color Schemes hyperlink in it instead of doing steps 1–2.*

3. Click the **Color Scheme** you want.

Customize a Color Scheme

1. If the Color Schemes task pane does not already appear:
   a. Click **Format** .... Alt+O
   b. Click **Color Schemes** C
2. Click **Custom color scheme**.
3. Open the **New** drop-down list for the color you want to change.
4. Click a different color on the palette that appears.

   OR

   Click **More Colors**, select a different color from the dialog box that appears, and click **OK**.

   OR

   Click **Fill Effects**, select a fill effect from the dialog box that appears, and click **OK**.

   ✓ *See Exercise 20 for more information on Fill Effects.*

5. Repeat steps 3–4 for each color you want to change.

6. (Optional) To save the modified scheme:
   a. Click **Save Scheme** button [Save Scheme...] .. Alt+V
   b. Type a name for new scheme.
   c. Click **OK** .... Enter
7. Click **OK** to apply new scheme to the current publication... Enter

Delete a Custom Color Scheme

1. Click **Format** .... Alt+O
2. Click **Color Scheme** C
3. Click **Custom color scheme**.
4. Click the **Standard** tab.
5. Click scheme you want to delete.

   ✓ *You can delete only custom color schemes (that is, schemes you have created). You cannot delete any of the standard schemes that come with Publisher.*

6. Click **Delete Scheme** button [Delete Scheme] .... D
7. Click **Yes**.
8. Click **OK**............................ Enter

Change the Layout

1. Click **Format**............... Alt+O
2. Click **Quick Publication Options** .... Alt+O

   ✓ *Substitute the publication type for Quick Publication in step 2 if you are working with a different type of publication (Brochure Options, Newsletter Options, etc.).*

   ✓ *If the task pane already appears on-screen, you can simply click the Quick Publication Options hyperlink in it instead of doing steps 1–2.*

3. Click the layout you want.

Choose a Font Scheme

1. Click **Format** .... Alt+O
2. Click **Font Schemes** .... N

   ✓ *If the task pane already appears on-screen, you can simply click the Font Schemes hyperlink in it instead of doing steps 1–2.*

3. Click the font scheme you want.

Exercise Directions

1. Start Publisher, if necessary.
2. Open the file **PUB10**. Save it as **10GEO**.
3. Change the Layout to include a graphic and a tear-off coupon.
4. Experiment with the other available layout options for flyers; then change the layout back to None for the graphic and None for the tear-offs.
5. Try several different publication designs; when you are finished, set the publication design to Mobile.
6. Try several different color schemes; when you are finished, set the color scheme to Tropics.
7. Change the Accent 1 color in the color scheme to dark green, and then save the color scheme under the name **Green Tropics**.
8. Try several different font schemes; when you are finished, set the font scheme to Industrial.
9. Set the text box containing the Calendar of Events to AutoFit Best Fit. Illustration A shows the finished flyer.
10. Save your work and exit Publisher.

On Your Own

1. Start Publisher, if necessary.
2. Begin a new publication using one of the Business Cards templates. Use these settings for the layout:
   - Logo: None
   - Orientation: Portrait
   - Copies per sheet: Multiple
3. Type your own contact information in the text placeholders on the card.
4. Change to a different color scheme.
5. Choose a different font scheme.
6. Change the design.
7. Change to Landscape orientation from the Business Card Options in the task pane.
8. Print a sheet of business cards (using plain paper).
9. Save your work as **10CARDS** and exit Publisher.

Illustration A

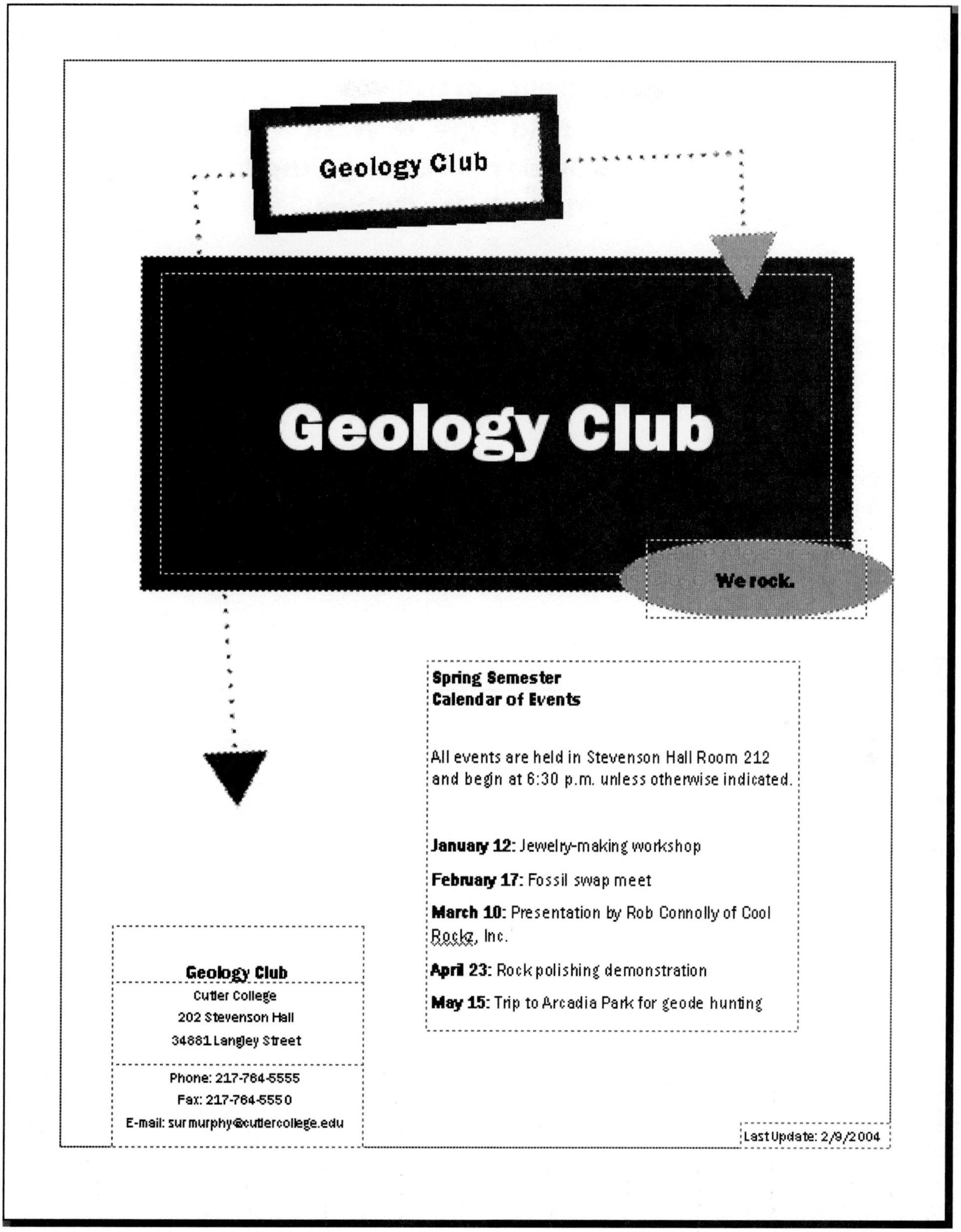

Exercise 11

Skills Covered:

◆ **Change the Paper and Fold Type** ◆ **Work with Special Papers**
◆ **Show/Hide Layout Guides** ◆ **Change the Layout Guides**
◆ **Place Ruler Guides**

On the Job

So far in this book, you've been working with normal 8.5" x 11" portrait-orientation pages, but there are many more possibilities, including special papers designed specifically for desktop publishing projects, which you can purchase from office supply outlets.

Anderson Farms is a fruit and vegetable farm that hosts special promotional events throughout the year. The owner, Jean Anderson, wants to create a flyer on special orange-colored paper she has ordered (8" x 10") announcing an upcoming pumpkin carving contest. She can do most of the work herself, but she isn't sure how to set up the non-standard paper size. In this exercise, you will help her by creating a new publication and setting up the paper size and orientation, margin guides, and grid guides.

Terms

Orientation The direction that the text runs on a page. Orientation can be portrait (text runs across the short edge) or landscape (text runs across the long edge).

Layout guides A generic term for grid guides and margin guides collectively.

Grid guides Blue, nonprinting lines on a page that show column and/or row margins in a multicolumn or multirow layout.

Margin guides Blue nonprinting lines on a page that show the page margins.

Baseline guides Yellow, nonprinting lines on a page that help position text baselines.

Ruler guides Green, nonprinting vertical or horizontal lines that you can display temporarily to help you align objects with one another.

Notes

Choose a Paper and Fold Type

- In the Page Setup dialog box (File, Page Setup), you choose a paper and fold type.
- Publisher refers to this setting as "Publication type" but this is *not* the same as the publication type you select when beginning the publication file (Quick Publication, Flyer, etc.). This setting determines your publication's size in relation to a standard sheet of paper.

✓ *This Publication type setting is important when creating a publication from scratch (that is, from a blank design), but if you start the publication based on a template, the appropriate publication type will have already been chosen for you.*

- The default is full page, which prints one copy of the publication on one sheet of paper. You can specify the paper size.

- Some types use only part of a page. For example, a business card might take up only a few inches of space on the page, so you could print multiple copies of it on a single sheet.
- Some types have more than one size. You can choose among available sizes from the Page size list.
- Some types allow you to select a page **orientation**: portrait or landscape. The Preview area in the Page Setup dialog box shows the effect of the change when you switch between them.

This special fold will create a folded 8.5" × 5.5" card from a single 8.5" × 11" sheet of paper

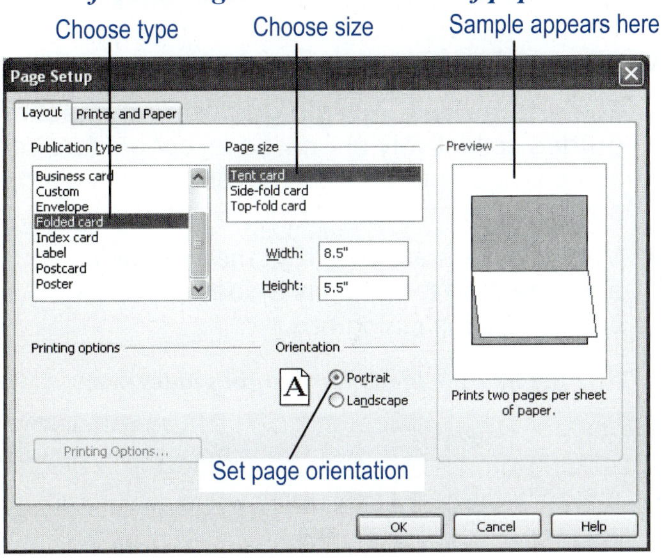

- Some types, such as Banner and Poster, require more than one sheet of paper. You can see dividers in the Preview area for such publication sizes, showing how many standard-size (8.5" x 11") sheets will be needed.

Some publication types require multiple sheets

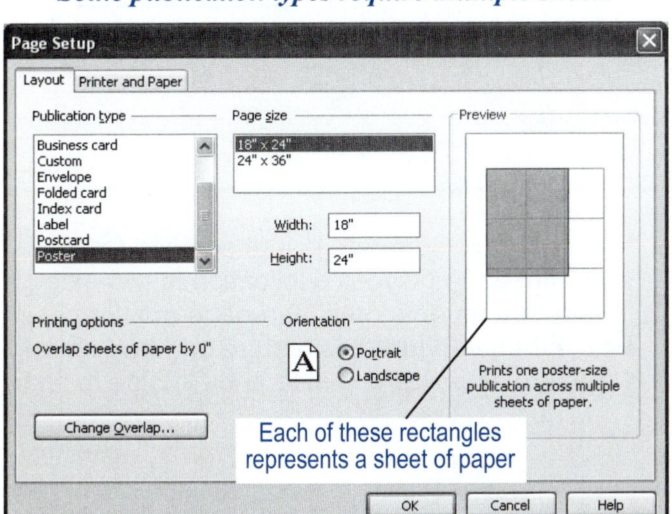

- On the Printer and Paper tab, you can choose the printer you want to print from (if you have more than one printer) and also specify the size of paper loaded into that printer.

You can choose a paper size independently from the publication size

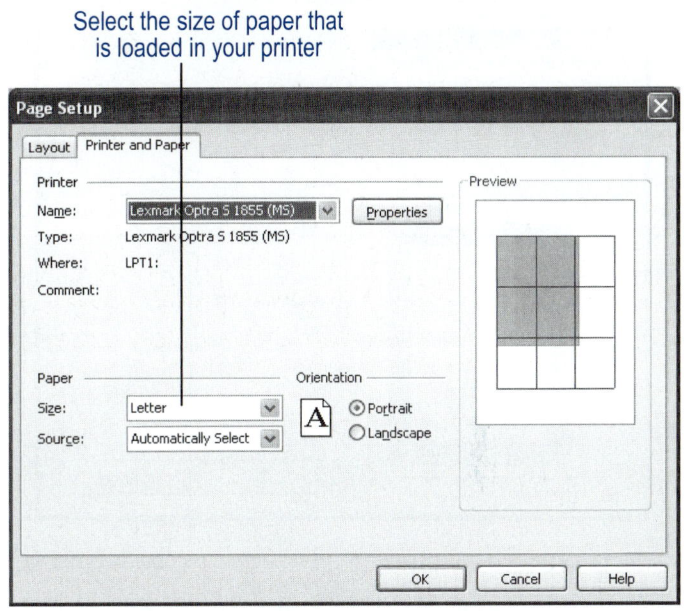

- Specifying the paper size is different from choosing the publication size, because some publications do not fit neatly onto one page.
- The Poster type shown in the dialog box above is a good example. You might have the same size poster, but it might be comprised of more or fewer sheets of paper depending on the paper size.

Work with Special Papers

- The Special Papers feature lets Publisher recognize and use any of several dozen special papers you may buy. They are manufactured by a company called Paper Direct.

  ✓ *You can buy paper online from Paper Direct at http://www.paperdirect.com.*

- When you choose View, Special Paper for the first time, you may be prompted to insert your Publisher 2003 CD-ROM to install it.
- Select your paper from the Special Paper dialog box. Or, if you have not yet bought the paper, browse the papers and make a note of the style number of the paper you want.

Select the special paper that you have bought for use with Publisher

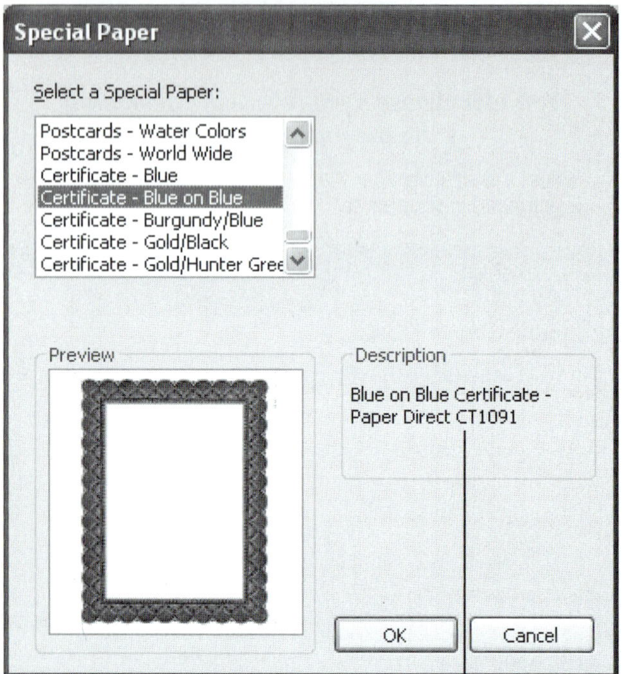

Style number to order

- When you select a special paper, the paper appears on-screen, and your page margins are adjusted for the graphics on the paper. That way you can see on the screen how the finished publication will appear when printed. However, the paper graphics you see on-screen will not print; you must buy and use the special paper on which the graphics are preprinted.

The special paper's design appears on-screen, but won't print

Special paper design (nonprinting)

Show/Hide Layout Guides

- The **layout guides** on-screen merely provide suggestions for object placement. You are free to place any object anywhere on the page you like.
  - ✓ *Layout guides are especially useful in multi-page publications, so you can be sure you are placing objects in a consistent way on each page.*
- To toggle the display of the layout guides, choose View, Boundaries and Guides or press Ctrl+Shift+O.
- Baseline guides are toggled on/off separately; choose View, Baseline Guides or press Ctrl+F7.

Change the Layout Guides

- The **grid guides, margin guides**, and **baseline guides** collectively are called *layout guides*. You can change both from the Layout Guides dialog box (choose Arrange, Layout Guides).
- Margin guides are blue. Set margin guide placement on the Margin Guides tab of the Layout Guides dialog box.

Set new positions for margin guides here

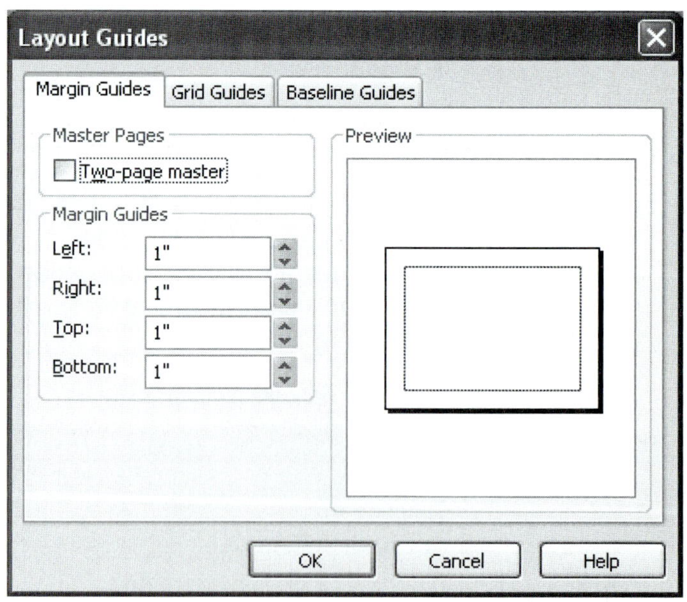

- You can have separate layout settings for left and right pages if your publication is two-sided. To set that up, mark the Two-page master check box. When you turn this feature on, the Left and Right boxes become Inside and Outside instead.

- Grid guides enable you to divide the page into multiple equal-sized sections. For example, if you wanted a page to be divided into eight equal sections, you could set up the grid guides to show where those sections should be.

Set new positions for grid guides here

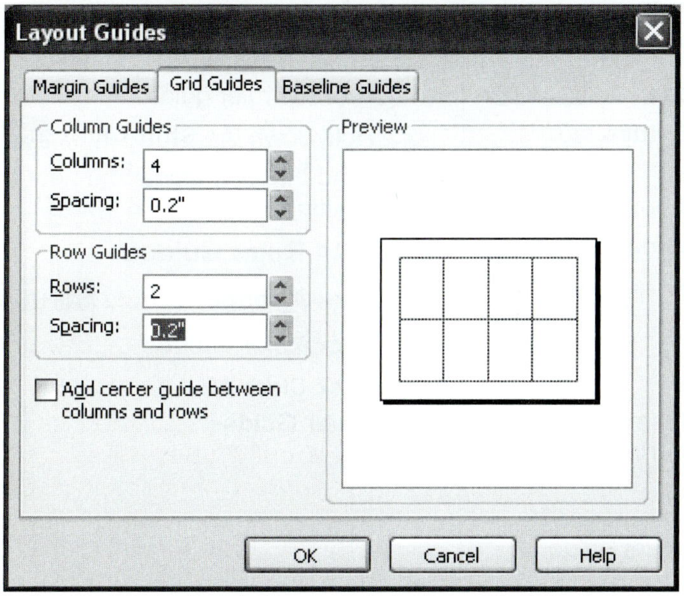

- By default, the grid consists of a single area (one row, one column), so grid guides are the same as margin guides.

- Baseline guides (new in Publisher 2003) enable you to set an alignment position for text so that the baselines of text across all columns line up.
- For baseline guides, you can set spacing and offset. Spacing is the space between the guides, and offset is the distance between the top margin guide and the first horizontal baseline below it.

  ✓ *As with other guides, baseline guides are merely suggestions to help with text box placement; they do not force text to lock with them.*

Place Ruler Guides

- **Ruler guides** are straight vertical or horizontal lines that you can temporarily place on your screen to assist you in aligning objects on a page. They do not print, and they can be easily removed at any time.
- To place a ruler guide, position the mouse pointer over a ruler and drag inward toward the center of the page to create and position a green guideline.
- To move a ruler guide after placement, hold down Shift while you drag it. You can drag it off the page to remove it.
- To clear ruler guides, choose Arrange, Ruler Guides, Clear All Ruler Guides.

Procedures

Choose a Publication Layout

1. Click **File** .... Alt+F
2. Click **Page Setup** .... U
3. Click a publication type on the Layout tab.
4. Set page size for chosen type.

   ✓ *Page size controls are not available for Full Page.*

5. Click **Portrait** or **Landscape** from the Choose an Orientation section (if available for type you chose in step 3).......... Alt+R/Alt+N
6. Click **OK**.................... Enter

Choose a Printer and a Paper Size

1. Click **File** .... Alt+F
2. Click **Page Setup** .... U
3. Click **Printer and Paper** tab.
4. Open **Name** drop-down list .... Alt+M
5. Click name of printer to use.
6. Click the **Size** drop-down list arrow .... Alt+Z, ↓
7. Select paper size to use.
8. Click **OK** .... Enter

Work with Special Papers

1. Click **View** .... Alt+V
2. Click **Special Paper**.......... S
3. Select the paper that you have purchased.

   ✓ *Compare the picture in the Preview area to the actual paper to make sure you are choosing correctly from the list.*

4. Click **OK**.................... Enter

Show or Hide Margin and Grid Guides

- Press
  Ctrl+Shift+O .... Ctrl + Shift + O

OR

1. Click **View** .... Alt + V
2. Click **Boundaries and Guides** .... B

Show or Hide Baseline Guides

- Press
  Ctrl+F7 .... Ctrl + F7

OR

1. Click **View** .... Alt + V
2. Click **Baseline Guides** .... E

Change the Layout Guides

1. Click **Arrange** .... Alt + R
2. Click **Layout Guides** L
3. Enter margin settings in the **Left**, **Right**, **Top**, and **Bottom** boxes on the Margin Guides tab.
4. If desired, click the **Two-page master** check box....... Alt + W
5. Click the **Grid Guides** tab.
6. Enter number of columns in the **Columns** box..... Alt + C
7. Enter number of rows in the **Rows** box .... Alt + R
8. Click **OK** .... Enter

Place Ruler Guides

1. Position the mouse pointer over either the vertical or horizontal ruler.
2. Drag toward the center of the page, placing a ruler guide.

Clear a Single Ruler Guide

1. Position the mouse pointer over the ruler guide.
2. Hold down the **Shift** key.... Shift
3. Drag the ruler guide off the page and drop it.

Move a Ruler Guide

1. Position the mouse pointer over the ruler guide.
2. Hold down the **Shift** key.... Shift
3. Drag the ruler guide to a new position.

Clear All Ruler Guides

1. Click **Arrange**............. Alt + R
2. Click **Ruler Guides** .... D
3. Click **Clear All Ruler Guides**......................... C

Exercise Directions

1. Start Publisher, if necessary.
2. Begin a new, blank publication and save it as **11PUMPKIN**.
3. Set the publication layout type to Custom and enter 8" for the width and 10" for the height.
4. Set the margin layout guides to 0.8" on all sides.
5. Place a vertical ruler guide at the 1.5" mark and a horizontal ruler guide at the 1.5" mark.
6. Create a 4" wide by 2" high text box beginning at the intersection of the ruler guides, and type **Pumpkin Carving Contest** in the text box.
7. Clear all ruler guides.
8. Save your work and exit Publisher.

On Your Own

1. Start Publisher, if necessary.
2. Create a new publication using one of the Greeting Card templates. Save it as **11CARD**.
3. In Page Setup, change the card to side-fold, landscape orientation, on legal-size paper.
4. In the Layout Guides dialog box, turn off the Two-page master setting.
5. Set the margin guides to be 0.5" on all sides.
6. Resize and reposition the objects on the front of the card to look good with the new page size.
7. Switch to a different design, and check the objects on the card for attractive placement. Adjust them if needed for the non-standard size.
8. Save your work and exit Publisher.

Exercise 12

Skills Covered:

◆ **Insert Pages** ◆ **Delete Pages** ◆ **Go to a Specific Page**
◆ **Work with Headers and Footers** ◆ **Use Page Numbering**

On the Job

So far in this book, you have worked with single-page publications, but a publication can have as many pages as you like. You may even layout an entire book in Publisher. When you begin working with multi-page publications, special challenges arise, such as how to keep repeated elements identical on every page and how to number the pages.

Marcela Lopez is a computer consultant who has been hired by a local dentist to research the availability of office management software. She has created the main report in Publisher and a separate cover sheet in Word. You will help her by combining the two publications and by setting up page numbering and a header and footer for her publication.

Terms

Header Text that is repeated at the top of each page in a multi-page document.

Footer Text that is repeated at the bottom of each page in a multi-page document.

Notes

Insert Pages

- You can insert any number of pages, either before or after the current page.
- To display the Insert Page dialog box, choose Insert, Page.
- You may wish to insert totally blank pages, or insert pages that already contain one or more text frames.
- If an existing page already contains text frames in the locations you want on the new page(s), you can duplicate all the objects from a particular page as you create the new ones.
  - ✓ *If you choose to duplicate objects on an existing page, that duplication includes any layout guides, ruler guides, and other page settings.*

Specify how many pages to insert and what objects to place on them to start with

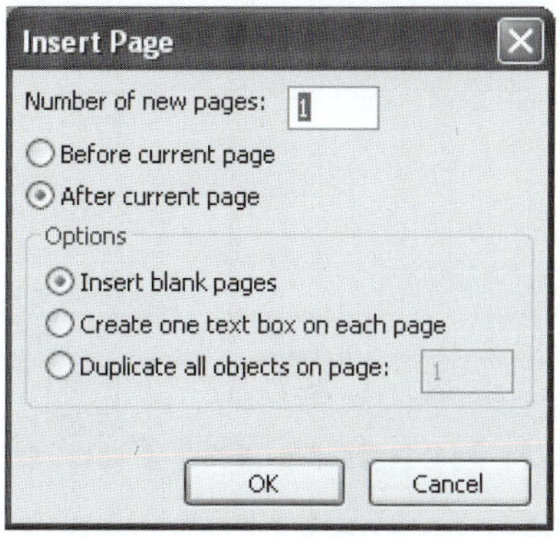

Delete Pages

- To delete a page, display the page and choose Edit, Delete Page. When you delete a page, all objects on that page are deleted, too. You can delete only one page at a time.

- If the page you're deleting contains a text frame that is part of a chain of linked frames (see Exercise 42), the text that was in that frame moves to the connected frames on the other pages.

View as a Two Page Spread

- When creating a publication that will be printed double-sided, such as a booklet, it may be helpful to see the pages in pairs.
- To view two pages at a time, choose View, Two Page Spread. Page 1 will be by itself, but all other pages will be paired.

Go to a Specific Page

- To display a page in a multi-page publication, click its page icon at the bottom of the screen.

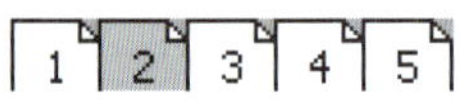

- If you are viewing the publication in Two Page Spread mode the page numbers are in pairs, and you select a two-page spread at once.

- If a publication has many pages, you may not be able to see the icons for all pages at the bottom. To go to a specific page, choose Edit, Go to Page and enter the page number you want.

Specify the number of the page you want to go to

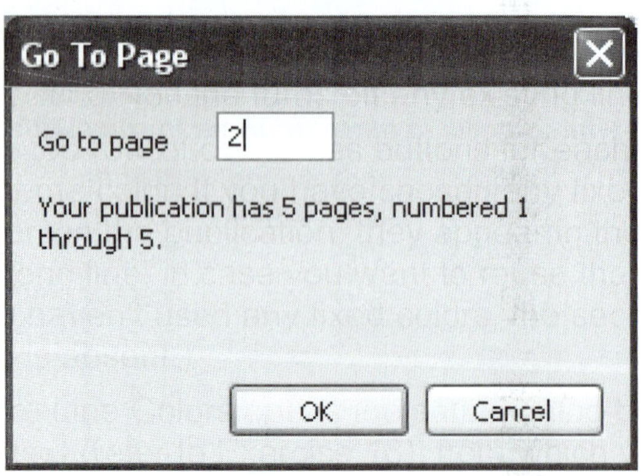

Work with Headers and Footers

- The **header** and **footer** areas enable you to enter text that you want to appear at the top or bottom of every page in the publication, such as the publication title for example.
- To work with the header and footer areas, choose View, Header and Footer. This makes the rest of the document gray (unavailable) and shows the header. You can scroll down on the page to see the footer.

Type text in the header (top) or footer (bottom) that should appear on every page

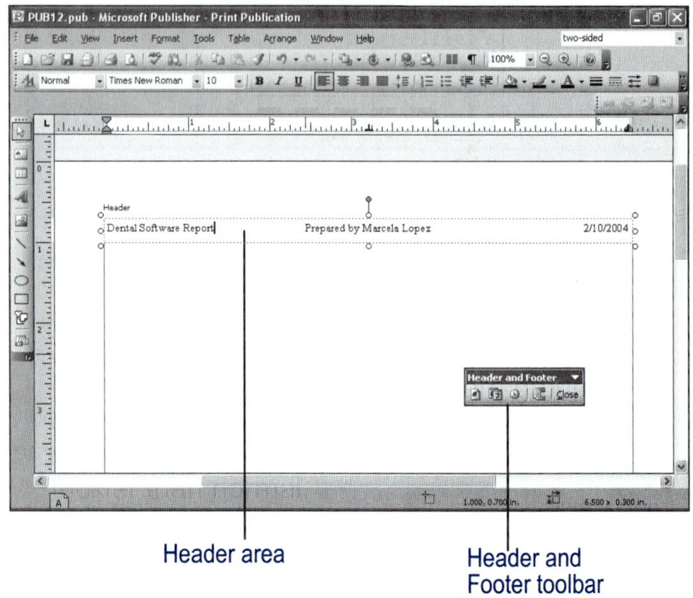

✓ *The header and footer text boxes are actually elements on the master page, which you'll learn about in Exercise 13.*

- The header and footer text boxes are like any other text box. You can type text into them and format it normally.
- The Header and Footer toolbar appears whenever the header and footer are displayed. It contains the following buttons:
  - Insert Page Number: Inserts a code that places page numbers on each page of the printout.
  - Insert Date: Inserts a code that places the current date on the printout.
  - Insert Time: Inserts a code that places the current time on the printout.
  - Show Header/Footer: Switches between the header and the footer.
- You can also insert page numbering in the header or footer using procedures explained in the following section.

- To leave the header/footer and return to working normally with the document, click the Close button on the Header and Footer toolbar or choose View, Header and Footer again.

Use Page Numbering

- If you need to quickly insert a page numbering code in the header or footer, one easy way is the Insert, Page Numbers command.
- Choosing Insert, Page Numbers opens the Page Numbers dialog box. From there, choose Top of page (Header) or Bottom of page (Footer) from the Position drop-down list.
- You can also choose an Alignment, which refers to the horizontal positioning of the code within the header, footer, or text box.
- To omit the page number on the first page, clear the Show page number on first page check box.

Specify where you want the page numbers to appear

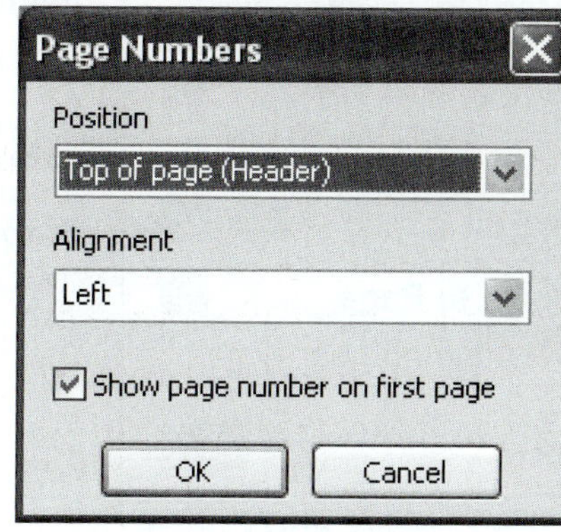

- If the insertion point was inside a text box when you issued the Insert, Page Numbers command, another option appears on the Position drop-down list: This Text Box. You can choose to place the page numbering code somewhere other than in the header or footer.

  ✓ *When you insert page numbers, or place things in the header and footer, you are actually working with a master page. Exercise 13 explains master pages.*

Procedures

Insert Pages

To insert a single blank page after the current page:

- Press **Ctrl+ Shift+N** .... Ctrl+Shift+N

To duplicate an existing page including all its content:

1. Right-click the page's icon 1 at the bottom of the screen
2. Click **Insert Duplicate Page** .... D

To insert any number of pages:

1. Open the **Insert Page** dialog box:
   a. Right-click a page icon 1 at the bottom of the screen.
   b. Click **Insert Page** .... P

   OR

   a. Click **Insert** .... Alt+I
   b. Click **Page** .... G
2. Enter the number of pages to insert in the **Number of new pages** box ...... Alt+N
3. Choose **Before current page** .... Alt+B

   OR

   Choose **After current page** .... Alt+A
4. Choose one of the following options:
   - **Insert blank pages** .... Alt+P
   - **Create one text box on each page** .... Alt+O
   - **Duplicate all objects on page** .... Alt+D
5. If you chose to duplicate objects, enter the page number from which to copy.
6. Click **OK** .... Enter

View Two-Page Spread

1. Click **View** .... Alt+V
2. Click **Two-Page Spread** ...... D

   ✓ *This is a toggle; repeat to go back to one-page viewing.*

Delete Pages

1. Display page you want to delete.
2. Do one of the following:
   a. Click **Edit** .... Alt+E
   b. Click **Delete Page** .... A

   OR

   a. Right-click the page's icon 1 at the bottom of the screen.
   b. Click **Delete Page** .... A
3. If the Delete page dialog box appears, choose one of the following:
   - **Both pages** .... B
   - **Left page only** L
   - **Right page only** .... R
4. Click **OK** .... Enter

Go to a Specific Page

- Click the page icon 1 at the bottom of the screen for the page you want.

OR

1. Display the **Go To Page** dialog box:
   - Press **F5** F5

   OR

   a. Click **Edit** .... Alt+E

   b. Click **Go to Page** .... G
2. Enter the page number to go to.
3. Click **OK**........................... Enter

Work with the Header and Footer

Display the header and footer:

1. Click **View** .... Alt+V
2. Click **Header and Footer** ... H

Switch between the header and the footer:

- Click the **Show Header/Footer** button.

Insert a code in the header or footer:

1. Position insertion point where you want the code.
2. Click a button on the Header and Footer toolbar:
   - **Insert Page Number**
   - **Insert Date**
   - **Insert Time**

   ✓ *To format the page number, date, or time, apply text formatting to the code.*

Insert a page numbering code with the Page Numbering dialog box:

1. Click **Insert**.................. Alt+I
2. Click **Page Numbers** .... U
3. Open the **Position** list and choose where you want the page numbers to appear .... Alt+P, ↓
4. Open the **Alignment** list and choose the horizontal alignment you want.............. Alt+A, ↓
5. (Optional) Clear the **Show page number on first page** check box........... Alt+S
6. Click **OK** .... Enter

Exercise Directions

1. Start Publisher, if necessary.
2. Open the file **PUB12**. Save it as **12DENTAL**.
3. Using Go To, view page 3.
4. Delete page 3.
5. Insert a new page at the beginning of the publication with a single text box on it, and insert **PUB12Import.doc** into it.
6. Resize the text box on page 1 so that the text appears centered on the page vertically.
7. Insert a page numbering code in the footer in the right corner, but omit it from the first page.
8. In the header, type **Report created by Marcela Lopez on** and then insert a date code from the Header and Footer toolbar.
9. Close the header and footer, returning to the document.
10. Print the document.
11. Save your work and exit Publisher.

On Your Own

1. Start Publisher, if necessary.
2. Create a new publication based on one of the Catalog wizards. Save it as **12CAT**.

   ✓ *Notice that the catalog is set up for a two-sided publication; you see two pages on-screen at once when you are viewing any page except the first one.*
3. Switch among the pages using the page icons at the bottom.

   ✓ *Notice that the page numbers are in the foreground, not in the header or footer.*
4. Add a new page using Insert, Page.

   ✓ *Notice that you are prompted by an Insert Catalog Pages dialog box to select layouts for left and right pages.*

   ✓ *Also notice that when you click OK, a message appears that you should insert the pages in groups of four. This is necessary because of the binding typical of catalogs. Go ahead and do so.*
5. Delete the page number text box from each page.
6. Place a page number code in the center of the footer.

   ✓ *Press the Tab key once in the footer to move to its center before you insert the code.*
7. Return to the foreground and preview the publication in Print Preview to check your work.
8. Save your work and exit Publisher.

Exercise 13

Skills Covered:

◆ **Work with Master Pages** ◆ **Name Pages** ◆ **Move Pages**

On the Job

One type of multi-page publication is a standard book-style report, where text flows from one page to the next as you saw in Exercise 12. You can ensure consistency among the pages with a background template called a master page. Most publications have a single master page, but Publisher 2003 enables you to create and use multiple master pages in a single publication if desired.

John Lowery, owner of The Hendricks Inn, has created a gift certificate in Publisher. He would like to be able to create an appropriate gift certificate whenever customers ask for a certain certificate type or value. You will use master pages to set this up for him.

Terms

Master Page The backdrop on which you place elements that should repeat on every page of the publication to which that master page is applied.

Foreground The "normal" part of the publication, where you place the text, graphics, and other objects that are unique to each page.

Notes

Work with Master Pages

- Each publication has a **master page**, on which you place any objects that you want to repeat the same way on every page in the publication. You can think of the master page as the solid "sheet" beneath each page and each page as a kind of transparency overlaid on top of it.

The master page holds elements to be repeated on each page

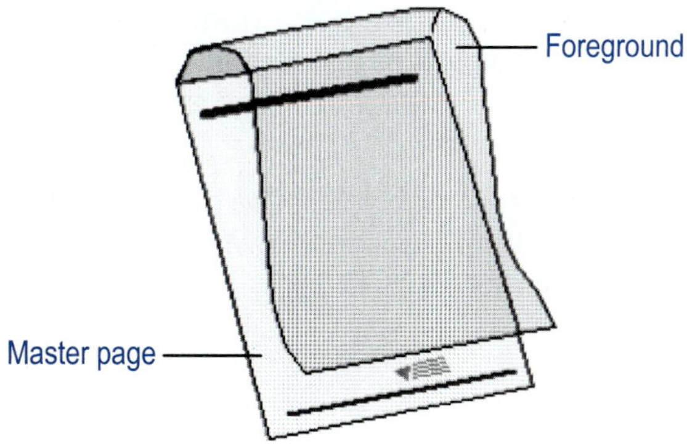

- The header and footer text boxes exist on this master page; when you were working with the header and footer, you were actually displaying and editing text boxes on the master page.
- You are not limited to the header and footer areas, however; you can place any object anywhere on the master page to make it repeat on each page. This could include text boxes, graphics, or other objects.
- Switch between master page and the **foreground** by choosing View, Master Page or by pressing Ctrl + M. Make sure you don't inadvertently add items to the background that belong on an individual page.
- By default the Master Page is blank; it contains content only if you placed any there, either manually or by using the Header and Footer or Page Numbering commands (see Exercise 12).

Master View shows the elements, if any, that are on the master page

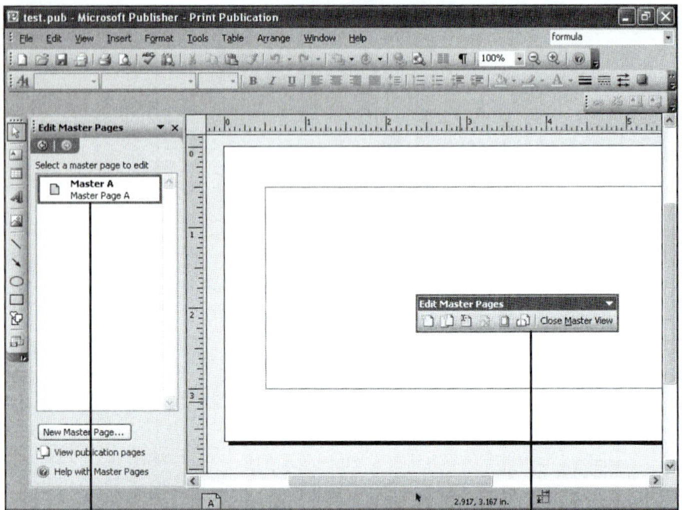

Master A is the default master page

Floating toolbar

Place Objects on the Master Page

- You can easily send objects back and forth between the master page and the foreground at any point.
- Select the object(s) and then choose Arrange, Send to Master Page.
- If there are multiple master pages in the publication (see the next section), and you use Send to Master Page, the object is sent to the master page that is currently applied to that page.
- When viewing the master page, you can select objects and choose Arrange, Send to Foreground to return them to the main publication.

Use Multiple Master Pages

- New in Publisher 2003, you can have multiple master pages. The default master page is called Master A.
- To create an additional master page, go into Master Page view (View, Master Page) and then click the New Master Page button.
- To duplicate an existing master page, click the Duplicate Master Page button.
- You can delete master pages, as long as at least one remains. (You cannot delete the last one.) From Master Page view, select it in the task pane and click the Delete Master Page button.

Apply a Master Page

- To apply a different master page to a certain page of the publication, close Master View and select that page. Then display the Apply Master Page task pane (Format, Apply Master Page) and choose the alternate master from the drop-down list there.

Use the Apply Master Page task pane to switch between master pages

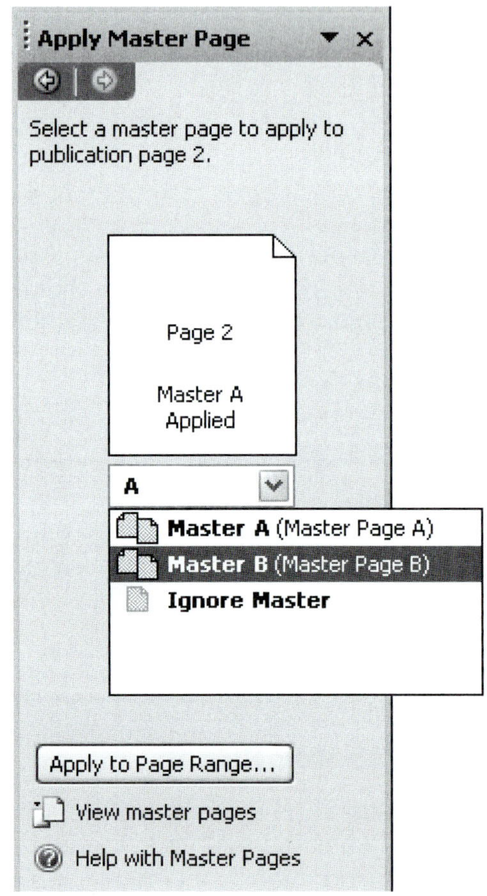

Name Pages

- Each page of your publication can have a unique name. This name does not show up when the publication is printed.
- The main purpose of a page name is to help you keep track of which page is which when you are constructing the publication and arranging pages.
- To name a page, right-click the page icon at the bottom of the publication window and choose Rename.

Move Pages

- You can rearrange the pages in your publication by dragging the page icons [1] at the bottom of the publication window to the left or right.
- You can also rearrange pages by choosing Edit, Move Page. Specify where you want the current page to move.

Move the current page before or after some other page in the publication.

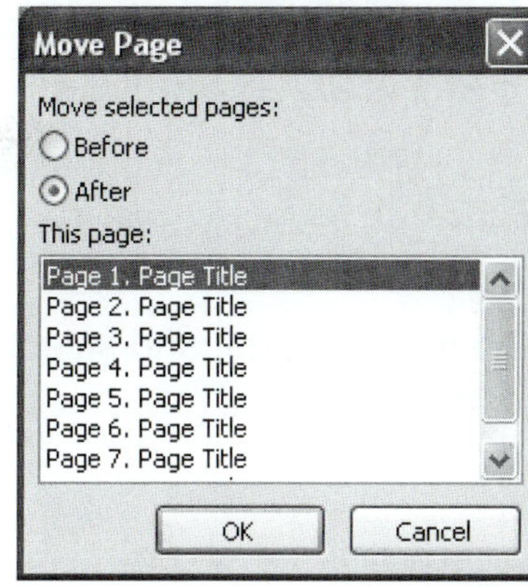

✓ *Notice above that each page's title is the generic "Page Title." If you name the pages as described in the preceding section, the new names will appear there instead, making it easier to identify them.*

Procedures

Switch Between Master Page and Normal Views

- Press **Ctrl+M** .... Ctrl+M

OR

1. Click **View** .... Alt+V
2. Click **Master Page** .... M

Send Objects to the Master Page

1. Select the objects(s).
2. Click **Arrange** .... Alt+R
3. Click **Send to Master Page** .... R

Send Objects to the Foreground from the Master Page

1. Select object(s) on the master page.
2. Click **Arrange** .... Alt+R
3. Click **Send to Foreground** .... F

Create a New Master Page

1. In Master Page view, click the **New Master Page** button.
2. Type a Description.
3. (Optional) Click in the **Page ID** box and type a different ID character if desired ...... Alt+P
4. (Optional) Click **Two-Page Master** .... Alt+W

   ✓ *Do step 4 if you want a double-sided publication with different master pages for left vs. right.*
5. Click **OK** .... Enter

Duplicate an Existing Master Page

1. In Master Page view, select the existing master.
2. Click the **Duplicate Master Page** button.
3. Type a Description.
4. (Optional) Click in the **Page ID** box and type a different ID character if desired ...... Alt+P
5. Click **OK** .... Enter

Rename a Master Page

1. In Master Page view, click the down arrow next to the master page to rename.
2. Click **Rename** .... Alt+N
3. Type a different Description.
4. (Optional) Click in the **Page ID** box and type a different ID character if desired ...... Alt+P
5. Click **OK** .... Enter

Delete a Master Page

1. In Master Page view, click the master in the Edit Master Pages task pane.
2. Click the **Delete Master Page** button.
3. Click **Yes** .... Y

Name a Page

1. Right-click the page icon [1].
2. Click **Rename** .... R
3. Type a new title.
4. Click **OK** .... Enter

Move a Page

- Drag the page icon [1] right or left.

OR

1. Click **Edit** .... Alt+E
2. Click **Move Page** .... M
3. Click **Before** .... B

   OR

   Click **After** .... A
4. Click an existing page.
5. Click **OK** .... Enter

Exercise Directions

1. Start Publisher, if necessary.
2. Open the file PUB13. Save it as **13GIFT**.
3. Select all objects (Ctrl+A) and send them to the Master Page.
4. Display the master page, and select only the following text boxes:
   - Number
   - Expires
   - Authorized by
   - The blank text box to the right of "This certificate entitles"
5. Send the selected text boxes to the foreground.
6. Rename this master **Fifty Dollars**.
7. Duplicate this master and call the copy **Twenty Dollars**. Edit that master so that the certificate is for $20, not $50.
8. Close Master View, and copy page 1 of the publication to a new page following it, duplicating its content.
9. Apply the Twenty Dollars master to page 2.
10. Fill out the gift certificates on both pages to a **Mr. and Mrs. Li Cho**:
    a. Type **100** and **101** in the Number boxes (respectively).
    b. Type your own name in the Authorized By box.
    c. Type **12/31/2006** in the Expires box.
11. Print both gift certificates.
12. Save your work and exit Publisher.

On Your Own

1. Start Publisher, if necessary.
2. Start a new publication based on one of the Letterhead templates. Use any design and color scheme you like.
3. Replace placeholder text with your own name, address, and other contact information.
4. Move all objects to the master page.
5. Duplicate the master page, and on the new master page, create a suitable template for subsequent pages of a multi-page letter. It should contain some of the same graphic elements as the "page 1" stationery page, but should not contain your contact information.
6. Close the master page, and create a new blank page in the publication. Apply the secondary master page to it.
7. Save the publication as **13LETTER** and print it.
8. Exit Publisher.

Exercise 14

Skills Covered:

◆ **Work with Master Sets** ◆ **Use the Design Checker**

On the Job

Most organizations need more than one type of publication. For example, a business might need business cards, stationery, brochures, and postcards. Publisher 2003 makes it easy to create many different types of publications using a common design, so that all the publications look like they are part of a cohesive marketing effort. In this exercise, you will learn about master sets and also about the Design Checker, a proofreader in Publisher that looks for layout errors.

John Lowery of The Hendricks Inn is so pleased with the gift certificate you designed in Exercise 13 that he has asked you to do some additional work for him. He has created a breakfast menu in Publisher that contains some layout problems; you will use the Design Checker to find and correct those errors. Then you will use a master set to help him create business cards that use the same design set as his menu.

Terms

Master set A group of publication templates that share a common design.

Design Checker A feature that proofreads your layout to help you find layout problems that might prevent the publication from looking good in print.

Notes

Work with Master Sets

- As you have created publications based on different types of templates in Publisher so far, you may have noticed some common design names across different types. Such related templates are part of a common **master set**.
- The master set contains all the templates of a particular design, but you can also work with subsets of the master set. Some of the available subsets include personal stationery sets, fundraiser sets, and holiday sets.
- To create new publications based on a set, choose Design Sets in the New Publication task pane. (Up to this point you have been choosing Publications for Print here.) Then choose the desired set, and all the available templates in it appear for your use.

Choose a template based on its design rather than its function

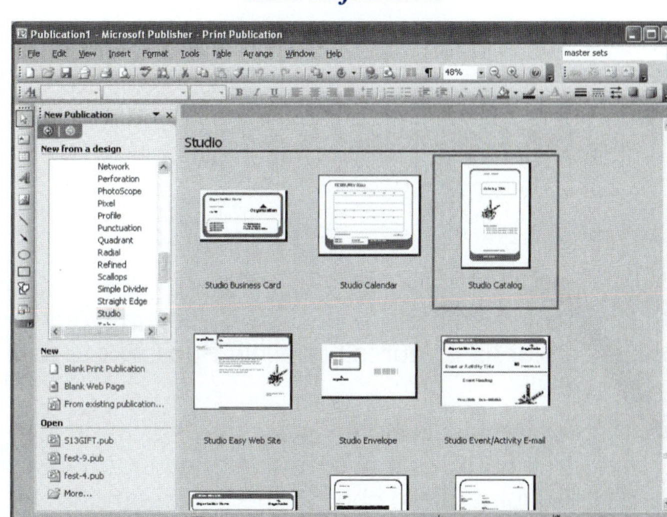

Use the Design Checker

- The **Design Checker** is very useful for identifying layout errors in a publication. It helps you find and fix errors that may cause problems when the publication is printed (either professionally or on your own printer) or when it is published to the Web.
- To run the Design Checker, choose Tools, Design Checker. The problems found appear in the task pane at the left.
- To jump to the found error in the publication, click it on the task pane.

Problems identified by the Design Checker

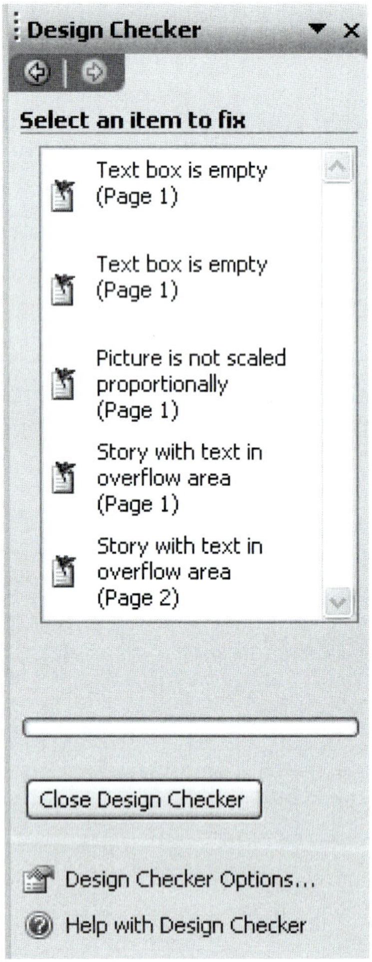

- Depending on the nature of the problem, you can either fix it yourself or allow Publisher to fix it for you.
- To allow Publisher to fix it, click the down arrow next to the found item on the task pane, opening a menu for it. Then choose the Fix command from the menu.

✓ *Think carefully about the best way to correct each error. The solution proposed by the Design Checker may not be the best one. For example, it may propose that you add a new page to continue the overflow text from a text box, when a better solution might be to simply enlarge the current text box slightly.*

When a problem is identified, choose what to do about it

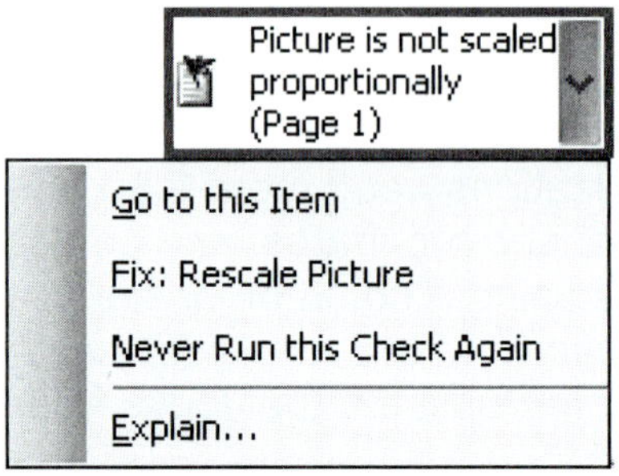

- The Design Checker looks for many types of errors. Here are the most common ones:
  - Empty frames—frames that no longer contain anything but are still present in the publication. These can probably be deleted without affecting the layout.
  - Covered objects—any object that is covering up (and possibly obscuring) another object. These may need to be moved.
  - Spot colors—unused spot colors, or more than two spot colors used. This is significant if you are paying by the color for color printing.
  - Text in overflow area—text that does not fit in the current text box and has nowhere else to flow. The text box may need to be enlarged, or you may need to decrease the font size.
  - Objects in nonprinting region—any object outside the page margins. Such objects may need to be moved inward in order to print.
  - Disproportional pictures—pictures that have been resized nonproportionally, so they no longer retain their original height/width ratio. These may need to be reset.
  - Spacing between sentences—inconsistent spacing after ending punctuation (such as a period or question mark).
- To prevent certain types of errors from being identified, choose Never Run this Check Again from a found error's menu, as shown above.

- Alternatively, you can manually edit the list of error types to identify. To do so, click the Design Checker Options hyperlink at the bottom of the task pane and then mark or clear check boxes on the Checks tab in the Design Checker Options dialog box.

Specify for which problems the Design Checker should look

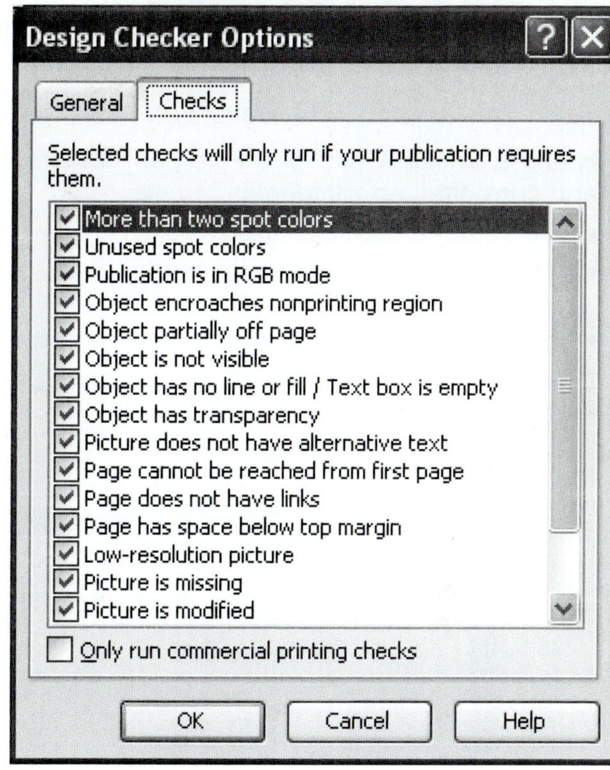

Procedures

Start a New Publication with a Master Set

1. Click **File** .... Alt+F
2. Click **New** .... N
3. Click **Design Sets**.
4. Click **Master Sets**.
5. Click the desired template.

Use the Design Checker

1. Click **Tools** .... Alt+T
2. Click **Design Checker** .... K
3. Click a found error in the task pane to jump to it.
4. Do one of the following:
   - Correct the error manually.

   OR

   a. Click the down arrow next to the error in the task pane.

   b. Click **Fix** .... F
5. Repeat steps 3 and 4 for each error.
6. Click **Close Design Checker**.

Set Design Checker Options

1. Click **Tools** .... Alt+T
2. Click **Design Checker** .... K
3. Click **Design Checker Options**.
4. Click **Checks** tab.
5. Mark or clear check boxes for design checker options.
6. Click **OK** .... Enter

Exercise Directions

1. Start Publisher, if necessary.
2. Open the file **PUB14**. Save it as **14MENU**.
3. Run the Design Checker on the publication, and correct all errors found:
   - Delete any empty text boxes found.
   - Allow the Design Checker to rescale disproportional pictures
   - Enlarge text boxes that contain overflow text.
4. Close the Design Checker task pane, and save and print the publication.
5. Close the publication.
6. Using the Master Sets feature, create a new publication that uses the same design (Studio) but is for business cards.
7. In the task pane, click None in the Logo area to remove the logo placeholder from the business card layout.
8. Enter the data shown in Illustration A and then save it as **14CARD** and close it.
9. Exit Publisher.

Illustration A

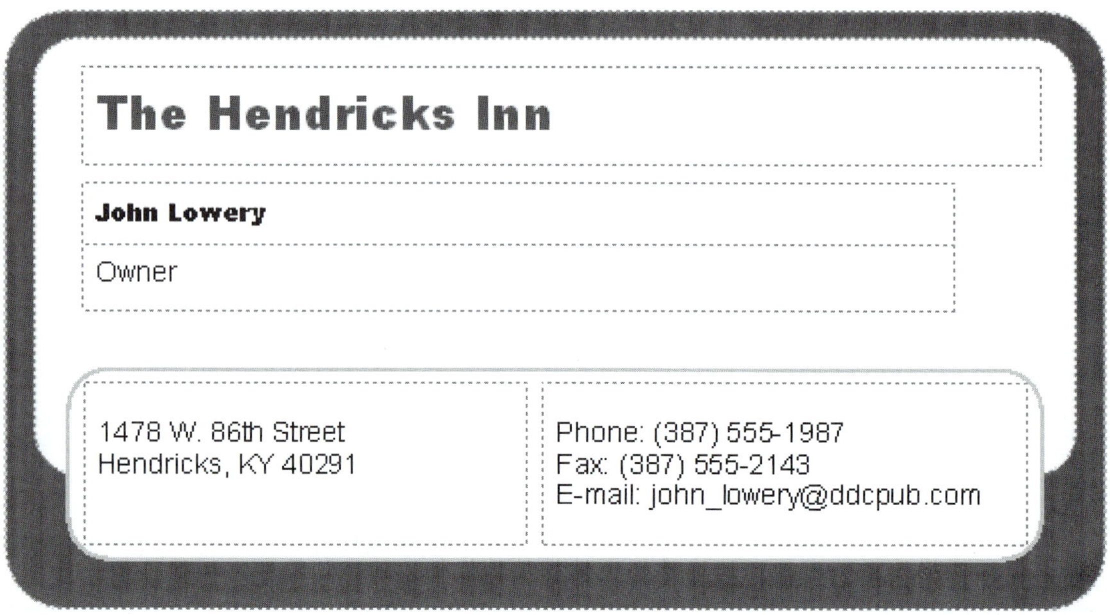

On Your Own

1. Start Publisher, if necessary.
2. Choose one of the Personal Stationery Sets under Master Sets, and create letterhead stationery for yourself, using your own name and address. Customize it any way you like. Save the file as **14MYSET1**.
3. Using the same Personal Stationery Set, create business cards, envelopes, and address labels for yourself. Save the files as **14MYSET2**, **14MYSET3**, and **14MYSET4**, respectively.

   ✓ *Save time by using a personal information set rather than retyping your contact information for each publication.*
4. Check each of your publications with the Design Checker, and correct any problems you encounter.

   ✓ *If you run into a "Space below top margin" error, this is harmless and can remain uncorrected.*
5. Save each publication and exit Publisher.

Exercise 15

Skills Covered:

◆ **Insert a Design Gallery Object** ◆ **Customize a Design Gallery Object**
◆ **Create Your Own Design Gallery Objects**

On the Job

As you've seen many times so far in this course, different templates apply different decorative flourishes and preset objects to publications, like graphics, coupons, tear-offs, and quotation boxes. Applying a design template is just one way to access these pieces; you can also manually insert them into any publication from the Design Gallery.

John Lowery of The Hendricks Inn wants to create a one-page flyer, including some quotations from happy customers and a coupon, to mail to potential customers. None of the Publisher templates have exactly what he wants, though. In this exercise, you will build one that meets his exact specifications using objects from the Design Gallery.

Terms

Design Gallery A collection of predesigned objects you can place in your publication, including mastheads, banners, logos, and more.

Attention-Getter A predesigned graphic accent that includes a few words of text.

Notes

Insert a Design Gallery Object

- The **Design Gallery** is a repository of special elements that can give your publications a more professional look. The Design Gallery includes coupons, **attention-getters**, tear-offs, logos, boxes, and lots of other elements.
- To open the Design Gallery, choose Insert, Design Gallery Object (or click the Design Gallery Object button on the Objects toolbar). Then locate an object and click the Insert Object button.

Select a Design Gallery object for use in your publication

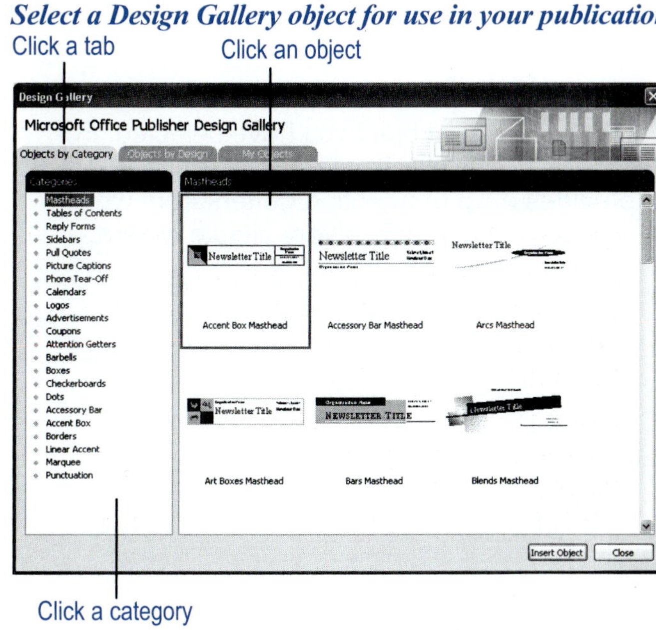

✓ *An Extra Content tab appears if there are objects in the publication that were removed or hidden when you changed publication designs at some point; you can use the Extra Content tab to reinsert them if they are needed. It does not appear in the figures shown here.*

- Once a Design Gallery object is in your publication, you can work with it (resize, move, etc.) as you would any other object.
- Objects may be selected either by design or by category. Browse them from the Objects by Category tab to see all mastheads, all logos, and so on, grouped by functionality.
- Browse from the Objects by Design tab to see all available objects grouped by design.

Customize a Design Gallery Object

- Many Design Gallery objects have special wizards associated with them. You can tell because a wizard button appears below the inserted object whenever it is selected. Click this button to run a wizard that helps you set up that object.

Wizard button below a selected object

- The exact controls that appear depend on which Design Gallery object you have selected. For example, the Attention Getter Designs Wizard provides a list of attention getters from which you can choose. It is a very simple wizard.

This attention getter from the Design Gallery can be customized by clicking the Wizard button

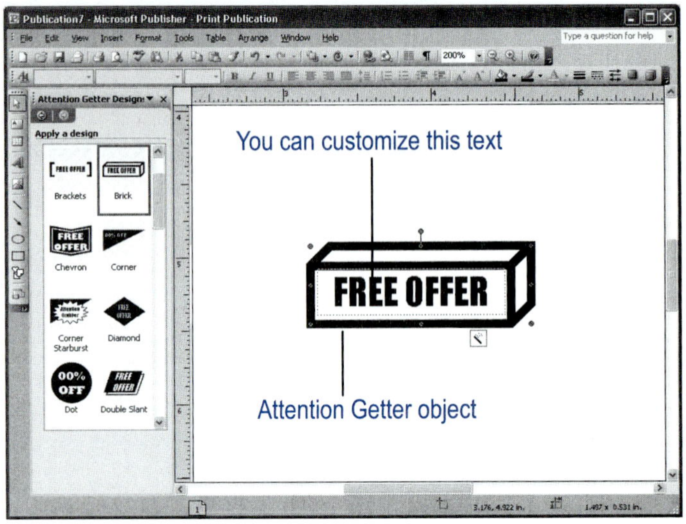

- Other wizards are more complex. For example, the Coupon Wizard shown below has two categories of settings: Coupon Options and Coupon Designs.

Click the Coupon wizard button for help with designing a coupon

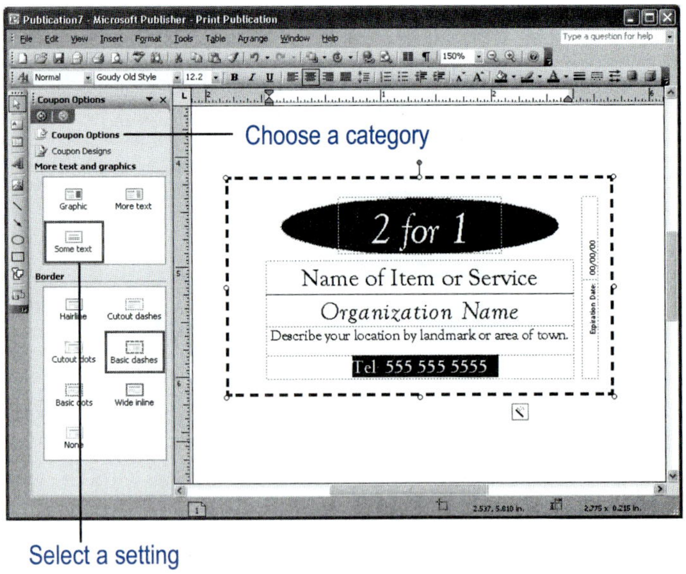

Create Your Own Design Gallery Objects

- You can add any object to the Design Gallery. Objects you add appear on the Your Objects tab. This way you can create a library of objects to reuse in the publication.
- These objects can either be items you create "from scratch" or existing Design Gallery objects that you have customized with your own information.
- To add an object to the Design Gallery, select it and then choose Insert, Add Selection to Design Gallery.
- The first time you save an object to the Design Gallery, you must create a category. (There are no predefined categories for the Your Objects tab.) For subsequent objects you can reuse your saved object from the same category or create new categories.

Add an object to the Design Gallery by naming and categorizing it

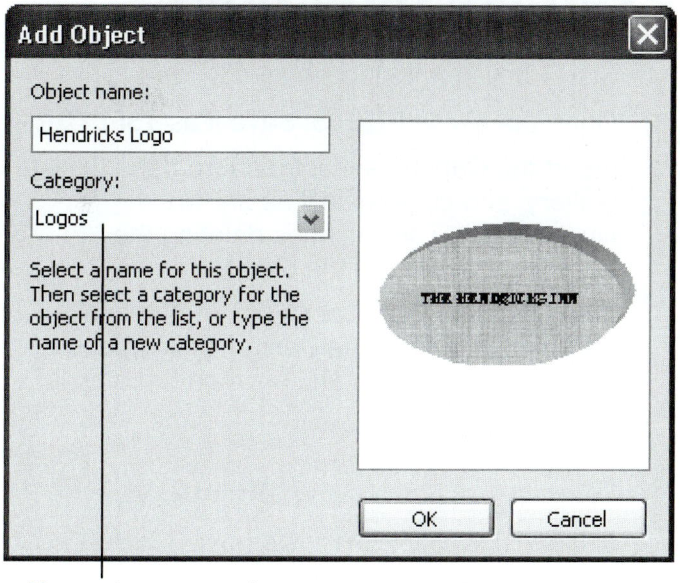

You can type a new category here or choose from the list

Procedures

Insert a Design Gallery Object

1. Click the **Design Gallery Object** button on the Objects toolbar.
2. Click the tab from which you want to select.
3. Click the category from which you want to select.
4. Click object you want to insert.
5. Click **Insert Object** ...... Alt+I

Customize a Design Gallery Object

Do any of the following:

- Move or resize the object by dragging it.
- If the object has a text box, replace the text placeholder in it with your own text.
- If the object has a **Wizard** button beneath it, click that button and use the controls in the task pane to customize the object.

Create Your Own Design Gallery Objects

1. Select an object's frame.
2. Click **Insert** .... Alt+I
3. Click **Add Selection to Design Gallery** .... A
4. Type a name for the object.
5. Choose a category from the **Category** list .... Alt+C

   OR

   Type the name of a new category to create in the **Category** box .... Alt+C
6. Click **OK** .... Enter

Exercise Directions

1. Start Publisher, if necessary.
2. Open the file PUB15. Save it as **15FLYER**.
3. Insert the Capsules masthead from the Design Gallery, and customize it as shown in Illustration A. This includes deleting the business name from the blue bar.
4. Insert the Bubbles, Capsules, and Fall pull quote objects from the Design Gallery, and type the text in them and arrange them as in Illustration A.
5. Insert the Tilted Box coupon at the bottom of the flyer.
6. Change the coupon to the Open Background coupon through its Wizard, and customize it as shown in Illustration A.
7. Add the masthead back into the Design Gallery as a custom object.
8. Print the publication, and then save your work and exit Publisher.

On Your Own

1. Start Publisher, if necessary.
2. Create a new, blank publication.
3. Insert four different kinds of Design Gallery objects, and customize each one. Try to choose types that were not represented in the exercise.
4. Add the customized objects back into the Design Gallery on the My Objects tab.
5. Save the presentation as **15DESIGN**.
6. Save your work and exit Publisher.

Illustration A

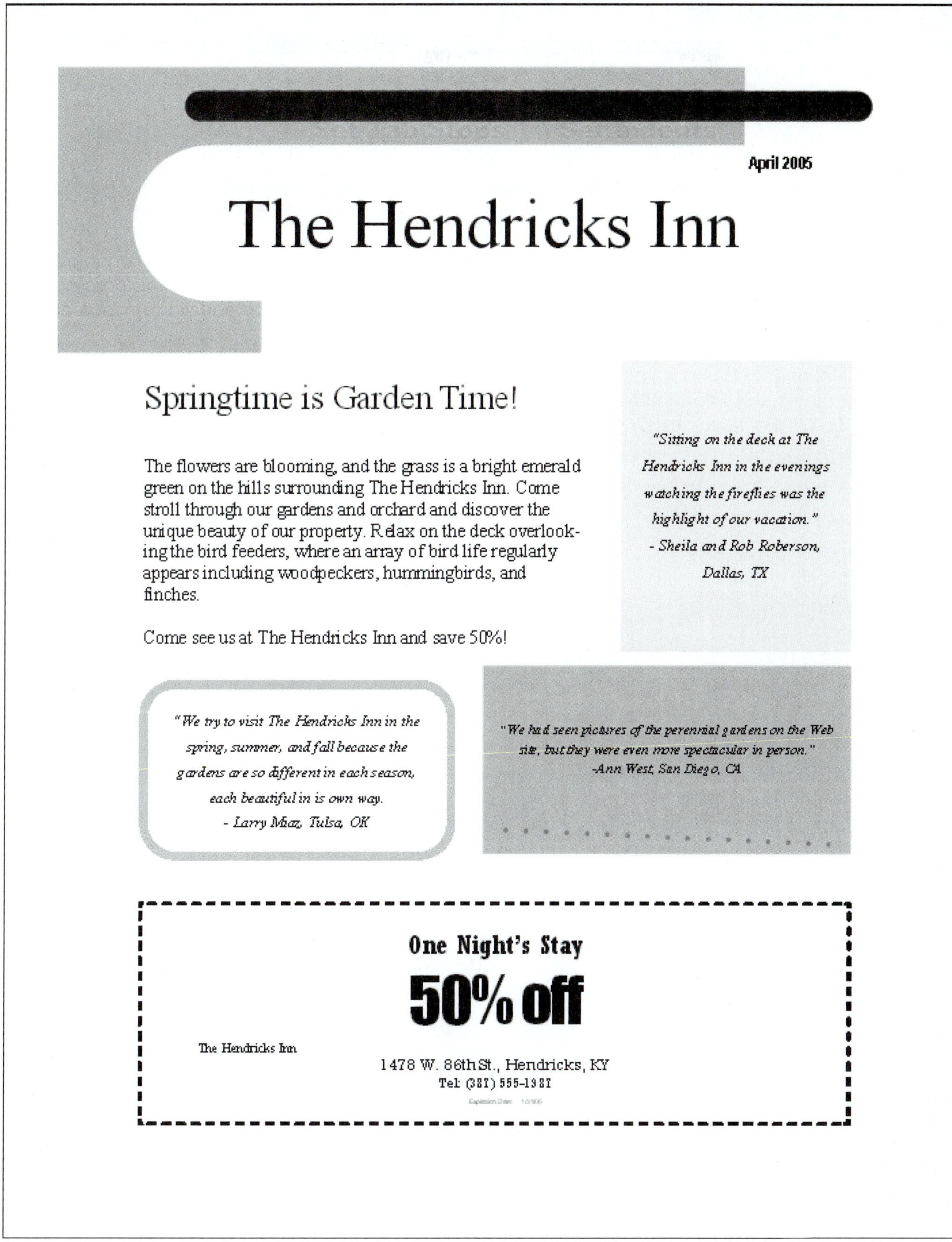

April 2005

The Hendricks Inn

Springtime is Garden Time!

The flowers are blooming, and the grass is a bright emerald green on the hills surrounding The Hendricks Inn. Come stroll through our gardens and orchard and discover the unique beauty of our property. Relax on the deck overlooking the bird feeders, where an array of bird life regularly appears including woodpeckers, hummingbirds, and finches.

Come see us at The Hendricks Inn and save 50%!

"Sitting on the deck at The Hendricks Inn in the evenings watching the fireflies was the highlight of our vacation."
- Sheila and Rob Roberson, Dallas, TX

"We try to visit The Hendricks Inn in the spring, summer, and fall because the gardens are so different in each season, each beautiful in is own way.
- Larry Miaz, Tulsa, OK

"We had seen pictures of the perennial gardens on the Web site, but they were even more spectacular in person."
-Ann West, San Diego, CA

One Night's Stay

50% off

The Hendricks Inn

1478 W. 86th St., Hendricks, KY

Tel: (381) 555-1381

Exercise 16

◆ **Critical Thinking**

Pet Rescue would like you to design some stationery and envelopes for their organization. You will use what you have learned about templates, designs, color schemes, and other objects to do this.

Exercise Directions

1. Start Publisher, if necessary.
2. Update the Secondary Business personal information set with this information if it is not already set from an earlier exercise:

   Name: **Ray James**

   Position: **Volunteer Coordinator**

   Organization Name: **Pet Rescue**

   Address: **2077 W. 166th St.**
   Indianapolis, IN 46240

   Phone, fax, and e-mail:
   Phone: 212-555-9191
   Fax: 212-555-9089
   E-mail: rjames@petrescueindy.org

   Tag line or motto: **Loving and caring for companion animals**
3. From the Batik personal stationery master set, create a new letterhead publication and apply the Secondary Business personal information set to it.
4. Set the Logo Options (in the task pane) so that there is no graphic for the logo.
5. Change the design to Blends.
6. Change the color scheme to Sunrise.
7. Customize the color scheme to use Gold instead of Pink for the Accent 3 color.
8. Insert the Balanced Barbell object from the Design Gallery, and place it at the bottom of the page.
9. Apply the Basis font scheme.

   ✓ *This will change the font sizes for some text; that's okay.*
10. Save the publication as **16LETTER**.
11. Print the publication.
12. Create a #10 envelope that matches the stationery, and save it as **16ENV**.
13. Save your work and exit Publisher.

Illustration A

Illustration B

Exercise 17

◆ **Critical Thinking**

Margaret Colvin is a training manager at Educate-U, a computer training facility. She would like to create certificates for students who have passed an introductory course in Microsoft Publisher 2003 and print them on some special paper she has bought.

Exercise Directions

Part I

1. Start Publisher, if necessary.
2. Create a new publication based on the Award Certificate—Maroon/Gray special paper. Save the file as **17CERTIF**.
3. In the Personal Information, enter **Introduction to Microsoft Publisher 2003** as the Business Name for the Primary Business set.
4. In the logo at the top of the certificate, change the text to **Educate-U**. Then use the logo's Wizard button to switch to a different style of logo.
5. Change **Certificate of Appreciation** to **Certificate of Completion**.
6. Change the text **in recognition of valuable contributions to** to **for successful completion of**.
7. Delete the bottom Signature line from the certificate so that it will be signed by only one person.
8. Replace the text **Signature** with **Margaret Colvin, Training Manager.**
9. Apply the Binary font scheme.
10. Add the logo to the Design Gallery as a new object called Educate-U Logo. Create a new category called Logos for it if there is not already such a category.
11. Delete the **Name of Recipient** text (but not its text box).
12. Send everything *except* the empty text box from step 11 to the master page.
13. Create 5 new pages, all of which duplicate all objects on page 1.
14. Open the Master Page for editing, and set the top text box to AutoFit Text – Best Fit. Then exit from master page view.
15. Go back to page 1 using the Go To Page dialog box.
16. On page 1, enter **Jennifer Simon** as the recipient, and print it. It should resemble Illustration A.
17. Type the following names on the 5 remaining certificate pages:
    - **Carol Simpson**
    - **Cindy Bell**
    - **Jamal Joyner**
    - **Maria Martinez**
    - **Joseph Jackson**
18. Save your work and exit Publisher.

Illustration A

Educate-U

Certificate of Completion

This certificate is awarded to

Jennifer Simon

for successful completion of

Introduction to Microsoft Publisher 2003

Margaret Colvin, Training Manager

Date

Lesson 3

Working with Fonts and Styles

Exercise 18

- Change the Font, Size, Style, and Color
- Change Character Spacing
- Create a Drop Cap

Exercise 19

- Apply Object Borders
- Change an Object's Fill Color

Exercise 20

- Apply a Patterned Border
- Use BorderArt
- Use Fill Effects

Exercise 21

- Align Text Horizontally
- Change Line Spacing
- Align Text Vertically

Exercise 22

- Set Tab Stops
- Set Indents

Exercise 23

- Create Bulleted Lists
- Create Numbered Lists

Exercise 24

- Copy Text Formatting
- Style Basics
- Apply a Style
- Create a Style
- Manage the Style List
- Import Styles from Other Publications

Exercise 25

- Create a Table
- Select Cells and Ranges
- Type in a Table
- Insert or Delete Rows and Columns
- Change Cell Height and Width

Exercise 26

- Format a Table
- Turn Off Automatic Hyphenation
- Merge Cells

Exercise 27

- Critical Thinking

Exercise 28

- Critical Thinking

Exercise 18

Skills Covered:

◆ **Change the Font, Size, Style, and Color**
◆ **Change Character Spacing** ◆ **Create a Drop Cap**

On the Job

As you have seen in Lessons 1 and 2, you can use AutoFit to allow Publisher to resize text in a text box, and you can use a font scheme to change the fonts in a publication. Sometimes, however, you will want to format text manually, applying a specific font, size, color, and so on. You may also want to manually adjust the spacing between letters, or make the first letter of a paragraph stand out with a drop cap.

The Hendricks Inn flyer is coming along nicely, but some of the text is too small and there is not much variety in its formatting. In this exercise, you will format the text to make it more readable and attractive.

Terms

Font A typeface; a style of lettering.

Point 1/72 of an inch, a font size measurement.

Scheme color A color placeholder that is defined by the chosen color scheme for the publication; it changes when you change the color scheme.

Fixed color A color that does not change when the color scheme changes. Publications do not use any fixed colors by default, but you can specify a fixed color for any object.

Character spacing The space between each letter in a block of text.

Scaling The width of characters in relation to a fixed default setting of 100%.

Tracking The spacing between the characters for a selected text box (Very Tight through Very Loose).

Kerning The spacing between certain characters based on their shapes and the way they fit together side-by-side.

Drop cap An ornamental capital letter at the beginning of a paragraph that is much larger than surrounding letters and that "drops" into the lines beneath it or rests on the baseline.

Notes

Change the Font, Size, and Style

- To choose a different **font**, select the text and then choose a font from the Font drop-down list on the Formatting toolbar. Your font list will probably have different fonts from those shown here.
- The fonts on the Font list appear with actual samples, so you can see how they will look when applied to text.
- You can also set the font from the Font dialog box; to display it choose Format, Font. (This dialog box also offers access to font size and text effects.)

Select a font from the Font list after selecting the text to affect

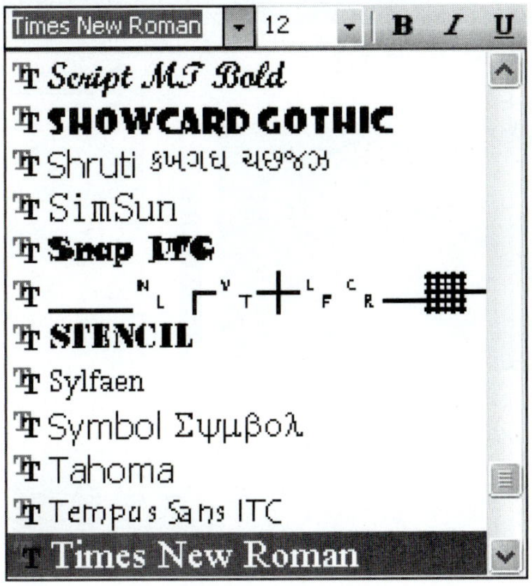

The Font dialog box lets you set several font controls at once

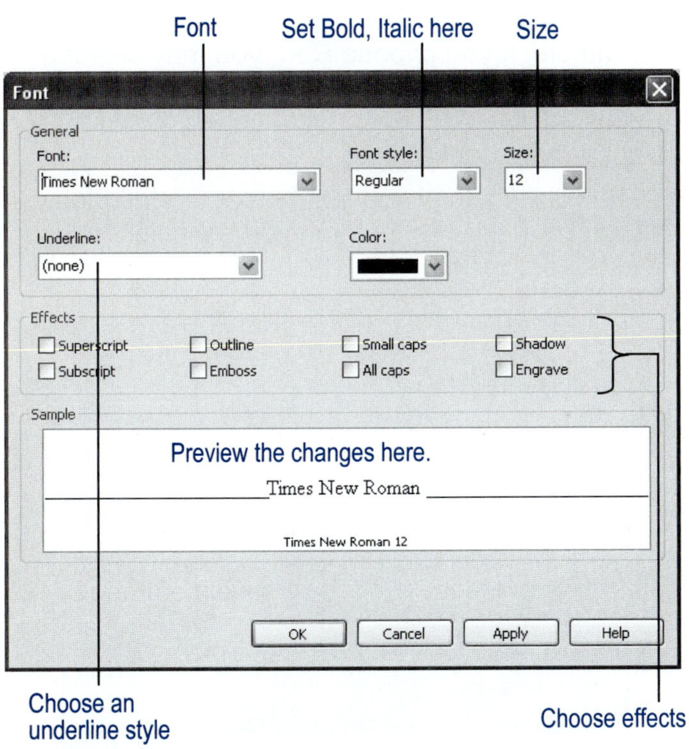

- To choose a different font size, select the text to affect and then choose from the Font Size drop-down list on the Formatting toolbar.
- Fonts are measured in **points**. A point is 1/72 of an inch. A typical size for body text is 10 or 12 points.

Select a font size from the Font Size list after selecting the text to affect

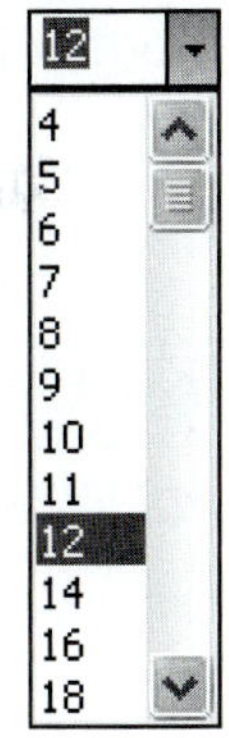

- The Font dialog box (Format, Font) also has a Size drop-down list.
- In addition, the Formatting toolbar has Decrease Font Size  and Increase Font Size  buttons, which you can use to increase or decrease the size of selected text by one size on the Font Size listing (usually one point) with each click.
- The font style can be regular, italic, bold, or bold italic.
- You can use the Bold  and Italic  buttons on the Formatting toolbar to toggle those attributes on or off for selected text. You can also choose the font style from the Font dialog box (Format, Font).
- You can use the Underline button  on the Formatting toolbar to toggle a plain, single underline on or off.
- The Font dialog box has an Underline drop-down list that lets you choose from many different underlining styles, such as double, dotted, words only, and more.
- You can apply text effects to copy to alter its appearance in subtle ways. Examples of text effects include superscript, subscript, outline, emboss, shadow, and so on.
- To apply a text effect, mark its check box in the Font dialog box.

Choose special text effects from the Font dialog box

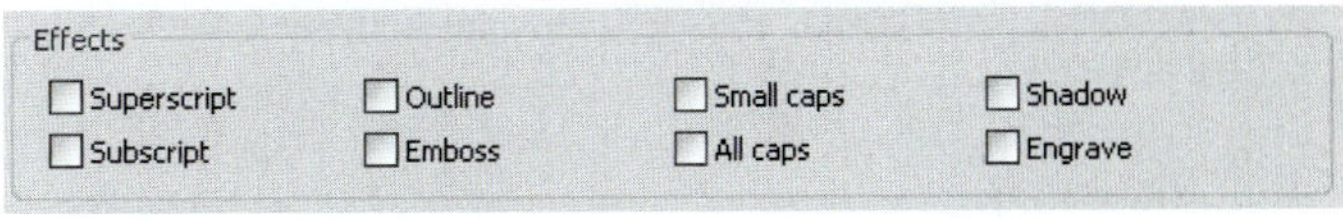

- You set the font color from the Color drop-down list in the Font dialog box or from the Font Color button 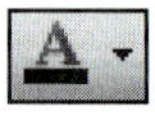 on the Formatting toolbar.

Either choose a scheme color or click the More Colors button

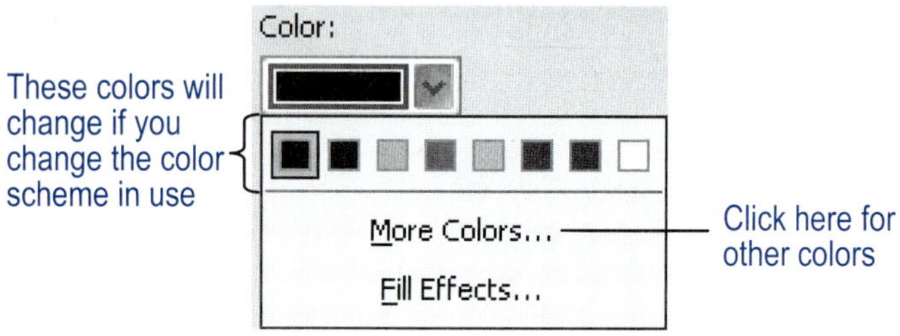

- You must decide whether you want to use **scheme colors** (which will change if you change the color scheme in use) or **fixed colors**.
- Using scheme colors ensures that the entire publication uses consistent colors.
- Using a fixed color gives you more colors to choose from and ensures that the color will not change regardless of later color scheme changes you make.
- If you choose More Colors, the Colors dialog box opens. You can click a colored hexagon on the Standard tab to choose from among many basic colors.

Select a basic color here

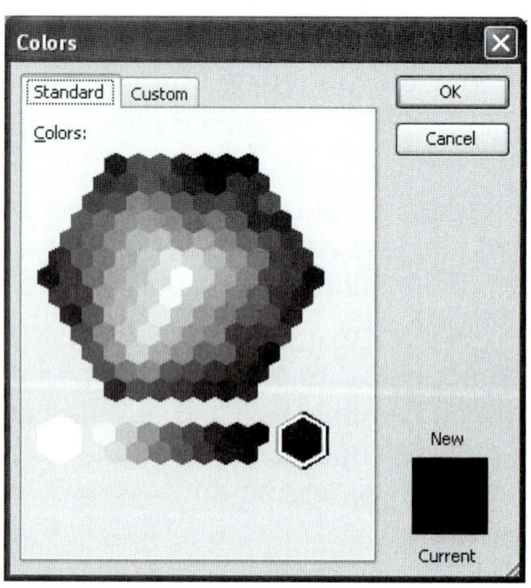

- Instead of Standard colors, you can click the Custom tab and then enter a color by its numeric code in any of a variety of color matching schemes, such as RGB, CMYK, and Pantone. This is useful when working with an official company logo, for example, that must be a precise color.

Select a custom color

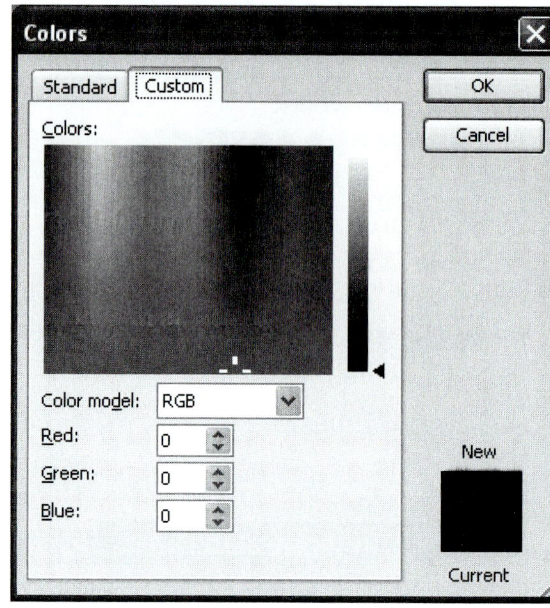

- Choosing Fill Effects from the Color drop-down list opens the Fill Effects dialog box, in which you can select a tint for the chosen color. For example, if you choose Red, you may select a bright red, a dark red, a pale red (pink), etc. This is useful if you want to use a scheme color but have more control over it.
- The Fill Effects dialog box has other options, such as gradients that you can set when working with fills; the Tint option is the only one available for text, however.

Select a shade for the chosen color

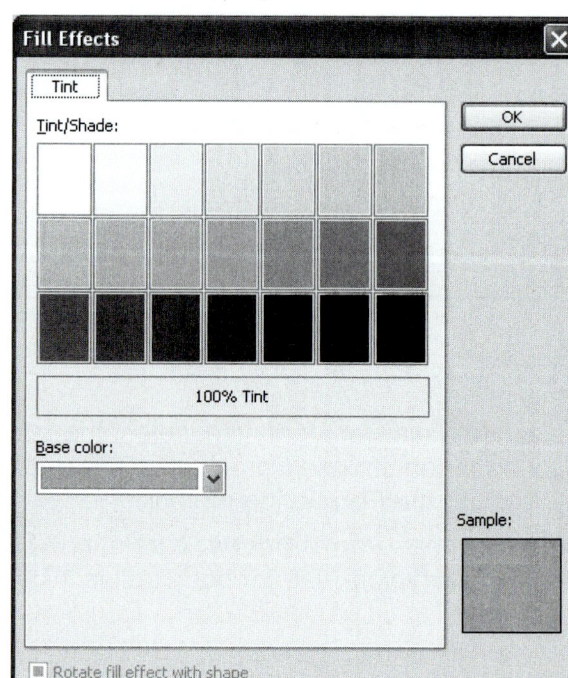

Change Character Spacing

- Publisher comes with some very sophisticated **character spacing** controls, accessible from the Character Spacing dialog box (Format, Character Spacing).
- **Scaling** sets the width of selected characters to more or less than the default (100%). For example, if you selected a capital *A* and then set its scaling to 200%, it would be twice as wide as normal, but the same height.
- **Tracking** controls the spacing between letters for a selected text box. You can set tracking to one of the presets (Very Tight, Tight, Normal, Loose, Very Loose) or to a specific percentage amount.
- **Kerning** controls fine-tune the spacing between certain characters based on their shapes. For example, when a capital V and a capital A appear next to one another, the spacing between them can be decreased without the letters running into each other because of the shape of the letters.

Set character spacing, scaling, and tracking here

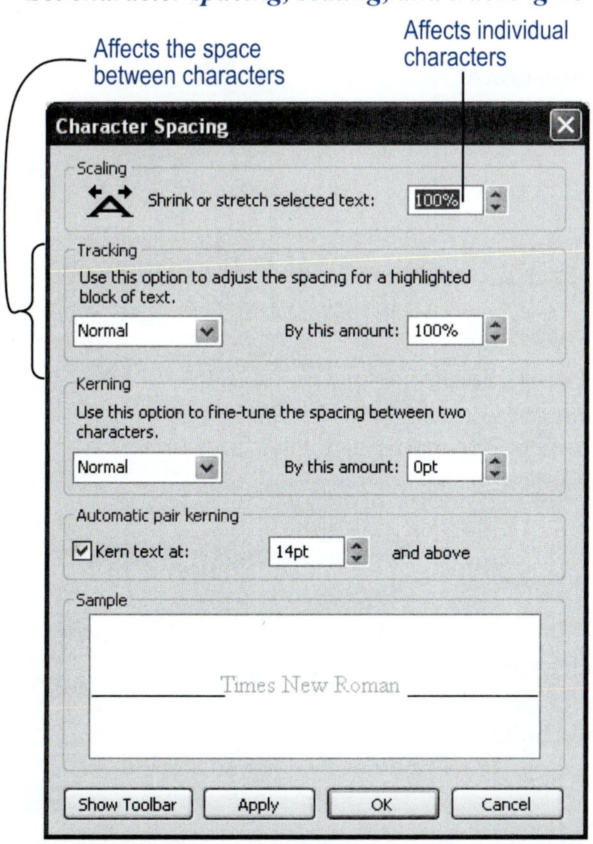

- Automatic pair kerning is turned on by default. It automatically kerns text whenever the font size is 14 point and above (or whatever size you specify).
- Character spacing tools are also available on the Measurement toolbar; click the Show Toolbar button in the Character Spacing dialog box to view it. (Or choose View, Toolbars, Measurement at any time.) It contains text boxes with increment buttons for each of the character spacing settings.

The Measurement toolbar lets you keep the character spacing controls on-screen as you work

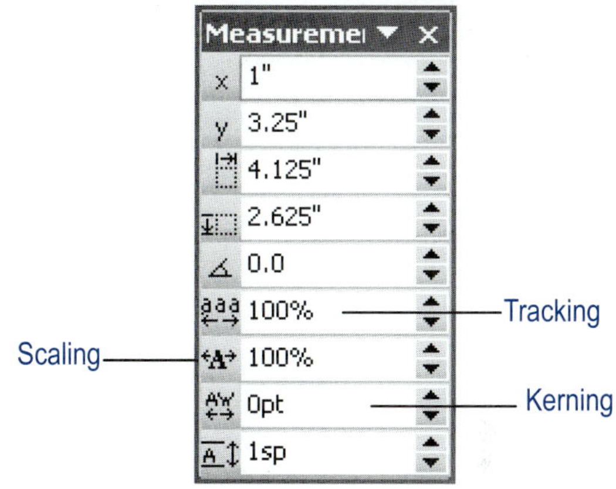

- You can close the Measurement toolbar by clicking its Close button.

Create a Drop Cap

- A **drop cap** is a large first letter in a paragraph. You have probably seen this text design in books at the beginning of a chapter. Publisher can create a variety of drop cap effects.
- To apply a drop cap to the first letter of a paragraph, select the letter and then choose Format, Drop Cap. In the Drop Cap dialog box, select a drop cap style that you like.

Select one of the preset drop cap styles

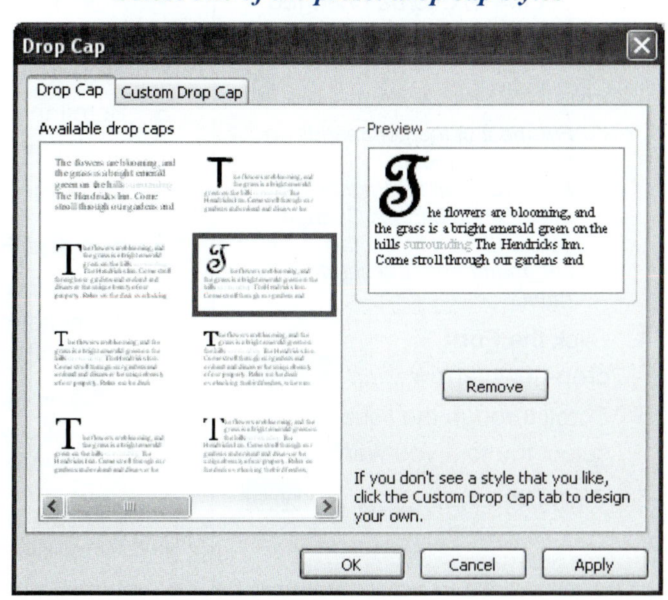

- To remove a drop cap, select it, and then click the Remove button in the Drop Cap dialog box.
- If you want to create your own new drop cap style, click the Custom Drop Cap tab and use the controls there to create it.

Create your own drop cap style, including the letter position, letter style, font, style, and color

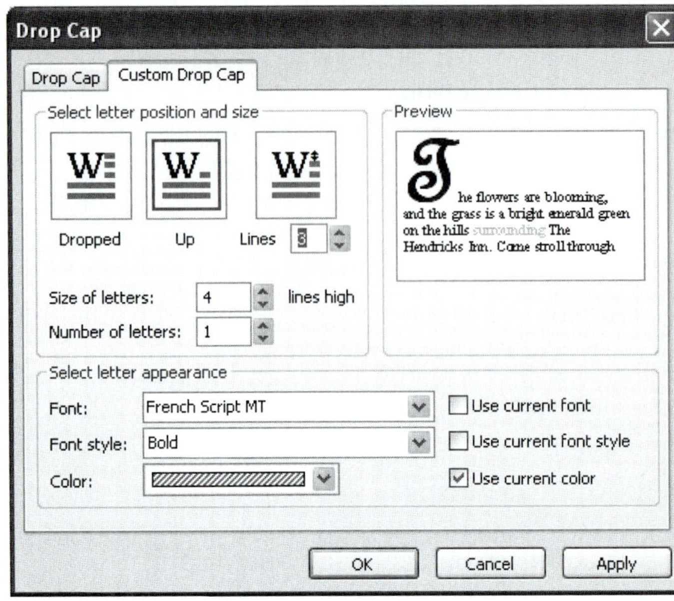

Procedures

Change the Font

1. Select the text to be changed.
2. Open the **Font** drop-down list [Times New Roman ▾] on the Formatting toolbar.
3. Scroll through the list and click the font you want.

   ✓ *You can type the first letter of a font's name to jump quickly to that part of the list.*

OR

1. Select the text to be changed.
2. Click **Format** .... Alt+O
3. Click **Font** .... F

   ✓ *For most of the commands on the Format menu, including Font, you can also right-click the text and choose Change Text and then select the command from the shortcut menu.*

4. Click the **Font** drop-down arrow .... Alt+F
5. Scroll through the list and select the font you want ...... ↓
6. Click **OK** .... Enter

Change the Font Size

1. Select the text to be changed.
2. Open the **Font Size** drop-down list [12 ▾] on the Formatting toolbar.
3. Scroll through the list and click the size you want.

OR

1. Select the text to be changed.
2. Click **Format** .... Alt+O
3. Click **Font** .... F
4. Click the **Size** drop-down arrow.......... Alt+S
5. Scroll through the list and select the size you want ...... ↓
6. Click **OK** .... Enter

Change the Font Style

1. Select the text to be changed.
2. To make the text italic (or turn italics off), click the **Italic** button [I] on the Formatting toolbar.
3. To make the text bold (or turn bold off), click the **Bold** button [B] on the Formatting toolbar.

OR

1. Select the text to be formatted.
2. Click **Format** .... Alt+O
3. Click **Font** .... F
4. Click the **Font style** drop-down arrow .... Alt+Y
5. Choose **Regular**, **Italic**, **Bold**, or **Bold Italic** .... ↓
6. Click **OK** .... Enter

Underline Text (Plain Underline)

1. Select the text to be underlined.
2. Click the **Underline** button [U] on the Formatting toolbar.

Underline Text (Choice of Styles)

1. Select the text to be underlined.
2. Click **Format** .... Alt+O
3. Click **Font** .... F
4. Click the **Underline** drop-down arrow .... Alt+U
5. Select an underline style on the list .... ↓
6. Click **OK** .... Enter

Change Text Effects

1. Select the text to be formatted.
2. Click **Format** .... Alt+O
3. Click **Font** .... F
4. Select or deselect any of the Effects check boxes as desired.
5. Click **OK** .... Enter

Change Font Color to a Scheme Color

1. Select the text to be formatted.
2. Click **Format** .... Alt+O
3. Click **Font** .... F
4. Click the **Color** drop-down arrow .... Alt+C
5. Select a different color from the scheme. .... ↓
6. Click **OK** .... Enter

Change Font Color to Another Color

1. Select the text to be formatted.
2. Click **Format** .... Alt+O
3. Click **Font** .... F
4. Click the **Color** drop-down arrow ... Alt+C, ↓
5. Click **More Colors** ... Tab+Enter
6. Select the color you want to use.

OR

- Do the following to specify a color by number:
  a. Click **Custom** tab.
  b. Click the **Color model** drop-down arrow ..... Alt+D
  c. Choose a color model ..... ↓
  d. Type numbers in the text boxes representing the color's values.

     ✓ *The box names change depending on the color model selected.*

7. Click **OK** .... Enter
8. Click **OK** .... Enter

Change Font Color to a Tint/Shade

1. Select the text to be formatted.
2. Click **Format** .... Alt+O
3. Click **Font** .... F
4. Click the **Color** drop-down arrow .. Alt+C, ↓
5. Click **Fill Effects** .... Tab+Tab+Enter
6. Click the **Base color** drop-down arrow and choose a color with which to start .... Alt+B, ↓

   ✓ *You can either choose a scheme color or click More Colors to select a different color, as in the preceding steps.*

7. Click a shade of the chosen color in the **Tint/Shade** area.
8. Click **OK** .... Enter
9. Click **OK** .... Enter

Change Character Spacing

1. Select the text to be affected.
2. Click **Format** .... Alt+O
3. Click **Character Spacing** .... R
4. Do any of the following:
   - Type a different scaling percentage in the **Scaling** box..... Alt+S, ↓
   - Open the **Tracking** drop-down list and choose a different tracking........... Alt+U, ↓
   - Open the **Kerning** drop-down list and choose a different kerning .... Alt+O, ↓
   - Select or deselect the **Kern text at** check box. If you select it, enter a point size at or above which text will be kerned .... Alt+K
5. Click **OK** .... Enter

Display the Measurement Toolbar

1. Click **Format** .... Alt+O
2. Click **Character Spacing** .... R
3. Click **Show Toolbar** ... Alt+T

OR

1. Click **View** .... Alt+V
2. Point to **Toolbars** .... T
3. Click **Measurement**.

Apply a Drop Cap

1. Click in the paragraph for which you want to set a drop cap.
2. Click **Format** .... Alt+O
3. Click **Drop Cap** .... D
4. Select a drop cap style.
5. Click **OK** .... Enter

Create a Custom Drop Cap

1. Click in the paragraph for which you want to set a drop cap.
2. Click **Format** .... Alt+O
3. Click **Drop Cap** .... D
4. Click the **Custom Drop Cap** tab.
5. Select a letter position:
   - **Dropped** .... Alt+D
   - **Up** .... Alt+P
   - **Lines** .... Alt+L
6. If you chose **Lines**, enter the number of lines.
7. Enter the size of the letters in the **Size of letters** box .... Alt+S
8. Enter the number of letters in the **Number of letters** box .... Alt+N
9. Choose a font from the **Font** drop-down list....... Alt+F, ↓
10. Choose a font style from the **Font style** drop-down list....... Alt+Y, ↓
11. Choose a color from the **Color** drop-down list....... Alt+C, ↓
12. Click **OK** .... Enter

Remove a Drop Cap

1. Click in the paragraph that contains the drop cap.
2. Click **Format** .... Alt+O
3. Click **Drop Cap** .... D
4. Click **Remove** .... Alt+R

Exercise Directions

1. Start Publisher, if necessary.
2. Open the file **PUB18**. Save it as **18FLYER**.
3. Select the text **Springtime is Garden Time!** and make it bold and bright blue.
4. Select the two paragraphs under the heading from step 3 and make them Arial, 11-point.
5. Set the scaling to 110% for these two paragraphs.
6. Create a drop cap from the first letter of the first paragraph (the **T** in the word **The**).
7. Use the Custom Drop Cap controls to make the drop cap 2 lines high rather than the default 4 lines high.
8. Select the text in the gray oval and remove the Bold and Italic attributes from it. Change its font color to dark green.
   - ✓ *You will need to use More Colors because there is no dark green in the current color scheme.*
9. Zoom in to 200% and look at the bottom of the coupon. Select the text describing the expiration date, and increase its size to 6 point. Zoom back out when finished.
   - ✓ *Since the expiration date label and date are in two separate text boxes you will need to format them separately.*
10. Select the text in the bright yellow text box, and set its size to 11 points and its font to Arial Narrow.
11. Remove the Bold attribute from the text from step 10 and set its Tracking setting to 109.1% using the Measurement toolbar.
12. Change to the Field color scheme.
    - ✓ *Notice that the title text changed color because it had been formatted with the blue from the scheme (step 3), but the text in the gray oval did not change color because it had been formatted with a fixed color (step 8).*
13. Print your publication. It should resemble Illustration A.
14. Save your work and close Publisher.

On Your Own

1. Start Publisher, if necessary.
2. Open **OPUB18**. Save it as **18LOST**.
3. Change the fonts and font sizes for the text on the flyer to make it more attractive and readable. Here are some suggestions, or you can use your own choices:
   - Bulleted list: Arial 18-point bold
   - **Last seen** text box: Arial 16-point
   - **Please help** text box: Arial Black, 26 point, italic
4. Increase the kerning in the **Last seen** text box to 0.4 pt.
5. Adjust any text box sizes as needed to make things fit.
6. Change the color of the **$200 REWARD** text to a bright color (such as bright yellow) that will stand out.
7. Change the **Please Call** text to the dark blue color in the color scheme.
8. Apply the Tint effect to that text so that it is a few shades lighter than the scheme color.
   - ✓ *If you were to change the color scheme, this dark blue would change to some other color, but the tint would continue to be in effect and would apply to the new color.*
9. Select the phone number, and apply the Shadow text effect to it to make it more prominent.
10. Save your work and exit Publisher.

Illustration A

April 2005

The Hendricks Inn

Springtime is Garden Time!

The flowers are blooming, and the grass is a bright emerald green on the hills surrounding The Hendricks Inn. Come stroll through our gardens and orchard and discover the unique beauty of our property. Relax on the deck overlooking the bird feeders, where an array of bird life regularly appears including woodpeckers, hummingbirds, and finches.

Come see us at The Hendricks Inn and save 50%!

"Sitting on the deck at The Hendricks Inn in the evenings watching the fireflies was the highlight of our vacation."
- Sheila and Rob Roberson, Dallas, TX

"We try to visit The Hendricks Inn in the spring, summer, and fall because the gardens are so different in each season, each beautiful in is own way.
- Larry Miaz, Tulsa, OK

"We had seen pictures of the perennial gardens on the Web site, but they were even more spectacular in person."
-Ann West, San Diego, CA

One Night's Stay

50% off

The Hendricks Inn

1478 W. 86th St., Hendricks, KY
Tel: (387) 555-1387
Expiration Date: 1/31/06

Exercise 19

Skills Covered:

- ◆ **Apply Object Borders**
- ◆ **Change an Object's Fill Color**

On the Job

Text boxes are transparent by default, so that the background on which they are placed shows through. However, sometimes you might want to give a text box a colored background. You also can apply a border in any thickness, line style, and color you want. In this exercise, you will work with text boxes, but these same skills apply to any type of object.

The Hendricks Inn flyer could benefit from some dressing up with text box formatting. In this exercise, you work with the borders and fills on some of the text boxes.

Terms

Object A generic term for any text box, picture, drawing, or other piece of data in a publication that is separately movable and resizable.

Border A line around the outside of an object that is visible when the publication is printed.

Hairline A very thin border.

Opaque Unable to be seen through; the opposite of transparent. An object's opacity is the measurement of how nontransparent it is.

Notes

Apply Object Borders

- In Publisher, every **object** is a free-floating entity on the page. You can move, resize, copy, and delete each object individually.
- Pull quote boxes inserted from the Design Gallery are similar to regular text boxes but behave somewhat differently in formatting because they actually are several objects grouped together.
- The border of the object appears in Publisher as a striped or dotted line (provided Boundaries and Guides are displayed; pressing Ctrl+Shift+O toggles them on/off). However, this line does not print unless you apply a **border** to the object.
- You can choose border formatting for any object so that its boundaries are visible when printed.
- One way to specify the border you want is with the Line/Border Style button  on the Formatting toolbar. Select the object and then click that button, and a drop-down menu of preset lines appears.
- The Line/Border Style button applies the same line on all sides of the object. Its options are rather limited; you cannot choose a line color from here, for example.

Select a line style for the selected object's border

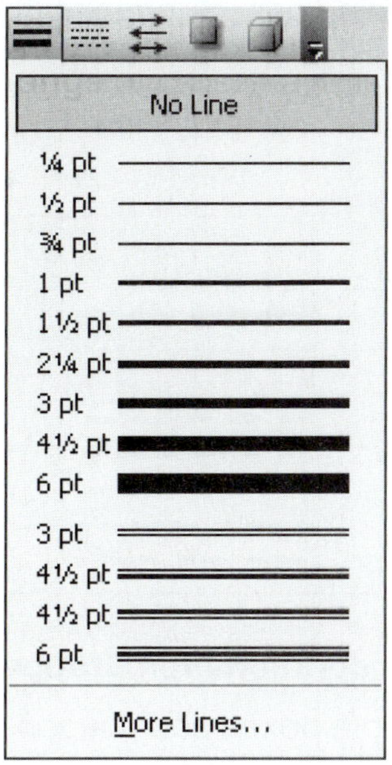

- For a wider selection of border options, choose More Lines from the menu. This opens the Colors and Lines tab of the Format Text Box dialog box. (If you are working with a type of object other than text box, the name will be different.)

  ✓ *Another way to open this same dialog box is to right-click the object and choose Format Text Box.*

- The Style setting in the Format Text Box dialog box is equivalent to the Line/Border Style button. Its drop-down list contains almost exactly the same options.

- The Weight setting enables you to enter a numeric value for the line thickness (in points). A point is 1/72 of an inch. This is useful because you can separate the line style (such as one of the double or triple lines from the Style setting) from its thickness.

  ✓ *You also can apply a shadow to an object, which makes the object appear as if it were floating over the page. (This is different from a border.) Access it with the Shadow button on the Formatting toolbar.*

Choose a thickness and color, and specify which sides it should appear on

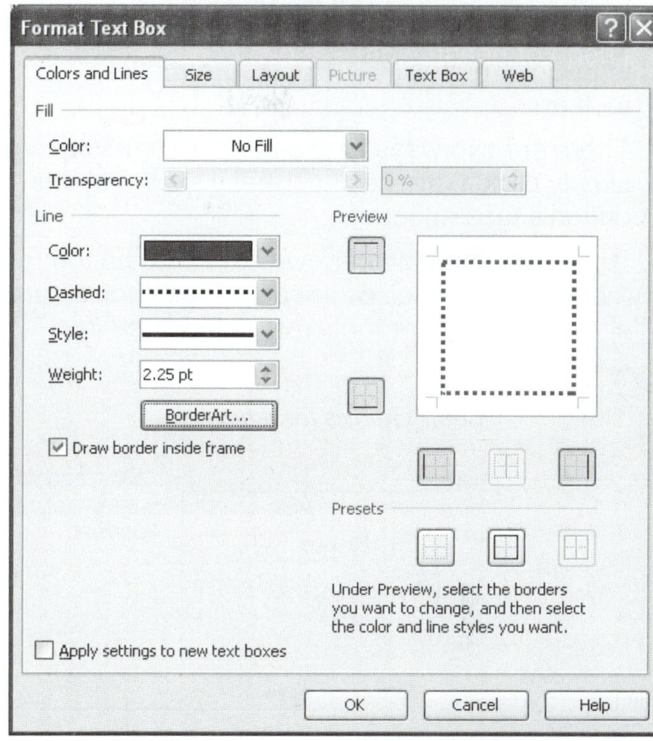

- One big advantage of using the dialog box to apply the border instead of the toolbar is that you can choose which sides of the object should be affected.

- By default, all four sides are turned on. You can turn off the border for a side by clicking the corresponding button around the sample area in the Format Text Box dialog box.

Turn on/off certain sides of border

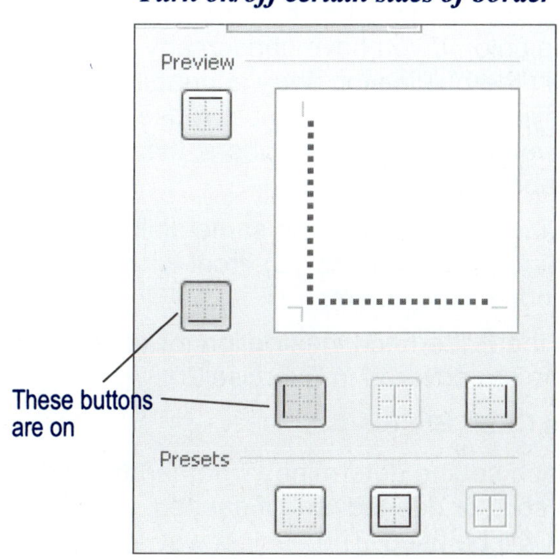

Choose a Border Color

- The easiest way to apply a border color to an object is to select the object and then use the Line Color button  on the Formatting toolbar.
- There are two ways to use the button. If you simply click it, the color currently shown on the button's face appears.
- If you click the down arrow next to the button, a menu of color choices appears. The choices are similar to those for fonts (as you learned in Exercise 18).

Color choices for a border

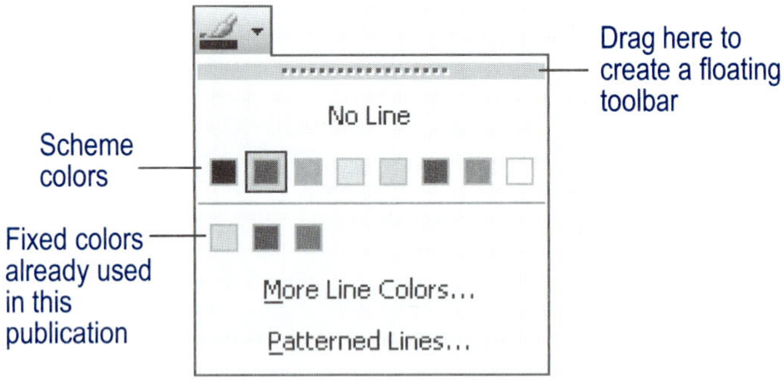

✓ *Notice the dotted horizontal line at the top of the list above. Whenever you see this, it indicates you can drag using the mouse to make the list into a floating toolbar that stays on-screen as you work.*

- This same menu of border color choices is available in the Format Text Box dialog box, too, by opening the Color drop-down list.
- Selecting No Line turns off any existing line.
- The top row of colors has buttons for each scheme color. If you have chosen any fixed colors in the publication, they appear in the second line, in case you want to reuse them. (If you haven't used any fixed colors, the second line is absent.)
- More Line Colors opens the same dialog box as for text (refer to Exercise 18), from which you can choose fixed colors.
- Ignore the Patterned Lines option for now. Patterns are covered in Exercise 20.

Choose a Dash Style

- The Dash setting determines whether the line will be solid or dashed, and if dashed, what pattern will be used. The easiest way to apply a dash style is with the Dash Style button on the Formatting toolbar.
- You can also apply a dash style from the Format Text Box dialog box, by opening the Dashed drop-down list.

Dash options

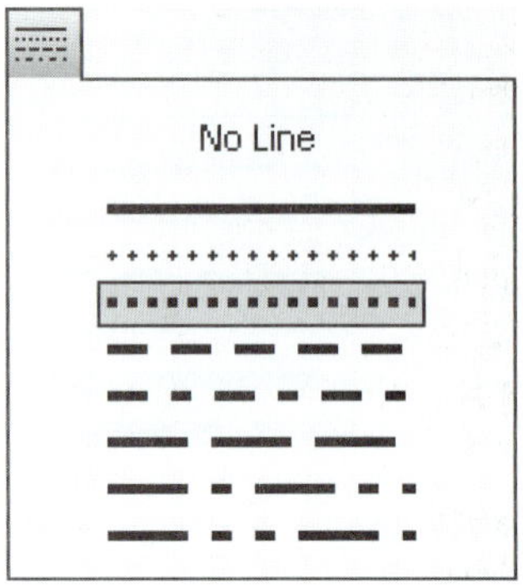

Special Considerations for Grouped Objects

- The pull quote boxes and coupon on the flyer you'll be using for this exercise are grouped objects—that is, they are comprised of multiple separate objects. This makes formatting a little trickier than normal.

  ✓ *You will learn how to group and ungroup objects in Exercise 33.*

- When you click on a grouped object to select it, you may see either round white selection handles, or gray selection handles with Xs in their centers. Clicking again on the object may change which handle type you see.
- To format a grouped object as a whole, it is important to first select it so that you see the gray circles with Xs surrounding the object as a whole, as shown here:

This grouped object is selected as a whole

- Applying a border or fill to the object when selected in this way will allow that formatting to apply to the entire object.

- In contrast, if you select the grouped object so that plain white circle selection handles appear around it, as shown here, a fill applied will affect the entire object but a border applied may not.

When white selection handles appear around a grouped object, the entire object may not receive formatting you apply

✓ *A grouped object that consists of a text box plus a drawn object such as an AutoShape will be considered an AutoShape when dealt with as a unit. Therefore when formatting such a grouped object, you would choose Format, AutoShape rather than the usual Format, Text Box.*

Change an Object's Fill Color

- By default, a text box is transparent, so whatever background is behind it shows through. You can set the background to be any color, however, including solid (**opaque**) white.
- The easiest way to choose an object's fill color is with the Fill Color button on the Formatting toolbar. As with text coloring, you can choose from the Scheme colors, More colors (solid ones), or Fill effects.

Select a fill color for the text box

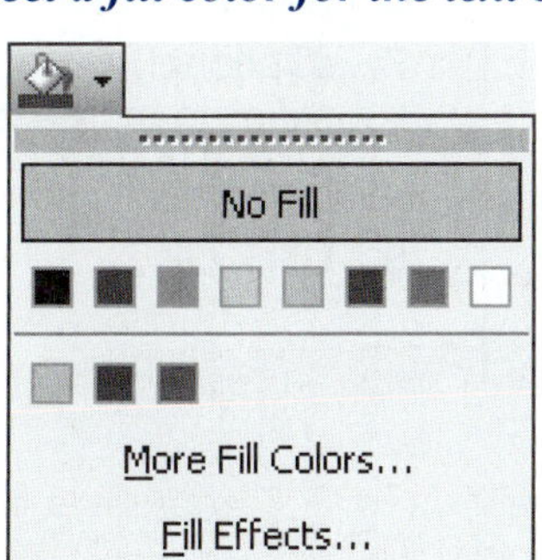

- Just like with text and lines, the first row of colored squares represents scheme colors. The second row, if present, shows fixed colors you have already used in this publication.
- Clicking More Fill Colors opens the More Colors dialog box, from which you can select specific fixed colors. (Refer back to Exercise 18 for information about fixed versus scheme colors.)
- To remove the fill from an object, choose No Fill.

✓ *The Fill Effects option is covered in Exercise 20.*

- You can also use the Color drop-down list in the Fill area of the Colors and Lines tab of the Format Text Box dialog box. Setting the fill color here has the advantage of allowing you to also set a Transparency setting.
- A transparency of 0% (the default) makes the colors very bright and vibrant. Dragging the Transparency slider to the right makes the color fill increasingly pale.

You can set a transparency level for the fill if you use the dialog box method to specify fill color

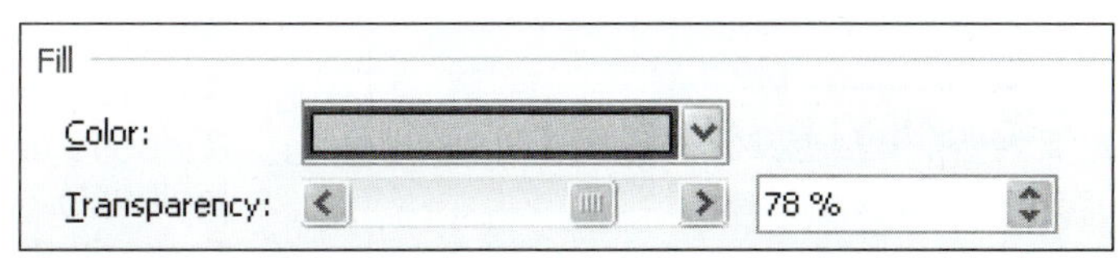

- Transparency might appear to have the same effect as the Tint effect covered in Exercise 18, but it is actually different. Transparency decreases the fill's opacity, so it becomes see-through. Tint mixes the color with varying degrees of white so it becomes paler but not less opaque.

Procedures

Apply an Object Border

Apply a border from toolbar:

1. Select the object.
2. Click the **Line/Border Style** button.
3. Click the line style you want.

   OR

   Click **No Line** to remove the current border.

Remove a border:

1. Select the object.
2. Click the **Line/Border Style** button.
3. Click **No Line**.

Apply current border color:

✓ *This applies the border color currently shown on the Line Color button's face.*

1. Select the object.
2. Click the **Line Color** button.

Choose border color from toolbar:

1. Select the object.
2. Click down arrow next to **Line Color** button.
3. Select a color.

   ✓ *Refer back to Exercise 18 to review scheme colors and fixed colors.*

Choose dash style from toolbar:

1. Select the object.
2. Click the **Dash Style** button.
3. Click dash style you want.

   OR

   Click solid line to remove dash.

Apply border from Format Text Box dialog box:

1. Select the object so that the border around it becomes visible.
2. Right-click object border.
3. Click **Format Text Box**........ O

   ✓ *The exact name of the command depends on the type of object.*

4. Click **Colors and Lines** tab.
5. Open **Color** drop-down list in Line area .... Alt+O

   ✓ *In the Format dialog box, you can click in the list box or click on the drop-down arrow to open the list or palette.*

6. Select a color.
7. Open **Dashed** drop-down list .... Alt+D
8. Select a dash style. (See "Choose dash style from toolbar.")
9. Open **Style** drop-down list .... Alt+S
10. Select a line style.
11. Type a line weight in the **Weight** box................. Alt+W

    OR

    Use the **up/down** increment buttons to increment the weight.

12. (Optional) Click a **border line** button to toggle on/off individual sides of the object border.
13. Click **OK** .... Enter

Select a Grouped Object to be Formatted

- Click the object border so that gray circle selection handles with Xs appear around its outer border.

  ✓ *You may need to click the object more than once. White round selection handles are not what you want in this case.*

Fill a Frame

Choose a fill color from the toolbar:

1. Select the object.
2. Click the down arrow on the **Fill Color** button on the Formatting toolbar.
3. Select a scheme color or fixed color.

Choose a fill color from Format Text Box dialog box:

1. Select the object so that the border around it becomes visible.
2. Right-click the object border.
3. Click **Format Text Box** .... O

   ✓ *The exact name of the command depends on the type of object.*

4. Click **Colors and Lines** tab.
5. Open **Color** drop-down list in Fill area .... Alt+C
6. Select a color.
7. (Optional) Drag **Transparency** slider to increase transparency of color fill............. Alt+T, ↑
8. Click **OK**.......................... Enter

Exercise Directions

1. Start Publisher, if necessary.
2. Open the file PUB19. Save it as 19FLYER.
3. Copy the text from the pale gold background pull quote box (the one that begins **Sitting on...**) to the Clipboard, and then delete the pull quote box.
4. Create a new text box in the spot where it was, and paste the text into the new text box.
5. Click at the beginning of the pasted text and press Enter as many times as needed to center the text vertically within the new text box.
6. Apply a 2-point dotted dark green (Accent 1 scheme color) border to the new text box.
7. Apply the same dark green (Accent 1 scheme color) as a fill for the text box, and then set its transparency to 85%.
8. Select the gold-background pull quote box so that selection handles appear around its outer border that are gray circles with Xs in the centers.
9. Choose Fill Effects for its fill, and on the Tint tab, choose a 70% tint.
10. Select the coupon box so that the gray circle-with-X selection handles appear around it, and change its dash style to 3-point square dot.
11. Print your publication.
12. Save your work and exit Publisher.

On Your Own

1. Start Publisher, if necessary.
2. Open the file OPUB19. Save it as 19BOARD.
3. Apply a different border and fill style to each of the text boxes. Include the following:
   - At least one dashed border
   - At least one border with a width of more than 6 points.
   - A different color for each border
   - A different color for each fill
   - At least one fill that uses a tint.
   - At least one fill set to more than 0% transparency.
4. Save your work and Exit Publisher.

Exercise 20

Skills Covered:

◆ **Apply a Patterned Border** ◆ **Use BorderArt** ◆ **Use Fill Effects**

On the Job

Publisher comes with a wide array of special effects that can dress up a publication. In addition to the standard frame borders that you learned about in Exercise 19, you can also apply patterned lines and BorderArt. To fill a frame, in addition to using solid colors, you can apply any of several fill effects.

You are still finding ways to improve the Hendricks Inn flyer. Now that you know about Publisher's special borders and fills, you would like to try using some of them to make the flyer more attractive.

Terms

BorderArt A small graphic that is repeated around the edge of an object, forming a border.

Gradient A fill effect that gradually progresses from one color to another that gives the appearance of how light falls on a shape or moving object.

Aspect ratio The ratio of height to width of an object. If the aspect ratio of a picture is allowed to change, the picture distorts.

Notes

Apply a Patterned Border

- When selecting a line color for a frame border, one of your choices is Patterned Lines.

Choose Patterned Lines as the line color

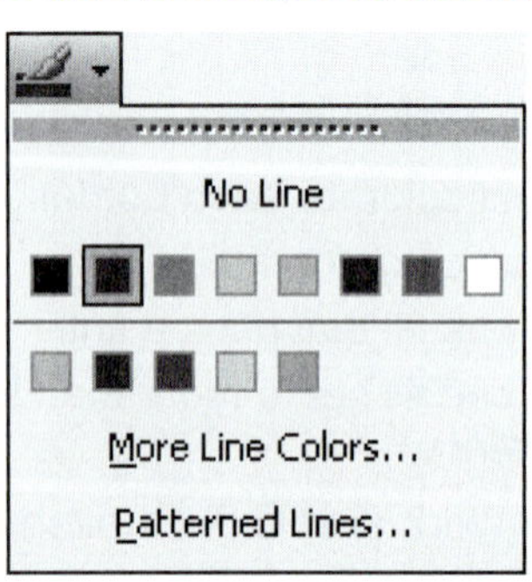

- Choosing Patterned Lines opens a Patterned Lines dialog box. It contains the Tint tab, the same as with text (see Exercise 18), but also a Pattern tab from which you can choose a line pattern if desired.

Line pattern choices

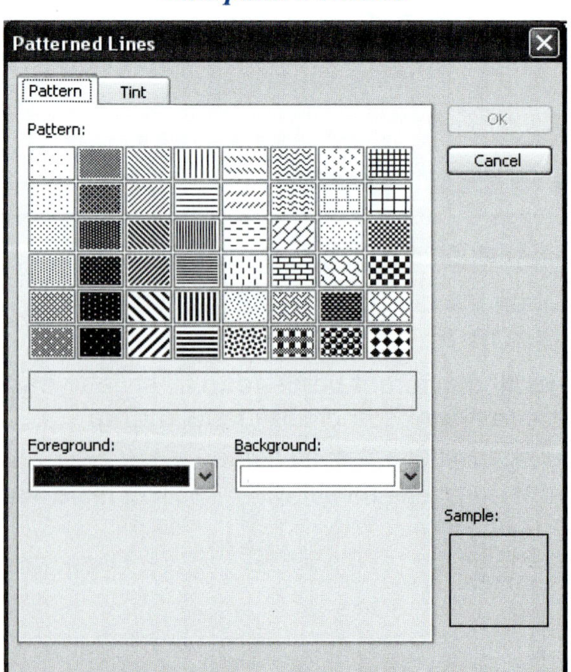

- For a pattern, choose a different color for Foreground and Background. The higher the contrast between the two colors chosen, the more apparent the pattern will be.
  - ✓ *Patterned lines do not look very good unless the border is very thick. Otherwise they just look like irregularly dotted lines. You will probably find patterns more useful for fills, covered later in this exercise, than for lines.*

A thick border (12 point shown here) accentuates the border pattern

Use BorderArt

- **BorderArt** is a repeated picture that serves as a border around a text box or other object.
- To open the BorderArt dialog box, click the BorderArt button in the Format Text Box dialog box (on the Colors and Lines tab).

Assign a graphical border with BorderArt

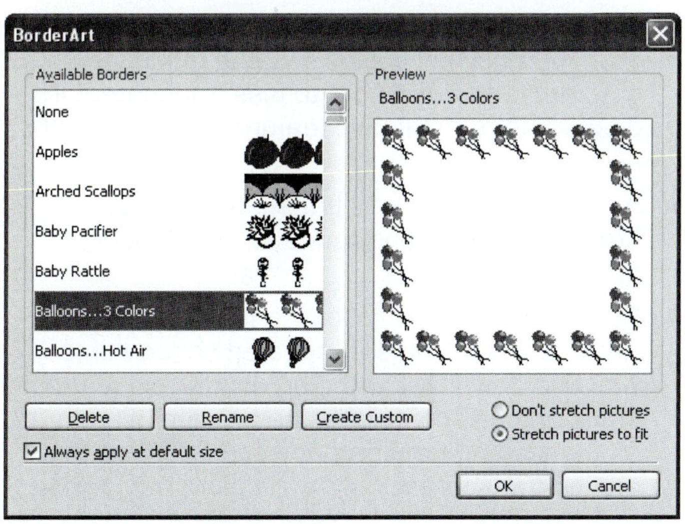

- BorderArt repeats a picture around the edge of the object frame.
  - ✓ *BorderArt can be overwhelming for individual text boxes. Use it sparingly.*
- If you choose Stretch pictures to fit, it makes each copy of the picture slightly wider or taller if needed to minimize the amount of blank space between pictures. The following figure shows the difference.

Notice the middle row of trees in the stretched versus unstretched versions

- If you leave the Always apply at default size check box marked, the BorderArt picture will remain the same size regardless of the frame size. When applied to a very small frame, this can result in only a few copies of the picture on each side of the frame.

A BorderArt image at default size can overwhelm a small object

- If you clear this check box, you can then specify a picture size in the Weight box of the Format Text Box dialog box to control the size of the BorderArt border.

You can specify a weight for the border to make the BorderArt graphic more appropriately sized

Use Fill Effects

- Fill Effects create special backgrounds in whatever object they are applied to (such as a text box).
- They include Tint and Pattern (which you have already learned about) and also Gradient, Texture, and Picture.

Tint Fill

- Just like with text, you can choose a tint for a fill. A tint is a shade of a particular color (the same hue but a different amount of light/dark). Refer to Exercise 18 for details.

Pattern Fill

- Just like with a line (earlier in this exercise), you can choose a pattern for a fill. You choose different colors for the background and foreground, and then choose a pattern to apply.
- The default background color for a pattern is white, but it can be set to any color.

A pattern applied as a background

Gradient Fill

- A **gradient** fill effect creates a sensation of movement, with one color fading into another. You can choose from a variety of gradient "directions" and specify the colors that will comprise it.

This gradient fill starts with white at the top and gradually fades to orange at the bottom

- You can have either a one-color or two-color gradient. If you choose one-color, the color it fades to is black or white.
- You can also choose a preset gradient, which includes two prechosen colors. These have evocative names like Late Sunset and Desert.

Select a gradient, and choose the colors for it

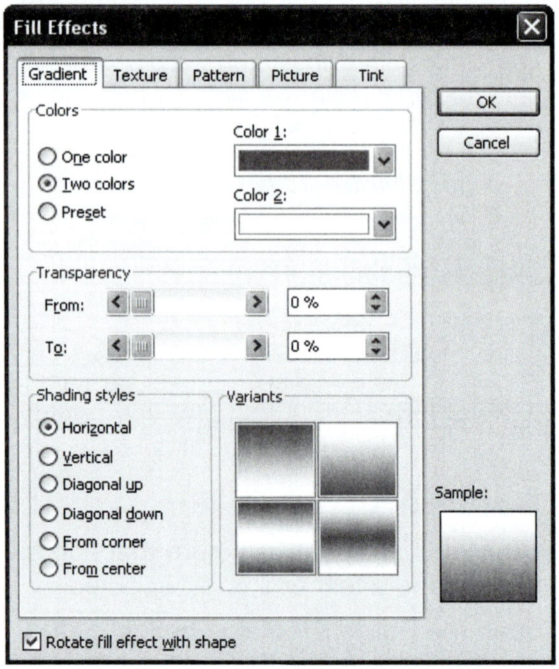

- After choosing the gradient colors, you fine-tune it by selecting a transparency level and shading style.
- Transparency level allows you to make the gradient fade from more to less transparent if desired. By default, this feature is set to 0%, for no transparency.
- As with single-color fill transparency, the Transparency setting refers to the amount of opaqueness.
- For example, in the following figure, a text box with the word "Vanish" repeated several times was laid down first and then overlaid with another blank text box containing the gradient fill with 0% as the starting transparency and 100% as the ending transparency, with all color set to White.

Transparency gradient can make different levels of transparency in different areas of the frame

- Shading styles let you specify which direction the fade will run. Within each shading style, you can choose from several Variants.

Choose a shading style and a variant

- The Rotate fill effect with shape check box lets you specify that if you later rotate the object that you are filling, the background gradient will rotate too. Gradient, Texture, and Picture all have this option.

  ✓ *You will learn about rotating objects in Exercise 35.*

Texture Fill

- Texture Fill enables you to apply a graphic as a background that resembles a certain type of material, such as paper, cloth, or wood.
- You can also use your own graphic as a texture by clicking Other Texture and selecting it.

Select a texture fill

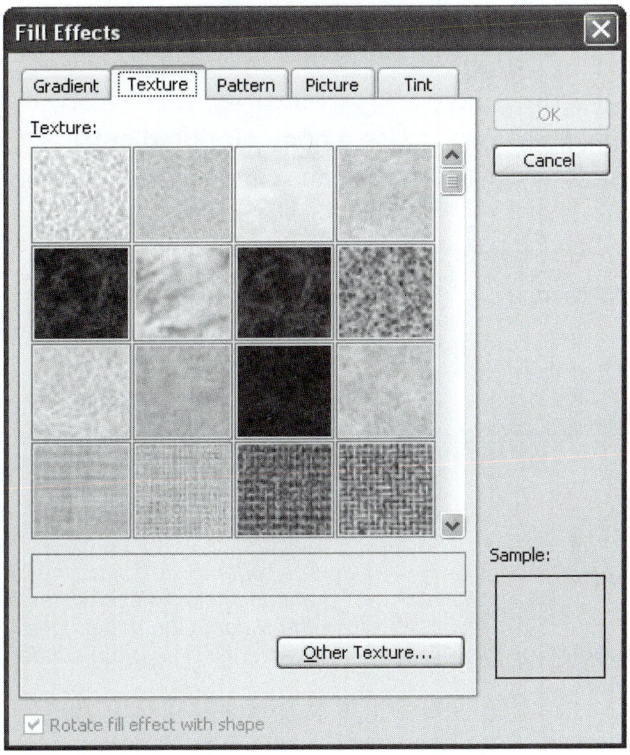

Picture Fill

- Picture Fill is like a texture fill, in that it fills the object with an image, but with Picture Fill you specify the image to use.
- The Picture tab starts out blank, with no picture displayed. You must click Select Picture and locate/select a picture to use. It then appears in the Picture preview area.

Specify a picture to use for the fill

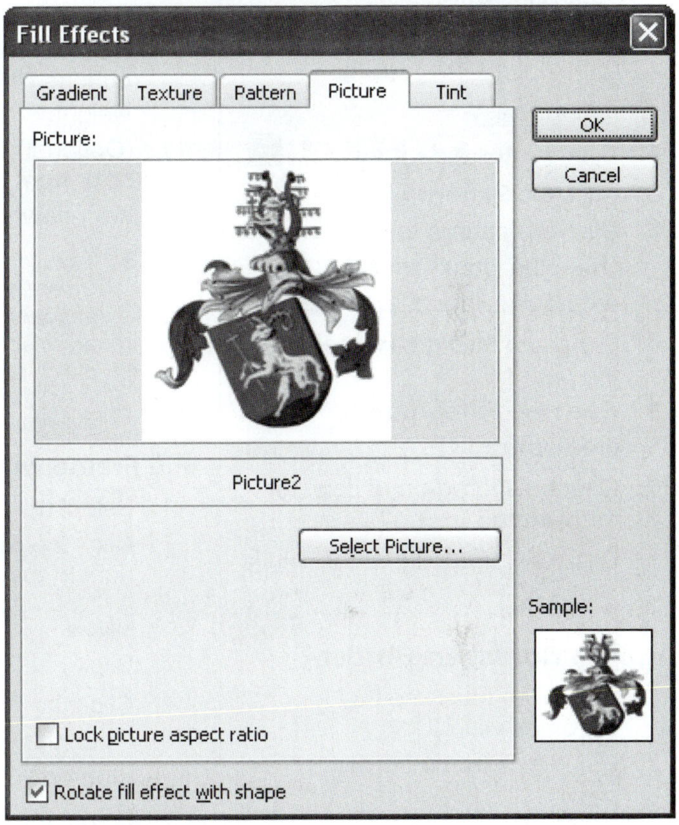

- The Lock picture **aspect ratio** check box ensures that the picture will not be distorted in order to fit more precisely in the frame. This is especially important if you are using a picture of a person.

  ✓ *A picture fill in a text box can make the text very difficult to read. Use such a fill very sparingly.*

Procedures

Create a Patterned Border

1. Select the frame.
2. Apply a border of the desired thickness.
   ✓ *A very thick border (at least 6 pts.) is recommended for use with patterns.*
3. Click the **down arrow** to the right of the **Line Color** button.
4. Click **Patterned Lines** .... P
5. Click the **Pattern** tab.
6. Click the pattern to use.
7. Open the **Background** drop-down list.............. Alt+B
8. Choose a background color for the pattern.
9. Open the **Foreground** drop-down list.............. Alt+F
10. Choose a foreground color for the pattern.
11. Click **OK**.......................... Enter
12. Click **OK**.......................... Enter

Apply a BorderArt Border

1. Select the frame so that it becomes visible.
2. Right-click frame border.
3. Click **Format Text Box** .... O
   ✓ *The name of the command depends on the type of frame.*
4. Click **Colors and Lines** tab.
5. Click the **BorderArt** button.......................... Alt+B
6. Click the border you want from the **Available Borders** list.......... Alt+V, ↓
7. If desired, clear the **Always apply at default size** check box.................... Alt+A
   ✓ *This allows you to specify the border width.*
8. Choose one:
   - **Don't stretch pictures**................ Alt+E
   - **Stretch pictures to fit**........................ Alt+F
9. Click **OK** .... Enter
10. If you cleared the check box in step 7, enter a weight in **Weight** box................. Alt+W

    OR

    Use the **up/down** increment buttons to increment the weight.
11. (Optional) Choose a different color from the **Color** drop-down list .... Alt+O
    ✓ *The Default setting on the Color list makes the BorderArt appear in its normal coloring, as selected in the BorderArt dialog box.*
12. Click **OK** .... Enter

Fill Frame with a Tint

1. Select the frame.
2. Click the **down arrow** to the right of the **Fill Color** button.
3. Click **Fill Effects**................. F
4. Click the **Tint** tab.
5. Open the **Base color** drop-down list .... Alt+B
6. Select the color to use.
7. Click the tint you want from the samples at the top of the dialog box.
8. Click **OK** .... Enter

Fill a Frame with a Pattern

1. Select the frame.
2. Click the **down arrow** to the right of the **Fill Color** button.
3. Click **Fill Effects**................. F
4. Click the **Pattern** tab.
5. Click the pattern to use.
6. Open the **Background** drop-down list .... Alt+B
7. Choose a background color for the pattern.
8. Open the **Foreground** drop-down list............. Alt+F
9. Choose a foreground color for the pattern.
10. Click **OK**.......................... Enter

Fill a Frame with a Gradient

1. Select the frame.
2. Click the **down arrow** to the right of the **Fill Color** button.
3. Click **Fill Effects** .... F
4. Click the **Gradient** tab.
5. Choose the color(s) option you want for your gradient. See one of the applicable sections following this procedure for details for selecting the desired color(s) or preset.
6. (Optional) Drag the **From** slider to the right to set the transparency for Color 1................. Alt+R, ↑
7. (Optional) Drag the **To** slider to the right to set the transparency for Color 2 (or for black or white, if you chose a one-color gradient)............... Alt+O, ↑
8. Select a shading style.
9. Select a variant.
10. Click **OK**.......................... Enter

Use a one-color gradient:

From the Gradient tab of the Fill Effects dialog box:

1. Click **One color**.......... Alt+N
2. Open the **Color 1** drop-down list............. Alt+1
3. Select a color.
4. Drag the **Dark/Light** slider to the right to set the darkness of the gradient .... Alt+K, ↑
   ✓ *With the slider toward dark, the second color will be black. With the slider toward light, the second color will be white. With the slider in the middle, the gradient will be more subtle.*

Use a two-color gradient:

From the Gradient tab of the Fill Effects dialog box:

1. Click **Two colors** .... Alt+T
2. Open the **Color 1** drop-down list .... Alt+1
3. Select a color.
4. Open the **Color 2** drop-down list .... Alt+2
5. Select a color.

Use a preset gradient:

From the Gradient tab of the Fill Effects dialog box:

1. Click **Preset** .... Alt+S
2. Open the **Preset Colors** drop-down list .... Alt+E
3. Select a named color setting .... ↑↓, Enter

Fill Frame with a Texture

1. Select the frame.
2. Click the **down arrow** to the right of the **Fill Color** button .
3. Click **Fill Effects** .... F
4. Click the **Texture** tab.
5. Select the texture you want .... Alt+T, ↑↓←→

   ✓ *You can click Other Texture to select a picture on your hard disk to use as a texture. When you use a picture as a texture, it repeats as needed to fill the frame. In contrast, when you fill the frame with a picture (see next procedure), a single copy of it appears.*
6. (Optional) Clear the **Rotate fill effect with shape** check box if desired .... Alt+W
7. Click **OK** .... Enter

Fill Frame with a Picture

1. Select the frame.
2. Click the **down arrow** to the right of the **Fill Color** button .
3. Click **Fill Effects** .... F
4. Click the **Picture** tab.
5. Click **Select Picture** button .... Alt+L
6. Select the picture to use.
7. Change to a different drive/folder if needed.
8. Click **Insert** .... Alt+S
9. (Optional) Select **Lock picture aspect ratio** if desired .... Alt+P
10. (Optional) Clear the **Rotate fill effect with shape** check box if desired .... Alt+W
11. Click **OK** .... Enter

Exercise Directions

1. Start Publisher, if necessary.
2. Open the file **PUB20**. Save it as **20FLYER**.
3. Select the pale green text box, and set its Transparency setting to 0%.
4. Apply a gradient fill to that text box that blends from bright green to pale green from top to bottom.

   ✓ *You can use a one-color gradient for this since you want two shades of the same color. Pick a bright green for the gradient color and then drag the gradient slider so that it fades to a paler shade of the same color.*
5. Select the gray-oval text box, so that gray selection handles with Xs appear around it, and then apply the Newsprint texture to it.
6. Select the coupon at the bottom of the flyer (gray selection handles), and apply the Coupon Cutout Dots BorderArt to it

   ✓ *If there appear to be multiple nested versions of the border in the box, choose Edit, Undo, make sure you have selected correctly, and then try again. Since the coupon is a grouped object, it consists of multiple text boxes, and you must make sure you apply the BorderArt only to the outer border.*
7. Change the light tan text box to a patterned fill using the Light Downward Diagonal pattern of the current color and white.
8. Print your publication. Illustration A shows the final result.
9. Save your work and exit Publisher.

On Your Own

1. Start Publisher, if necessary.
2. Open the file **OPUB20**. Save it as **20BOARD**.
3. Apply different fill effects to each of the text boxes.
4. Apply a patterned border to at least one of the text boxes.
5. Apply a BorderArt border to at least one of the text boxes.
6. Save your work and Exit Publisher.

Illustration A

April 2005

The Hendricks Inn

Springtime is Garden Time!

The flowers are blooming, and the grass is a bright emerald green on the hills surrounding The Hendricks Inn. Come stroll through our gardens and orchard and discover the unique beauty of our property. Relax on the deck overlooking the bird feeders, where an array of bird life regularly appears including woodpeckers, hummingbirds, and finches.

Come see us at The Hendricks Inn and save 50%!

Sitting on the deck at The Hendricks Inn in the evenings watching the fireflies was the highlight of our vacation."
- Sheila and Rob Roberson, Dallas, TX

"We try to visit The Hendricks Inn in the spring, summer, and fall because the gardens are so different in each season, each beautiful in is own way.
- Larry Miaz, Tulsa, OK

"We had seen pictures of the perennial gardens on the Web site, but they were even more spectacular in person."
-Ann West, San Diego, CA

One Night's Stay

50% off

The Hendricks Inn

1478 W. 86th St., Hendricks, KY

Tel: (381) 555-1981

Expiration Date: 1/31/06

Exercise 21

Skills Covered:

◆ **Align Text Horizontally** ◆ **Change Line Spacing**
◆ **Align Text Vertically**

On the Job

Text alignment within a text box can make a big difference in the look of a publication. Publisher lets you adjust the spacing between paragraphs and between lines of an individual paragraph, as well as set alignment options for text both vertically and horizontally.

You'll finish up the Hendricks Inn flyer in this exercise by adjusting the alignment in some of its text boxes to make it more visually appealing and readable.

Terms

Justified Text stretched out with extra spacing as needed so that all lines align evenly on both the right and left.

Line spacing The whitespace between lines.

Vertical alignment The vertical positioning of text within a text frame. The default is Top.

Notes

Align Text Horizontally

- You may choose among Left, Center, Right, and **Justified** alignment for each paragraph. To do so, click in the paragraph and then click one of the alignment buttons on the Formatting toolbar.
  - Left
  - Center
  - Right
  - Justified

  ✓ *If one or more of the alignment buttons is missing, click the >> button at the right end of the toolbar; perhaps the button is hidden and can be found on the drop-down list of extra buttons.*

- You also can select an alignment from the Paragraph dialog box. Choose from its Alignment drop-down list on the Indents and Spacing tab.

Control alignment and spacing here

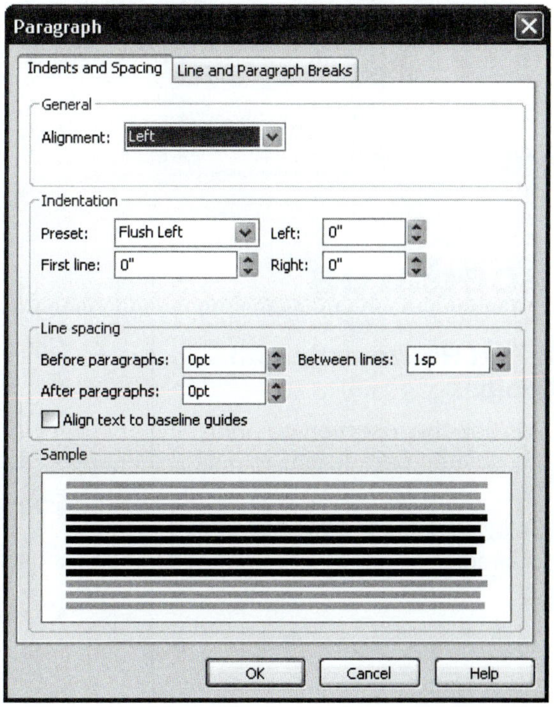

- The default alignment is Left for manually placed text boxes; for placeholder boxes the alignment varies depending on the template.
- To affect more than one paragraph at once, select the paragraphs first.

Change Line Spacing

- There are three kinds of **line spacing** you can set: Between lines, Before paragraphs, and After paragraphs.
- Line spacing settings apply only to the paragraph in which the insertion point lies when you make the change. To affect more than one paragraph at once, select them before making the change.
- Set line spacing from the Paragraph dialog box (Format, Paragraph) on the Indents and Spacing tab.
- You also can set line spacing from the Measurement toolbar. To turn it on, click the Show Toolbar button in the Line Spacing dialog box, or choose View, Toolbars, Measurement.

The Measurements toolbar offers line spacing controls

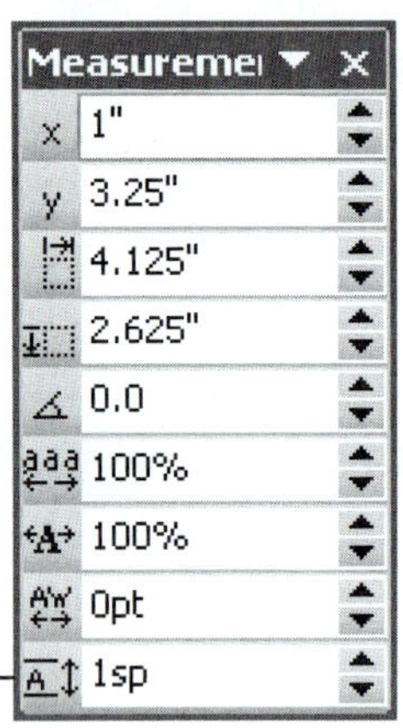

Set line spacing here

Align Text Vertically

- **Vertical alignment** refers to the vertical position of the text within the text frame. The default vertical alignment is Top, but Publisher offers Middle or Bottom as well.
- To choose an alignment, place the insertion point in the paragraph to affect (or select multiple paragraphs) and then choose Format, Text Box. Then on the Text Box tab, change the Vertical alignment setting.

Select a vertical alignment

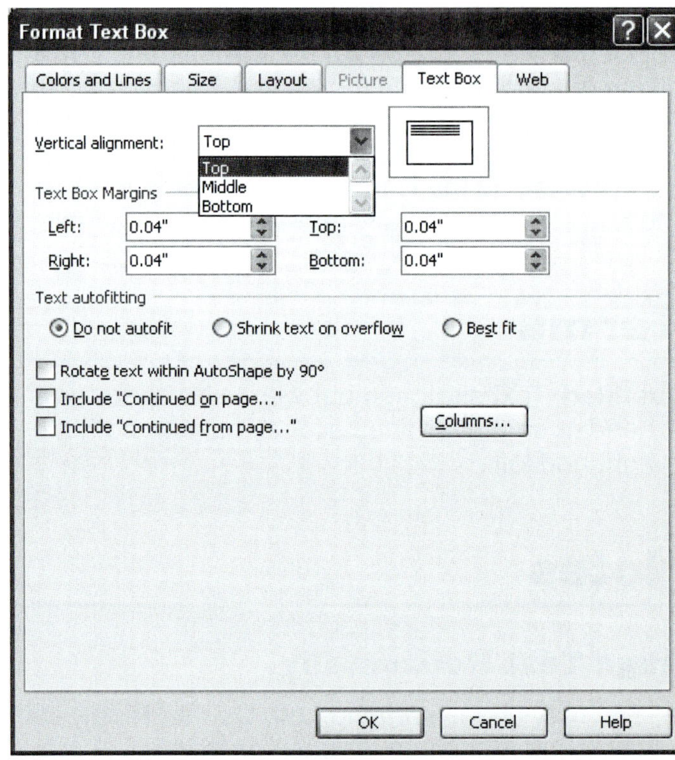

Procedures

Align Text Horizontally with the Toolbar

1. Position the insertion point in the desired paragraph.
   OR
   Select multiple paragraphs to affect.
2. Click one of the alignment buttons on the Formatting toolbar:
   - **Left**
   - **Center**
   - **Right**
   - **Justified**

Change Line Spacing with the Paragraph Dialog Box

1. Position the insertion point in the desired paragraph.
   OR
   Select multiple paragraphs to affect.
2. Click **Format** .... Alt+O
3. Click **Paragraph** .... P

4. Click **Indents and Spacing** tab.
5. Enter a number of points of space in the **Before paragraphs** box .... Alt+B
6. Enter a number of points of space in the **After paragraphs** box .... Alt+E
7. Enter a number of lines in the **Between lines** box ...... Alt+W

   ✓ *It need not be a whole number in step 7; you can enter **1.25** for one and a quarter spaces, for example.*

8. Click **OK** .... Enter

Change the Line Spacing with the Measurement Toolbar

1. If the Measurement toolbar does not appear, display it by doing the following:
   a. Click **View** .... Alt+V
   b. Point to **Toolbars** .... T
   c. Click **Measurement**.
2. Position the insertion point in the desired paragraph.

   OR

   Select multiple paragraphs to affect.
3. Enter a new measurement in the **Line Spacing** box on the Measurement toolbar.

   OR

   Click the **up** or **down** increment buttons next to the Line Spacing box to increase or decrease the number shown.

Align Text Vertically

1. Position the insertion point in the desired paragraph.

   OR

   Select multiple paragraphs to affect.
2. Click **Format** .... Alt+O
3. Click **Text Box** .... E
4. Click the **Text Box** tab.
5. Open **Vertical alignment** drop-down list............. Alt+V
6. Click vertical alignment desired.
7. Click **OK** .... Enter

Exercise Directions

1. Start Publisher, if necessary.
2. Open the file **PUB21**. Save it as **21FLYER**.
3. Click the heading (**The Hendricks Inn**) and set it to Center alignment.

   ✓ *Notice that it doesn't change. Can you guess why? It's because the text box in which it sits is exactly the minimum width required to hold that text. Whenever there is no extra space in the width, a different horizontal alignment setting will have no effect.*

4. Set the **April 2005** text to Center alignment.
5. In the green text box, set the vertical alignment to Middle.
6. In the gray-border text box, change the spacing between the lines of text to 1.10sp and the horizontal alignment to Left.

   ✓ *The "sp" stands for spaces.*

7. On the coupon, select **The Hendricks Inn** and center it.
8. Change the alignment of both paragraphs under the **Springtime is Garden Time** heading to Left alignment.
9. Print your publication. Illustration A shows the finished product.
10. Save your work and exit Publisher.

On Your Own

1. Start Publisher, if necessary.
2. Open the file **OPUB21**. Save it as **21BOARD**.
3. Set each box on the bulletin board to have a unique combination of vertical and horizontal alignment. No two boxes should have the same combination.
4. For the red text box, set the line spacing of the body paragraph to 1.5sp, and set the space After Paragraph for the heading in that box to 10 point.
5. Change the line spacing for at least two other text boxes, including both between-line spacing and spacing either before or after paragraphs.

   ✓ *As an experiment, try setting the spacing between lines to less than 1sp.*

6. Save your work and exit Publisher.

Illustration A

April 2005

The Hendricks Inn

Springtime is Garden Time!

The flowers are blooming, and the grass is a bright emerald green on the hills surrounding The Hendricks Inn. Come stroll through our gardens and orchard and discover the unique beauty of our property. Relax on the deck overlooking the bird feeders, where an array of bird life regularly appears including woodpeckers, hummingbirds, and finches.

Come see us at The Hendricks Inn and save 50%!

Sitting on the deck at The Hendricks Inn in the evenings watching the fireflies was the highlight of our vacation."
- Sheila and Rob Roberson, Dallas, TX

"We try to visit The Hendricks Inn in the spring, summer, and fall because the gardens are so different in each season, each beautiful in is own way.
- Larry Miaz, Tulsa, OK

"We had seen pictures of the perennial gardens on the Web site, but they were even more spectacular in person."
-Ann West, San Diego, CA

One Night's Stay

50% off

The Hendricks Inn
1478 W. 86th St., Hendricks, KY
Tel: (381) 555-1981
Expiration Date: 1/31/06

Exercise 22

Skills Covered:

◆ **Set Tab Stops** ◆ **Set Indents**

On the Job

Tabs and indents can be employed to make text align neatly on a page. If you have worked with a word processing program before, such as Microsoft Office Word, you may already be familiar with these; they work the same in Publisher as they do there.

You'll start a new project for The Hendricks Inn in this exercise. You will create an information card, with a telephone extension directory on it, to place in each room.

Terms

Leader A repeated character appearing between some text and the next tab stop that helps the eye follow the text across the page. It is commonly used in tables of contents, for example, between a title and its associated page number.

Indent Extra horizontal space inserted on one or both sides of a paragraph.

Hanging Indent An indent style in which the first line is set with a negative indent in relation to the rest of the paragraph, so it sticks out farther to the left. (These terms use hanging indents.)

Notes

Use Tab Stops

- A tab stop marks a certain horizontal location within a text box. When the insertion point is to the left of the tab stop, you can press the Tab key to move it to the stop. Any text to the right of the insertion point will be pushed to the tab stop as well.
- Each paragraph has its own separate tab stop settings. To change the tab stops for more than one paragraph at once, first select the paragraphs to affect.
- Each paragraph has default tab stops every ½".
- Any custom tab stops you create for a paragraph will appear as symbols on the ruler when the insertion point is in the paragraph for which they are set. The default tab stops do not appear on the ruler.

  ✓ *When you set a custom tab stop for a paragraph, all of the default tab stops to its left are cleared, but the default tab stops to its right remain.*

Set or Remove a Custom Tab Stop

- To set a tab stop, click inside the paragraph then click the ruler to place a stop at the desired location.

Set a tab stop by clicking on the ruler

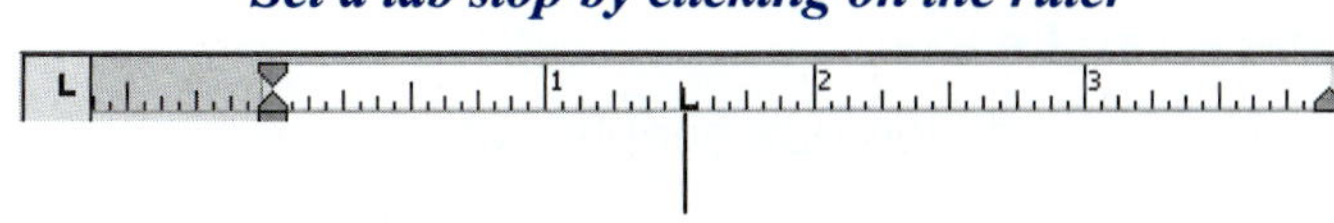

- To remove a tab stop, drag it off the ruler and drop it anywhere else.
- You can drag custom tab stops to the right or left on the ruler to reposition them.
- You also can set tab stops with the Tabs dialog box (Format, Tabs). To set a tab stop from here, type a ruler position (in inches) in the Tab stop position text box, and then choose an alignment and leader character and click Set. (You'll learn about alignments and leader characters shortly.)

You can set tabs from the Tabs dialog box

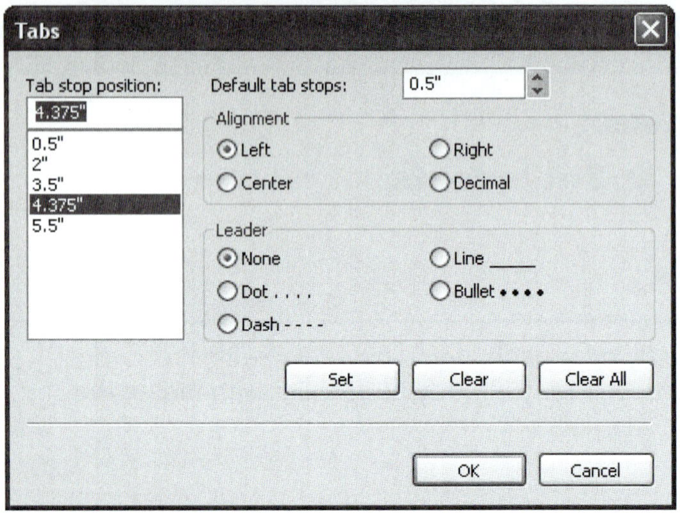

Tab Stop Types

- The default tab stop is a Left one; text that you type after you press Tab to move to it begins at the tab stop and runs to the right.
- Other tab stop types available are Center, Right, and Decimal.
  - A center tab stop centers the text under the tab stop.
  - A right tab stop adjusts the text placement so that the text ends exactly under the tab stop.
  - A decimal tab stop works like a right tab stop until a decimal point (or period) appears in the text; then it begins to work like a left tab stop from that point, so the decimal point remains exactly under the stop.
- To change a tab stop to a different type, double-click it to open the Tabs dialog box, and then choose a different alignment.

Use a Tab Leader

- The Tabs dialog box enables you to set a **leader**.
- A leader is useful if you want to help a reader's eye follow the text from one side of a page to another without skipping a line, such as in a table of contents. The leader character appears between the text and the next tab stop to the right.

Publisher lets you choose from a variety of leader characters such as these

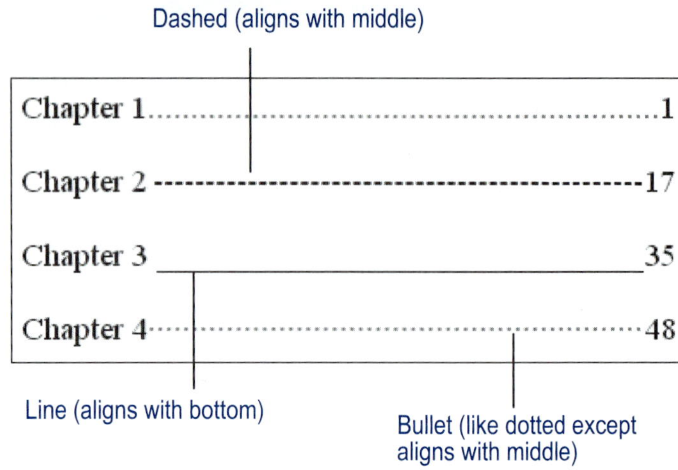

Redefine the Default Tab Stops

- The Default tab stops setting in the Tabs dialog box enables you to redefine the interval at which default tab stops occur.
- Use the increment buttons to increase or decrease the value if desired.

Set Indents

- **Indents** increase the amount of white space to the left and/or right of a paragraph. You might want to indent a paragraph, such as a quotation, for emphasis.

  ✓ *Do not confuse indents with left/right margins. Margins are for the entire text box or entire page, while indents are for individual paragraphs only.*

- You also can set a first-line indent for a paragraph. This controls the indent for only the first line of the paragraph. Some people like to indent the first line of each paragraph ½", for example.

Create a Left Indent with the Toolbar

- Left indentation of the entire paragraph is the most common type of indent. You can create a 0.5" left indent for a paragraph with the Increase Indent button  on the Formatting toolbar.

  The Decrease Indent button  does the opposite, "outdenting" the paragraph by 0.5".

Adjust Indents with the Ruler

- Another way to set indents for a paragraph is to drag the indent markers on the ruler when that paragraph is selected. The indent markers on the left consist of two triangles and a rectangle.
- Drag the top triangle to set the first-line indent, or the bottom triangle to set the indent for subsequent lines. Or, drag the rectangle to set the overall left indent (all lines together).
- The indent marker on the right is much simpler: a single triangle. Drag it to set the right indent for all lines of the paragraph together.

An easy way to set indents is to drag the indent markers

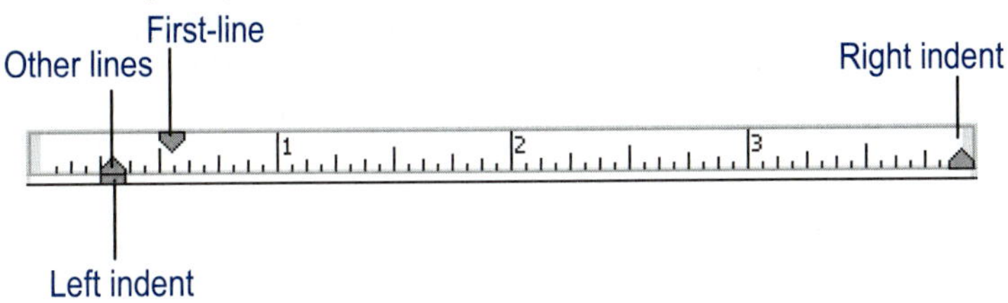

Adjust Indents with the Paragraph Dialog Box

- You also can set indents with the Paragraph dialog box (Format, Paragraph) on the Indents and Spacing tab.
- There are several preset indents from which to choose on the Preset drop-down list. These include Flush Left, 1st Line Indent, **Hanging Indent**, and Quotation. They set the Left, First line, and Right settings of a paragraph automatically.
  ✓ *To remove all indents, choose Flush Left.*
- If you wish, you may enter your own Left, First line, and Right settings for a specific indentation for the paragraph.

Control indentation precisely using the Paragraph dialog box

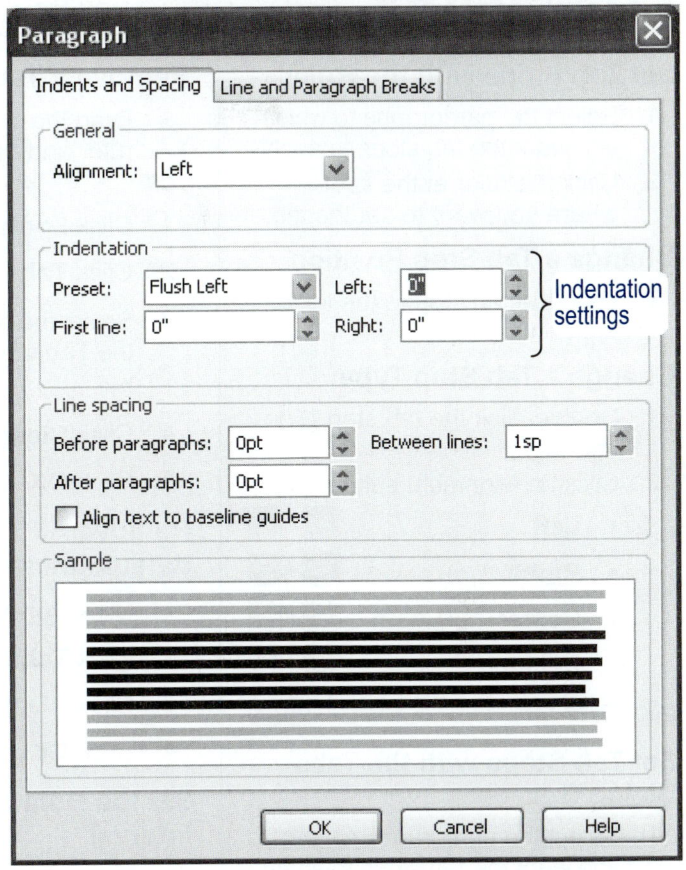

✓ *Hint: Don't get so wrapped up in paragraph indents that you forget that you can change the positioning of all text in the text box with one easy step—drag the left side of the text box toward the center. It's not cheating—it's efficient.*

Procedures

Set Tab Stops with the Ruler

1. Select the paragraphs to which you want the tab stops to apply.
2. Click the ruler at the spot where you want to set the tab.

Change a Tab Stop Position

- Drag the tab stop to the left or right on the ruler.

Change a Tab Stop Type

1. Double-click the tab stop on the ruler.
2. Click an Alignment button:
   - **Left** .... Alt+L
   - **Right** .... Alt+R
   - **Center** .... Alt+C
   - **Decimal** .... Alt+D
3. Click **OK** .... Enter

Set Tab Stops with the Tabs Dialog Box

1. Select the paragraphs to which you want the tab stops to apply.
2. Click **Format** .... Alt+O
3. Click **Tabs** .... T
4. Enter the exact position desired in the **Tab stop position** box .... Alt+T
5. Click an Alignment button:
   - **Left** .... Alt+L
   - **Right** .... Alt+R
   - **Center** .... Alt+C
   - **Decimal** .... Alt+D
6. If desired, click a Leader:
   - **Dot** .... Alt+O
   - **Dash** .... Alt+H
   - **Line** .... Alt+I
   - **Bullet** .... Alt+B
7. Click **Set** .... Alt+S
8. Repeat steps 4–7 to set each desired tab stop.
9. Click **OK** .... Enter

Remove a Tab Stop

- Drag the tab stop down off the ruler and drop it.

OR

1. Click **Format** .... Alt+O
2. Click **Tabs** .... T
3. Select the desired tab stop on the **Tab stop position** list .... Alt+T, ↓
4. Click **Clear** .... Alt+E
5. Click **OK** .... Enter

Remove All Tab Stops (except default ones)

1. Click **Format** .... Alt+O
2. Click **Tabs** .... T
3. Click **Clear All** .... Alt+A
4. Click **OK** .... Enter

Set the Default Tab Stop Interval

1. Click **Format** .... Alt+O
2. Click **Tabs** .... T
3. Enter a new interval in the **Default tab stops** box .... Alt+F
4. Click **OK** .... Enter

Set Indents on the Ruler

Select the paragraphs to which you want the indent setting to apply.

- Drag any of the following indent markers on the ruler to a new position.
- Drag the **First Line indent** marker to change the left indent for the first line of each selected paragraph.
- Drag the **Other Lines indent** marker to change the left indent for all lines of the selected paragraphs except the first lines.
- Drag the **Left indent** marker to change the left indent for all lines of the selected paragraphs together.
- Drag the **Right indent** marker to change the right indent for the selected paragraphs.

Set Indents with the Paragraph Dialog Box

1. Select the paragraphs to which the indent setting should apply.
2. Click **Format** .... Alt+O
3. Click **Paragraph** .... P
4. Open the **Preset** drop-down list and select a preset indent style .... Alt+P

   OR

   Enter indent amounts in the following text boxes:
   - **First Line** .... Alt+F
   - **Left** .... Alt+L
   - **Right** .... Alt+R
5. Click **OK** .... Enter

Exercise Directions

1. Start Publisher, if necessary.
2. Open the file PUB22. Save it as 22INFO.
3. In the **Telephone Extensions** section, select all the paragraphs containing extensions and then use the Tabs dialog box to insert a right-aligned tab stop with a bullet leader at the 4.5" mark.
4. Click between the name and the extension and press Tab on each of the lines. The text after the tab should right-align, as in Illustration A.
5. Select all of the phone extensions and drag the right-aligned tab marker on the ruler to the 4.75" mark.
6. Indent the paragraphs under the **Check-Out** and **Restaurant Reservations** headings by 0.5" using the Increase Indent button on the toolbar.
7. Using the Paragraph dialog box, set Left and Right indents of 0.5" each for the first paragraph under **Personal Items**.
8. Apply a 0.5" left indent to the list of personal items by selecting the text and dragging the left indent marker on the ruler.
9. Print your publication.
10. Save your work and exit Publisher.

Illustration A

Telephone Extensions

Front Desk/Information ·· *1
Room Service ·· *2
Housekeeping ·· *3
Wake-up calls: ·· *4
Guest rooms: ································ *7 plus room number
Outside line (local calls): ································ 9
Time and Temperature: ························ 9, then 555-9291

On Your Own

1. Start Publisher, if necessary.
2. Open the file OPUB22. Save it as 22TOC.
3. Use tab stops to create a three-column listing of the items at the top. You choose which tab stop type is most appropriate for each column of information.
4. Use tab stops with leader characters to format the table of contents beneath the listing. Make it readable and easy to understand by assigning different formatting and indentation for each outline level.
5. Print the publication.
6. Save your work and exit Publisher.

Exercise 23

Skills Covered:

◆ **Create Bulleted Lists** ◆ **Create Numbered Lists**

On the Job

Bulleted and numbered lists are organizational devices that help you present data to your readers in more interesting and readable formats. Both require a hanging indent for the first line, but the Bullets and Numbering feature in Publisher sets up those indents for you automatically so the process is nearly painless.

Your client at The Hendricks Inn would like the list at the bottom of the information sheet from Exercise 23 to be a numbered list. In this exercise, you will make it so, and you'll also add some custom bulleted lists to a room service menu he has given you to work with.

Terms

Bullet A character that appears to the left of the first line of a paragraph to call attention to that paragraph's beginning point.

Separator character The character that follows the number in a numbered list item. For example, a period is a common separator character.

Notes

Create Bulleted Lists

- For a quick bulleted list from existing paragraphs, select the text and then click the Bullets button on the Formatting toolbar.
- This applies a plain, round **bullet**, or whatever bullet style was last used in this publication (if different).
- Publisher also allows you to create a bulleted list as you type. Click the Bullets button to turn bullets on, and then type your list, pressing Enter between items. Publisher will continue assigning bullets to each paragraph until you press Enter twice without typing any text, or click the Bullets button again.
- To choose a different bullet character, or control the indentation for bulleted paragraphs, choose Format, Bullets and Numbering, and click the Bullets tab.

Specify bullet character, bullet spacing, and so on

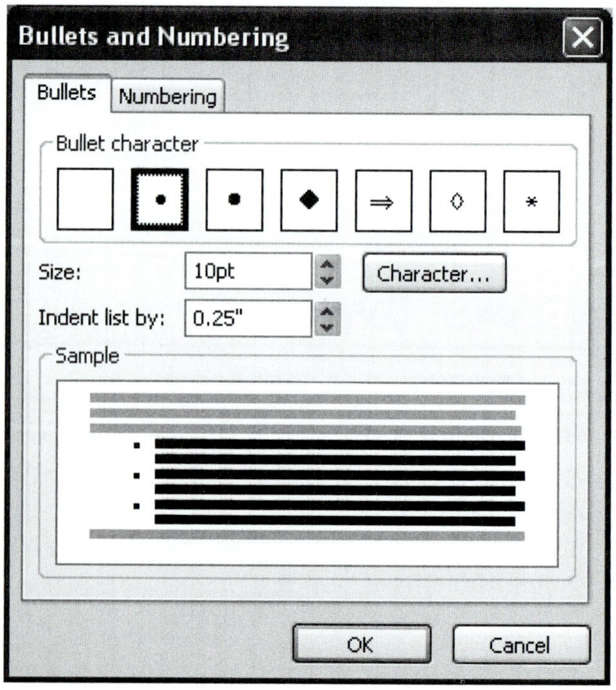

- Set the size of the bullet in the Size box. By default it is the same size as the paragraph's text.
- Use the Indent list by box to specify how much indent the text should have. This does not affect the bullet character's positioning—only the text.

To affect the bullet character's positioning, adjust the hanging indent for the first line in the Paragraph dialog box, as in Exercise 22.

- If none of the bullet characters appeals to you, you can select a different character by clicking the Character button. In the Bullet Character dialog box that appears, choose a font and then select a character from that font to use as your bullet.

  ✓ *Some useful fonts for bullets include Wingdings, Webdings, Symbol, and Marlett.*

Choose a different bullet character from any font installed on your PC

Choose a font

Click a character

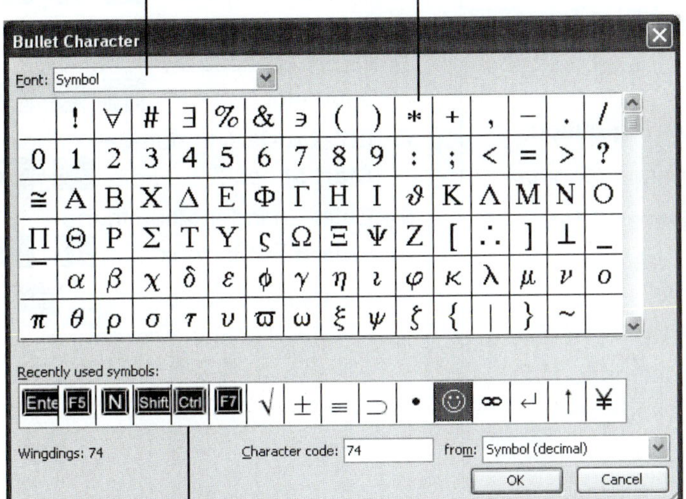

Recently used characters

Create Numbered Lists

- For a quick numbered list, select the text and then click the Numbering button on the Formatting toolbar. This applies a number in the same font as the paragraph text, with a period and tab stop after it.
- Just as with bullets, you can create a numbered list while you type. Click the Numbering button to turn bullets on, and then type your list, pressing Enter after each item.
- Press Enter twice, or click the Numbering button again, to turn numbering off.
- To change the formatting of the numbered list, choose Format, Bullets and Numbering, and click the Numbering tab.
- You may choose a number format from the Format drop-down list. Your choices include Arabic numbers (1, 2, 3, 4), lowercase letters (a, b, c, d), or uppercase letters (A, B, C, D).
- The **separator character** is the character that follows the number. By default, it is a period, but you may choose from a variety of characters (or no character).

Set numbered list options here

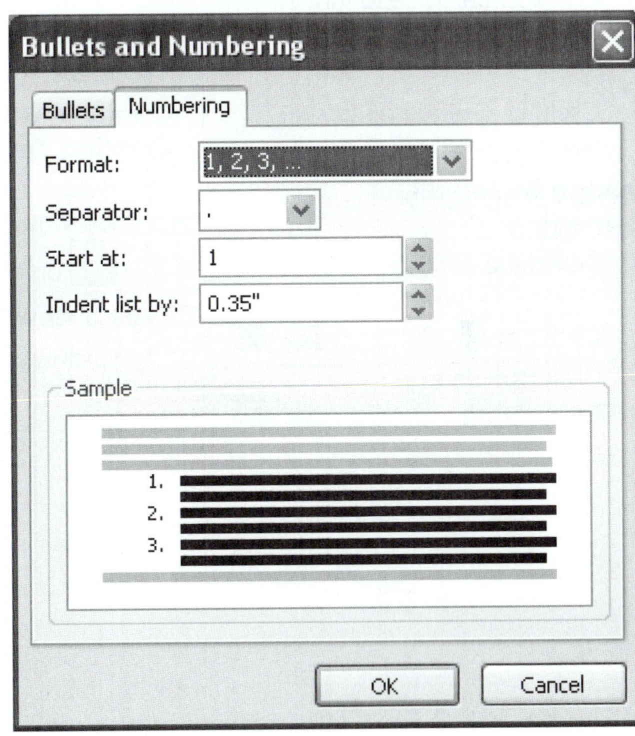

- Start At lets you start the numbering at some other number than 1 if desired. This is useful when you are continuing a numbered list from elsewhere in the document, for example.
- Indent list by is the same for numbered lists as for bulleted ones; it specifies where the text should begin. It has no effect on the number or separator character position.

Procedures

Create a Bulleted List from Existing Text

1. Select the text.
2. Click the **Bullets** button on the Formatting toolbar.

Type a New Bulleted List

1. Click where you want to begin the list.
2. Click the **Bullets** button on the Formatting toolbar.
3. Type the first list item and press **Enter** .... Enter
4. Continue typing and pressing **Enter** until the list is complete.
5. Press **Enter** twice to turn off the bullets.

   OR

   Click the **Bullets** button again to turn it off.

Change Bulleted List Formatting

1. Select the paragraphs in which to use the custom bullets.
2. Click **Format** .... Alt+O
3. Click **Bullets and Numbering** .... B
4. Click the **Bullets tab.**
5. Select the bullet character to use in the **Bullet character** area .... Alt+U, →

   OR

   Do the following:

   a. Click the **Character** button .... Alt+C

   b. Open the **Font** drop-down list and choose the font you want .... Alt+F

   c. Select a character in that font to use for the bullet.

   d. Click **OK** .... Enter
6. Enter an indentation in the **Indent list by** box.......... Alt+I
7. (Optional) Use the **Size** increment buttons to increase or decrease the bullet size.
8. Click **OK** .... Enter

Create a Numbered List from Existing Text

1. Select the text.
2. Click the **Numbering** button on the Formatting toolbar.

Type a New Numbered List

1. Click where you want to begin the list.
2. Click the **Numbering** button on the Formatting toolbar.
3. Type the first list item, and press **Enter** .... Enter
4. Continue typing and pressing **Enter** until the list is complete.
5. Press **Enter** twice to turn off the numbering.

   OR

   Click the **Numbering** button again to turn it off.

Change Numbered List Formatting

1. Select the paragraphs in which to use the custom numbering.
2. Click **Format** .... Alt+O
3. Click **Bullets and Numbering** .... B
4. Click the **Numbering** tab.
5. Open the **Format** drop-down list and choose a format .... Alt+F, ↓
6. Open the **Separator** drop-down list and choose a separator .... Alt+S, ↓
7. Enter a starting number in the **Start at** box .... Alt+T
8. Enter an indentation in the **Indent list by** box .... Alt+I
9. Click **OK** .... Enter

Exercise Directions

1. Start Publisher, if necessary.
2. Open the file **PUB23A**. Save it as **23INFO**.
3. Format the list of personal items at the bottom of the flyer as a numbered list that uses lowercase letters as the numbers (a, b, c). Use a colon (:) as the separator character.
4. Use the Paragraph dialog box to set the left indent for the paragraphs of the list to 1".
5. Save and close the file.
6. Open **PUB23B** and save it as **23MENU**.
7. Make all the choices on the menu bulleted list items that use a blank square 12-point checkbox as the bullet character.

   ✓ *There is an appropriate square in the Wingdings font.*
8. Remove the checkboxes from **Toast**, **Jelly/Jam**, and **Eggs** and indent them so that they align with the other surrounding text that still has bullets.

   ✓ *You could use the Paragraph dialog box to set their left indent to 0.25" or you could drag the indent marker on the ruler.*
9. Indent each of the italicized items under the items from step 8 by an extra 0.25". See Illustration A.
10. Print the publication.
11. Save your work and exit Publisher.

On Your Own

1. Start Publisher, if necessary.
2. Open the file **OPUB23**. Save it as **23PARTY**.
3. Turn off AutoFit for the text in the main text box.
4. Make the party details (**Date**, **Time**, **Dress**, **Bring**) into a bulleted list. Choose a bullet character that looks festive (such as a starburst or a happy face).
5. Make the bullets larger, so they are more prominent.
6. Adjust the spacing so that there is plenty of room between the bullet character and the text.
7. Make the text in the Bring section into a separate bulleted list that is subordinate to the Bring bullet. Use a different bullet character for it.
8. Print the flyer.
9. Save your work and exit Publisher.

Illustration A

Room Service Breakfast Menu

Select one coffee:

☐ Regular

☐ Decaf

Select one juice:

☐ Orange

☐ Grapefruit

☐ Grape

☐ Apple

Select one bread :

Toast:

- ☐ *White*
- ☐ *Wheat*

☐ Bagel

☐ Muffin

☐ Biscuit

Select one meat:

☐ Sausage links

☐ Sausage patties

☐ Ham

☐ Bacon

☐ Vegetarian "sausage links"

Select up to two main course items:

☐ Biscuits and gravy

☐ Hash browns

Eggs:

- ☐ *Fried (style: ____________)*
- ☐ *Scrambled*
- ☐ *Poached*

☐ Pancakes

☐ French toast

Select as many of the following as desired:

☐ Butter

☐ Margarine

Jelly/Jam:

- ☐ *Strawberry jam*
- ☐ *Grape jelly*
- ☐ *Orange marmalade*

☐ Ketchup

☐ Salt and pepper

☐ Sugar

☐ Cream

☐ Artificial sweetener

☐ Maple syrup

☐ Sugar-free maple syrup

☐ Cream cheese

Exercise 24

Skills Covered:

◆ **Copy Text Formatting** ◆ **Style Basics** ◆ **Apply a Style**
◆ **Create a Style** ◆ **Manage the Style List**
◆ **Import Styles from Other Publications**

On the Job

Now that you know how to format text, it's time to learn a few formatting shortcuts. You can copy all the formatting from one text block to another with the Format Painter feature. You can also create named styles that contain groups of formatting specifications, and apply those styles to any text you choose.

The menu from Exercise 23 is formatted with manual formatting, but it may be better and easier to maintain with styles instead. In this exercise, you will change its formatting to a style-based system.

Terms

Format Painter A feature that enables you to copy the formatting from existing text and "paint" it onto other text.

Style A set of predefined formatting specifications that you can apply to certain text. For example, formatting for the style Heading 1 might include bold, italic, 24-point Arial, and centered.

Notes

Copy Text Formatting

- To copy formatting from one section of text to another, select the text that is already formatted correctly, and then click the **Format Painter** button on the Standard toolbar. The mouse pointer becomes a paintbrush. Drag across the text to be formatted, and the formatting is copied.
- If you click in the paragraph of the text to be formatted instead of dragging over specific text, the entire paragraph receives the formatting.
- Format Painter copies all attributes of the text: font, size, text effects, underline style, color, and so on.
- If you double-click the Format Painter button, you can then drag over multiple sections of text. Click the button again to turn the feature off when finished.

Copy formatting

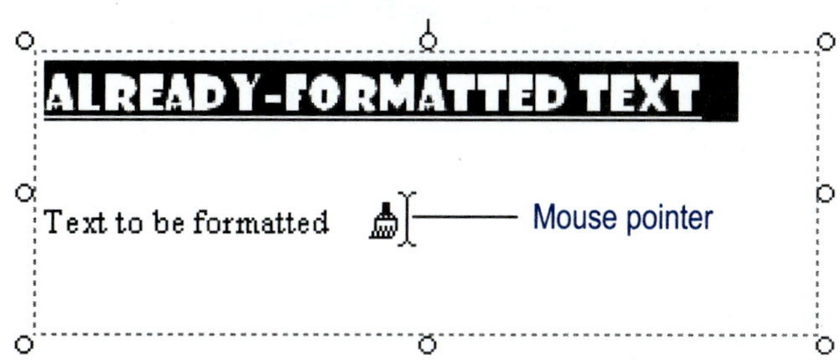

✓ *Depending on how you use Format Painter, its copying can include the paragraph style or not. If you drag across the text to paint the format onto it, the text receives all the formatting of the source but the style is not applied. However, if you single-click the paragraph to paint it, the style is copied.*

Style Basics

- A **style** is a named set of formatting specifications that you can apply with a single command. Using styles saves formatting time and also ensures consistency in a publication.
- The leftmost drop-down list on the Formatting toolbar is the Style list.
- If you start with a template, there will be several styles already.
- If you start with a blank publication, the only default style on this list is Normal, so you will probably want to create other styles.

Apply a Style

- To apply a style, position the insertion point in the paragraph that you want to apply the style to, and open the Style drop-down list on the Formatting toolbar and select the style's name.
- Alternatively, you can click the style's name in the Formatting and Styles task pane (shown at right).
- To turn on the Formatting and Styles task pane, click the Styles and Formatting button, or choose Format, Styles and Formatting.
- When you hover your mouse pointer over a style in the task pane, the attributes of that style appear in a ScreenTip.

Create a Style

- To create a style by example, format some text the way you want it, select the text, and then type a new style name in the Style box on the toolbar. When you press Enter, the Create Style by Example dialog box opens. Confirm the selections there to create the new style.

Create a new style by example

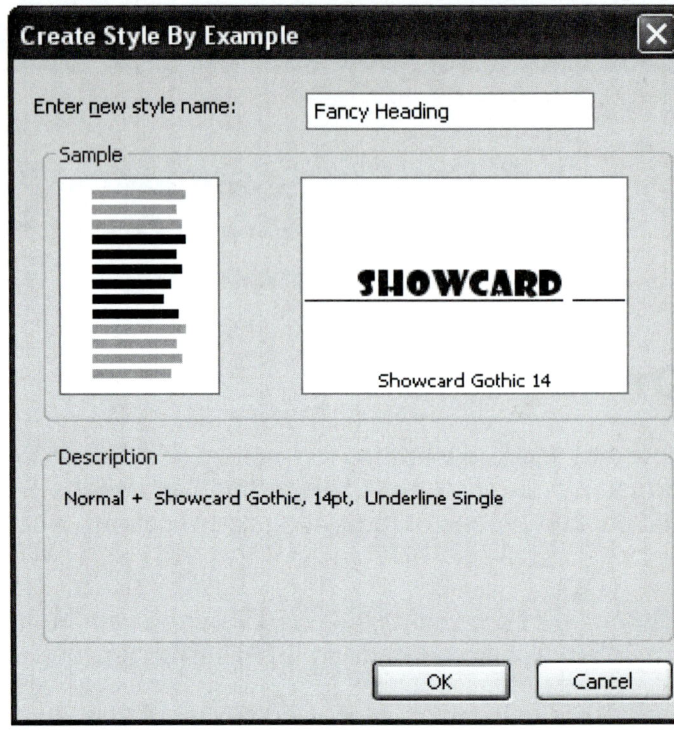

- You can also start new styles from the Styles and Formatting task pane.
- Clicking the Create new style button on the task pane opens the Create New Style dialog box. There you can precisely define all the settings for a new style to be created.

Start a new style from the task pane

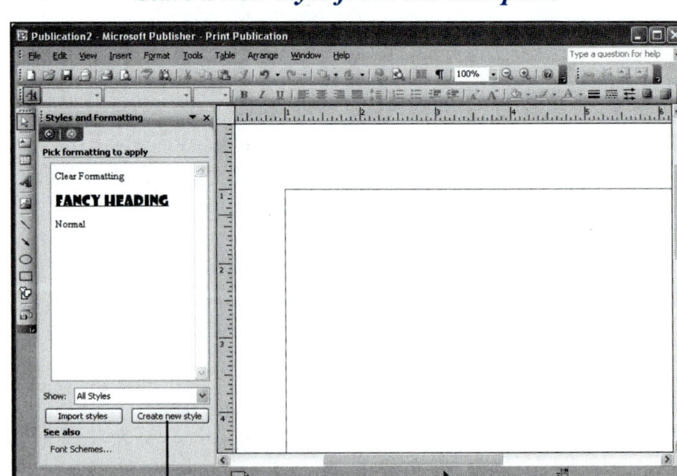

Click here to define a new style

- In the New Style dialog box, the buttons in the Click to change section lead to various other dialog boxes you have already worked with in this lesson, for specifying font, alignment, spacing, and so on.

Create a new style by defining it manually

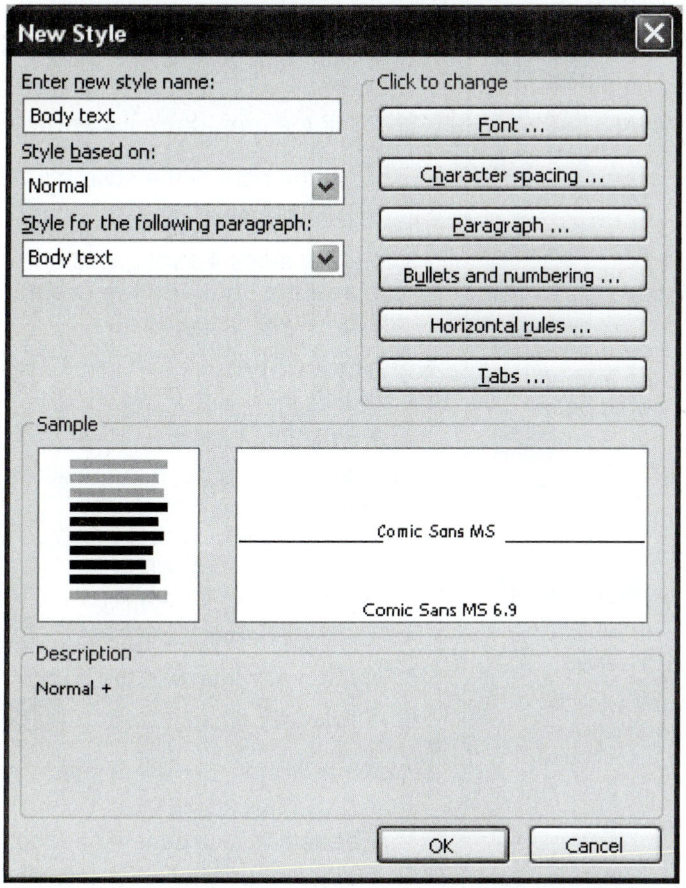

- When you define a style, you define it in relation to the Normal style. For example, if you want a style to be just like Normal except center aligned, center alignment is the only style attribute you need to define.
- The Style for the following paragraph setting lets you specify what style will be applied to a new paragraph created by pressing Enter within a paragraph of this style. For headings, you will probably want a non-heading text style to follow them; for a non-heading style, you will probably want more of the same style.

Manage the Style List

- After creating styles, you can manage them from the Styles and Formatting task pane.
- Point to a style in the task pane, and a down arrow appears next to it. Click that down arrow, and a menu appears. From this menu you can modify, rename, or delete a style.

Click the down arrow next to a style in the task pane to work with it

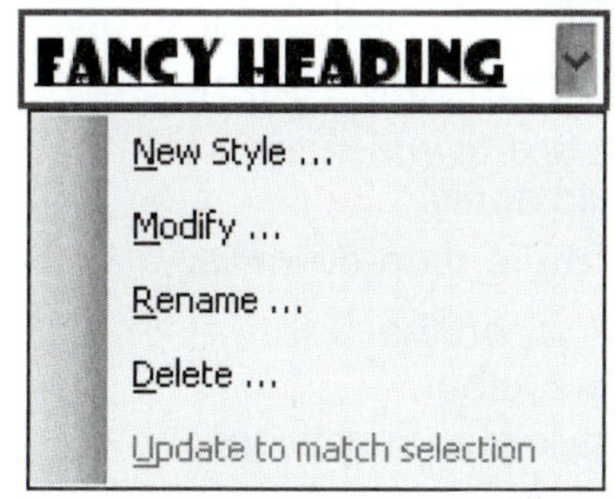

- When you choose Modify, the Change Style dialog box appears. It is almost identical to the Create New Style dialog box; you can use it to redefine the style's settings.
- The Update to match selection menu item changes the style to whatever formatting is applied to the currently selected text (or to the paragraph in which the insertion point lies, if no text is selected). If the insertion point is not in a text box, the command is unavailable (as shown above).

  ✓ *Using Update to match selection is an easier way to change a style than the Change Style dialog box.*

- You can modify the Normal style just as you would change any other style. When you change the Normal style, all other styles change, too, because they are all based on it.
- You cannot delete the Normal style, but you can delete any other styles you have created. Open the style's menu (see above) and choose Delete.

Import Styles from Other Publications

- If you have styles set up in one publication, you can use them in another publication.
- On the Styles and Formatting task pane, click the Import styles button. Choose the publication to import from and click OK, and all of that publication's styles are instantly transferred to your new publication.

  ✓ *You might want to create a "dummy" publication for the sole purpose of storing styles. Then you can import the styles from that publication each time you need styles in a new publication.*

Procedures

Copy Text Formatting

1. Select the text that is already formatted correctly.
2. Click the **Format Painter** button.
3. Drag across the text to copy the formatting.

Apply a Style from the Toolbar

1. Select the text to which the style should apply.
2. Open the **Style** drop-down list [Normal] on the Formatting toolbar.
3. Click the style you want to apply.

Create a Style by Example

1. Select text that is formatted the way you want the style to be.
2. Click in the **Styles** box [Normal] on the Formatting toolbar.
3. Type a new style name.
4. Press **Enter**.
5. Click **OK** .... Enter

Display the Styles and Formatting Task Pane

- Click the **Styles and Formatting** button.

OR

1. Choose **Format** .... Alt+O
2. Click **Styles and Formatting** .... S

OR

1. Click **View** .... Alt+V
2. Click **Task Pane** .... K
3. Click the down arrow at the top-right corner of the task pane.
4. Click **Styles and Formatting**.

Create a Style with the Create New Style Dialog Box

1. Display the Styles and Formatting task pane (see above).
2. Click **Create new style** button [Create new style].
3. Type a name in the **Enter new style name** box ... Alt+N
4. Click the button for the style attribute you need to be different from Normal style:
   - **Font** .... Alt+F
   - **Character spacing** ... Alt+H
   - **Paragraph** .... Alt+P
   - **Bullets and Numbering** .... Alt+U
   - **Horizontal rules** .... Alt+R
   - **Tabs** .... Alt+T
5. Make changes to the formatting in the dialog box that appears.
6. Click **OK** .... Enter
7. Repeat steps 4-6 as needed to change other parts of the style.
8. Click the **Style based on** drop-down list arrow...... Alt+B, ↓
9. Choose the style on which the new one should be based.

   ✓ *Any formatting not explicitly defined for the new style will match the style you choose here.*

10. Click the **Style for the following paragraph** drop-down list arrow...... Alt+S, ↓
11. Choose the style for paragraphs that follow ones of this type.
12. Click **OK** .... Enter

Change a Style by Example

1. Display the Styles and Formatting task pane if needed.
2. Apply the style to a paragraph.
3. Make formatting changes to the text.
4. Point to the style in the task pane.
5. Click the drop-down list arrow to the right of the style.
6. Click **Update to match selection** .... U

Change a Style with the Modify Style Dialog Box

1. Display the Styles and Formatting task pane if needed.
2. Point to the style in the task pane.
3. Click the drop-down list arrow to the right of the style.
4. Click **Modify** .... M
5. Follow steps 4 through 12 of "Create a Style with the Create New Style dialog box."

Rename a Style

1. Display the Styles and Formatting task pane if needed.
2. Point to the style in the task pane.
3. Click the drop-down arrow to the right of the style.
4. Click **Rename** .... R
5. Type a new name in the To box.
6. Click **OK** .... Enter

Delete a Style

1. Display the Styles and Formatting task pane if needed.
2. Point to the style in the task pane.
3. Click the drop-down list arrow to the right of the style.
4. Click **Delete** .... D
5. Click **Yes** .... Y

Import Styles from Other Publications

1. Display the Styles and Formatting task pane if needed.
2. Click **Import styles** button [Import styles].
3. Select the publication you want to import styles from.
4. Click **OK** .... Enter
5. If messages appear that any style names are duplicate, click **Yes** or **No** to accept new style or not.

Exercise Directions

1. Start Publisher, if necessary.
2. Open the file PUB24. Save it as **24MENU**.
3. Modify the Body Text style to be 36-points in size.
4. Select the **Select one coffee** text and define a new style called Minor Heading based on it. Then apply that new style to all the other minor headings above the checkboxes on the menu.
5. Define a new style called **Major Bullet** based on the first bullet under the **Select one coffee** heading.
6. Modify the Major Bullet style so that it has only 3 points of space after the paragraph.
7. Apply the Major Bullet style to all bulleted paragraphs except those that are indented (such as the various kinds of toast, for example).

   ✓ *One easy way to do this is with Format Painter. Double-click the Format Painter button so it stays "on," and then click on each of the paragraphs to receive the style. (Click on them, don't drag across them.)*

8. Delete the unused styles (Title, Organization Name, and Address).
9. Rename the Minor Heading style to **Head01**.
10. Save your work and close the file.
11. Create a new, blank publication and copy the styles from **24MENU** into it.
12. Save the new publication as **24COPY**.
13. Save your work and exit Publisher.

On Your Own

1. Start Publisher, if necessary.
2. Open the file OPUB24. Save it as **24STYLES**.
3. Copy the styles from OPUB24IMP. When asked about the duplicate style, click No to change the definition of Normal.

   ✓ *OPUB24IMP has only one style in it—Normal—so step 3 simply redefines the Normal style in the publication to match the Normal style in OPUB24IMP. No text changes immediately in the flyer because no text is currently formatted with Normal style.*

4. Apply Normal style to the bottom paragraph (**No gifts, please**).
5. Change that paragraph's font size to 18 points and then redefine the Normal style to match it.
6. Create new styles called **Smiley Bullet** and **Star Bullet** based on the two types of bulleted lists on the flyer.

   ✓ *Since some but not all text is bold on the Smiley Bullet paragraphs, do not include the bold in the style definition.*

7. Create a new style called **Title** based on the Party text and redefine it so that it is centered rather than left-aligned.
8. Save your work and exit Publisher.

Exercise 25

Skills Covered:

◆ **Create a Table** ◆ **Select Cells and Ranges**
◆ **Type in a Table** ◆ **Insert or Delete Rows and Columns**
◆ **Change Cell Height and Width**

On the Job

Tables help organize data. If you have lists of numbers and text to display, need to make comparisons, and the like, create tables to communicate your content to readers.

The Hendricks Inn needs an informational flyer listing some of the local attractions. The owner has experimented with making this a bulleted list, but finds that there are too many items and it looks overwhelming. In this exercise, you will provide him an alternative in a tabular format.

Terms

Cell The intersection of a row and a column in a table. You type text in cells.

Range A rectangular block of cells selected as a group.

Notes

Create a Table

- To create a table, click the Insert Table button in the Objects toolbar and drag on the publication to create a box in which the table appears. A Create Table dialog box opens in which you can set the number of rows, the number of columns, and the table format.
- You may choose a table format as you are creating the table, or apply one later using the Table, Table AutoFormat command. You can also format tables manually. You will learn how to format a table in Exercise 26.
  - ✓ *Table formats assume that the top row and left column contain header text, not data, so if that's not true for your table you may find it more convenient to simply choose None as the table format and then format the table manually.*

Enter details about the new table you want to create

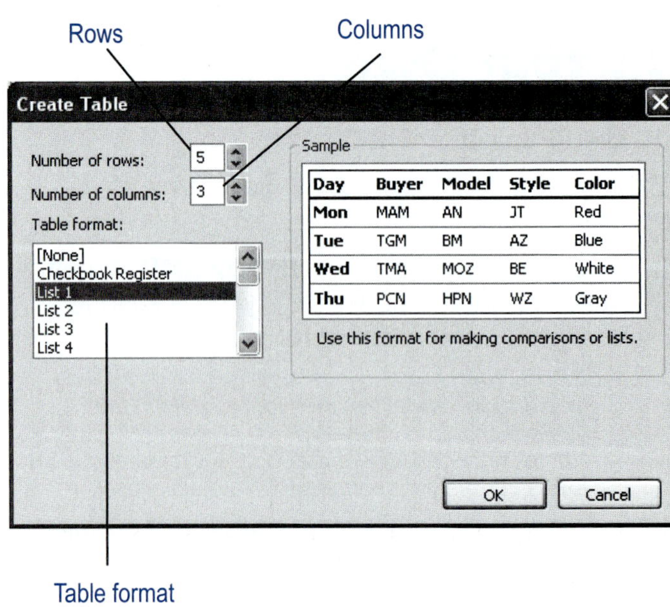

Select Cells and Ranges

- To select a **cell** in a table, click it.
- To select a **range** of cells in a table, drag across them.
- To select the entire table, click inside a table cell and then press Ctrl+A twice. The first time selects the cell, and the second time selects the whole table.
- To select an entire row, move the mouse pointer to the left edge of the row, so the mouse pointer becomes a right-pointing arrow ➡, and then click.
- To select an entire column, do the same thing at the top of a column, so the mouse pointer becomes a down-pointing arrow ⬇.

Select a row in the table

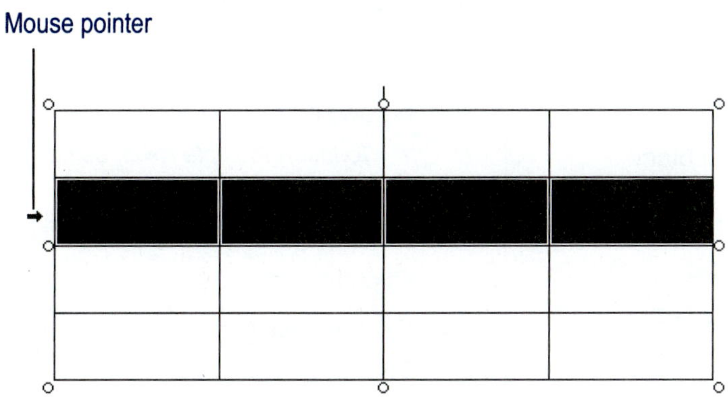

- You also can select various parts of the table with the Table, Select command. It opens a submenu from which you can choose Table, Column, Row, or Cell. The mouse method is easier, and you may seldom use the command method.

Type in a Table

- Click in a cell to move the insertion point there, and then type.
- To move to the next cell (to the right, or to the next row if you are already in the rightmost column), press Tab.
- To move to the previous cell, press Shift + Tab.
- If you press Tab while in the bottom-right cell in the table, it starts a new row.
- To fill a series of cells with the same data (for example, to repeat a name in a whole row or column), type the data in the first cell and then select it and all the cells you want to fill. Then choose Table, Fill Right (or Table, Fill Down).

Insert or Delete Rows and Columns

- To insert rows or columns, position the insertion point in a cell adjacent to where you want to insert, and then choose Table, Insert to open a submenu as shown below.

Choose what you want to insert (rows or columns), how many of them, and where you want them

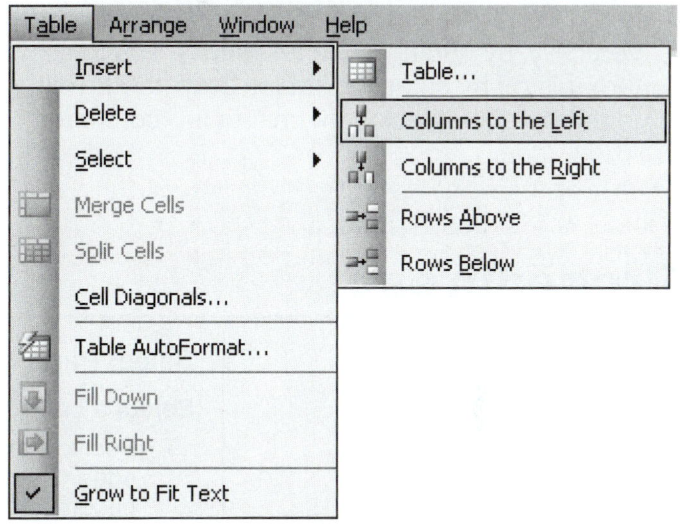

✓ *You can also right-click the table and choose Change Table for access to many of the Table menu's commands, including Insert.*

- If you want to insert multiple rows or columns at once, select multiple rows or columns before issuing the Insert command. For example, to insert three rows, select three rows first.
- To delete a row or column, select it and then choose Table, Delete and then choose Columns or Rows.

Delete rows or columns from a table

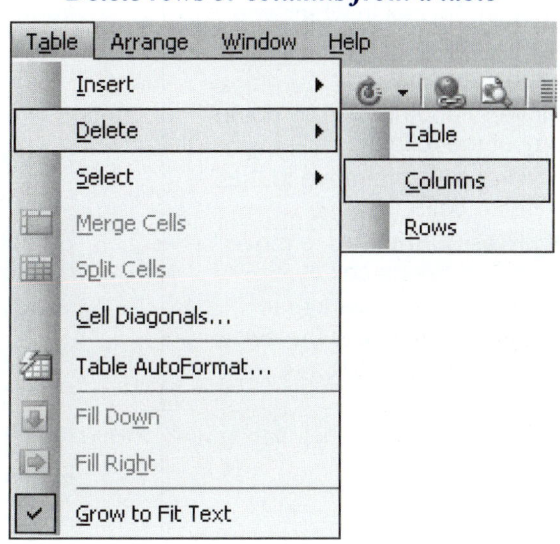

- To delete the entire table, choose Table, Delete, Table. You can also select the table frame and press the Delete key.

Change Cell Height and Width

- By default, each row and column is set to grow automatically to fit the text within it. That means if you add lots of text to a cell, or use very large text, the cell will expand as needed (usually vertically, by adding more text lines). You can turn this off by selecting Table, Grow to Fit Text to remove the checkmark next to the command.
- You also can manually resize a row or column. Position the insertion point on the divider between two rows or columns. The mouse pointer becomes a double-headed arrow. Drag the row or column to its new size.

Resize a row or column by dragging in the header area

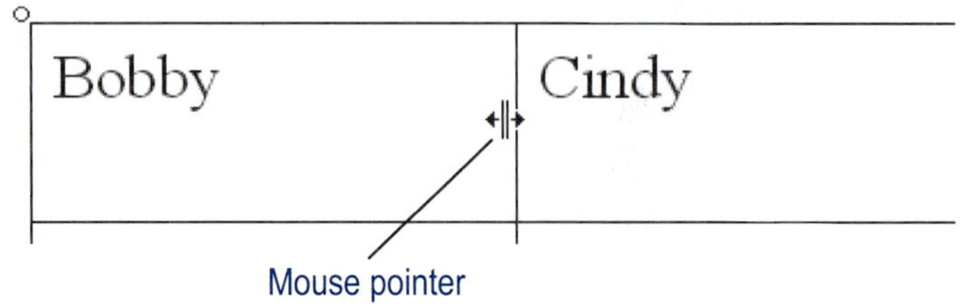

Procedures

Create a Table

1. Click the **Insert Table** button on the Objects toolbar.
2. Drag a box on the publication where you want the table.
3. Enter a number of rows in the **Number of rows** box.. Alt+R
4. Enter a number of columns in the **Number of columns** box .... Alt+C
5. Select a format from the **Table format** list .... Alt+F
6. Click **OK**.......................... Enter

Type in a Table

1. Click to position the insertion point in the cell in which you want to type.
2. Type your text.
3. Move to another cell by doing any of the following:
   - Press **Tab** to move to the next cell.
   - Press **Shift+Tab** to move to the previous cell.
   - Press an **arrow key** to move one cell in the arrow direction.

Select Parts of a Table

Select a cell:

1. Position mouse pointer at left edge of cell, so pointer becomes diagonal black arrow ↗.
2. Click left mouse button.

Select a range of cells:

- Drag across or the range to select.

Select a row:

1. Position mouse pointer at left edge of row, so pointer becomes black arrow ➡.
2. Click the left mouse button.

Select a column:

1. Position mouse pointer at top edge of column, so pointer becomes black arrow ⬇.
2. Click the left mouse button.

Select multiple rows or columns:

1. Select a row or column.
2. Hold down **Shift**................ Shift
3. Select additional rows or columns.

Select the entire table:

1. Position insertion point inside a cell in the table.
2. Press **Ctrl+A** .... Ctrl+A
3. Press **Ctrl+A** again...... Ctrl+A

Insert a Row

1. Select the row where the new row will appear above (or below) it.
   ✓ *To insert multiple rows, select multiple rows.*
2. Click **Table** .... Alt+A
3. Click **Insert**......................... I
4. Click **Rows Above**............. A
   OR
   Click **Rows Below**............. B

Insert a Column

1. Select the column adjacent to where the new one should appear.
   ✓ *To insert multiple columns, select multiple columns.*
2. Click **Table** .... Alt+A
3. Click **Insert**......................... I
4. Click **Columns to the Left**.. L
   OR
   Click **Columns to the Right**............................ R

Delete a Row

1. Select the row(s) to be deleted, or click anywhere within the row.
2. Click **Table** .... Alt+A
3. Click **Delete**........................ D
4. Click **Rows**......................... R

Delete a Column

1. Select the column(s) to be deleted, or click anywhere within the column.
2. Click **Table**.................. Alt + A
3. Click **Delete** .... D
4. Click **Columns**...................... C

Change Cell Height or Width

1. Position the mouse pointer between two rows or columns, so pointer becomes double-headed arrow.
2. Drag the row or column to a new height or width.

   ✓ *You can double-click a divider between two rows or columns to AutoFit it to the text.*

Exercise Directions

1. Start Publisher, if necessary.
2. Open the file **PUB25**. Save it as **25FLYER**.
3. Zoom out to Whole Page view.
4. Drag the bulleted list text box off to the side of the flyer, so it is still visible but not on the flyer itself. (You will use it for reference.)
5. In the space where the text box was, create a table of 4 rows and 5 columns. For the table format, choose None.
6. Select two of the columns, and delete them.
7. Select one of the rows, and insert a new row above it.
8. Resize the table so it once again fills the available space without overrunning it.
9. Redefine the Normal style to be 16 point.
10. In the second row of the table, enter **Dining**, **Museums**, and **Sports**, each in a separate cell, and apply Bold formatting to the text.
11. On the bulleted list text box, remove the bullets (use the Bullets button on the Formatting toolbar).
12. Cut-and-paste the items from the list into the table under the appropriate headings, and apply Normal style to each item. When you are finished, delete the empty text box.
13. Drag the bottom border of the heading row (Dining, Museums, Sports) upward so that the row's height is decreased, as in Illustration A.
14. Print the publication. The final product is shown in Illustration B.
15. Save your work and exit Publisher.

Illustration A

Dining	**Museums**	**Sports**
Mateo's Italian Ristorante	Conner Prairie Museum	Glenn Acre Sta-bles trail rides
Alexander's Ice Cream	Hendricks County Art Museum	Just Boats water-craft rentals
Bongi's Pub and Grill	The Children's Museum	Mission Road bi-cycle rentals

Illustration B

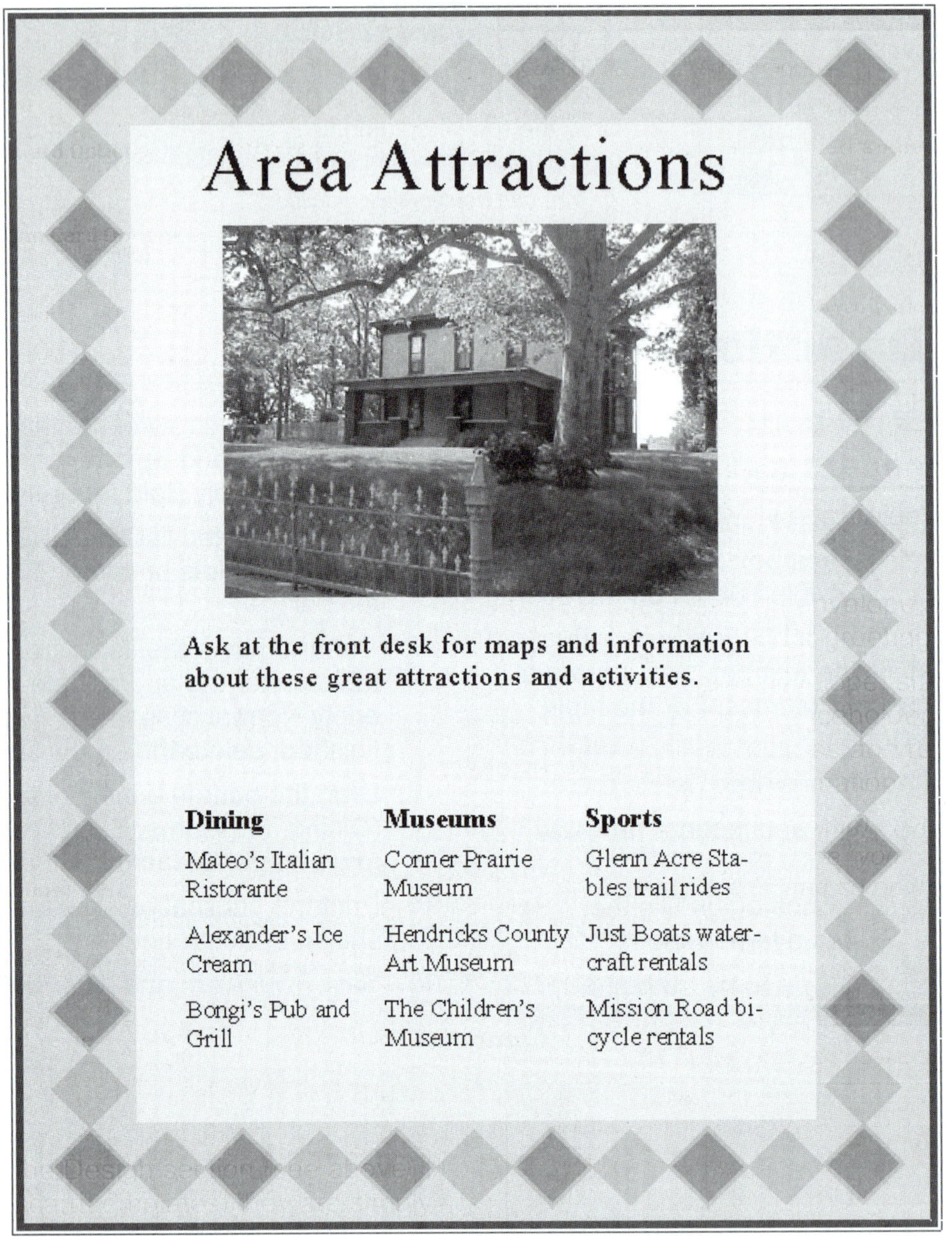

Area Attractions

Ask at the front desk for maps and information about these great attractions and activities.

Dining	Museums	Sports
Mateo's Italian Ristorante	Conner Prairie Museum	Glenn Acre Stables trail rides
Alexander's Ice Cream	Hendricks County Art Museum	Just Boats watercraft rentals
Bongi's Pub and Grill	The Children's Museum	Mission Road bicycle rentals

On Your Own

1. Start Publisher, if necessary.
2. Open a new, blank publication and save it as **25CAL**. Set its page orientation to Landscape.
3. Create a table that takes up the entire page. Give the table 7 columns and 7 rows and use the List with Title 3 table format.
4. In the top cell (black), enter the current month and year and format the text as 48 point.
5. In the second row, enter the days of the week starting with Sunday, and decrease the height of that row so that the text exactly fits.
6. In the remaining rows, enter the numbers to create a calendar for the current month and year. Delete any unused rows.
7. Select all the rows that contain numbers (not the first two rows) and set the alignment to Left.
8. Print and save your work and exit Publisher.

Exercise 26

Skills Covered:

◆ **Format a Table** ◆ **Turn Off Automatic Hyphenation** ◆ **Merge Cells**

On the Job

You can greatly improve a table's appearance by applying formatting to it, in much the same way as you apply formatting to a text box and its text. You can use either automatic formatting or manual. You can also improve a table's readability to turning off automatic hyphenation of its text.

The flyer you began in Exercise 25 needs some formatting to be more attractive and readable. In this exercise, you will format its table, including merging some cells and applying cell borders and shading.

Terms

No new vocabulary in this exercise.

Notes

Format a Table

- You can select a different table format by choosing Table, Table AutoFormat. This opens the Auto Format dialog box.
- Choosing None removes any existing auto-formatting.
- Click the Options button at the bottom of the dialog box to display the Formats to apply check boxes. All are marked by default, but you can clear one or more to prevent certain formatting aspects from being applied.
  - ✓ *Auto Format assumes that the first row and first column contain headings, and treats them differently than the others. You can't prevent this. It's one of the weaknesses of the Table AutoFormat feature in Publisher 2003.*

Select a different format, excluding certain aspects of it if unwanted

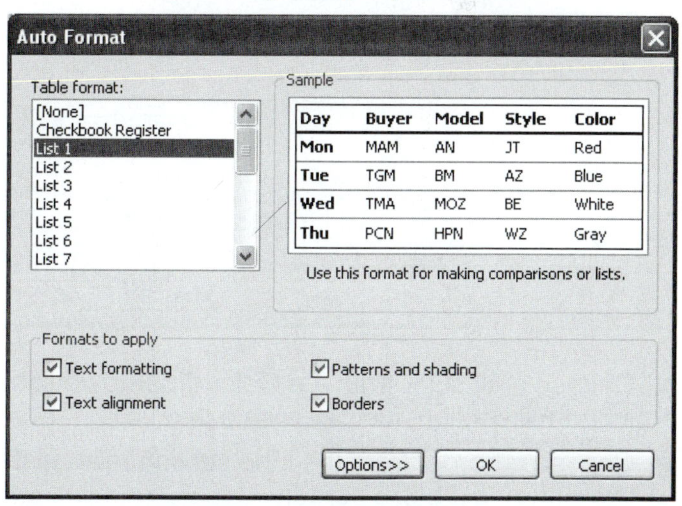

Format Table Text

- You can format a table's text manually, using any of the text box formatting controls you have learned about in earlier lessons. Nearly all the commands on the Format menu work with table cells, including Font, Paragraph, and Character Spacing.

Format the Table Manually

- To manually format the table itself, select the portion of the table you want to affect (or the entire table) and choose Format, Table. This opens the Format Table dialog box.
- The changes you make with the Format Table dialog box apply only to whatever portion of the table was selected before you issued the command. So, for example, if the insertion point was in a cell, it would affect only that one cell.

Colors and Lines

- You can apply borders and shading to individual cells or groups of selected cells on the Colors and Lines tab.

Format the border and fill for cells in a table

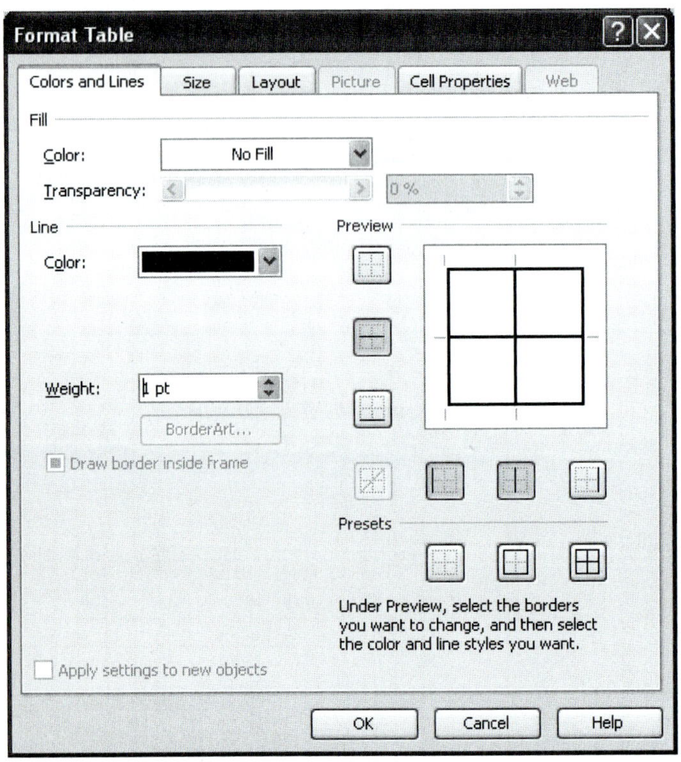

- Choose a fill color from the Color drop-down list in the Fill section, just like with a text box.
- Choose a border from the Line section, also just like with a text box's border.
- The main difference with a table is that there are lines in-between cells in the selection, and a special button on the sample area to format those lines.
- There is also a button in the Presets area that applies the chosen line to all borders of all cells in the selection.

✓ *Formatting table cell borders can be tricky; select the border on the sample area first, and then choose the color and width you want. Refer to the Sample area to make sure you get the results you expect; click the No Border button in the Presets area to clear everything and start fresh if needed.*

- Another way to apply a border to one or more cells is with the Line/Border Style button on the Formatting toolbar, just like with text boxes (Exercise 19). Select the cells to affect first.
- Using the Line/Border Style button places an outside border around the selection, so if you select multiple cells, the border will apply to the outer edges of the selection, not to each individual cell.
- You can use the Line Color button, also on the Formatting toolbar, to change the color of the border, just like with a text box (Exercise 19).
- The Fill Color button works to fill the selected cells as well, just like with a text box.

Table Size

- On the Size tab, you can specify the exact size of the table in inches, or you can scale it by a percentage of its current value. This is an alternative to the simpler method of resizing the table by dragging a selection handle.
- You can also set a rotation for the table, in degrees. 90 degrees is sideways; 180 degrees is upside-down.

Table Layout

- On the Layout tab you can specify a position on the page for the table. This is an alternative to the simpler method of moving the table by dragging its border.
- You can also specify wrapping settings for the table. This controls how any text in a text box will interact with the table if the text box and the table overlap. Such layout options will be covered in Lesson 4 when we look at graphics.

Cell Properties

- On the Cell Properties tab you can choose a vertical alignment for the text within the selected cell(s): Top, Middle, or Bottom. This is just like with a text box, but in this case each cell has its own setting.
- You can also enter internal margin settings for the cell, just like you do for text boxes.

Set Cell Properties including internal margins

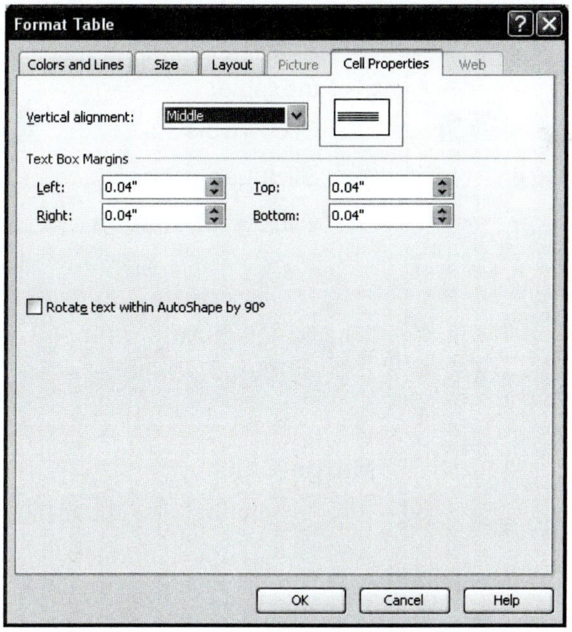

Turn Off Automatic Hyphenation

- Whenever you are working with short lines of text, as in a table cell, Publisher's automatic hyphenation feature can produce too many undesirable line breaks, interfering with the readability of the text. You will probably want to turn off automatic hyphenation when working with text in a table.
- To do so, choose Tools, Language, Hyphenation, and deselect the Automatically hyphenate this story check box. The hyphenation on/off setting applies only to the current story (in this case, the current table frame).

Turn off automatic hyphenation

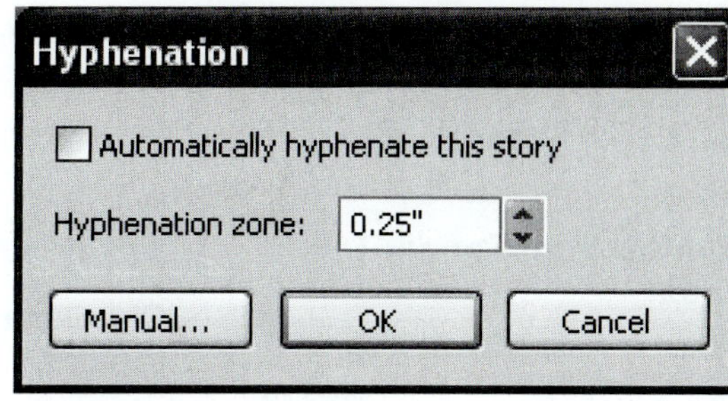

✓ *Hyphenation is very useful when you are trying to fit the maximum amount of text on a page, for example, because it allows a few extra characters to appear on a line than would normally fit.*

Merge Cells

- You might occasionally want to merge two or more cells in a table. The most common reason for this is to create a large single cell in the first row, in which you might center a title.
- To merge two or more cells, select the cells and then choose Table, Merge Cells. Any text in the separate cells is placed together in the new, common cell, separated by spaces.
- To return merged cells to individual cells, use the Table, Split Cells command.

  ✓ *You can also split cells diagonally, with the Table, Cell Diagonals command. You may want to experiment with this on your own.*

Procedures

Change the Table AutoFormat

1. Click **Table**.................. Alt+A
2. Click **Table AutoFormat**...... F
3. Click a new format on the list.
4. To see more table controls, click the **Options** button Options>> .... Alt+O
5. Deselect any check boxes for formatting features you want to exclude.
6. Click **OK**.......................... Enter

Apply a Table Border

Apply a border from toolbar:

1. Select the cells to affect.
2. Click the **Line/Border Style** button.
3. Click the line style you want.

   OR

   Click **No Line** to remove the current border.

Remove a border:

1. Select the cells to affect.
2. Click the **Line/Border Style** button.
3. Click **No Line**.

Apply current border color:

✓ *This applies the border color currently shown on the Line Color button's face.*

1. Select the cells to affect.
2. Click the **Line Color** button.

Choose border color from toolbar:

1. Select the frame.
2. Click down arrow next to **Line Color** button.
3. Select a color.

Apply border from Format Table dialog box:

1. Select the cells to affect.
2. Click **Format** .... Alt+O
3. Click **Table** .... E
4. Click **Colors and Lines** tab.
5. (Optional) To clear existing borders click the **No Border** button.
6. Open **Color** drop-down list in Line area........... Alt+O
7. Select a color.
8. Type a line weight in the **Weight** box .... Alt+W

   OR

   Use the **up/down** increment buttons to increment the weight.
9. Click one or more of the **border line** buttons to toggle on/off individual sides of the frame border.
10. Click **OK** .... Enter

Apply a Fill to Table Cells

Choose a fill color from the toolbar:

1. Select the cells to affect.
2. Click the down arrow on the **Fill Color** button on the Formatting toolbar.
3. Select a scheme color or fixed color.

Choose a fill color from Format dialog box:

1. Select the cells to affect.
2. Click **Format**............... Alt+O
3. Click **Table**......................... E
4. Click **Colors and Lines** tab.
5. Open **Color** drop-down list in Fill area....................... Alt+C
6. Select a color.
7. (Optional) Drag **Transparency** slider to increase transparency of color fill .... Alt+T, ↑
8. Click **OK** .... Enter

Turn Off Automatic Hyphenation for a Table

1. Position insertion point within the table.
2. Click **Tools**................. Alt+T
3. Click **Language** L
4. Click **Hyphenation**............. H

   ✓ *You can press Ctrl+Shift+H instead of doing steps 2–4.*
5. Deselect **Automatically hyphenate this story**. Alt+A
6. Click **OK**.......................... Enter

Merge Cells

1. Select the cells to merge.
2. Click **Table** .... Alt+A
3. Click **Merge Cells** .... M

Split Merged Cells

1. Select the merged cell.
2. Click **Table** .... Alt+A
3. Click Split Cells .... P

Exercise Directions

1. Start Publisher, if necessary.
2. Open the file **PUB26**. Save it as **26FLYER**.
3. Merge all the cells in the first row (the empty row) into a single cell.
4. Cut the text from the text box above the table and paste it into the newly merged row.
5. Delete the empty text box, and increase the height of the table to fill the space it occupied.
6. Apply a light gray background (use the gray in the color scheme) to row 1.
7. Apply a 1-point bottom-only purple border (use the purple in the color scheme) in row 2, so that the headings look like they have an underline separating them from the lists beneath them.
8. Set the vertical alignment of the cells in row 2 to Bottom.
9. For rows 3, 4, and 5, turn off automatic hyphenation.
10. For rows 3, 4, and 5, set the internal right margin to 0.2".
11. Print the publication. The final table is shown in Illustration A.
12. Save your work and exit Publisher.

Illustration A

Row 1 merged and shaded gray

Row 2 with bottom border

Ask at the front desk for maps and information about these great attractions and activities.		
Dining	**Museums**	**Sports**
Mateo's Italian Ristorante	Conner Prairie Museum	Glenn Acre Stables trail rides
Alexander's Ice Cream	Hendricks County Art Museum	Just Boats watercraft rentals
Bongi's Pub and Grill	The Children's Museum	Mission Road bicycle rentals

On Your Own

1. Start Publisher, if necessary.
2. Open the file **OPUB26**. Save it as **26CAL**.
3. Use what you have learned in this lesson about borders and shading to format this calendar attractively.
4. Format the text if needed using normal text formatting, to make it easier to read.
   ✓ *You can do what you like with it, but make sure it is easy to read and attractive when printed; use Print Preview to check your work as you go.*
5. Save your work and exit Publisher.

Exercise 27

◆ Critical Thinking

Pet Rescue is having a silent auction to benefit their organization and would like your help in designing a flyer for it.

Exercise Directions

1. Start Publisher, if necessary.
2. Open the file **PUB27**. Save it as **27PET**.
3. Make the Silent Auction text 48 point, bold, and centered. Use any font you choose.
4. Change the **Silent Auction** text's color the text white. (Don't worry that it disappears; this is temporary.)
5. Apply a texture as a background fill in the Silent Auction text box. Choose one of the darker textures for best results.
6. Select all the text in the second text box, and make it all Arial 14 point. Create a new style called Body and define it to match that text.
7. Make the **Date**, **Time**, and **Place** text bold and italicized, and dark blue in color.
   - ✓ *There is no dark blue in the color scheme, so you will need to use More Colors.*
8. Apply a BorderArt border to the entire page.
   - ✓ *Hint: Draw a large text box that covers the whole page, and apply the BorderArt to it.*
9. Create a table in the remaining space on the flyer, with 8 rows and 3 columns. Merge the cells in the first row. Apply 14-point Arial formatting to the entire table.
10. Delete the bottom two rows and resize the table so that it takes up the same space as it did before the deletion.
11. Apply a 1/4-point black border to every side of every cell in the table except the first row.
12. Enter the text shown in Illustration A into the table.
13. Save your work and exit Publisher.

Illustration A

Silent Auction

Please join Pet Rescue for an evening of fun, food, and prizes as we raise money for our mission of finding homes for homeless dogs and cats.

Date: September 30
Time: 7:00 p.m.
Place: Plankston Armory, 3487 West McGovern St.

A sampling of items to be auctioned off:

Car washes	B&B weekends	Movie tickets
CDs	DVDs	Books
Garden supplies	Plumbing services	Carpentry services
Online classes	Pet care products	Catering
Clothing	Tuxedo rentals	Handbags
Tools	Lawn care services	Gourmet baskets

Exercise 28

◆ Critical Thinking

A friend who works for Garden Gate Supply is trying to come up with a sales flyer for the company's big spring sale and has asked for your help. All the text is there, but the formatting is not very attractive. In this exercise you will improve the flyer by applying text formatting.

Exercise Directions

1. Start Publisher, if necessary.
2. Open the file **PUB28**. Save it as **28GARDEN**.
3. Make the **Spring Planting Sale** text 48 points in size.
4. In the text box with the green text, apply the following attributes to that text:
   a. Left-aligned
   b. 14 points in size
   c. Bright blue (use placeholder color)
   d. Not bold or italic
   e. Spacing between lines in the paragraphs: 1.25sp
5. Delete the empty text box below the one from step 4.
6. Swap the positions of the text box from step 4 and the text box that contains the two-column bulleted list.
   ✓ *It's okay if the round black attention-getter overlaps the text box; the text will wrap around it. Expand the text box as needed to make sure all the text fits.*
7. Change the font size of the bulleted list to 12 point.
8. Change the bullet character to a symbol that looks like a flower (any style, from any font set). If needed, adjust the indent or bullet placement for attractiveness.
9. Expand the bulleted list text box as needed so that all the bullet points continue to fit in two equal-length columns.
10. In the three text boxes at the bottom of the flyer, increase the text by 3 points. (So, for example, the 11-point text becomes 14 point and the 8-point text becomes 11 point.)
11. Print the publication. Illustration A shows an example of the finished product.
12. Save your work and exit Publisher.

Illustration A

Lesson 4

Working with Pictures and WordArt

Exercise 29
- Insert Clip Art
- Work with the Clip Organizer
- Format Clip Art

Exercise 30
- Insert a Picture from a File
- Acquire an Image from a Scanner or Digital Camera
- Save an Acquired Image to Disk

Exercise 31
- Crop a Picture
- Wrap Text Around a Picture

Exercise 32
- Draw Lines
- Draw Ovals and Rectangles
- Draw AutoShapes

Exercise 33
- Format Lines and Shape Borders
- Fill a Shape
- Apply 3-D Effects
- Apply Shadows Effects
- Group and Ungroup Objects

Exercise 34
- Create WordArt
- Edit WordArt Text
- Format WordArt

Exercise 35
- Align Objects
- Distribute Objects
- Flip Objects
- Rotate Objects
- Nudge Objects
- Set Object Layering

Exercise 36
- Insert Objects
- Insert an Existing File
- Copy Data from Another Program
- Edit an Embedded Object
- Update Links

Exercise 37
- Critical Thinking

Exercise 38
- Critical Thinking

Exercise 29

Skills Covered:

◆ **Insert Clip Art** ◆ **Work with the Clip Organizer** ◆ **Format Clip Art**

On the Job

Clip art can enliven an otherwise boring publication. Publisher comes with hundreds of clip art images, and you can download more from Microsoft's Web site on the Internet.

The Hendricks Inn is co-sponsoring an open house with the Central Kentucky Land Trust, and John Lowery, the owner, would like an advertising flyer to help spread the word. He has started a flyer, and in this exercise you will improve it by adding clip art.

Terms

Clip art Ready-to-use artwork. The name comes from the days when professional designers could buy books full of generic drawings, with many on each page. They would then "clip" the desired drawing out of the book with scissors and paste it directly onto their page layout.

WMF Short for Windows Metafile, the format in which Publisher provides its clip art. Clip art you buy or download from another source may be in a different format.

Clip Organizer An organizer that displays and manages the clip art images. Publisher uses the same Clip Organizer as Word, Excel, and other Microsoft Office programs.

Aspect ratio The ratio of width to height. If you resize one dimension more than another, the picture can become distorted.

Notes

Insert Clip Art

- To select a piece of **clip art** for use in your publication, choose Insert, Picture, Clip Art. The Clip Art controls appear in the task pane.

  ✓ *The first time you access clip art, you are prompted to catalog the clips. Click Now to do so; it takes several minutes. You can also choose to do it later, and you will be reminded to do it each time until you do. Cataloging clips makes searches more effective, so you should do it as soon as possible.*

- You can also click the Picture Frame button on the Objects toolbar (left side of screen) and then click Clip Art on the pop-out menu.

- From the Clip Art task pane, you can search for a clip matching your needs.

  ✓ *Most of the clips that come with Publisher are in Windows Metafile, or **WMF**, format. This format allows you to scale (resize) pictures without losing any image quality.*

- Each clip has one or more keywords associated with it. Type the keyword you are looking for in the Search text box and click Search.

Clip art controls in the task pane

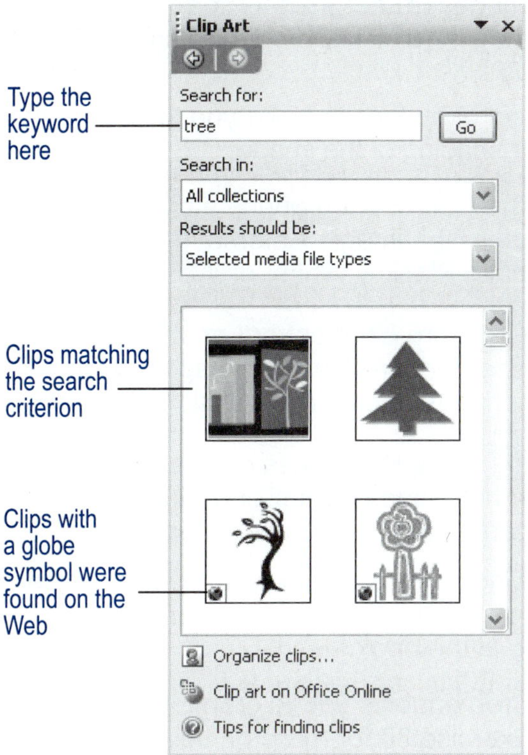

- An assortment of clips that have the word you typed as a keyword appear.

  ✓ *If you have an active Internet connection, Publisher will search the Office Online Web site and you'll see additional clips from which to choose; the clips from online have a globe symbol on them.*

- Click the clip you want, and it appears in your publication, in its own frame. You can move and resize that frame as needed.

Click the clip to place it in your publication

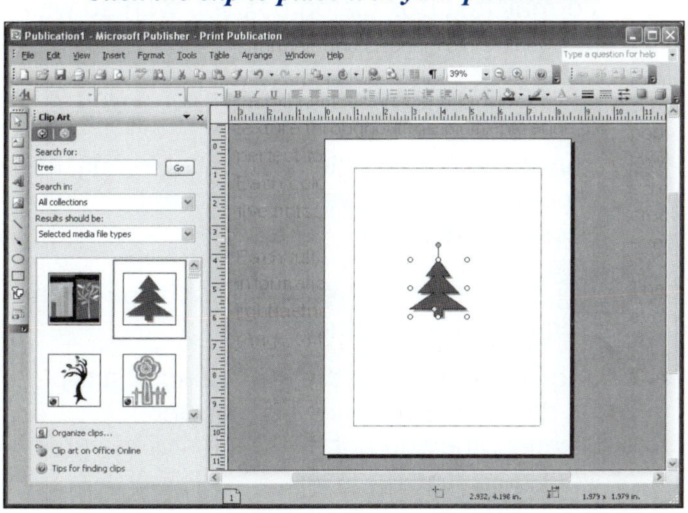

- If not very many clips appear, try connecting to the Internet and then searching again, so that it can pull from the online clips as well.

Work with the Clip Organizer

- If you want to browse all available clip art, rather than search by keyword, you can use the **Clip Organizer**.
- In the Clip Art task pane, click the Organize clips… hyperlink. This opens the Microsoft Clip Organizer window. Then click a folder on the Collection List to see the pictures within it.

Browse and organize clips in the Clip Organizer

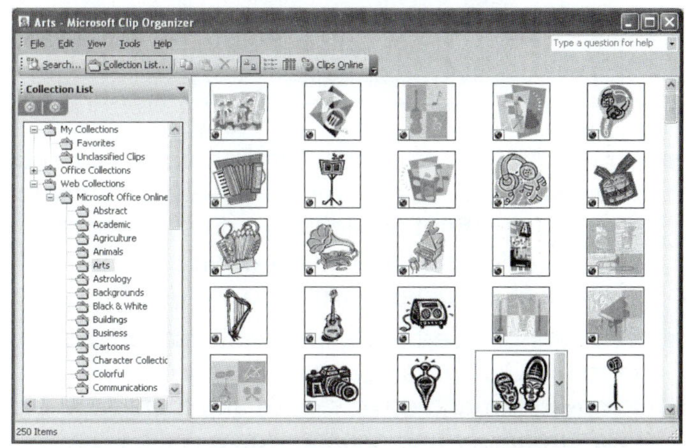

- The folders on the Collection List were cataloged based on what the Clip Organizer found when it searched for and organized your clips initially, the first time you used clip art. A separate folder appears for each folder in which it found pictures of any type, not just clip art.
- The clip art that comes with Publisher is in a folder called *Office Collections*. Within that folder are subfolders by category. Click a category to browse the clips within it.
- The *Web Collections* folder contains subfolders that link to Office Online, Microsoft's online repository of clip art. You can directly browse the clip art available from the Microsoft Web site through these folders.

  ✓ *The Clip art on Office Online hyperlink in the task pane opens a Web page from which you can browse available clips at Office Online, as an alternative to using the Web Collections folder. The same clips appear either way.*

- To work with a particular clip in the Clip Organizer, point to it, so that an arrow appears to its right. Then click the arrow to open a menu.

Each clip has a menu of actions you can perform on it

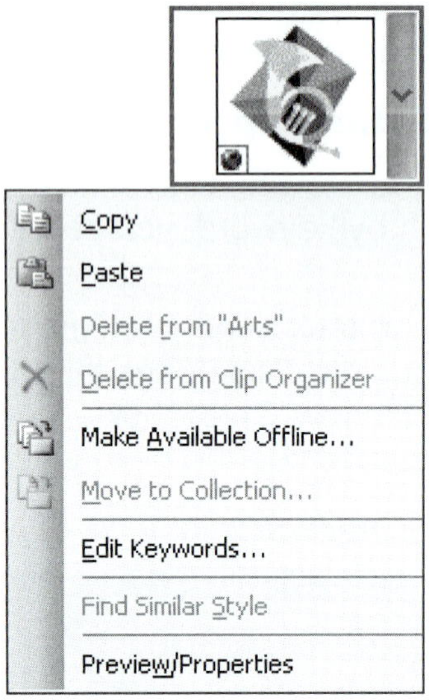

- You might want to copy a clip from the Internet to your own hard disk so you can use it later when the Internet is not available. To do so, choose Make Available Offline. Then when prompted, select a local folder in which to store it.
- You cannot insert a clip into a publication directly from the Clip Organizer, but you can copy it (Copy command on its menu) and then close the Clip Organizer and choose Paste (Edit, Paste). You can also drag-and-drop from the Clip Organizer into a document.

Format Clip Art

- You can move or resize a picture just like a text box.
- To move a picture, position the mouse pointer anywhere over it (except over a selection handle) and drag.
- To resize a picture, drag a selection handle. To maintain the **aspect ratio** of the picture, drag a corner handle; to distort the image, drag a side handle.
- The Picture toolbar appears when clip art is selected in your publication. You can use its tools to change how the picture appears.

  ✓ *These same tools appear for pictures from a file, or from your scanner or camera. You'll learn about those types of pictures in Exercise 30.*

This toolbar provides formatting buttons you can use for the selected clip

- The first two buttons are for bringing in different types of images, rather than for formatting an existing image. You'll learn about them in Exercise 30.
- The next set of buttons enables you to change the coloring or shading of the image:
  - The Color button opens a menu of settings for the image: Automatic (color), Grayscale, Black & White, or Washout.
  - More Contrast or Less Contrast increases or decreases the image's contrast by increments each time you click on them.
  - More Brightness or Less Brightness makes the image brighter or darker by increments each time you click on them.
- The following buttons enable you to change the picture's area or border and are covered elsewhere in the book:
  - Crop enables you to crop the image. (See Exercise 30 for more on this.)
  - Line/Border Style enables you to add a border to the picture, just like with a text box. (See Exercise 19.)
  - Text Wrapping lets you control how text in overlapping text boxes will interact with the picture. (See Exercise 30.)
- The final three buttons on the Picture toolbar offer miscellaneous adjustments:
  - Format Picture opens the Format Picture dialog box, which is much like the Format Text Box dialog box you worked with in Lesson 2.
  - Set Transparent Color enables you to choose a color in the picture that will be transparent. This button is available only for clips that do not have a transparent background.
  - Reset Picture returns all settings for the picture to their defaults.
- Changes you make to the formatting of a clip apply only to the copy in your current publication; they do not affect the stored version on your hard disk or online.

Procedures

Display the Clip Art Task Pane

1. Click the **Picture Frame** button on the Objects toolbar
2. Click **Clip Art** C

OR

1. Click **Insert** .... Alt+I
2. Click **Picture** .... P
3. Click **Clip Art** C

Insert Clip Art

1. Display page of publication on which clip should appear.
2. Display the Clip Art task pane.
3. Type keyword to search for in the **Search for** text box.
4. Click **Go** .... Go.
5. Click clip to insert.

Resize a Clip

1. Click the clip frame to select it.
2. Position mouse pointer over a selection handle, so pointer turns into double-headed arrow.
3. Hold down left mouse button.
4. Drag the handle to a new position, resizing the clip.
   ✓ *Hold down the Shift key as you drag if you don't want to maintain the aspect ratio, or drag a side handle rather than a corner.*
5. Release the mouse button.

Move a Clip

1. Click the clip frame to select it.
2. Position mouse pointer over the clip (but not on a selection handle), so pointer turns into a Move pointer.
3. Hold down left mouse button.
4. Drag the clip to a new position.
5. Release the mouse button.

Browse Clips in Clip Organizer

1. Display the Clip Art task pane.
2. Click **Organize clips** hyperlink.
3. Click plus sign next to the **Office Collections** folder (or whatever collection you want to view).
4. Click clip art category's folder to browse.
   ✓ *The clips in that category appear, if there are any clips in it.*

Insert Clip from Clip Organizer

1. Locate the clip in the Clip Organizer. (See "Browse Clips in Clip Organizer.")
2. Point to clip.
3. Click arrow to right of clip.
4. Click **Copy** .... Alt+C
5. Close Clip Organizer window.
6. Display page of publication on which clip should appear.
7. Click **Paste** button .... Ctrl+V

Make Clip Available Offline

1. Locate the clip in the Clip Organizer. (see "Browse Clips in Clip Organizer.")
2. Point to clip.
3. Click arrow to right of clip.
4. Click **Make Available Offline** .... Alt+A
5. Click folder in which to store the clip.
6. Click **OK** .... Enter

Change Clip Art Appearance

1. Click clip to select it.
   ✓ *The Picture toolbar appears. If it does not, choose View, Toolbars, Picture.*
2. Click **Color** button.
3. Click color option you want:
   - **Automatic** .... A
   - **Grayscale** .... G
   - **Black & White** .... B
   - **Washout** .... W
4. (Optional) Click a button to change the image appearance:
   - **More Contrast**
   - **Less Contrast**
   - **More Brightness**
   - **Less Brightness**

Reset a Picture's Appearance

1. Click the picture to select it.
2. Click **Reset Picture** button.

Exercise Directions

1. Start Publisher, if necessary.
2. Open the file PUB29. Save it as **29OPEN**.
3. Search for clip art using the keyword **wetlands**, and select a clip that looks appropriate for this flyer.
   - ✓ *If you don't have the picture shown in Illustration A, choose a similar picture.*
4. Move and resize the picture as shown in Illustration A, maintaining the aspect ratio.
5. Increase the contrast for the picture.
6. Try out each of the four settings on the Color button's menu; then leave it set for Automatic.
   - ✓ *Notice that changing the Color button's setting resets the brightness and contrast settings to the default.*
7. Increase the brightness for the picture by two levels (that is, two clicks of the More Brightness button).
8. Print the publication.
9. Save your work and exit Publisher.

On Your Own

1. Start Publisher, if necessary.
2. Create a new publication based on one of the Quick Publications. Choose a layout that includes a picture.
3. Replace the picture with one of the pictures from the Clip Art task pane.
4. Use your imagination to create a flyer that fits the picture you chose.
   - ✓ *Remember that you can move, resize, and arrange text boxes and other graphical elements on the page as needed to create the effect you want.*
5. Use the Clip Organizer to browse the Web Collections and find a similar (but different) piece of art to the one you chose.
   - ✓ *If you do not have Web access in the classroom, find a different piece in the Office Collections instead.*
6. Replace the current piece of clip art in your publication with the one you found.
7. Save your work as **29ART** and exit Publisher.

Illustration A

The text automatically wraps around the picture

Open House and Wetlands Tour

Join the Central Kentucky Land Trust (CKLT) at The Hendricks Inn for an open house and a rare opportunity to tour **Burr Oak Bend**, the CKLT wetland preservation area just across the street from The Hendricks Inn. This 120-acre stretch of wetland is the home of countless species of wildlife including birds, fish, and small mammals. Come see what CKLT has been doing to help preserve this wildlife habitat, and tour the beautiful Hendricks Inn.

When: September 2, 1:00 p.m. to 5:00 p.m.

Where: The Hendricks Inn
1478 W. 86th Street
Hendricks, KY 40291

Who: The public is invited

What: Tours of The Hendricks Inn
Hiking tours of Burr Oak Bend
Refreshments
Raffle drawing

Exercise 30

Skills Covered:

- ◆ **Insert a Picture from a File**
- ◆ **Acquire an Image from a Scanner or Digital Camera**
- ◆ **Save an Acquired Image to Disk**

On the Job

The clip art that comes with Publisher can be useful, but you might need to use other artwork. For example, you may have to acquire a photograph from a scanner or digital camera, or a picture stored on a disk or sent via an e-mail attachment.

The Central Kentucky Land Trust would like you to use a photo on the flyer for the open house rather than clip art. In this exercise, you will insert a picture that they have provided in JPG format and make that picture available in the Clip Organizer.

Terms

Picture A generic term for artwork, including photographs, line drawings, cartoons, and other graphic creations.

Embedded graphic A graphic that is stored inside the Publisher file rather than as a separate image.

Linked graphic A graphic that is stored outside the Publisher file and referenced by its file name and location for display within Publisher.

Notes

Insert a Picture from a File

- When you want to use a **picture** that isn't in the Clip Organizer, use the Picture Frame button.
- When you click the Picture Frame button and choose Picture from File, the mouse pointer becomes a crosshair. Drag to draw a box where you want the picture frame or single-click on the page to use a default size.
- Next, the Insert Picture dialog box opens. Use it to choose the picture you want.
- If you do not see previews of the pictures, open the Views button's drop-down list in the Insert Picture dialog box and choose Thumbnails.

The Insert Picture dialog box

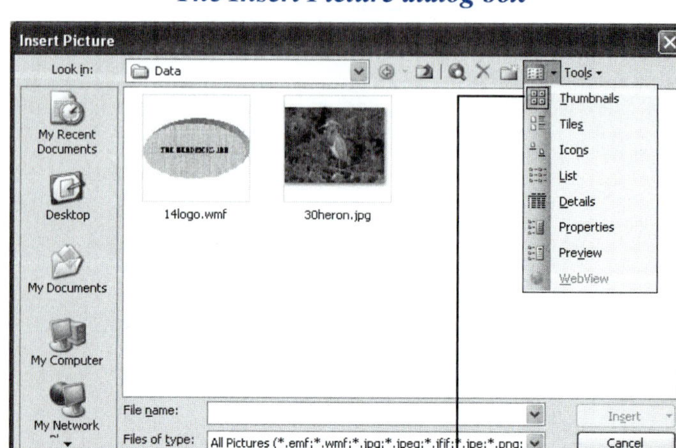

Thumbnails view

✓ *You can also open the Insert Picture dialog box by choosing Insert, Picture, From File. When you do this instead of creating the frame first, Publisher places the picture at a default size in the center of the page, and you must move and resize it after insertion.*

- You can download pictures from the Internet or receive them as e-mail attachments from others. You can also create pictures yourself with a digital camera, or convert a hard-copy photo to a picture file with a scanner.

  ✓ *If you use a picture you have acquired from a Web page, make sure it is not copyrighted and that you have permission to use it. Otherwise you might be subject to legal penalties.*

- Publisher accepts a wide variety of graphic formats, so you should not have to worry about the format being compatible. Some of the formats Publisher accepts include PCX, BMP, JPG, GIF, PNG, TIF, CGM, Kodak Photo CD, CorelDraw, Postscript, and Macintosh PICT.
- You can move and resize a picture exactly as you learned to do for clip art in Exercise 29.
- Inserted pictures are **embedded graphics**, which means they are stored inside the Publisher file. See "Save an Acquired Image to Disk" to learn how to make them linked instead (that is, existing outside the publication file).

Acquire an Image from Scanner or Digital Camera

- Publisher 2003 has an interface through which you can interact directly with a scanner or digital camera, rather than first using that device to save the file to disk.

  ✓ *This feature works only with devices that are on Microsoft's hardware compatibility list for your operating system. Check http://www.microsoft.com/hcl. In addition, it also works only under Windows XP, not Windows 2000.*

- Choose Insert, Picture, From Scanner or Camera to begin. (Alternatively, if the Picture toolbar appears, you can click the Insert from Scanner or Camera button .)
- On the Device list, choose the device to acquire from, adjust any other settings, and then click Insert (or Custom Insert).

Inserting a picture from a digital camera

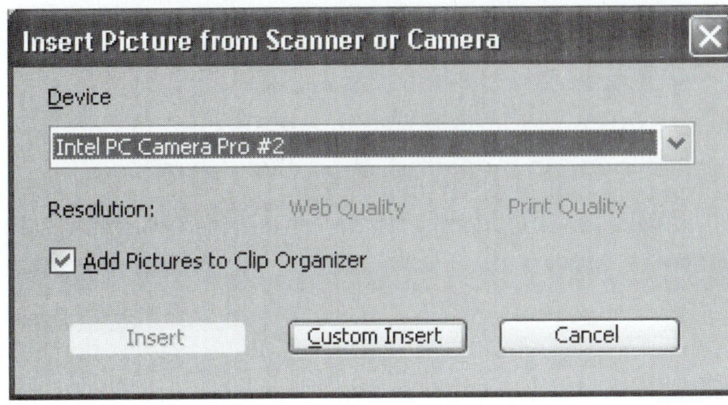

✓ *The Insert button is not available in the preceding figure because the device is a video camera that contains multiple stored images. For a scanner, clicking Insert will acquire the single image on the scanner glass.*

- Custom Insert opens a dialog box from which you can select the stored image in the camera that you want to use in your publication. The figure below shows a video camera; the dialog box is slightly different for a still camera.

Custom insertion for a video camera device

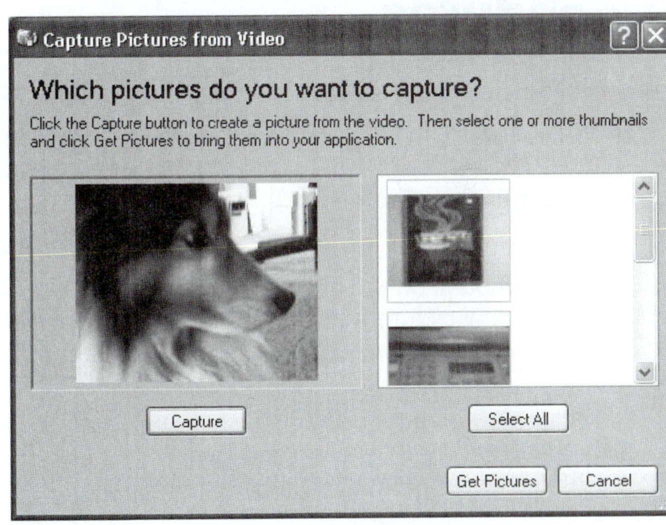

Save an Acquired Image to Disk

- Acquiring from a scanner or camera embeds the picture in the publication. It does not exist outside that publication.
- If you think you might want to use the picture again in the future in some other publication or application, you should save it to your hard disk for later reuse.
- To save an embedded graphic, use the Graphics Manager. Choose Tools, Graphics Manager to display the Graphics Manager task pane.

- Point to a picture, and then click the down arrow to the right of its name. From the menu that appears, choose Save as Linked Picture.
- In the Save As dialog box, change the file name and location if desired; then click Save.

Save an embedded graphic as a linked picture

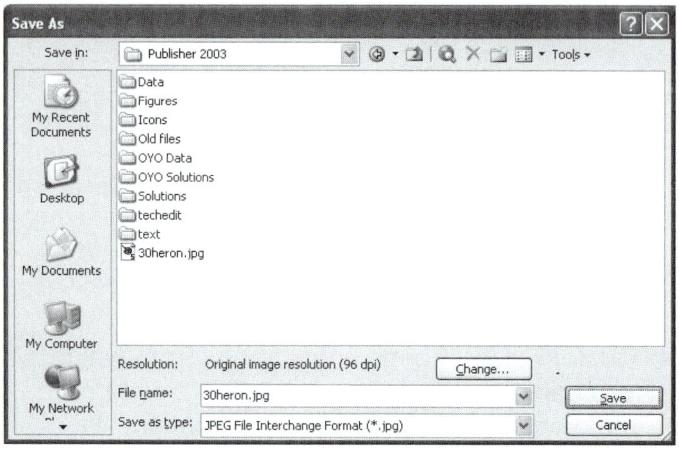

✓ *Notice the Resolution setting. If the resolution of the picture is currently higher than the display resolution (which is 96 dpi usually), you can click the Change button to decrease the picture's resolution at which it will be saved. This can save disk space but will degrade the quality of the image so that it is no longer good enough for a print publication.*

Embed a Linked Picture

- After saving the picture, it becomes a **linked graphic** rather than embedded; in other words, the picture file is stored outside of the Publisher file. This might be a problem if you send the publication file to someone else but you do not send the picture.
- Therefore, after saving the picture to disk, you may want to convert it back to an embedded picture through the Graphics Manager.
- Point to the picture, and then click the down arrow to the right of its name. From the menu that appears, choose Convert to Embedded Picture.

Procedures

Insert a Picture from a File

1. Display page on which picture should appear.
2. Click the **Picture Frame** button.
3. Drag the mouse on the page to draw the new picture frame.
4. Release the mouse button.

   ✓ *You can choose Insert, Picture, From File instead of doing steps 1–3 if desired, but you will need to resize and move the inserted picture afterward.*

5. Locate and select the picture file you want to insert.

   ✓ *To preview the pictures, make sure Thumbnails view is turned on. To do so, open the* ***Views*** *button's menu in the Insert Picture dialog box and click* ***Thumbnails***.

Insert a Picture from Scanner or Camera

1. Display page on which picture should appear.
2. Click **Insert** .... Alt+I
3. Point to **Picture** .... P
4. Click **From Scanner or Camera** .... S
5. Choose device to acquire from.
6. Select **Web quality** or **Print quality**.

   ✓ *Web quality is lower quality and uses less disk space for storage. Depending on the device, the options in step 6 might not be available.*

7. (Optional) If you do not want the picture added to the Clip Organizer, clear the **Add Pictures to Clip Organizer** check box .... Alt+A
8. Click **Insert** (if available) .... Alt+I

   OR

   Click **Custom Insert** ... Alt+C
9. Use any additional controls that appear to select and acquire from the chosen device.

   ✓ *The controls vary depending on the device type.*

Save an Acquired Image to Disk

1. Click **Tools** .... Alt+T
2. Click **Graphics Manager** .... N
3. Point to the image name in the taskbar
4. Click the down arrow.
5. Click **Save as Linked picture** .... S
6. Change the save location if desired.
7. Change the file name if desired.
8. Click **Save** .... Enter

Embed a Linked Image

1. Click **Tools** .... Alt+T
2. Click **Graphics Manager** .... N
3. Point to the image name in the taskbar
4. Click the down arrow.
5. Click **Convert to Embedded Picture** C

Exercise Directions

1. Start Publisher, if necessary.
2. Open the file **PUB30**. Save it as **30OPEN**.
3. Delete the clip art image and replace it with **30heron.jpg**. Make the photo the same size and positioning as the clip art was. See Illustration A.
4. Using the Graphics Manager, save **30heron.jpg** as a new file on your hard disk named **30link.jpg**.
5. Re-embed **30link.jpg** into the presentation file by using Convert to Embedded Picture.
6. Print the publication.
7. Save your work and exit Publisher.

Illustration A

Open House and Wetlands Tour

Join the Central Kentucky Land Trust (CKLT) at The Hendricks Inn for an open house and a rare opportunity to tour **Burr Oak Bend**, the CKLT wetland preservation area just across the street from The Hendricks Inn. This 120-acre stretch of wetland is the home of countless species of wildlife including birds, fish, and small mammals. Come see what CKLT has been doing to help preserve this wildlife habitat, and tour the beautiful Hendricks Inn.

When:	September 2, 1:00 p.m. to 5:00 p.m.
Where:	The Hendricks Inn 1478 W. 86th Street Hendricks, KY 40291
Who:	The public is invited
What:	Tours of The Hendricks Inn Hiking tours of Burr Oak Bend Refreshments Raffle drawing

On Your Own

✓ ***Note:*** *This exercise requires a scanner or digital camera.*

1. Start Publisher, if necessary.
2. Start a new, blank publication.
3. Place a scanned or digital camera image on the page, so that is centered horizontally of the page and is at least 5" wide.
4. Add a text box below it with a caption explaining the picture's content and how you acquired it (scanner or camera), plus your name and the current date.
5. Save the publication as **30IMAGE**. See Illustration B for a sample solution.
6. Save your work and exit Publisher.

Illustration B

Exercise 31

Skills Covered:

◆ **Crop a Picture** ◆ **Wrap Text Around a Picture**

On the Job

Sometimes you may want to zoom in on one part of a picture. You can do this with Publisher's cropping tools. Wrap text around a picture for professional results.

The flyer you did in Exercise 30 for The Hendricks Inn has come back from the event planning committee with some changes made to it, including some more text and some different artwork that the owner would prefer to use. Faced with this new material, you now need to make the flyer attractive by cropping and wrapping text around the artwork.

Terms

Crop To remove part of an image on one or more sides.

Wrap To flow text around a picture or other graphic object.

Notes

Crop a Picture

- You can **crop** any kind of image, including clip art, but you will probably need to crop a photo more often. Cropping removes one or more edges of the picture, zooming in on the part you want to use.

The picture on the left is uncropped; the one on the right has been cropped and enlarged

- Use the Crop button on the Picture toolbar to crop a picture. When you click it to turn the feature on, the mouse pointer becomes a Crop pointer, and the selection handles turn to black corners.
- Position the mouse pointer over a black corner, and the pointer changes to a corner, too. Then drag inward to crop the image.

The lines show where the crop will be

- Click the Crop button again to turn the feature off when you are finished with it.
- You can "uncrop" a picture the same way you cropped it. Simply turn on the cropping feature, and then drag one of the selection handles outward instead of inward.
- You can also use the Reset Picture button on the Picture toolbar to undo a crop.

Wrap Text Around a Picture

- **Wrapping** style controls the way that text in a text box interacts with a graphic when the two objects overlap.
- You make the change to the wrapping style in the graphic's settings, not the text box's settings.
- Choose a wrapping style from the Text Wrapping button on the Picture toolbar.

Wrapping for a picture can also be set from the Picture toolbar

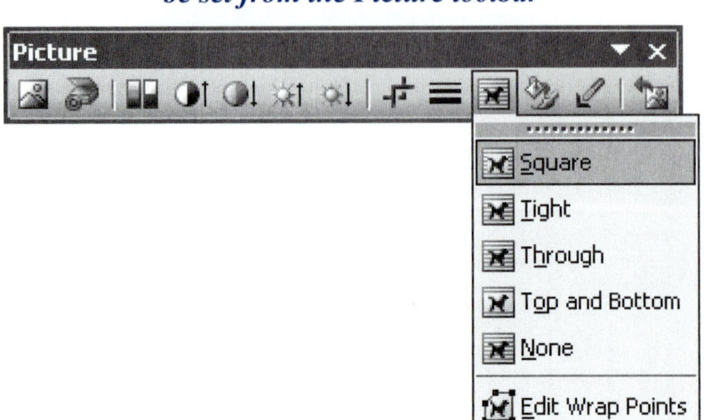

- The available wrapping styles are as follows:
  - Square: Text wraps around the rectangular frame of the other object.

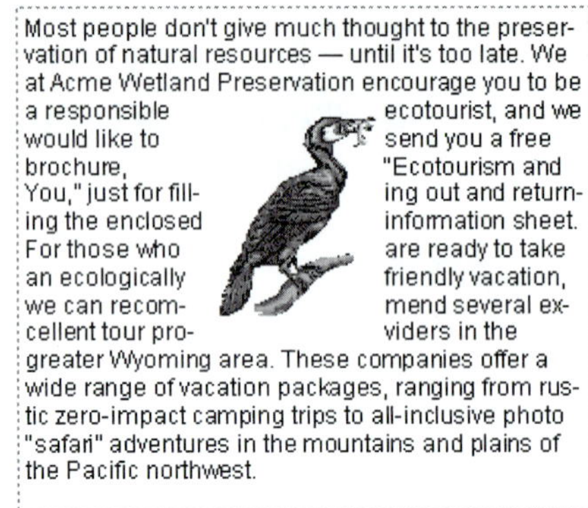

  - Tight: Text wraps around the object inside the frame. (This is different from Square only if the object itself is not rectangular.)

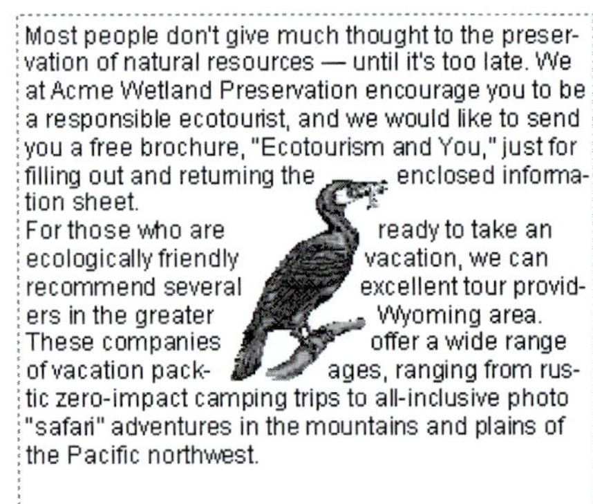

  - Through: Text runs through the object frame, but wraps around certain parts of the object. Depending on the object, it can appear the same as either Tight or None.
  - Top and bottom: Text wraps around the top and bottom of the object, but not the sides.

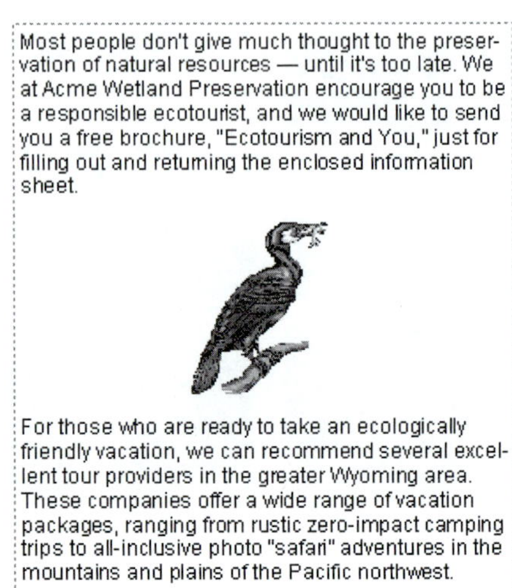

- None: Text does not wrap around the frame.

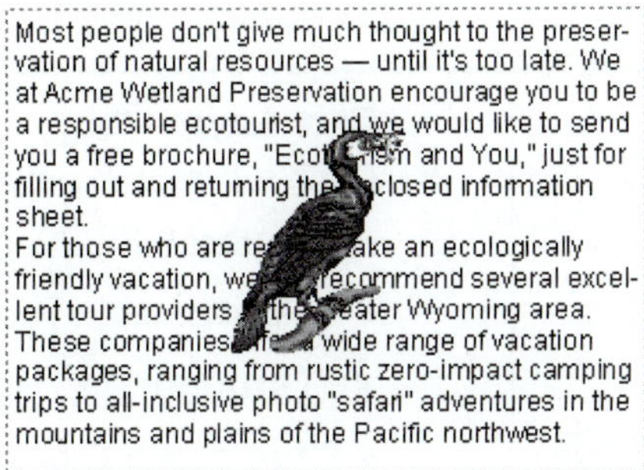

- Another way of controlling the wrapping is from the Format Picture dialog box (Layout tab). Select the picture and then choose Format, Picture or click the Format Picture button on the Picture toolbar. Then click the Layout tab and choose a wrapping style.
- In addition to a wrapping style, you can also choose which sides to wrap on. These settings apply only if you choose a wrapping style (above) that allows wrapping on the sides.
  - Both sides: Wraps text on both sides of the object.
  - Left only: Wraps text only on the left.
  - Right only: Wraps text only on the right.
  - Largest only: Wraps text only on the side where there is the most room (either left or right).

Control text wrapping for the current picture or other object

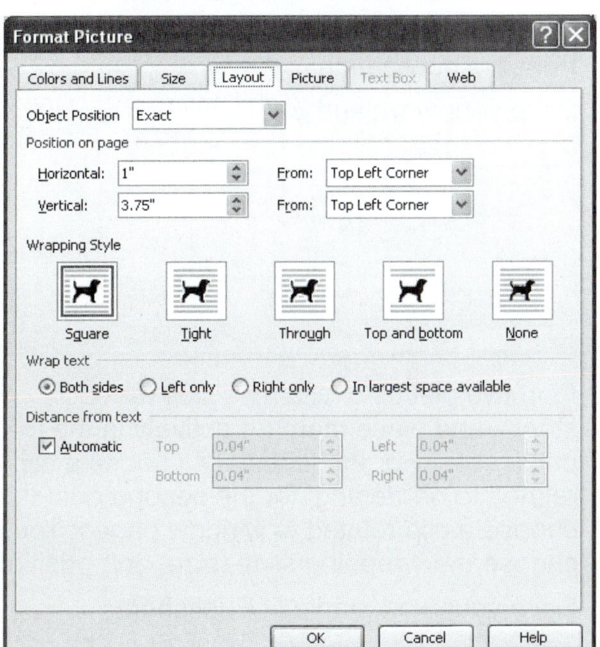

- The Distance from text controls let you specify the amount of white space between the object and the wrapped text. Clear the Automatic checkbox and then enter spacing settings.

Edit Wrap Points

- The clip art that comes with Publisher has predefined wrap points. These wrap points determine where the text will flow in a Tight wrap. Other objects, such as WordArt, also have predefined wrap points.
- You can change the wrap points for an object by setting the wrapping to Tight and then choosing Arrange, Text Wrapping, Edit Wrap Points.
- You can also choose Edit Wrap Points from the Text Wrapping button on the Picture toolbar, as shown in the preceding page.
- An outline appears around the object, comprised of lines with squares at each juncture. You can drag a square to change the wrap shape.

- You can also specify margins for all sides of the picture. This adds additional white space around the picture (within the frame) so the finished layout will look as though the picture is farther away from the wrapped text.

Procedures

Crop a Picture

1. Click the picture to select it.
2. Click the **Crop** button on the Picture toolbar.
3. Position mouse pointer over a selection handle. The pointer changes to a Crop icon.
4. Drag inward, holding down left mouse button, to crop picture.
5. Crop other parts of the picture as desired.
6. Click the **Crop** button again to turn off the feature.

Change the Wrapping Setting with Toolbar

1. Select the picture you want to affect.

   ✓ *If the Picture toolbar does not appear automatically, choose View, Toolbars, Picture to display it.*

2. Click **Text Wrapping** button.

   ✓ *Instead of step 2 you can choose Arrange, Text Wrapping if you prefer.*

3. Click a wrapping style:
   - **Square** .... S
   - **Tight** .... T
   - **Through** .... H
   - **Top and bottom** .... O
   - **None** .... N

Change Wrapping Setting with Dialog Box

1. Select picture (or other object) that text should wrap around.
2. Click **Format** .... Alt+O
3. Click **Picture** .... E

   ✓ *You can click the Format Picture button on the Picture toolbar instead of doing steps 2–3.*

4. Click **Layout** tab.
5. Click a Wrapping style:
   - **Square** .... Alt+Q
   - **Tight** .... Alt+T
   - **Through** .... Alt+U
   - **Top and bottom** .... Alt+B
   - **None** .... Alt+N
6. (Optional) Set other wrapping options.
7. Click **OK** .... Enter

Edit Wrap Points

1. Select the picture.
2. Click **Text Wrapping** button.
3. Click **Edit Wrap Points** .... E
4. Drag one of the handles around the image to adjust wrapping.
5. Click away from picture to turn off wrap editing.

Exercise Directions

1. Start Publisher, if necessary.
2. Open the file **PUB31**. Save it as **31OPEN**.
3. Crop the photo on the left and right sides so that it is square, and then enlarge it to fill the available space. See Illustration A.
4. Resize and reposition the heron clip as shown in Illustration A, and edit its wrap points as shown.
5. Print the publication.
6. Save your work and exit Publisher.

On Your Own

1. Start Publisher, if necessary.
2. Open the file **OPUB31**. Save it as **31NEWS**.
3. Find two pieces of clip art – one for each story—and place them attractively in the publication. For the first story, choose a clip related to gardening; for the second one, choose a clip related to window panes. You choose the wrapping style, size, and position.
4. Save your work and exit Publisher.

Illustration A

Open House and Wetlands Tour

Cropped and resized photo

When: September 2,
1:00 p.m. to 5:00 p.m.

Where: The Hendricks Inn
1478 W. 86th Street
Hendricks, KY 40291

Who: The public is invited

What: Tours of The Hendricks Inn.
hiking tours of Burr Oak Bend,
Refreshments, Raffle drawing

Join the Central Kentucky Land Trust (CKLT) at The Hendricks Inn for an open house and a rare opportunity to tour **Burr Oak Bend**, the CKLT wetland preservation area just across the street from The Hendricks Inn. This 120-acre stretch of wetland is the home of countless species of wildlife including birds, fish, and small mammals. Come see what CKLT has been doing to help preserve this wildlife habitat, and tour the beautiful Hendricks Inn.

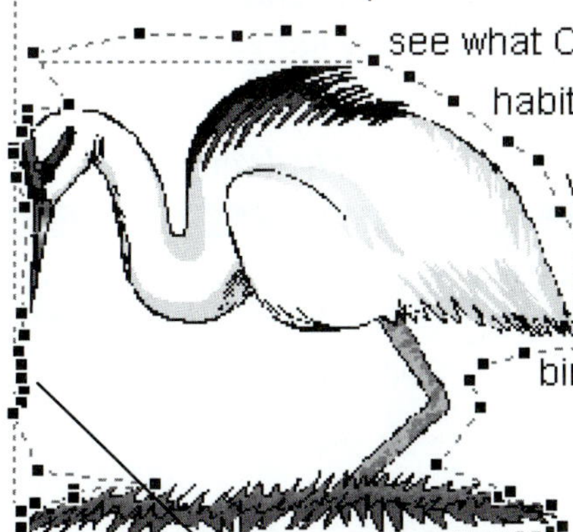

Walking tours will leave every half hour from The Hendricks Inn, and will traverse a one-mile path next to the waterway. So bring your boots and your binoculars for this one-of-a-kind opportunity.

Wrap points edited

Exercise 32

Skills Covered:

◆ **Draw Lines** ◆ **Draw Ovals and Rectangles** ◆ **Draw AutoShapes**

On the Job

You aren't limited to ready-to-use artwork in Publisher; you can also draw your own simple lines and shapes using Publisher's Drawing tools. These are not sophisticated tools, but they can come in very handy when you want to draw a few simple objects without leaving Publisher.

People attending the open house for The Hendricks Inn will need directions. A new page has already been created containing those directions, but they would be much clearer with an accompanying map. In this exercise you will create a simple map using the drawing tools.

Terms

AutoShapes Any of a variety of shapes that Publisher provides (besides ovals and rectangles).

Notes

Draw Lines

- Drawn lines can be useful for separating one section of a publication from another, or for drawing arrow pointers to call attention to an object.
- You can draw a straight line anywhere on the publication. It can be vertical, horizontal, or at any angle—your choice.
- To draw a line, click the Line button on the Objects toolbar, and then drag on the publication where you want the line. If you want the line to have an arrow at one or both ends, use the Arrow button instead.
- To make the line perfectly vertical, horizontal, or an angle of a multiple of 15 degrees (15, 30, 45, and so on), hold down the Shift key as you draw.
- After creating a line, you can format it in a variety of ways, as you will learn in Exercise 33. You can change the line thickness, change its style (solid vs. dashes vs. dotted), and change its color.

Drag to draw a line

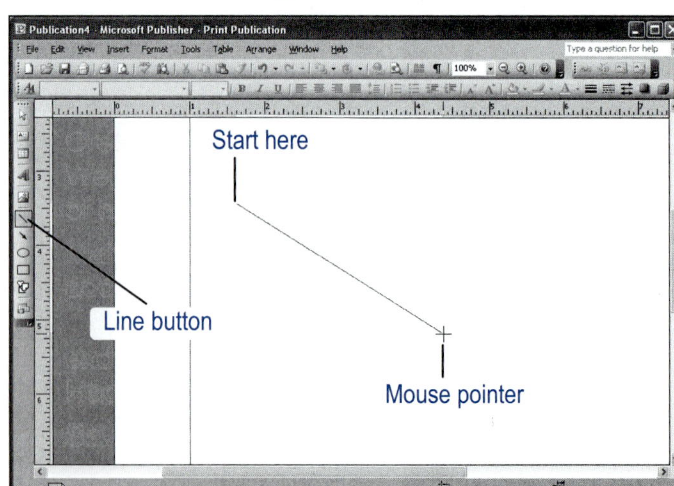

Draw Ovals and Rectangles

- Ovals and rectangles can be used to build simple drawings or call attention to other objects on the page.
- To draw an oval, click the Oval button on the Objects toolbar and then drag to draw the oval. To draw a rectangle, use the Rectangle button the same way.
- To draw a perfect circle or square, hold down Shift as you drag. To make a perfect 1" by 1" square or circle, click on the publication rather than dragging.

Draw AutoShapes

- **AutoShapes** help you create more complex shapes without having to draw them with a series of lines. They include block arrows, starbursts, and a variety of polygons (such as pentagons, hexagons, triangles, and so on).
- To draw an AutoShape, click the AutoShapes button on the Objects toolbar.
- This opens a menu of shape categories. Point to a category, and then click the shape you want to draw.
- Then drag in the publication to create it.

Select an AutoShape and then drag to create it

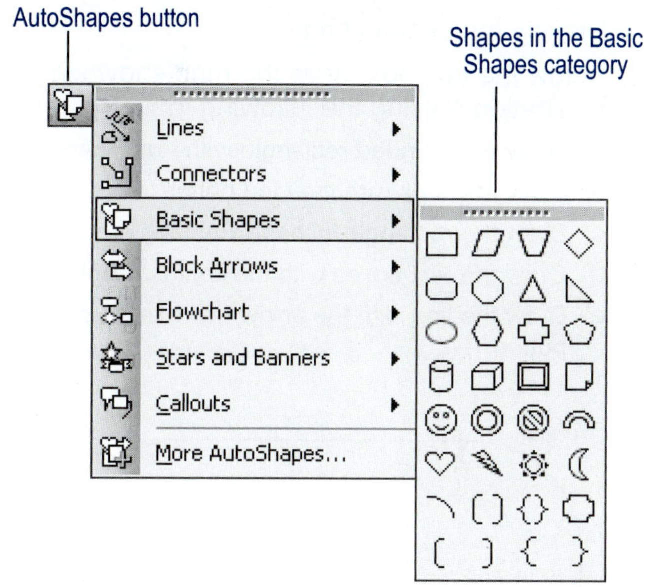

Procedures

Draw Lines

1. Click the **Line** button.
2. Position the mouse pointer where you want the line to start.
3. Hold down the left mouse button.

   ✓ *To draw a perfectly vertical, horizontal line or at an angle that's a multiple of 15° hold down the **Shift** key* Shift.
4. Drag the mouse where you want the line to end.
5. Release the mouse button (and **Shift** key if necessary).

Draw Arrow Lines

1. Click the **Arrow** button.
2. Position the mouse pointer where you want the non-arrow end of the line to start.
3. Hold down the left mouse button.
4. Drag the mouse where you want the tip of the arrow to be.
5. Release the mouse button.

Draw Ovals or Circles

1. Click the **Oval** button.
2. Position the mouse pointer where you want the shape to start.

   ✓ *To draw a perfect circle, hold down the **Shift** key* Shift.
3. Hold down the left mouse button.
4. Drag the mouse where you want the shape to stop.
5. Release the mouse button (and **Shift** key if necessary).

Draw Rectangles or Squares

1. Click the **Rectangle** button.
2. Position the mouse pointer where you want the shape to start.

   ✓ *To draw a perfect square, hold down the **Shift** key* Shift.
3. Hold down the left mouse button.
4. Drag the mouse where you want the shape to stop.
5. Release the mouse button (and **Shift** key if necessary).

Draw AutoShapes

1. Click the **AutoShapes** button.
2. Point to the shape category you want to view.
3. Click the shape you want to draw.
4. Position the mouse pointer where you want the shape to start.

   ✓ *To draw the shape exactly as shown on its button, hold down the **Shift** key* Shift.
5. Hold down the left mouse button.
6. Drag the mouse where you want the shape to stop.
7. Release the mouse button (and **Shift** key if necessary).

Exercise Directions

1. Start Publisher, if necessary.
2. Open the file PUB32. Save it as **32OPEN**.
3. Display the second page.
4. Below the text box, draw the map shown in Illustration A using the following tools:
   a. Draw the rounded rectangle with AutoShapes.
   b. Draw the lines with the Line button.
   c. Draw the rectangle with the Rectangle button.
   d. Draw the text boxes with the Text Box button.
   e. Draw the line with the arrow using the Arrow button.
5. Print the publication.
6. Save your work and exit Publisher.

Illustration A

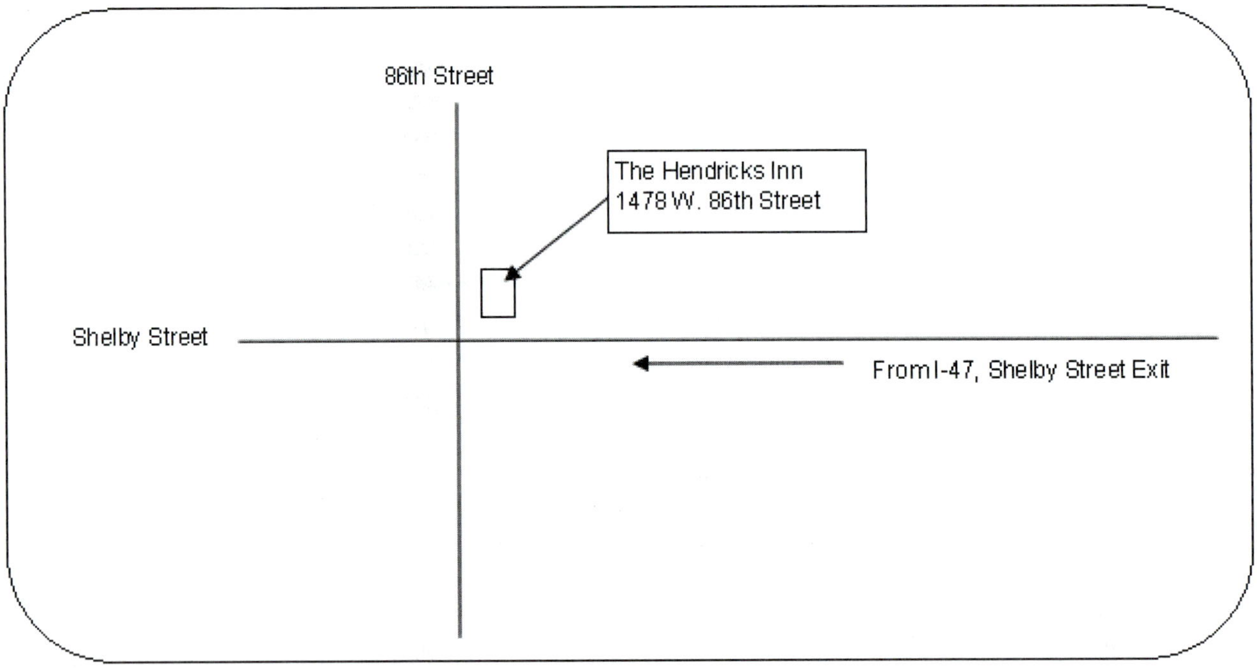

On Your Own

1. Start Publisher, if necessary.
2. Open a new, blank publication and save it as **32DRAW**.
3. Pick one of the following and draw it, as best you can, using the Publisher drawing tools:
   - A man walking a dog
   - A city street, with buildings and cars
   - An aquarium with fish and plants

   ✓ *Don't worry if lines show through overlapped shapes at this point. All shapes are transparent by default. In the next exercise you will learn how to make them solid.*
4. Save your work and exit Publisher.

Exercise 33

Skills Covered:

◆ **Format Lines and Shape Borders** ◆ **Fill a Shape**
◆ **Apply 3-D Effects** ◆ **Apply Shadows Effects**
◆ **Group and Ungroup Objects**

On the Job

The plain, transparent shapes you learned to draw in Exercise 32 are fairly simple, but you can easily enliven them by formatting with borders and fills. Then, after creating the separate elements of your drawings, you can group them together as a whole.

Here you'll format the lines and shapes of the map you created in Exercise 32 and then group the individual shapes together to form a single object.

Terms

3-D (Three-dimensional) An object with 3-D effects applied appears to have depth as well as height and width.

Group To link multiple objects together so that they can be selected, moved, and/or resized as a single entity.

Ungroup To reverse a Group operation, so that objects that were formerly separate are once again separate.

Notes

Format Lines and Shape Borders

- Drawn shapes have borders just as text boxes do. You can set a shape border's color and style in the same way as for text boxes (as you learned in Exercise 19), using various tools on the Formatting toolbar.
- Use the Line Color button's drop-down list to choose a border color. You can select a scheme color or click More Line Colors or Patterned Lines for additional color choices.

Select a border color for the shape

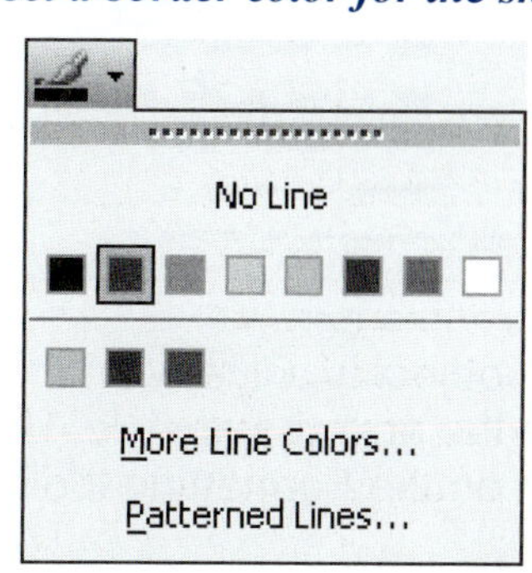

- Use the Line/Border Style button to choose a border thickness. You can select one of the preset thicknesses or click More Lines to open a dialog box with more choices. This works exactly as it did for text frames in Exercise 19.

Select a border thickness

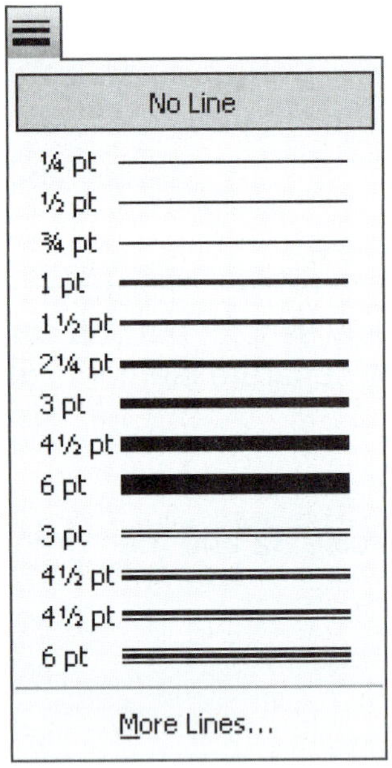

- You can also specify whether the border will be solid or broken (and if broken, in what way). Set the dash style with the Dash Style button.

Select a dash style from the Dash Style button's drop-down list

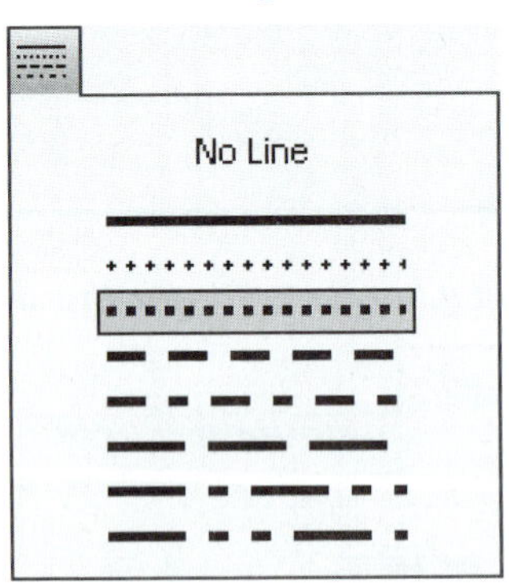

- If the drawn object is a line with an arrow, you can change the arrowhead style. Use the Arrow Style button on the Formatting toolbar to do so.

Select an arrow style

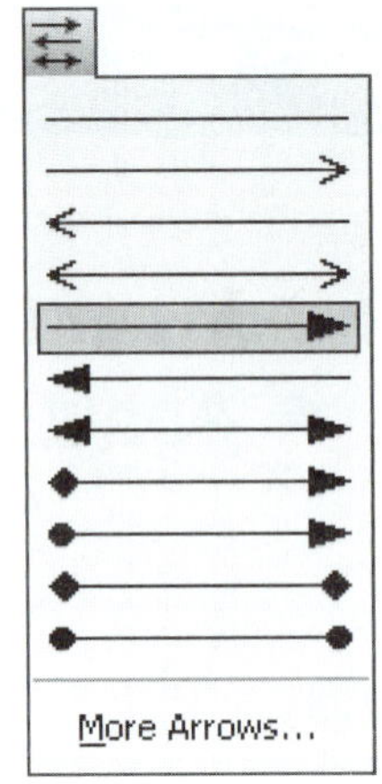

- For more arrow choices, click the More Arrows option.
- When you choose "More" of some formatting option (lines, arrows, etc.), the Format dialog box for the drawn object appears.
  - ✓ *Regardless of the type of object (line, shape, or AutoShape), the dialog box is titled* Format AutoShape.
- In the Format AutoShape dialog box, you can choose a line style, thickness, and color and an arrow shape and size (for lines only).

A full range of line/border formatting controls is available in the Format AutoShape dialog box

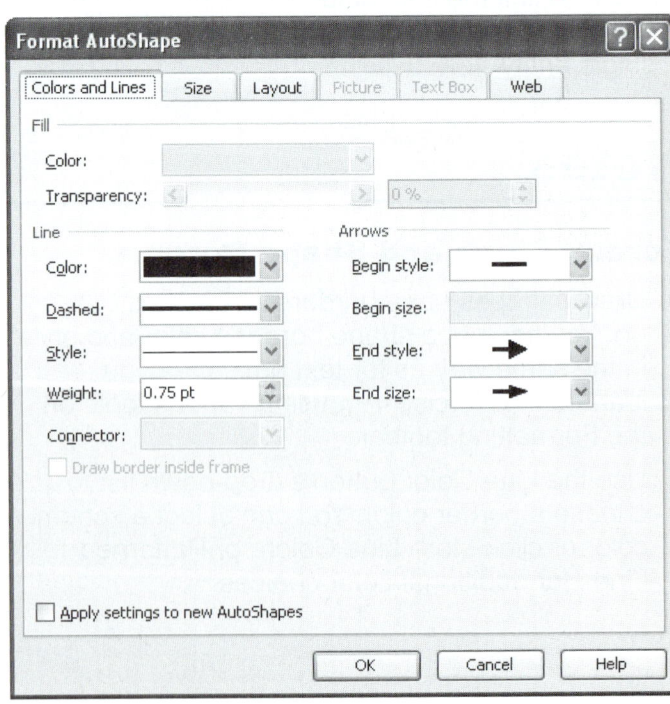

- You can also open the Format AutoShape dialog box by double-clicking the drawn line or shape.

Fill a Shape

- A shape can be filled with one of the scheme colors, or with any other solid color. You fill a shape the same way that you filled a text box in Exercise 20—by selecting a color from the Fill Color button's drop-down list (or from the Format AutoShape dialog box).

Select a fill color from the scheme or go with More Fill Colors or Fill Effects

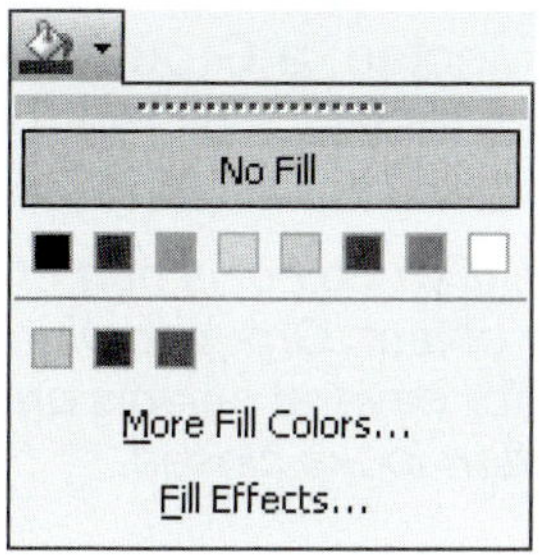

- To remove a fill, choose No Fill.
- Choosing More Colors opens the Colors dialog box, from which you can select any fixed color. (Again, this is just like in Exercise 11.)

Select a fixed color to fill the shape if desired

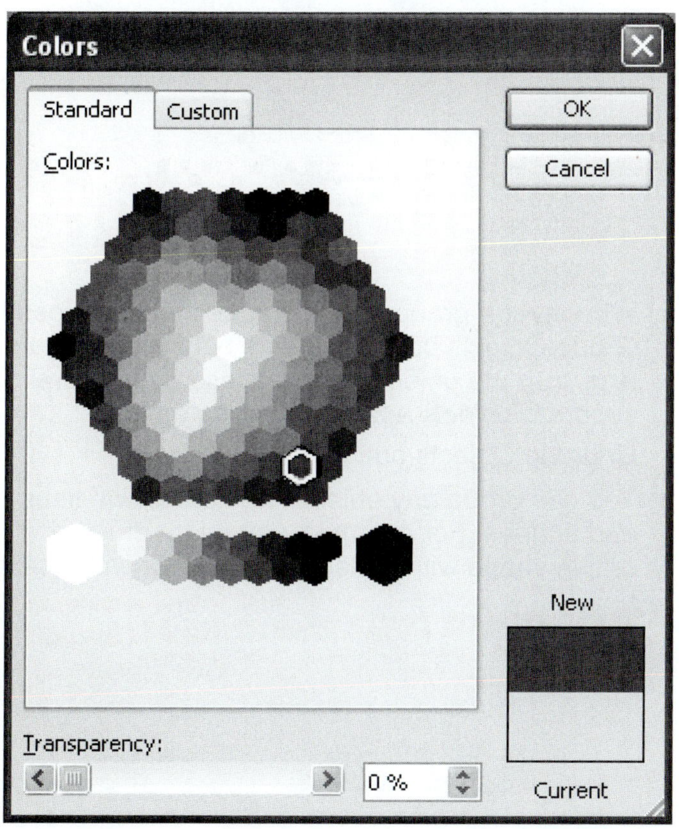

- Choosing Fill Effects opens the Fill Effects dialog box, which you worked with in Exercise 20.

Apply 3-D Effects

- You can apply **3-D** effects to almost any object in Publisher, but they are especially effective and dramatic on drawn shapes.
- 3-D effects make an object look like it has depth as well as height and width, as shown below.

A rectangle with 3-D applied

- To select a 3-D effect, click the 3-D Style button on the Formatting toolbar, and then select from the palette of effects.

Choosing a 3-D effect

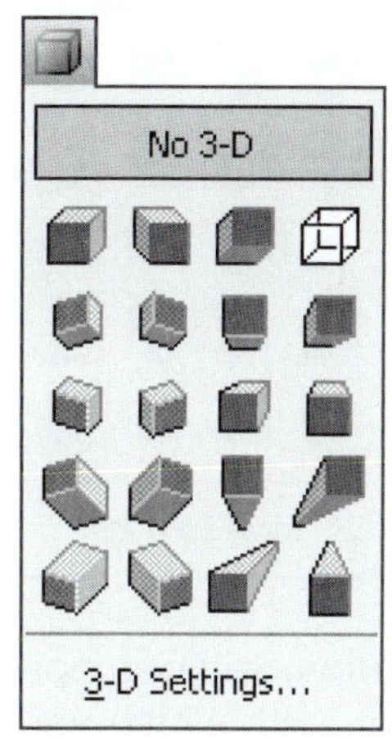

- Choosing 3-D Settings at the bottom of the palette opens the 3-D Settings toolbar, which contains buttons for fine-tuning the 3-D effect.

The 3-D Settings toolbar

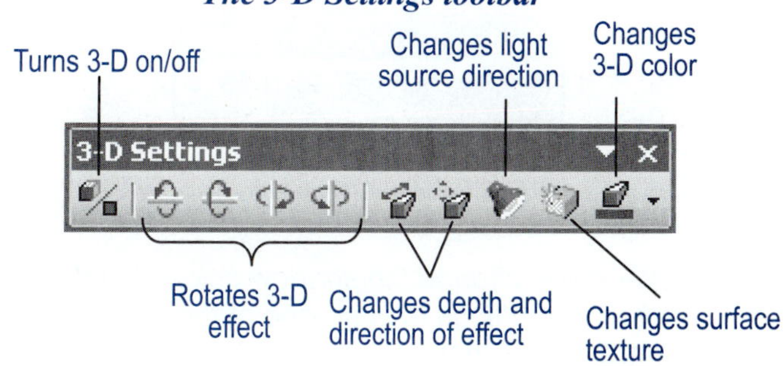

Apply Shadow Effects

- Shadow effects are similar to 3-D effects except instead of making a solid-looking object, they apply a two-dimensional shadow behind the object.

A rectangle with shadow applied

- To apply a shadow, use the Shadow Style button on the Formatting toolbar.

Applying a shadow style

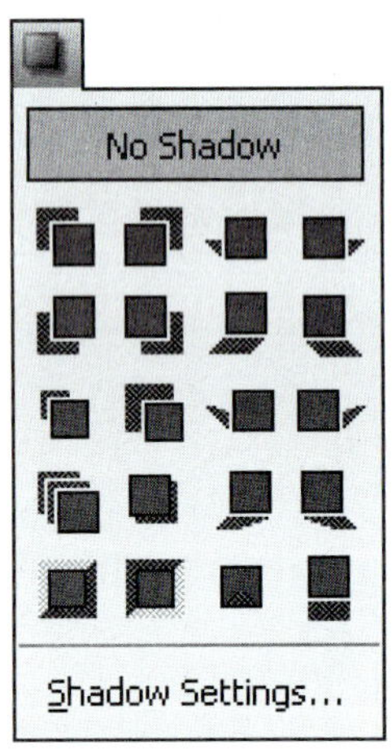

- Choosing Shadow Settings opens the Shadow Settings toolbar, with which you can fine-tune the shadow.

The Shadow Settings toolbar

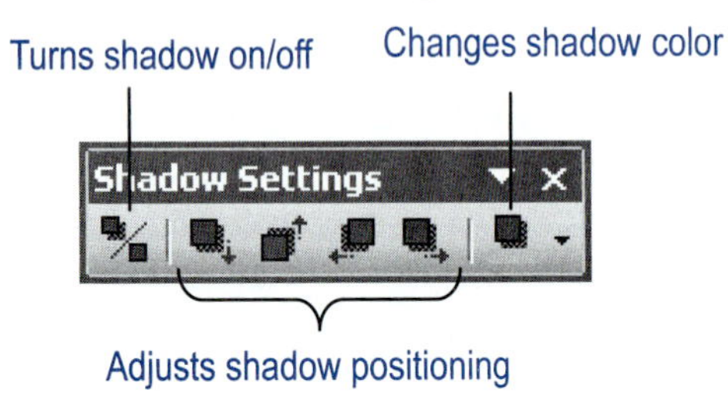

✓ *When you change the shadow color from the Shadow Settings toolbar, one of the choices on that button's menu is Semitransparent Shadow. If you select it, the shadow will be lighter than normal in color and partially see-through.*

Group and Ungroup Objects

- If you draw a picture that uses multiple shapes and lines, you may wish to **group** them so you can work with the picture as a single object. This makes it easier to move or resize the picture.
- To group objects, select them by clicking each one as you hold down the Shift key, or use the pointer tool to drag a rectangle around all the objects you want to group. When multiple objects are selected, a Group Objects button appears below them. Click that button to group them.

  ✓ *You can tell if an object is part of a group by clicking the object. Grouped objects have one set of handles for several objects and the Group Objects button looks closed.*

Group these individual objects by clicking the Group Objects button

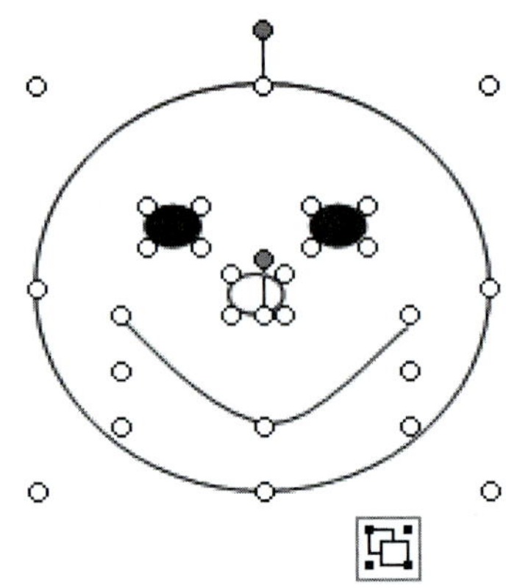

- Whenever a grouped object is selected, a closed Group Objects button appears below it. You can **ungroup** the object so that it becomes several separate objects again by clicking on the Ungroup Objects button.
- You can group any objects, not just drawn lines and shapes. For example, you might group a drawn shape with a piece of clip art or with a text box.

Procedures

Format Lines/Borders

Apply a scheme color to a line or shape border:

1. Select the line or shape.
2. Click the down arrow to the right of the **Line Color** button.
3. Click one of the scheme colors.

Apply a fixed color to a line or shape border:

1. Select the line or shape.
2. Click the down arrow to the right of the **Line Color** button.
3. Click **More Line Colors** .... M
4. Click the color you want.
5. Click **OK** .... Enter

Change a line or shape border width:

1. Select the line or shape.
2. Click the **Line/Border Style** button.
3. Click one of the preset thicknesses.

   OR

   Click **More Lines** .... M
4. Click a style from the **Style** list .... S

   OR

   Type an exact thickness in the **Weight** box .... W
5. Click **OK** .... Enter

Apply a dash style to a line:

1. Select the line.
2. Click the **Dash Style** button.
3. Click the dash style you want.

Add or change an arrow:

1. Select a line, with or without an arrow.
2. Click the **Arrow Style** button.
3. Click the arrow style you want.

   OR

   Click **More Arrows** .... M
4. Select an arrow style (or a plain line with no arrow) from the **Begin style** list ...... Alt+B
5. Select an arrow size from the **Begin size** list .... Alt+I
6. Select an arrow style (or a plain line with no arrow) from the **End style** list .... Alt+E
7. Select an arrow size from the **End size** list .... Alt+Z

   ✓ *If you chose a plain line with no arrow in step 4 or 6, the size list in step 5 or 7 will not be available.*
8. Click **OK** .... Enter

Format Shapes

Fill a shape with a scheme color:

1. Select the shape.
2. Click the down arrow to the right of the **Fill Color** button.
3. Click one of the scheme colors.

Fill a shape with a fixed color:

1. Select the shape.
2. Click the down arrow to the right of the **Fill Color** button.
3. Click **More Fill Colors** .... M
4. Click the color you want.
5. Click **OK** .... Enter

   ✓ *You can also apply fill effects to a shape, the same as with a text box. Refer back to Exercise 12.*

Shadows and 3-D Effects

Apply 3-D effect:

1. Select the object.
2. Click **3-D Style** button on the toolbar.
3. Click the desired effect.

   ✓ *You can choose 3-D Settings to open a toolbar with additional 3-D effect choices.*

Remove a 3-D effect:

1. Select the object.
2. Click **3-D Style** button on the toolbar.
3. Click **No 3-D**.

Apply a shadow:

1. Select the object.
2. Click **Shadow Style** button on the toolbar.
3. Click the desired effect.

   ✓ *You can choose Shadow Effects to open a toolbar with additional shadow choices.*

Remove a shadow:

1. Select the object.
2. Click **Shadow Style** button on the toolbar.
3. Click **No Shadow**.

Grouping

Group objects:

1. Click the first object.
2. Hold down the **Shift** key..... Shift
3. Click on the other objects, one by one, that you want to include.

   OR

   Drag a box around objects you want to include, selecting them.
4. Click the **Group Objects** button.

Ungroup objects:

1. Click the grouped object.
2. Click the **Ungroup Objects** button.

Exercise Directions

1. Start Publisher, if necessary.
2. Open the file **PUB33**. Save it as **33OPEN**.
3. Display page 2.
4. Zoom in so you can see the map clearly.
5. Format the vertical line with the following attributes:
   - 6 points
   - Bright blue
6. Format the horizontal line with the following attributes:
   - 4 1/2 points
   - Dashed (your choice of styles)
   - Dark blue
7. Color the small rectangle representing the Hendricks Inn building a bright orange and remove its border.
8. Apply a white background fill to the text box containing **The Hendricks Inn**, and then apply 3-D Style 1 to that text box.
9. Select the outer border (rounded rectangle) of the map and make it bright orange (the same color as in step 7) and 3 points in thickness. Apply a shadow to it.
10. Select all the components of the map (text boxes and drawn objects) and group them. Illustration A shows the finished version.
11. Save your work and exit Publisher.

Illustration A

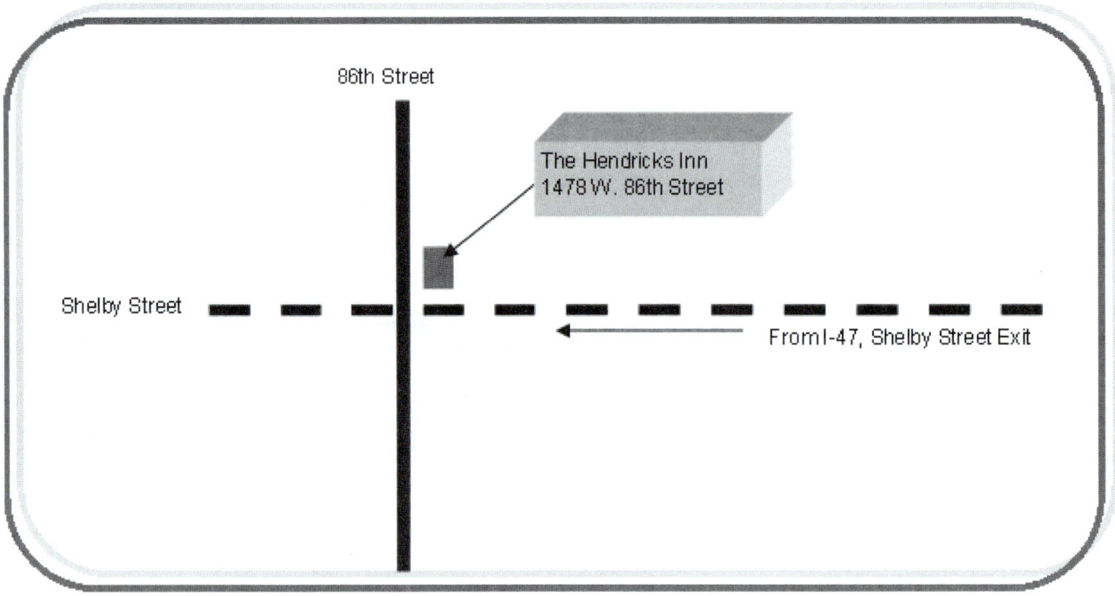

On Your Own

1. Start Publisher, if necessary.
2. Open the drawing you created in Exercise 32 (it should be in the file **32DRAW**), or open the file **OPUB33** if you don't have a drawing.
3. Save the files as **33DRAW**.
4. Color your picture using the fill and border controls you learned about in this exercise.
5. Use 3-D effects and/or shadows to enhance your drawing.
6. Group all the objects in the drawing together into a single object.
7. Save your work and exit Publisher.

Exercise 34

Skills Covered:

◆ **Create WordArt** ◆ **Edit WordArt Text** ◆ **Format WordArt**

On the Job

WordArt helps you stylize your text with twists, arches, fancy patterns, 3-D effects, and other enhancements. You won't want to set your entire publication in WordArt, of course, but it can make for some stunning headings and attention getters.

The flyer for the open house and wetlands tour is nearly complete. In this exercise you will replace the ordinary title text with a piece of WordArt.

Terms

Even height All characters are the same height regardless of their capitalization.

Vertical text Text running vertically, but with each letter appearing in normal orientation.

Notes

Create WordArt

- WordArt enables you to enter a few words of text and then manipulate that text in a variety of ways, as if it were a graphic. You can create some very interesting special effects with it.
- To start a new piece of WordArt, click the Insert WordArt button on the Objects toolbar. The WordArt Gallery appears. Select a WordArt style to use as a starting point.

  ✓ *If you want to convert regular text into WordArt, place it in its own text box and select that text box before clicking the Insert WordArt button.*

Select a WordArt design to start with

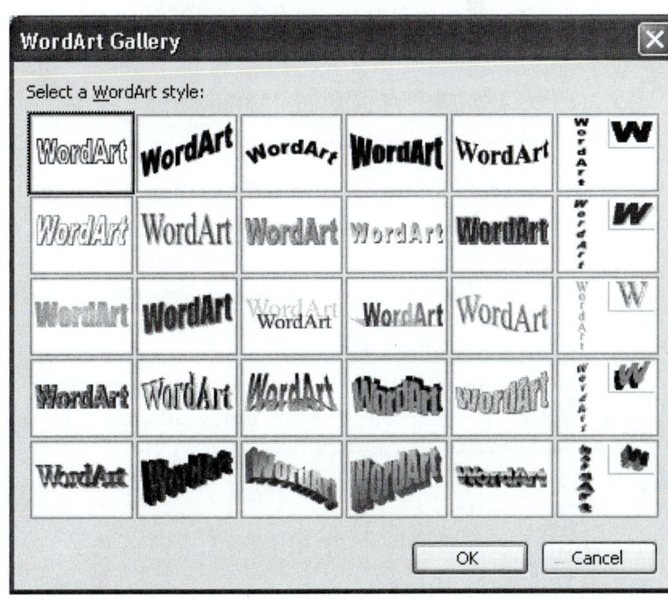

- After selecting the initial design, type the text to use in the Edit WordArt Text dialog box. Then click OK, and the WordArt appears.

Enter the text to use for the WordArt

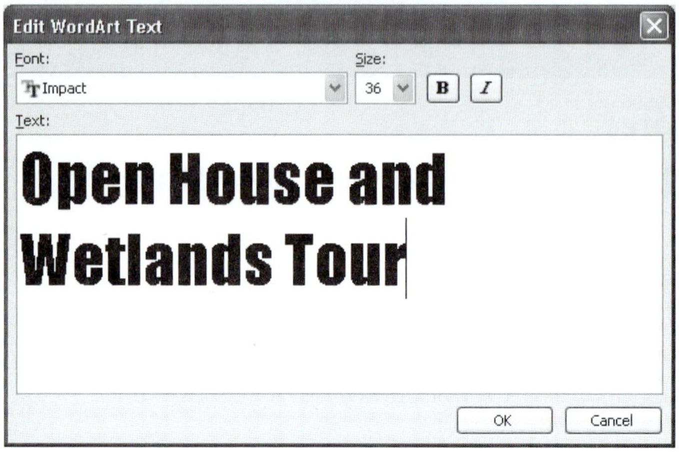

- Don't worry if it doesn't look exactly the way you want at first; there are many ways to change WordArt appearance.

Edit WordArt Text

- If you need to edit the text, double-click the WordArt to reopen the Edit WordArt Text dialog box.
  - ✓ *You can also click the Edit Text button on the WordArt toolbar.*

Format WordArt

- When a piece of WordArt is selected, the WordArt toolbar appears. It contains buttons you can use to modify the WordArt appearance.

  - ✓ *WordArt formatting applies to the entire piece of WordArt; you cannot format one part of it differently from another. Create two separate pieces of WordArt if you need that capability.*

- The WordArt Gallery button reopens the WordArt Gallery dialog box, which you used to create the WordArt originally. You can use it to select a different style to start with.

- The Format WordArt button opens a Format WordArt dialog box, very similar to the Format Picture and Format Text Box dialog boxes you have seen in earlier lessons. You can use it to control the border, fill, and wrapping options for the WordArt, among other settings.

- The WordArt Shape button opens a palette of alternative shapes you can apply to the WordArt, instead of the one that came with the style you chose initially from the gallery.

Select a shape from the WordArt Shape button's menu

- You can also change the WordArt shape by dragging a yellow diamond on the WordArt.

Yellow diamonds

- The yellow diamonds are reshaping handles. Dragging one of them modifies the chosen object without changing its basic shape; for example, for a wave, dragging the diamond makes the wave more dramatic or more subtle.
  - ✓ *Some WordArt has a single yellow diamond; other WordArt has two. It depends on the shape you chose.*

- The Text Wrapping button works just like with clip art; it controls how text in an overlapping text box interacts with the WordArt.

- The WordArt Same Letter Heights button toggles the letters between normal size and **even heights** (that is, all letters the same height, including capitals).

- The WordArt **Vertical Text** button toggles between normal layout and stacked layout (that is, the letters running vertically but appearing in normal orientation, as shown here).

This WordArt uses vertical text

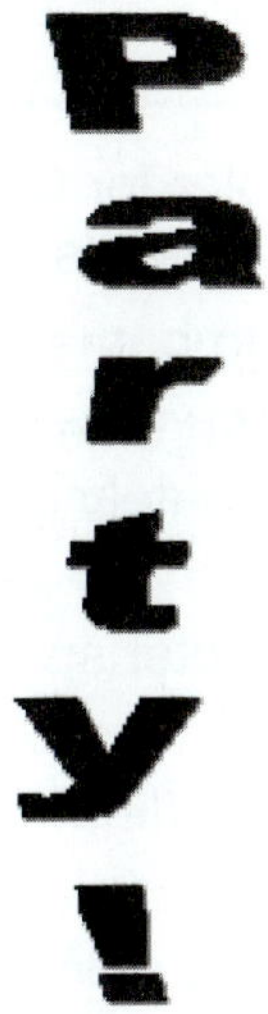

- To adjust the horizontal alignment within the frame, click the WordArt Alignment button. This opens a drop-down list of alignments from which to choose.
- The WordArt Character Spacing button opens a drop-down list of character spacing choices, such as Loose and Tight. These are like the spacing choices you learned about in Exercise 18.
- In addition to the buttons on the WordArt toolbar, you can apply many of the formatting features you have learned about in earlier lessons.
- For example, you can apply fill and border coloring, fill effects, 3-D effects, and shadows.

Procedures

Create WordArt

1. Display page on which you want to place the WordArt.
2. Click the **Insert WordArt** button on the Objects toolbar.
3. Click a WordArt style.
4. Click **OK**.......................... Enter
5. Type the text for the WordArt.

   ✓ *Try to limit your WordArt to two or three words. WordArt begins to look distorted when there is too much text.*
6. Select basic font formatting for the WordArt:
   - **Font**........................ Alt+F
   - **Size**........................ Alt+S
   - **Bold**............................ B
   - **Italic**............................ I
7. Click **OK**.......................... Enter

Edit WordArt Text

1. Double-click the WordArt.
2. Edit the text.
3. Change the basic font formatting if desired:
   - **Font**........................ Alt+F
   - **Size**........................ Alt+S
   - **Bold**............................ B
   - **Italic**............................ I
4. Click **OK**.......................... Enter

Change WordArt Style

1. Click the WordArt to select it.

   ✓ *The WordArt toolbar appears.*
2. Click **WordArt Gallery** button.
3. Click new style to use.
4. Click **OK**.......................... Enter

Change WordArt Shape

1. Click the WordArt to select it.

   ✓ *The WordArt toolbar appears.*
2. Click **WordArt Shape** button.
3. Click new shape to use.
4. (Optional) Drag yellow diamond on WordArt to fine-tune shape.

Format WordArt

1. Click the WordArt to select it.

   ✓ *The WordArt toolbar appears.*
2. Do any of the following:
   - Click **Text Wrapping** button and select new text wrap setting.
   - Click **WordArt Same Letter Heights** button to toggle letter height uniformity.
   - Click **WordArt Vertical Text** button to toggle vertical text.
   - Click **WordArt Alignment** button and select new alignment setting.
   - Click **WordArt Character Spacing** button and choose spacing setting.

     ✓ *You can also change WordArt fill color, border color, border style, shadow, and 3-D effect using the skills you have learned in earlier exercises.*

Exercise Directions

1. Start Publisher, if necessary.
2. Open the file **PUB34**. Save it as **34OPEN**.
3. Delete the **Open House and Wetlands Tour** text box.
4. Create a new WordArt object at the top of the space that says **Wetlands Tour** and then create another one directly below it that says **Open House**.
   - ✓ *For each piece of WordArt, begin with the third style in the top row of the WordArt Gallery, and with Arial 32-point Bold text.*
5. For each WordArt object, change the font to Times New Roman 36 point.
6. Change the shape of the Wetlands Tour WordArt so that it is a downward arch, rather than an upward one.
7. Change the fill color for Open House to bright yellow, and for Wetlands Tour to bright green.
8. Apply a shadow to both pieces.
9. Resize the WordArt objects if needed so they are each approximately 5" in width, and center them horizontally on the page.
10. Change the character spacing on Wetlands Tour to Loose.
11. Change the border (line) color on Wetlands Tour to dark green.
12. Create a new piece of WordArt that says **and**. Place it between the other two pieces. Use any style and formatting that you think is attractive.
13. Print the publication. Illustration A shows the finished WordArt.
14. Save your work and exit Publisher.

Illustration A

On Your Own

1. Start Publisher, if necessary.
2. Start a new, blank publication.
3. Create six different WordArt objects on the page, with the following phrases:
   - **Sale**
   - **Check Us Out**
   - **New and Improved**
   - **Please Recycle**
   - **Good News!**
   - **Welcome**
4. Use completely different formatting for each of them. Make it a challenge to see how different each WordArt object can be.
5. Save your work as **34WORDART** and exit Publisher.

Exercise 35

Skills Covered:

◆ **Align Objects** ◆ **Distribute Objects** ◆ **Flip Objects**
◆ **Rotate Objects** ◆ **Nudge Objects** ◆ **Set Object Layering**

On the Job

Now that you know how to place and create different kinds of objects on a page (drawn shapes, WordArt, clip art, and so on), have some fun with them! Publisher includes commands that let you rotate and flip objects, align them precisely with one another, and even stack them.

You'll start a new project in this exercise. The Literacy League is awarding All-Star Volunteer prizes to some of its volunteers, and they need some help with their flyer. You will align the pictures with one another, position them precisely, and layer them with some drawn shapes to add interest.

Terms

Free Rotate To rotate an object by a precise amount, instead of one of the presets (90 or 180 degrees). In earlier versions of Publisher it is called *custom rotate*.

Nudge To move an object in one direction by a precise amount.

Notes

Align Objects

- Sometimes you might want some objects to align neatly with one another. For example, if you have three pictures side by side, you might want the tops of them to align vertically.
- You can align all kinds of objects with one another; they need not be the same type or even similar. You could align a picture with a text box, for example.
- To align objects with one another, select the objects (by holding down the Shift key as you click on each one). Then choose Arrange, Align or Distribute, and then an align command (Align Top, Align Left, etc.).

Set alignment for the selected objects

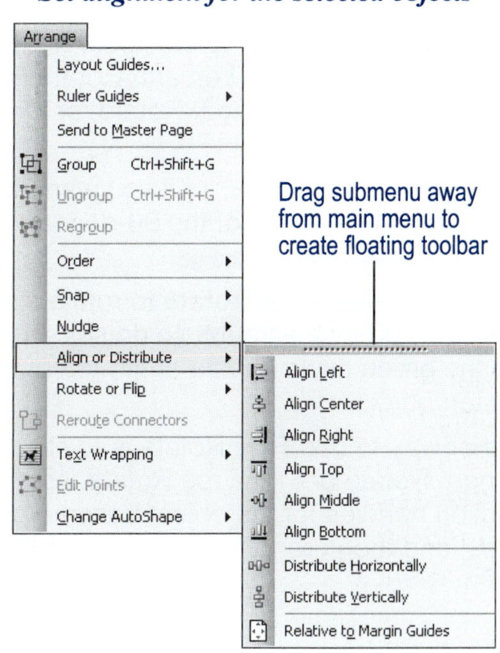

- The Relative to Margin Guides command is an on/off toggle. It's off by default. When you turn it on, all alignment commands refer to positioning in relation to the margin guides rather than in relation to the other selected objects.
- For example, when Relative to Margin Guides is off, and you choose Align Left for two objects, it determines the leftmost one and then moves the others to match it. When Relative Margin Guides is on, it moves both items to align with the left margin guide, regardless of their former positions.

✓ *Most of the submenus on the Arrange menu can be dragged off it to create floating toolbars. If you need to apply commands from one repeatedly, this can be a great time saver. Drag it by the dotted line at the top of the submenu.*

Distribute Objects

- When you select three or more objects, the Distribute commands become available. Distribution spaces out the objects evenly so that there is the same amount of blank space between each object and the others.
- You can distribute either vertically or horizontally.

Flip Objects

- You can flip an object along its vertical or horizontal axis.
- Select the object and then choose Arrange, Rotate or Flip, and then either Flip Vertical or Flip Horizontal.

Rotate Objects

- You can rotate an object to the left or right 90 degrees with the Rotate Left and Rotate Right commands (on the Arrange, Rotate, or Flip menu).
- Rotations are cumulative, so if you want to rotate 180 degrees, issue one of the 90-degree rotation commands twice.
- You can also use **Free Rotate** to rotate an object by a precise amount. To do so, simply drag the green circle handle at the top of the selected object.
- Another way to use Free Rotate is to choose Arrange, Rotate or Flip, Free Rotate, so that the selection handles for the object become green circles, and then drag one of those handles.
- There is also a Rotation box on the Measurement toolbar. (Choose View, Toolbars, Measurement to display it.)

You can adjust the rotation from the Measurements toolbar, too

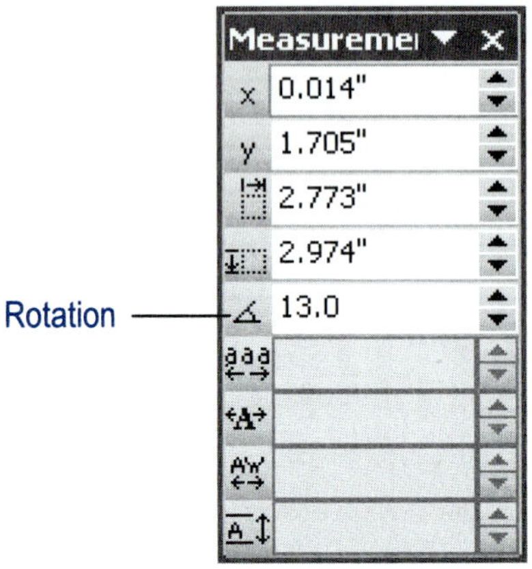

Nudge Objects

- **Nudging** an object moves it a precise amount in a certain direction. It's useful when you are having trouble making an object align precisely where you want it by dragging it into place.
- To nudge an object, select it, and press an arrow key. Each time you press the arrow, the object moves by a certain amount (the default is 0.13").
- You can also use the menu system to nudge. Choose Arrange, Nudge, and then the direction you want to nudge (Right, Left, Up, or Down).

✓ *To change the default nudge amount, choose Tools, Options, and on the Edit tab, mark the Arrow keys nudge objects by check box and then enter a different value into its text box.*

Set Object Layering

- You can stack objects in Publisher to create interesting special effects. For example, you might stack a photo on top of a drawn shape to create a mat or frame for the picture.
- When you stack objects, the objects created most recently appear at the top of the stack. You can change the stack order, however.
- To change an object's position in the stack, select the object and then choose Arrange, Order, and then a placement.

Select an arrangement from the Arrange, Order menu

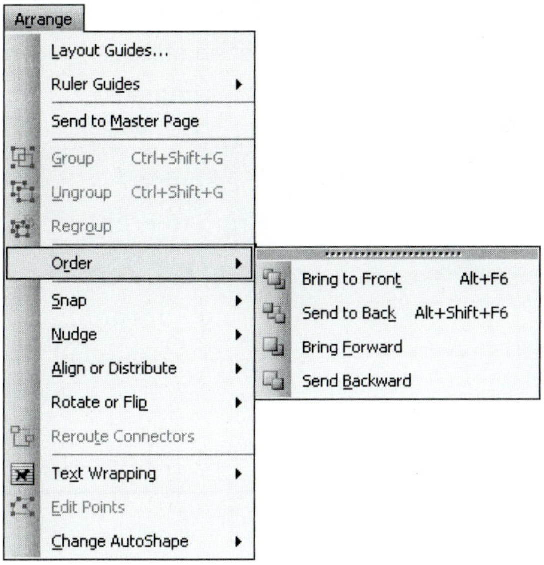

- Bring to Front moves the object to the top of the stack. A shortcut is Alt+F6.
- Send to Back moves the object to the bottom of the stack. A shortcut is Alt+Shift+F6.
- Bring Forward moves the object one position toward the top of the stack.
- Send Backward moves it one position toward the bottom.

Procedures

Align Objects

1. (Optional) If you want to align relative to margin guides, do the following first:
   a. Click **Arrange** .... Alt+R
   b. Point to **Align or Distribute** .... A
   c. Click **Relative to Margin Guides** .... O
2. Select the object(s) to align.
   ✓ *For alignment relative to margin guides, you can select a single object; for all other alignments, you must select at least two objects.*
3. Click **Arrange** .... Alt+R
4. Point to **Align or Distribute** .... A
5. Click an alignment option:
   - **Align Left** L
   - **Align Center** C
   - **Align Right** .... R
   - **Align Top** .... T
   - **Align Middle** .... M
   - **Align Bottom** .... B

   ✓ *If you have turned on Relative to Margin Guides, you must repeat step 1 to turn it off again before you can do any other kind of alignment.*

Distribute Objects

1. Select at least three objects to distribute.
2. Click **Arrange** .... Alt+R
3. Point to **Align or Distribute** .... A
4. Click **Distribute Vertically** V

   OR

   Click **Distribute Horizontally** .... H

Flip an Object

1. Select an object.
2. Click **Arrange** .... Alt+R
3. Click **Rotate or Flip** .... P
4. Click one of the following:
   - **Flip Horizontal** .... H
   - **Flip Vertical** V

Rotate an Object by 90 Degrees

1. Select an object.
2. Click **Arrange** .... Alt+R
3. Click **Rotate or Flip** .... P
4. Click one of the following:
   - **Rotate Left 90°** L
   - **Rotate Right 90°** .... R

Free Rotate

1. Select an object.
2. Position mouse pointer over **rotation handle** (green circle) at top of object.
3. Drag to rotate object.

OR

1. Select an object.
2. Click **Arrange** .... Alt+R
3. Click **Rotate or Flip** .... P
4. Click **Free Rotate** .... T
   ✓ *Selection handles of object turn into green circles.*
5. Drag any selection handle to rotate object.

Nudge Objects

1. Select an object.
2. Press an **arrow key** for direction you want it to move .... [arrow keys]

Adjust Nudge Amount

1. Click **Tools** .... Alt + T
2. Click **Options** .... O
3. Click **Edit** tab.
4. Click **Arrow keys nudge objects by** .... Alt + N
5. Enter a nudge amount.
6. Click **OK** .... Enter

Set Object Layering (Alt+F6/ Alt+Shift+F6)

1. Select an object.
2. Click **Arrange**............. Alt + R
3. Click **Order**.......................... R
4. Click an order:
   - **Bring to Front** .... T
   - **Send to Back** .... K
   - **Bring Forward** .... F
   - **Send Backward** .... B

Exercise Directions

1. Start Publisher, if necessary.
2. Open the file **PUB35**. Save it as **35AWARDS**.
3. Top-align the pictures with one another.
4. Crop the pictures as needed so they are all the same height.
5. Use Align Center to align each caption beneath its picture, and then group the picture with the caption.
6. Distribute the pictures horizontally.
7. Select all three pictures and the WordArt and group it all into a single object.
8. Center the object vertically and horizontally in relation to the margin guides.
9. Ungroup the object.
10. Behind the leftmost picture, place the Explosion 2 AutoShape, as shown in Illustration A, with a bright yellow fill.

    ✓ *Explosion 2 is the second AutoShape in the Stars and Banners category.*
11. Copy the AutoShape, and flip the copy horizontally. Place the copy behind the rightmost picture, as in Illustration A.
12. Bottom-align the two AutoShapes with one another.
13. Print the publication.
14. Save your work and exit Publisher.

Illustration A

On Your Own

1. Start Publisher, if necessary.
2. Create a new, blank publication.
3. Choose a piece of clip art and insert it. Then copy the clip art twice and place the copies side by side.
4. Top align the copies and distribute them horizontally. Flip the middle copy horizontally, and flip the right copy vertically.
5. Place a different AutoShape (each filled with a different color or other fill) behind each picture as a background matte.
6. Place a large rectangle over the top of all clips and AutoShapes, covering them completely, and then move it to the back of the stack so it functions as a background.
7. Save your work as **35SHAPES** and exit Publisher.

Exercise 36

Skills Covered:

◆ **Insert Objects** ◆ **Insert an Existing File**
◆ **Copy Data from Another Program**
◆ **Edit an Embedded Object** ◆ **Update Links**

On the Job

Sometimes the data you want to include in a publication is in another program's format. You might have a table in Excel, for example, or a chart in PowerPoint. There are a number of ways to include such data in your Publisher publication.

In this exercise, you will continue to work with the All-Star Volunteers flyer. You'll create a link to part of an Excel spreadsheet on a second page, showing some information about each of the award-winning volunteers.

Terms

Object An object is anything that appears in a publication in its own frame. It can be a picture, a piece of WordArt, a drawn shape, and so on. *Object* can also mean a block of data that comes from another program. (This latter definition is the operative one for this exercise.)

Embedding A method of maintaining a connection between a foreign object in Publisher (that is, an object created using a different program) and the program that created it, so that when you double-click the object, the original program opens to help you edit it.

Link The connection between a copy of an object and its original source. When the source changes, the copy changes, too.

Notes

Insert Objects

- You have already seen in earlier lessons how to insert certain types of objects, such as pictures and text.
- Other **object** types, such as data from Excel, PowerPoint, or Access, do not have special menu commands, so you must rely on the generic Insert, Object command.
- Choosing Insert, Object opens the Insert Object dialog box. Here you can choose to create a new, embedded object or place an existing file as an object.
- When you create a new object within Publisher, the new object is **embedded**. You can double-click that object at any time to reopen it for editing in whatever program it was created in.
- To create a new object, click the Create New button in the Insert Object dialog box. Then choose the object type from the list. The object types on the list come from the installed programs on your system, so your list may look different from the one shown.

Select the type of object you want to create

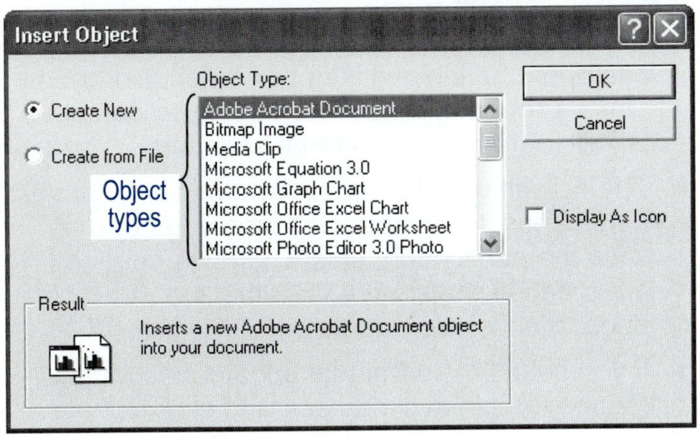

- After you choose an object type and click OK, the chosen application opens, and you can create the new object using it. Depending on the application chosen, the controls may be integrated with the Publisher window, as shown below, or they may be in an entirely separate window.

Here, a new Excel worksheet is being created within Publisher

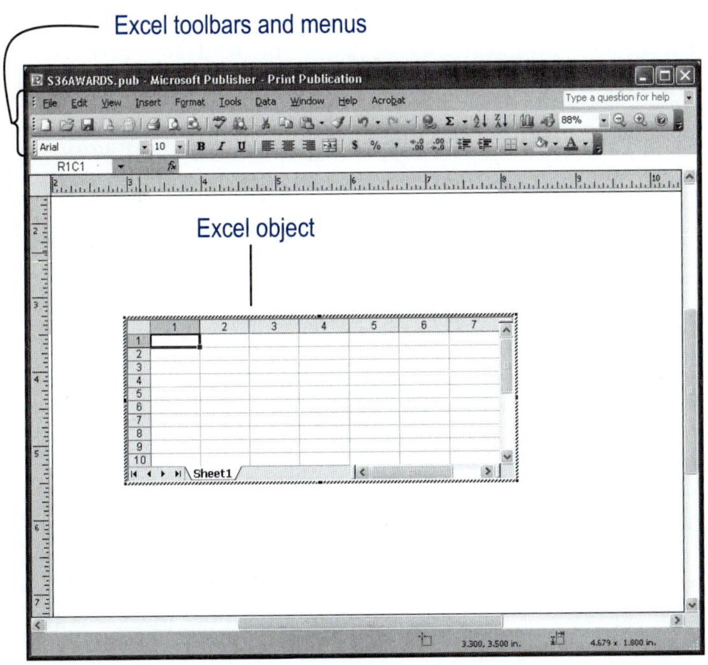

- When you're finished editing the object, click the Publisher page (outside the object) to return to Publisher. Or, if the application opened in a separate window, open the File menu and choose the Exit & Return to {*publication name*} command. (If you do not see this command, simply use the regular File, Exit command.)

Insert an Existing File

- Clicking the Create from File button in the Insert Object dialog box displays a File text box, in which you can type the path to the file you want. (You can also click Browse to locate it if needed.)

Use Create from File to specify an existing file to insert

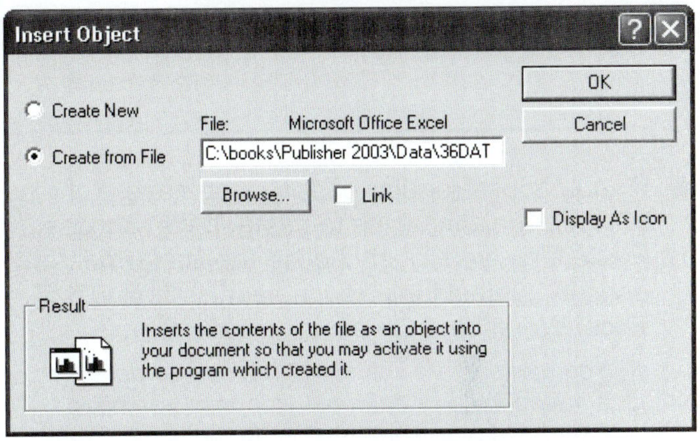

- Inserting an existing file inserts the entire document in that file; you can't choose a specific portion of the document. See the following section if you want only a certain part of the file (such as a few specific cells from a spreadsheet).
- If you want to create a **link** between the original and the copy in your publication, mark the Link check box. Don't mark this unless you need the feature, however, because it increases file size and slows down file saving and opening.

Copy Data from Another Program

- You can use the Clipboard to copy and paste data between applications, just as you learned to do with text blocks in Lesson 1.
- If you want to copy and create a link, or copy in a specific format, use the Edit, Paste Special command instead of regular pasting. Doing so opens the Paste Special dialog box.
- In the Paste Special dialog box, you can choose between regular pasting (Paste) and link pasting (Paste Link).

Paste in a particular format, or paste as a link

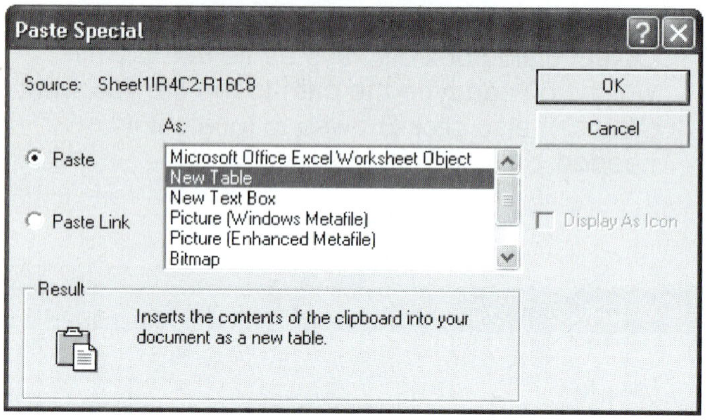

- If you choose regular pasting, you have a choice of file formats in which to paste. If you choose Paste Link, you must choose the file format that ends in "Object Link" (such as Microsoft Office Excel Worksheet Object Link, for example).
  - ✓ *You can paste a link only if the copied data is from a saved file. For example, suppose you open Excel and type some text in the cells, and then copy that text to the Clipboard. You cannot use Paste Special to Paste Link unless you have saved your work in Excel, because otherwise there is no Excel file name to create the link to.*

Edit an Embedded Object

- To edit an embedded object, double-click on it. The object opens in the program that created it. If it is a linked object, the original file opens; if merely embedded, it opens as a new file.

Update Links

- In a publication that contains linked objects, you can open the Links dialog box by choosing Edit, Links. From the Links dialog box, you can set a link for automatic or manual updating.
- The default update setting for a link is Automatic; that means it updates each time you open or save the publication, plus whenever changes are made to the source file while the Publisher publication is open, too.
- If you set a link to Manual update, you must reopen the Links dialog box and click Update Now every time you want to update it.

Set each link to either Automatic or Manual

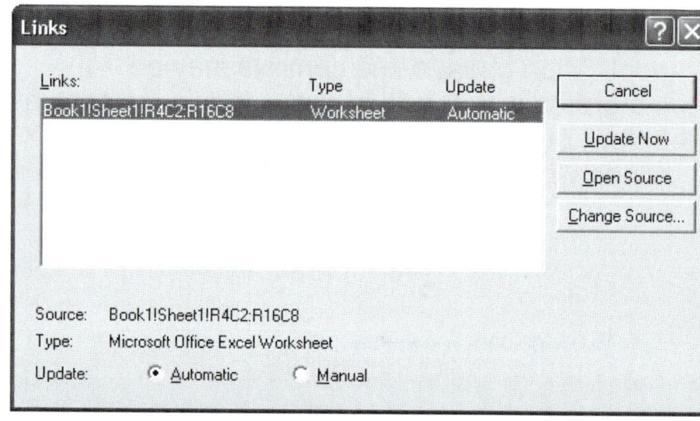

✓ *If you have many links in your publication, your PC's performance may slow down while it takes the time required to update each link in the file. This can make the process of opening and saving the file unnecessarily drawn out. Setting all links to Manual prevents the link updating from slowing you down.*

Procedures

Create a New Embedded Object

1. Click **Insert** .... Alt+I
2. Click **Object** .... O
3. Click **Create New**........ Alt+N
4. Click an object type on the **Object Type** list.......... Alt+T
5. Click **OK**........................ Enter
6. Create the new object using the program controls that appear.
7. Do one of the following to return to Publisher:
   - If the program opened in the Publisher window, click on the Publisher page, outside of the object.
   - If the program opened in its own window, click **File** and then click **Exit & Return to *{publication name}***.

Insert an Existing File

1. Click **Insert** .... Alt+I
2. Click **Object**........................ O
3. Click **Create from File** .... Alt+F
4. Click **Browse** .... Alt+B
5. Locate and select the file you want to insert.
6. Click **Insert**................. Alt+I
7. If you want to create a link, click the **Link** check box.................... Alt+L
8. Click **OK**.......................... Enter

Copy Data from Another Program

1. Open the program containing the data and select it.
2. Click **Edit** .... Alt+E
3. Click **Copy** C
4. Switch back to Publisher, and display the page on which you want to place the copy.
5. Click **Edit** .... Alt+E
6. Click **Paste Special** .... S
7. Click one of the following:
   - **Paste** to paste the data without a link .... Alt+P
   - **Paste Link** to paste the data and link it .... Alt+L
8. Click the format you want from the **As** list. (You do not have a choice if you chose Paste Link.) .... Alt+A
9. Click **OK** .... Enter

Edit an Embedded Object

1. Double-click the object to open it.
2. Edit the object.
3. Do one of the following to return to Publisher:
   - If the program opened in the Publisher window, click on the Publisher page, away from the object.
   - If the program opened in its own window, click **File** and then click **Exit & Return to *{publication name}*** or **Exit**.

Set Link Updating

1. Click **Edit** .... Alt+E
2. Click **Links** .... K
3. Click the link you want to change.
4. Click **Automatic** .... Alt+A

   OR

   Click **Manual** .... Alt+M
5. Click **Close** .... Enter

Update a Link Manually

1. Click **Edit** .... Alt+E
2. Click **Links** .... K
3. Click the link you want to update.
4. Click **Update Now** .... Alt+U
5. Click **Close** .... Enter

Exercise Directions

✓ *This exercise requires Microsoft Excel. If you do not have Excel, try linking content from some other program on your own instead, such as Word, Notepad, or Paint.*

1. Start Publisher, if necessary.
2. Open the file **PUB36**. Save it as **36AWARDS**.
3. Insert a new, blank page after the first one, and display the blank page.
4. Insert the Excel file **36DATA.xls** as a linked object in the center of the page.
5. Double-click the object, opening it in Excel for editing.
6. Make the first row bold, and center-align the first row.

   ✓ *If you need help working in Excel, ask your instructor for assistance.*
7. Return to Publisher, closing Excel and saving your work.
8. Set the link to manual updating.
9. Open the file **36DATA.xls** in Excel, and center the text in the Years of Service column. Then close Excel, saving your work.
10. Return to Publisher and update the link. The Excel data should appear with the formatting you applied, as shown in Illustration A.
11. Print the publication.
12. Save your work and exit Publisher.

Illustration A

Name	Profession	Years of Service	Quote
Henry Gonzalez	Carpenter	4	"I love helping people learn to read because it opens up their minds to new and exciting ideas and possibilities."
Richard Vargas	Pastor	3	"Children are naturally loving, gentle souls; it's up to us to help them get back to that natural state when their life situations have made them lose touch with that."
Cinda Jackson	Student	2	"All kids deserve the chance to learn to read, even if they don't always learn it in regular school."

On Your Own

1. Start Publisher, if necessary.
2. Start a new publication and save it as **36ART**.
3. Create a new embedded drawing in the center of the page using the Paint program that comes with Windows. Make the object size 6" by 6" in Publisher.
   ✓ *Choose the Paintbrush Picture object type to create.*
4. Create a drawing using any of the tools in Paint. Then return to Publisher.
5. Resize and reposition the new object in Publisher as desired.
6. Place a border around it, and add a shadow.
7. Save your work and exit Publisher.

Exercise 37

◆ **Critical Thinking**

The Pet Rescue staff has added some text to the back side of the flyer you created in Exercise 27. In this exercise, you will dress it up by adding some graphics to it.

Exercise Directions

1. Start Publisher, if necessary.
2. Open the file **PUB37**. Save it as **37PET**.
3. Display page 2.
4. Insert **37DOG.jpg** and crop it to show only the dog's head.
5. Place the image to the right of the first paragraph using Square wrapping.
6. Insert a picture of a dog from the Clip Organizer and place it to the left of the **What is the Pet Rescue Process?** paragraph with Tight wrapping.
   - ✓ *Make sure you search the clips in the Web collection; there are many good pictures of dogs there.*
   - ✓ *If any text appears to the left of the clip, use the Format Picture dialog box to prevent this from happening. To do this, choose Right Only from the Layout tab.*
7. Draw an AutoShape heart over the top of the last paragraph, and set its wrapping to None.
8. Color the heart with a Fill Effects pattern (any) that uses pale pink and white, and set its border to None.
9. Use Send to Back to send the heart behind the text. Illustration A shows the finished page.
10. Save your work and exit Publisher.

Illustration A

What is Pet Rescue?

Pet Rescue is a non-profit corporation that exists for the betterment of homeless companion animals. We are based in Decatur, Illinois but our operations extend all over the Midwest. Our ultimate goal is to place homeless animals in permanent homes, but we also maintain a system of foster homes where animals await permanent placement. While in the Pet Rescue system, animals receive any necessary veterinary care through our network of veterinarians.

What is the Rescue Process?

When we receive an animal, it goes through an evaluation with one of our staff members, and is checked by a veterinarian. If it is immediately ready for placement, volunteers try to find it a permanent home while it lives with a foster family. If some training or rehabilitation is required, the animal goes to a special foster home specializing in that type of treatment.

What is the Adoption Process?

Potential permanent owners must undergo an in-home interview and for dog adoption must show proof of a fenced yard. There are no fees associated with adoption, but a voluntary donation of $50 is requested to cover placement and veterinary costs if possible.

What Support is Available?

Pet Rescue offers pet ownership classes for new dog and cat owners once a month in several cites throughout the Midwest. Classes are free to the public, including Pet Rescue adoptive families, but a $25 donation is requested if possible.

Exercise 38

◆ **Critical Thinking**

Garden Gate Supply is preparing for a special sale and needs your help with a pricing mailer. The data is there already, and in this exercise you will improve it by adding graphics.

Exercise Directions

1. Start Publisher, if necessary.
2. Open the file **PUB38**. Save it as **38SALE**.
3. Under the Payment Policies, insert **38garden.jpg** and size it to fit the available space in that column.
4. Under the Seed Sale box at the right side of page 1, insert some clip art from the Clip Organizer that shows a flower or plant.
   - ✓ *Make sure you include the Web collections in your clip art search for best results.*
5. In the right column on page 1, ungroup the Garden Gate Supply text box from the orange frame around it.
6. Delete the Garden Gate Supply text box and replace it with WordArt that says the same thing. Then group the WordArt with the orange frame. The finished page 1 is shown Illustration A.
7. Insert another clip art image at the bottom left corner of page 2.
8. Place an AutoShape on top of the second piece of clip art, fill it with one of the scheme colors, and then move it behind the clip art so that it makes a matte behind the image.
9. Apply a shadow to the AutoShape.
10. Group the clip art and the AutoShape. The finished page 2 is shown in Illustration B.
11. Print the publication.
12. Save your work and exit Publisher.

Illustration A

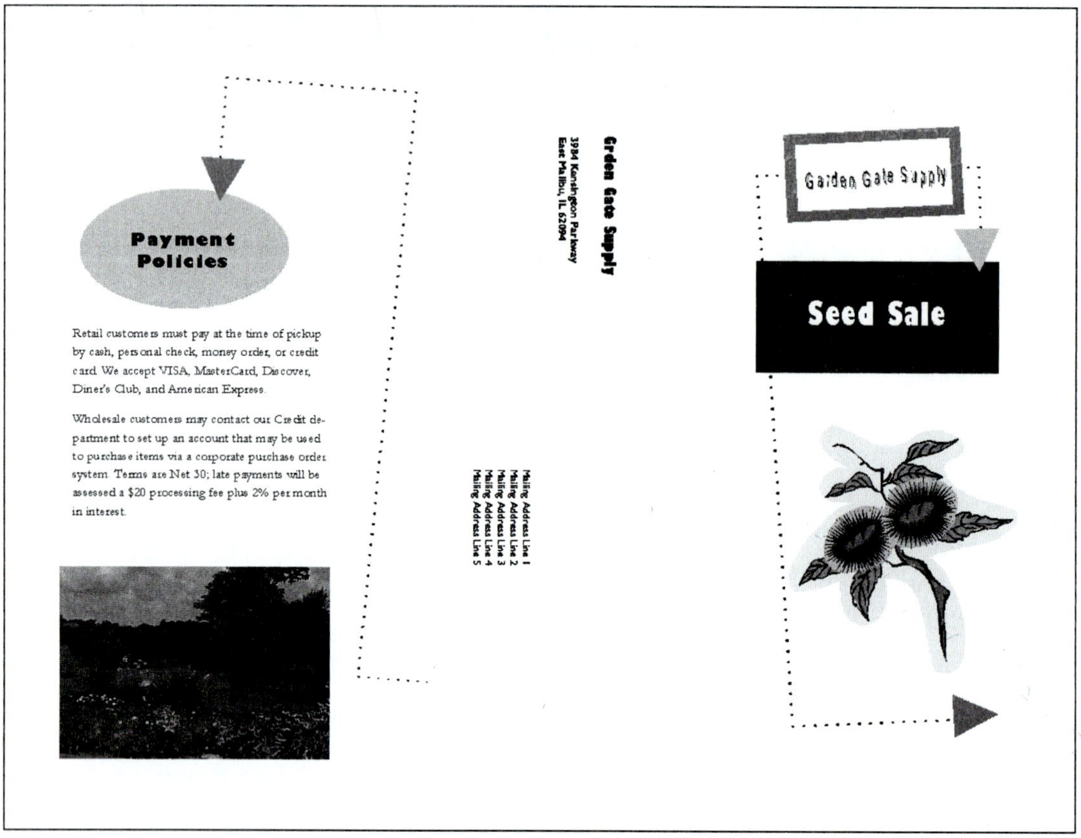

Illustration B

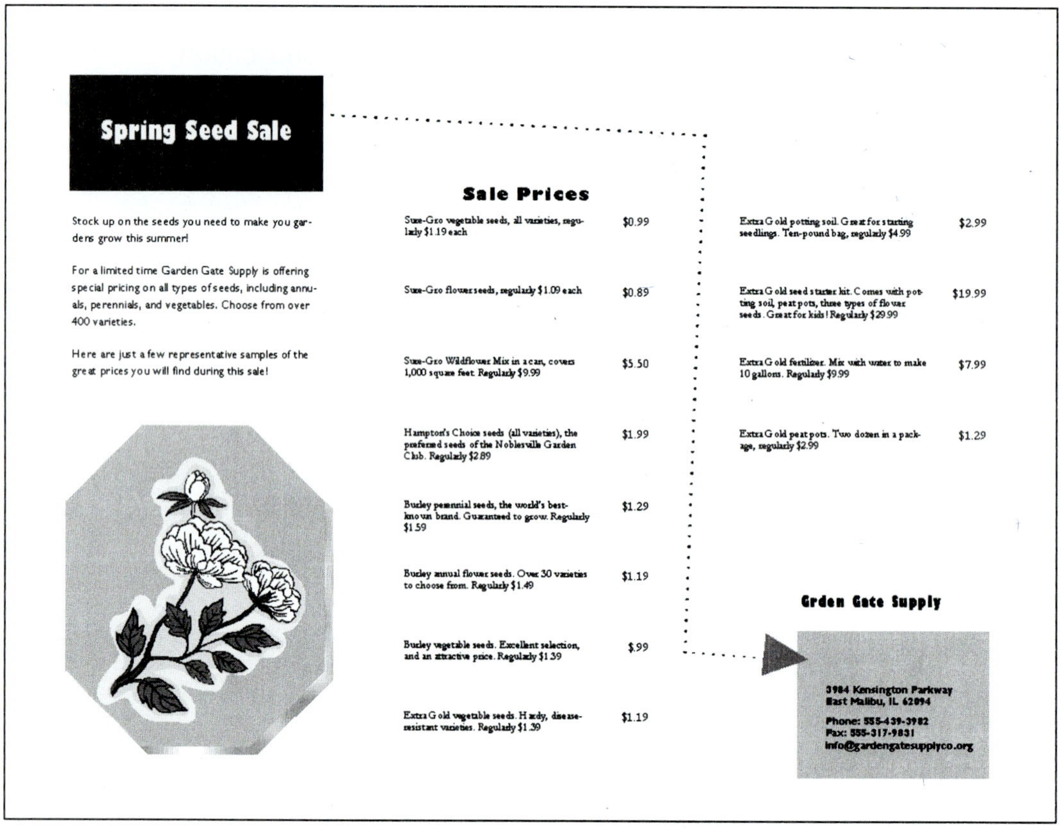

Lesson 5

Creating Various Publications

Exercise 39

- Use a Flyer Template
- Manually Place Tear-off Elements
- Customize Forms
- Customize Logos

Exercise 40

- Create a Greeting Card
- Create an Envelope
- Print an Envelope

Exercise 41

- Create Business Cards
- Use a Background

Exercise 42

- Use the Newsletter Wizard
- Enter Your Own Content in the Newsletter
- Link Text Frames
- Move Among Linked Frames
- Break a Frame Link
- Add a "Continued" Notation

Exercise 43

- Create Mailing Labels
- Mail Merge Basics
- Create an Address List in Publisher
- Edit an Address List
- Set Up a Mail Merge with the Wizard
- Set Up a Mail Merge Manually

Exercise 44

- Use the Postcard Wizard
- Merge Addresses from Outlook
- Merge Addresses from an External File
- Filter and Sort a Merge

Exercise 45

- Create a Brochure
- Choose a Color Model
- Use Specific Colors
- Use Trapping
- Link to External Graphics Files
- Embed Fonts
- Use Pack and Go

Exercise 46

- Critical Thinking

Exercise 47

- Critical Thinking

Exercise 39

Skills Covered:

◆ **Use a Flyer Template** ◆ **Manually Place Tear-off Elements**
◆ **Customize Forms** ◆ **Customize Logos**

On the Job

You've spent a lot of time so far in this book working with simple one-sheet flyers. But flyers need not be so simple! There are a variety of sophisticated Design Gallery objects you can place on a flyer, including tear-offs, coupons, and forms.

Paula Watson is starting a dog grooming service and would like to create some flyers to advertise. She wants two versions: one with phone tear-offs to post in local businesses and one with coupons to hand-deliver to the homes in her neighborhood. You will help create flyers for her in this exercise.

Terms

Flyer A single-page sheet designed for mass distribution.

Tear-off A special element designed to be torn or removed from a flyer, such as a coupon or a response form.

Notes

Use a Flyer Template

- The **Flyer** templates offer many different designs. These designs are more than just cosmetically different from one another, as with the Quick Publication Wizard; they actually include different placeholders, graphics, and **tear-off** options.
- As you can see in the figure at right, you can choose whether to have a graphic placeholder and/or a customer address, and you can select which tear-off element you want to include, if any.
- If you choose Customer Address, an additional page will be added to the publication for the back side of the flyer.
- The available tear-off elements include coupons, order forms, response forms, and sign-up forms.

Select the flyer options, including tear-offs, from the task pane

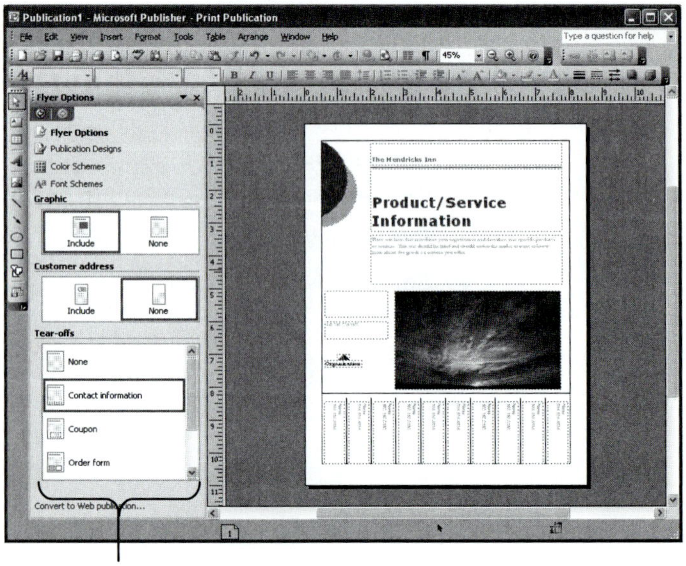

Select a tear-off

Manually Place Tear-off Elements

- You can also place tear-offs manually, with the Design Gallery.
- Some Design Gallery objects, such as coupons, have an associated wizard. You can click the Wizard button below the object to work with it.
- Other objects do not have a wizard; you simply place them in the publication from the Design Gallery and then edit their text.
- For example, the Phone Tear-off object from the Design Gallery starts with a series of identical placeholders for name and phone number. You simply click and type in one of the tear-off frames. When you click away from that box, all the other boxes update automatically to match.

Each of the boxes in a Phone Tear-off block is linked, so a change in one makes the change in the others

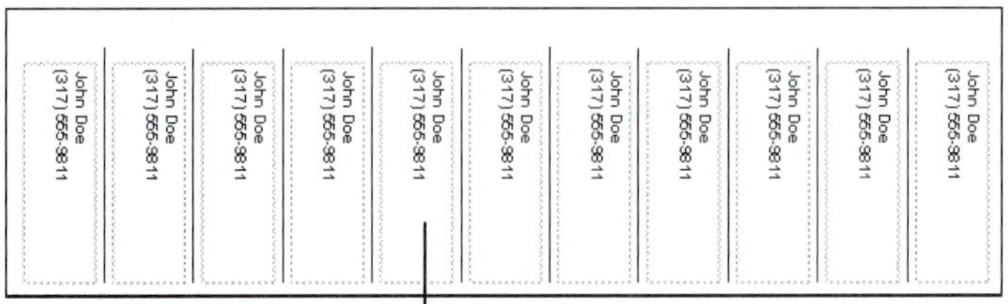

Type in any of these to change them all

✓ *Another unique feature of the Phone Tear-off element is that when you resize it horizontally, instead of each tear-off box getting wider, more boxes are added.*

- Order, response, and sign-up forms can be inserted either with a Flyer template or through the Design Gallery.
- Like a phone tear-off, these forms have no wizard attached to them; you simply type in the text boxes they create, changing the placeholder text, and adding your own names for the various blanks to be filled in.

Sample order form from Design Gallery

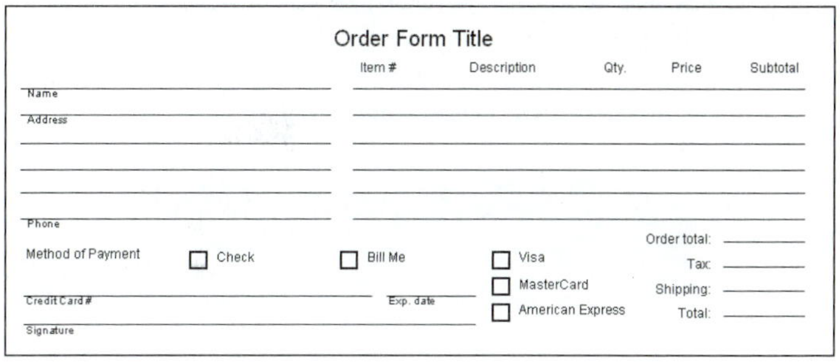

Order Form Title

Item # | Description | Qty. | Price | Subtotal

Name

Address

Phone

Method of Payment ☐ Check ☐ Bill Me ☐ Visa ☐ MasterCard ☐ American Express

Credit Card # Exp. date

Signature

Order total: Tax: Shipping: Total:

Customize Logos

- Many templates, including the Flyer template, enable you to add a logo to the publication. You can also add a logo manually with the Design Gallery.
- After placing a logo in the publication, you will want to customize it for your own company. Logos use a wizard for customization; you can click the Wizard button beneath a logo to open a task pane of options for it.
- There are two sections in the task pane when customizing a logo: Logo Options and Logo Designs.
- Logo Options provides the following settings:
  - New or existing: If you choose Publisher design, it will use the logo design you select under Logo Designs.

    If you choose Inserted picture, the Choose picture button becomes active, and you can import a graphic from a file to use as your logo. Then all other options become unavailable.
  - Graphic: Choose to use a graphic as part of the logo, or choose None to omit it.

    ✓ *To change the graphic in one of Publisher's logos, select the logo and ungroup it. Then delete the current graphic and insert your own graphic, either from disk or clip art. Move and resize it as needed, then regroup the logo with the new graphic in place.*

- Lines of text: Select the number of text boxes that the text portion of the logo should include.

Fine-tune the design with these options

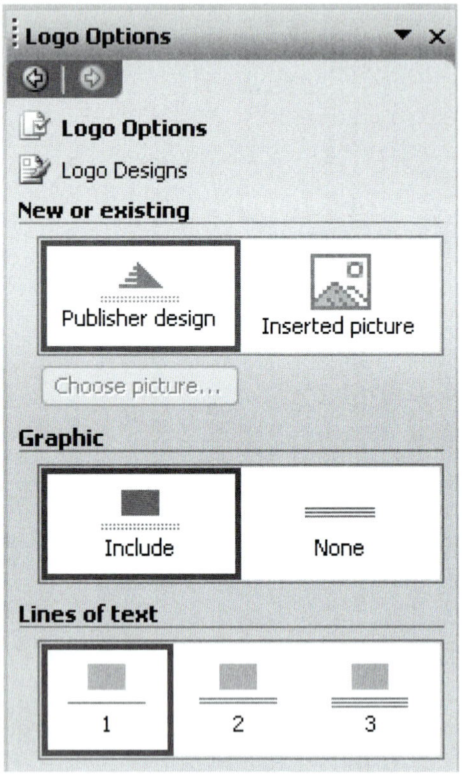

- Logo Designs lets you choose from a variety of basic logo shapes and styles.

Select a logo design

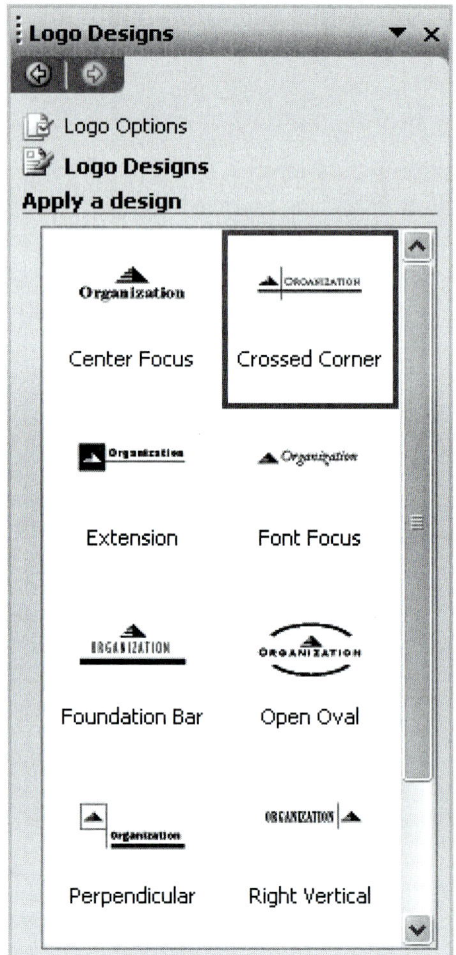

Procedures

Create a Flyer

1. Start Publisher.
2. Click **Publications for Print** on the task pane.
3. Click **Flyers**.
4. Click the category of flyer you want.
5. Click a flyer design.
   ✓ *The Flyer Options appear in the task pane.*
6. Under Graphic, if available, click **Include** or **None**.
7. Under Customer address, click **Include** or **None**.
8. Under Tear-offs, if available, click the tear-off type desired, or click **None**.
9. Click **Color Schemes** and choose a color scheme.
10. Click **Font Schemes** and choose a font scheme.
    ✓ *See Exercise 10 for help with color and font schemes.*
11. Replace the text and graphics on the flyer with your own.

Insert Design Gallery Object

1. Display page on which object should appear.
2. Click **Insert** .... Alt+I
3. Click **Design Gallery Object** .... D
4. Click the desired category.
5. Click the desired object.
6. Click **Insert Object** .... Enter
7. Customize the object as needed.

Customize Phone Tear-offs

1. Click in any of the text frames in the Phone Tear-off area.
2. Select the existing text there.
3. Type new text, replacing the existing text.
4. Click outside the text frame. All other frames are updated, too.

Customize a Form

1. Click in any of the form's text boxes.
2. Select the text there that you don't want.
3. Type new text, replacing the old text.
4. Format text, changing size, font, and other attributes as desired.
   - ✓ *Refer to Exercise 18 for help formatting text.*

Customize a Logo

1. Insert a logo from Design Gallery if there is no logo already in the publication.
   - ✓ *See "Insert Design Gallery Object."*
2. Select logo object.
3. Click **Wizard** button below logo.
   - ✓ *Logo options appear in the task pane.*
4. Click desired logo design.
5. Click **Logo Options**.
6. Under Graphic, click **Include** or **None**.
7. Under Lines of Text, click **1**, **2**, or **3**.
   - ✓ *You will probably want to zoom in for a closer view of the logo at this point.*
8. Edit logo text as needed.

Import an Existing Graphic as a Logo

1. Follow steps 1–3 under "Customize Logo."
2. Click **Logo Options**.
3. Under New or existing, click **Inserted Picture**.
4. Click **Choose picture** ...... Enter
5. Select the picture to use.
6. Click **Insert** .... Enter

Exercise Directions

1. Start Publisher, if necessary.
2. Start a new flyer using the Blends Special Offer design of the Flyer template.
3. Choose a different color scheme (your choice).
4. In the task pane, choose None for the flyer's graphic.
5. Delete the "2 for 1" attention getter graphic at the top.
6. Edit the text on the flyer to match Illustration A, deleting any text boxes that you don't need.
   - ✓ *If you are in a hurry and don't want to type all that text, open the file* **PUB39** *and use that file.*
7. Save your work as **39WASH**.
8. Use the Flyer Options to insert phone tear-offs (called *Contact information* in the task pane listing).
   - ✓ *Notice that the logo is now missing.*
9. Use the Flyer Options to remove the phone tear-offs. (Set the tear-off setting to None.)
10. Move the logo so that it is no longer in the space where the tear-off should go.
11. Insert the phone tear-off object from the Design Gallery.
    - ✓ *If asked whether you want to change to a design that includes tear-offs, click No. Such designs omit the logo placeholder, and we want to keep it.*
12. Move and resize the inserted tear-off as needed so it fills the blank space at the bottom of the flyer.
13. Customize the tear-offs with the following information:

    Paw Washer
    (387) 555-5585
14. Delete the **Paw Washer** text box at the top of the flyer, and move the logo into its place.
15. Replace the **Organization** text on the logo with **Paw Washer**.
16. Using the Logo Wizard, change to the Extension design for the logo.
17. Remove the logo graphic using Logo Options.
18. Enlarge the logo to an attractive and readable size. See Illustration B.
19. Save your work, and then save it again as **39COUPON**.
    - ✓ *If asked whether you want to save the new logo as the default, choose No.*
20. Delete the phone tear-off, and place a coupon in that spot (from the Design Gallery) offering 15% off for first-time customers. Set the expiration date to 1/1/2006. Illustration C shows an example.
21. Print the publication.
22. Save your work and exit Publisher.

Illustration A

PAW WASHER — *18 point*

Dog Grooming

88 South May Drive
Springfield, IL 62187
Phone: (387) 555—5585
— *14 point*

With today's busy schedules, it's easy to overlook your dog's grooming. Whether your pet needs a bath, a manicure, or just a good brushing, let me take care of it for you!

I am a dog lover with three of my own, and will treat your pet with care. Your dog will come back sweet-smelling and tidy, making him or her a more pleasant companion for you.

And because Paw Washer is a mobile service, I come to you! No need to pick up or drop off your pet.

Available Services

- Baths
- Nail clipping
- Haircuts
- Removing dead hair
- Show grooming
- Teeth cleaning

12 point

Organization

Illustration B

Paw Washer — *Customized logo*

Dog Grooming

88 South May Drive
Springfield, IL 62187
Phone: (387) 555—5585

With today's busy schedules, it's easy to overlook your dog's grooming. Whether your pet needs a bath, a manicure, or just a good brushing, let me take care of it for you!

I am a dog lover with three of my own, and will treat your pet with care. Your dog will come back sweet-smelling and tidy, making him or her a more pleasant companion for you.

And because Paw Washer is a mobile service, I come to you! No need to pick up or drop off your pet.

Available Services

- Baths
- Nail clipping
- Haircuts
- Removing dead hair
- Show grooming
- Teeth cleaning

Phone tear-offs

Paw Washer (387) 555-5585	Paw Washer (387) 555-5585	Paw Washer (387) 555-5585	Paw Washer (387) 555-5585	Paw Washer (387) 555-5585	Paw Washer (387) 555-5585	Paw Washer (387) 555-5585	Paw Washer (387) 555-5585	Paw Washer (387) 555-5585	Paw Washer (387) 555-5585

Illustration C

First Service Visit

15% off

Paw Washer

New customers only

Call (387) 555-5585 for an appointment

Expiration Date: 01/01/06

On Your Own

1. Start Publisher, if necessary.
2. Start a new publication based on the any of the flyer templates. Save it as **39SALE**.
3. Place a Response form on the flyer and remove the picture. Include a Customer Address placeholder. (Do all these things through the Flyer Options task pane, rather than manually.)
4. Edit the text on the flyer to sell a product of your choice. (How about multi-vitamins or dog collars?)
5. Customize the logo to make it appropriate for the type of business that would sell such a product.
6. Change the Response form to an Order form.
7. Edit the order form to make it appropriate for ordering your product. Then group the entire order form into a single object and make it as large as possible, while still fitting in its spot.
8. Save your work and exit Publisher.

Exercise 40

Skills Covered:

◆ **Create a Greeting Card** ◆ **Create an Envelope** ◆ **Print an Envelope**

On the Job

Publisher can create good-looking greeting cards and invitations, either on plain paper or on specially designed cardstock of various types. It can also print the recipient's name and address directly on the envelope.

Miriam Goldstein would like to send an anniversary card to her parents Nathan and Ruth. In this exercise, you will create a card, and print an envelope in which to send it.

Terms

Half-fold A card made by folding a piece of paper in half.

Quarter-fold A card made by folding a piece of paper in half, and then in half again.

Notes

Create a Greeting Card

- Publisher can create many types of greeting cards, from thank-you notes to holiday and special-occasion greetings.
- Click Page Options in the task pane to see the available sizes. A card can be half-fold or quarter-fold:
  - A **half-fold** card takes an 8.5" x 11" sheet and folds it in half; the resulting card is 8.5" x 5.5".
  - A **quarter-fold** card folds a half-fold again, resulting in a card that is 4.25" x 5.5".
- You can also specify a custom paper size when creating a card, so that the finished product is a different size when folded up.

  ✓ *See Exercise 11 for information about special papers and custom paper sizes.*

Page options in the task pane include half- versus quarter-fold

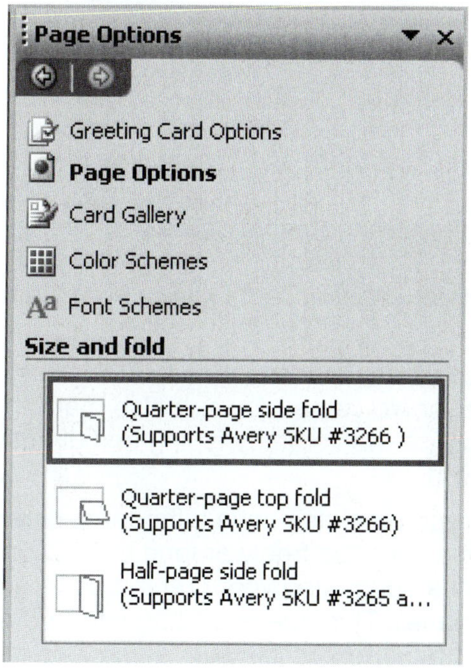

- Click Greeting Card Options in the task pane to see the available layout and design options.

Greeting Card Options include design and suggested verse

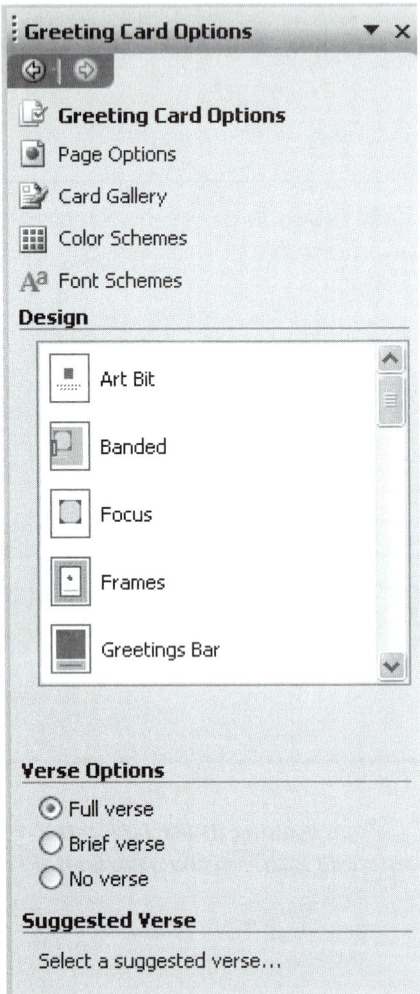

- The designs in the Design section (see above) are not different card templates; they are simply different arrangements of the same template content. If you want to choose a different template, choose Card Gallery from the task pane.
- Under Verse Options, choose Full verse, Brief verse, or No verse. You can also manually customize the verse by typing text directly onto the card.
- Different templates have different verses, but you may choose freely among them by clicking Select a suggested verse (at the bottom of the task pane). This opens a Suggested Verse dialog box from which you can choose according to occasion.

Select a greeting card verse

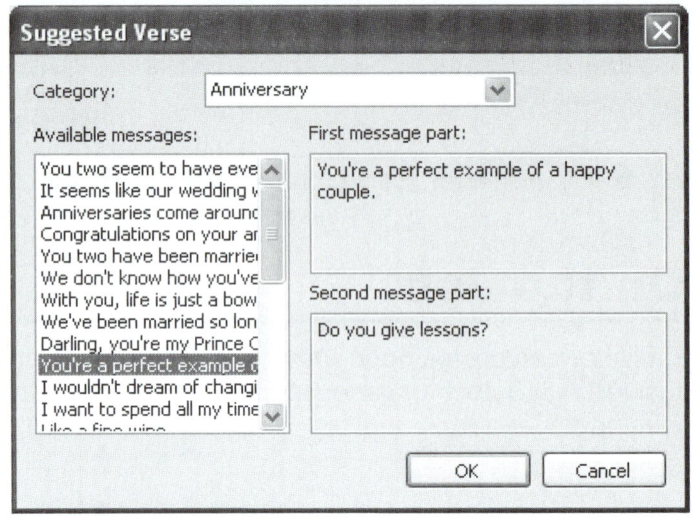

Create an Envelope

- Publisher treats an envelope as a separate publication from your greeting card.
- To create a new envelope, start with an envelope design. Placeholder text boxes appear for the mailing address and return address; simply fill in the information.
  - ✓ *There is no blank (plain) envelope template. If you want a plain envelope, you can delete any design elements, logos, and so on from the envelope layout.*

Create an envelope

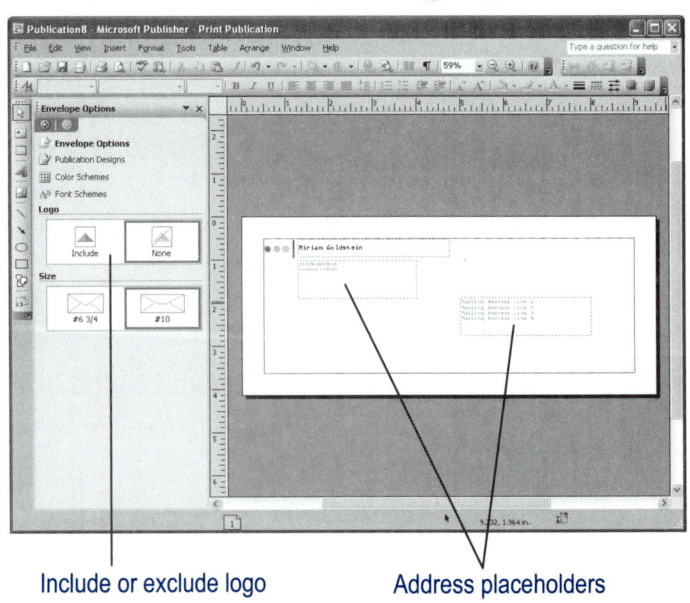

- The available envelope designs are roughly the same as the available designs for letterhead publications, so in many cases you can select an envelope design that matches your publication.
- In the task pane you can choose between two common envelope sizes: #6 ¾ and #10. If you need a different size than that, use Page Setup to set it up.
- The half-fold and quarter-fold greeting cards you create by folding up a standard sheet of paper will not fit neatly into any of the standard business sizes of envelope.
- You will need to buy special envelopes if you plan to send Publisher-created greeting cards regularly, and then set them up as a custom paper size (see Exercise 11). Look for an envelope that is approximately 4.5" x 5.75" for a quarter-fold card.

Print an Envelope

- If your printer accepts envelopes, you can inform Publisher of that fact by changing the paper type to the envelope size you are using.
- Choose File, Page Setup and then, on the Layout tab, change the Size setting to the type of envelope you have.

Choose an envelope as the Size

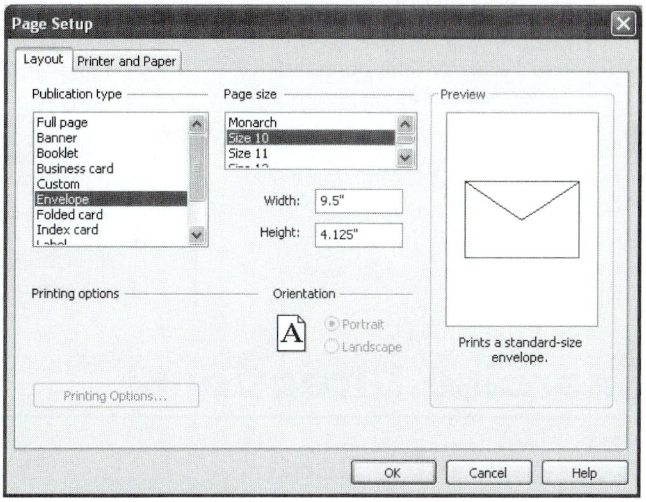

✓ *Make sure you set the Size for the same size of envelope that you chose for the envelope itself (on the Layout tab or in the task pane).*

- On the Printer and Paper tab, select the feed source from the Feed drop-down list. For example, if your printer has multiple paper trays, and one of them contains envelopes, select that tray.
- If you must manually feed envelopes into your printer, choose Envelope, Manual Feed as the source (if available) to make the printer prompt you to insert the envelope. This is useful because the printer won't forge ahead with the printing until you load the envelope and press a button on the printer to continue.

Procedures

Create a Greeting Card

1. Start Publisher, if needed.
2. Display the New Publication task pane, if needed.
3. Click **Greeting Cards** on the task pane.
4. Click a greeting card occasion.
5. Click a card template.
6. Click a design in the task pane.
7. Click a verse option: **Full verse**, **Brief verse**, or **No verse**
8. Click the Page 2 icon 2 to display page 2 (the inside of the card).
9. Type different text if desired, or see "Choose a Greeting Card Verse"
10. Click **Page Options**
11. Click a size and fold.
12. Click **Color Schemes**
13. Click a color scheme
14. Click **Font Schemes**
15. Click a font scheme

Choose a Greeting Card Verse

1. Click **Greeting Card Options** in the task pane.
2. Click **Select a suggested verse**.
3. Click the **Category** drop-down list arrow and select an occasion .... Alt+C
4. Click a message on **Available messages** list.
5. Click **OK** .... Enter

Create an Envelope

1. Display the New Publication task pane, if needed.
2. Click **Envelopes** on the task pane.
3. Click a design.

   ✓ *The task pane changes to show Envelope Options.*
4. Under Logo, click **Include** or **None**.
5. Under Size, click the envelope size to use.

   ✓ *If the size you want does not appear, see "Set a Custom Envelope Size" on the next page.*
6. Type the mailing address, replacing the placeholder text.

7. Type your return address, if it is not already correct.
   ✓ *Publisher pulls the return address from the personal information set.*
8. Delete any unwanted design elements or text boxes from the envelope.

Set a Custom Envelope Size

1. Click **File** .... Alt+F
2. Click **Page Setup** .... U
3. Click **Layout** tab.
4. Click the Page **size** drop-down list arrow and select envelope size .... Alt+S
   ✓ *Choose Custom and enter the size manually if needed.*
5. Click the **Printer and Paper** tab.
6. Click the **Source** drop-down list arrow and select envelope feed source for your printer .... Alt+C
7. Click **OK** .... Enter

Exercise Directions

Create Greeting Card

1. Start Publisher, if needed.
2. Create an anniversary greeting card using the following settings:
   - Anniversary Card 3 from the Congratulations category
   - Picture Squares design
   - Quarter-page top fold
   - Lagoon color scheme
   - Etched font scheme
3. Choose any of the verses from the Anniversary category in the Suggested Verse dialog box.
   ✓ *Choose one that would be appropriate from child to parents.*
4. Place a text box on page 3 with the following text:

   Hope you have a great anniversary,
   Mom and Dad. Love, Miriam.
5. Format the text in a script-type font (your choice).
6. Save your work as **40CARD**.
7. Print the card; then fold up the printout as a card.

Create Envelope

✓ *You do not have to possess an envelope in the size needed for this exercise, as you will not be printing the envelope publication.*

1. Start a new Envelope publication using the following settings:
   - Arrows Envelope design
   - Custom envelope size of 5.75" x 4.5".
   - Sunrise color scheme
   - Economy font scheme
   - No logo
2. Use the following for the return address:

   Miriam Goldstein
   722 Wilmington Avenue
   Boston, MA 02145
3. Use the following for the mailing address:

   Mr. and Mrs. Nathan Goldstein
   1933 Pelican Terrace #5
   Miami, FL 24113
4. Save your work as **40ENV** and exit Publisher.

On Your Own

1. Start Publisher, if necessary.
2. Create a thank-you card for your instructor to thank him or her for helping you learn Publisher. Use any settings and options you like.
3. Save the card as **40THANKS** and print it.
4. Create a party invitation, inviting your friends to celebrate a friend's birthday. Make the settings and options as different as possible from the ones you used for the thank-you card.
   ✓ *Notice that Invitations is a separate category from Greeting Cards.*
5. Save the card as **40BDAY** and print it.
6. Save your work and exit Publisher.

Exercise 41

Skills Covered:

- **Create Business Cards**
- **Use a Background**

On the Job

Many people find that Publisher can create good-quality business cards without the expense of commercial printing. The Background feature in Publisher is especially good for business cards, as it helps add interest and make the cards look more professional.

Miriam Goldstein was so pleased with the birthday card you created in Exercise 40 that she would now like you to make her some business cards for her scrapbook supplies shop, The Paper Forest.

Terms

Vertical gap The amount of space between the bottom of one copy and the top of the next one, when printing multiple copies per page.

Horizontal gap The amount of space between the right edge of one copy and the left edge of the other, when printing multiple copies per page.

Background A fill or effect applied to the entire publication, rather than an individual object.

Notes

Create Business Cards

- Publisher can help you design and print your own business cards.
- It can use plain paper or specialty paper, whichever you prefer.
  - ✓ *See Exercise 11 for help with special papers.*

A simple business card created in Publisher

- The Business Card templates work just like the other publication types you have seen in this book. You can change the design, the color scheme, and the font scheme as usual.
- The Business Card Options (in the task pane) offer the following settings:
    - Logo: Include or None
    - Orientation: Portrait or Landscape
    - Copies per sheet: One or Multiple

Card Size

- In the United States, the standard size for business cards is 3.5" x 2". You can change to a card size appropriate to either Europe or East Asia in the Page Setup dialog box.

    ✓ *It is usually not a good idea to use a nonstandard size for your business cards, because then they won't fit in business card holders and organizers in which people might want to store your card.*

Choose a business card size

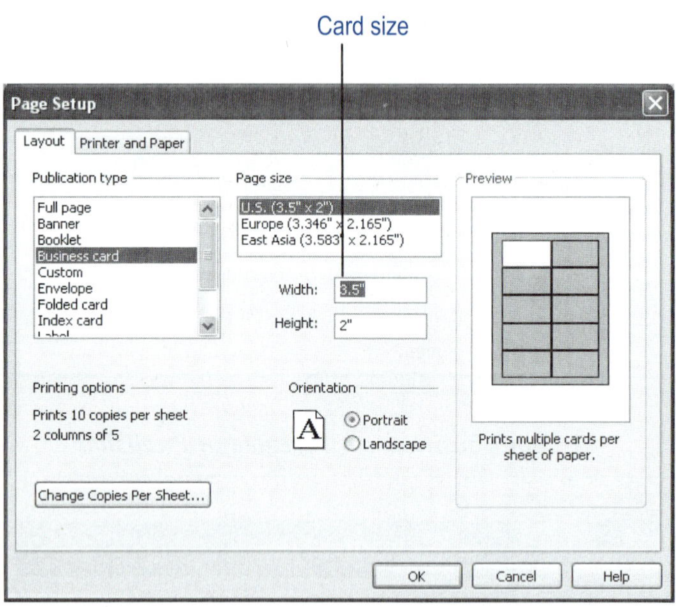

Number of Copies per Sheet

- Along with card size, you can also specify a different number of copies to print per sheet, and specify a **vertical gap** and/or **horizontal gap** between the copies on the printed page.
- When creating business cards, most people do not use a vertical or horizontal gap, so copies print flush against one another. This is useful when cutting out the cards because it minimizes the amount of trimming you must do.

    ✓ *If you change the card size, the number of copies per sheet, or either of the gaps, your printout will be out of alignment with any special paper or perforated cardstock you might print out.*

- For USA-sized business cards (3.5" × 2"), ten cards can fit on a standard letter-sized sheet, with no vertical gap or horizontal gap. To change this setting, click the Change Copies per Sheet button on the Layout tab of the Page Setup dialog box (above).
- This opens the Small Publication Print Options dialog box, where you can specify the number of rows, number of columns, and gaps between copies.

Specify how many copies per sheet and where they will be placed

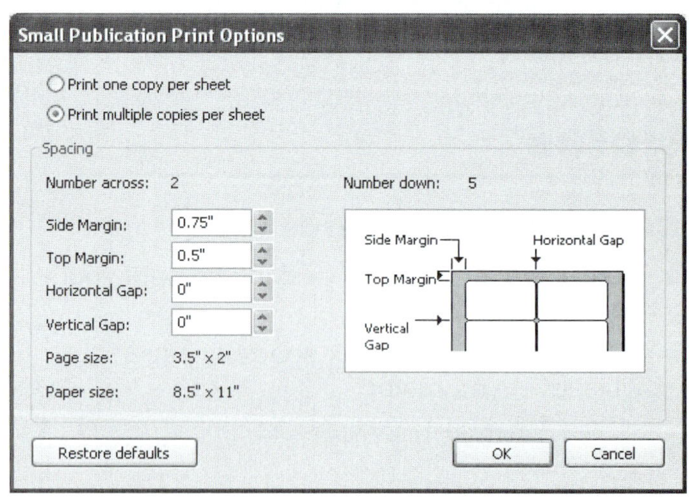

- You can also turn off multi-copy printing from the above dialog box, by choosing Print one copy per sheet.

Use a Background

- You have already seen in earlier exercises how to apply a background fill to a text box or other object. You can also apply such a fill to an entire page, or to the entire publication (if multiple pages).
- To apply a **background** to the whole page, choose Format, Background. This opens the Background task pane.
- The Background task pane contains thumbnail images of a variety of different background fill effects, including several textures, gradients, and patterns. Click the one you want to apply it.
- If the background you want does not appear, click More backgrounds. This opens the Fill Effects dialog box, which you worked with in Exercise 33.

Choose a background

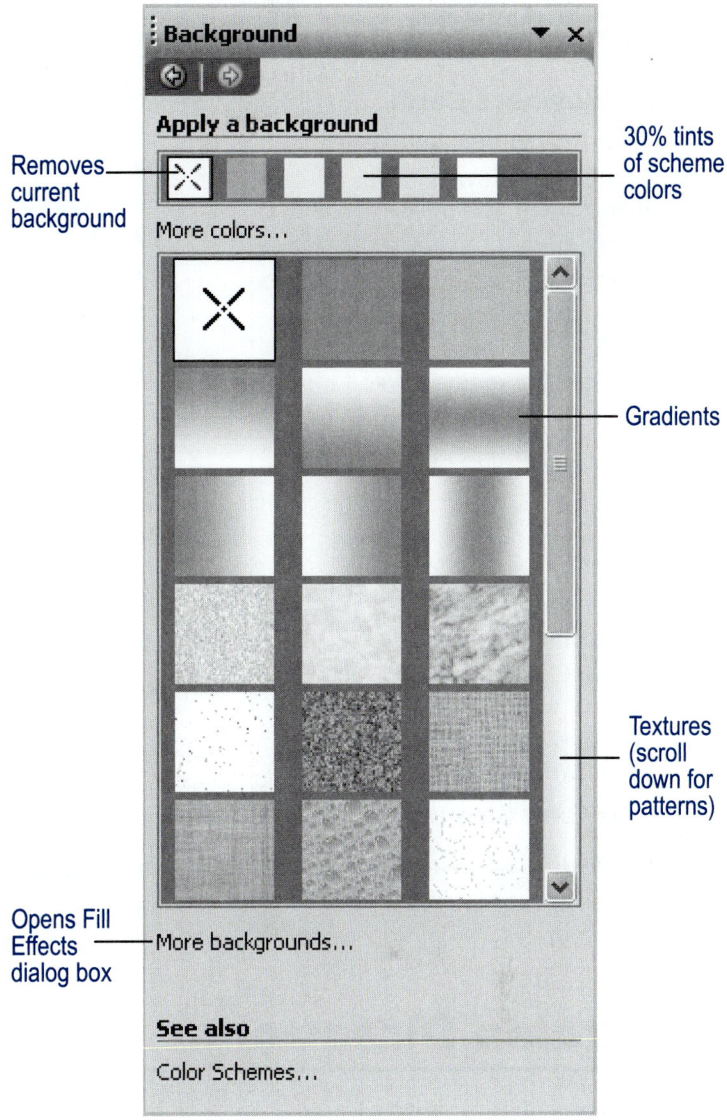

Procedures

Create Business Cards

1. Start Publisher, if needed.
2. Display the New Publication task pane, if needed.
3. Click **Business Cards** on the task pane.
4. Click **Plain Paper** or **Special Paper**.
   - ✓ *Use Special Paper only if you have purchased business card paper from PaperDirect and want to use it now.*
5. Click a business card design.
6. Under Logo in the task pane, click **Include** or **None**.
7. Under Orientation, click **Portrait** or **Landscape**.
8. Under Copies per Sheet, click **One** or **Multiple**.
9. Replace placeholder text with your own text.

Change Card Size

1. Click **File** .... Alt+F
2. Click **Page Setup** .... U
3. In **Page size**, click a region.......................... Alt+S

   OR

   Type specific size in **Height** and **Width** boxes .... Alt+H / Alt+W
4. Click **OK** .... Enter

Change Copies Per Sheet

1. Click **File**...................... Alt+F
2. Click **Page Setup** .... U
3. Click **Change Copies Per Sheet** button .... Alt+O
4. Click **Print multiple copies per sheet** if not already selected .... Alt+M
   - ✓ *The number of copies per sheet is calculated automatically based on the following settings. You cannot directly specify it.*
5. Change values in **Side Margin** and **Top Margin** boxes, if needed......... Alt+S / Alt+T
6. Increase **Horizontal Gap** and/or **Vertical Gap** settings, if needed .... Alt+Z / Alt+V
7. Click **OK** .... Enter
8. Click **OK** .... Enter

Add a Page Background

1. Click **Format** .... Alt+O
2. Click **Background** .... K
3. Click a preset background on task pane.
   - ✓ *You can choose from tints, gradients, textures, and patterns.*

   OR

   a. Click **More Backgrounds**.

   b. Select a background from the Fill Effects dialog box.

   c. Click **OK**...................... Enter
   - ✓ *You might want to set the backgrounds of objects on the page, such as text boxes, to No Fill so the page background shows through.*

Exercise Directions

1. Start Publisher, if needed.
2. Create a business card using the Blocks design. Make the business card landscape in orientation and do not include a logo.
3. Apply the Moss color scheme and the Archival font scheme.
4. Change the placeholder text to reflect Miriam Goldstein's business, using the contact information shown in Illustration A.
5. Insert the image **40PIC.EMF** and place it near the upper-right corner.
6. Apply the Newsprint texture as the background.
7. Make all text boxes except the one for **The Paper Forest** transparent (No Fill) so the background shows through them. See Illustration A.
8. Save your work as **41PAPER**.
9. Print a whole page full of the cards.
10. Save your work and exit Publisher.

Illustration A

On Your Own

1. Start Publisher, if necessary.
2. Create business cards for yourself, for either your current job or a job you would someday like to have.
3. Add a background to the card, if you did not use one originally.
4. Change the size of the card to European.
5. Save the card as **41MYCARD** and print a single copy of it.
6. Save your work and exit Publisher.

Exercise 42

Skills Covered:

◆ Use the Newsletter Wizard ◆ Enter Your Own Content in the Newsletter ◆ Link Text Frames ◆ Move Among Linked Frames ◆ Break a Frame Link ◆ Add a "Continued" Notation

On the Job

A newsletter layout can be tricky to create from scratch with all its columns, headings, and other frames. With Publisher's Newsletter Wizard, though, anyone can have a nicely designed newsletter. Just fill in the articles. Most newsletters rely on a multicolumn format, so the main skill to master in working with newsletters is linking text frames so that each article flows smoothly from one frame to the next.

Jaime Cruz, the owner of a local art supply store, needs your help in assembling a customer newsletter. He wants to place an article on the first page and have it continue to the second page. In this exercise, you will create a new newsletter, import text from Microsoft Office Word, and link the appropriate text frames to place the article where Jaime wants it.

Terms

Story The text in a frame plus any frames that are linked to it. A single story can span several text frames on several pages, as in a newspaper or magazine.

Link To join two frames together so that any text that does not fit in the first one will flow into the second one.

Unlink To break a link between frames.

Notes

Use the Newsletter Wizard

- The Newsletter templates work like any other publication template. Just select a design and then customize it using the options in the task pane.
- The task pane offers two special sections for the newsletter template publications: Newsletter Options and Page Content.
- For Newsletter Options, you have two decisions to make:
  - One- or two-sided printing: specifies whether there should be separate right and left master pages.
  - Customer address: specifies whether there should be an area on the back page for placing customer mailing addresses.

Newsletter options in the task pane

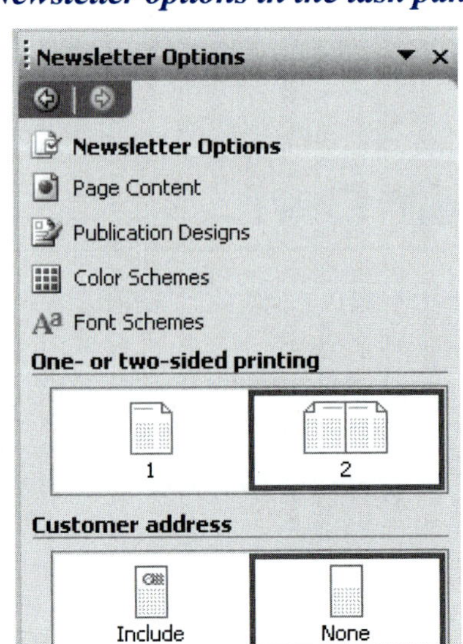

- The Page Content options in the task pane let you choose the number of columns for text boxes on each page. You set this on a page-by-page basis.

Select a number of columns for the articles on the page

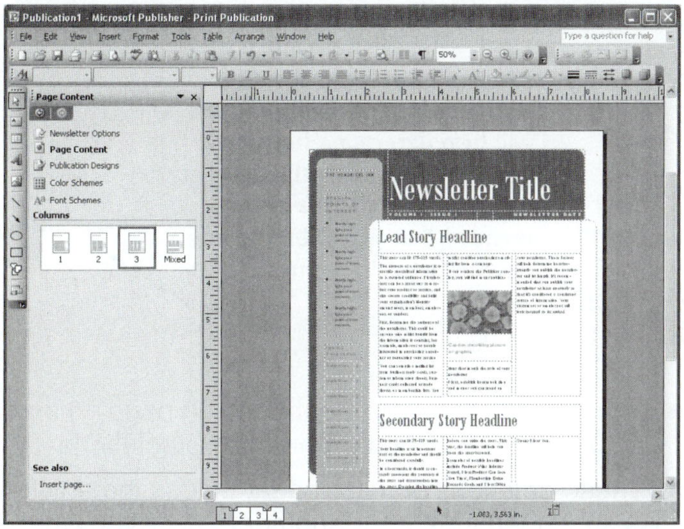

✓ *The number of columns you choose is in addition to the thin extra column along the side. So, if you choose three columns, for example, you actually have four columns—three for regular text and one for special elements.*

Enter Your Own Content in the Newsletter

- Newsletters, like newspapers, usually consist of a collection of short articles. Publisher calls these *stories*. Each **story** can continue from one page to another independently of the others.
- It can be somewhat awkward to type new text in a multicolumn newsletter format. You may want to create an entire story first in another program, such as Word, and then flow it into text frames afterward.
- In a perfect world, all articles would fit exactly in the text frames provided on the layout. However, that is seldom the case.
- If the article is too short and doesn't fill the frames, you can delete the extra frames or resize the frames so that it fits exactly. (Then, of course, you'll need to figure out how to fill the extra blank space on your page layout.)
- When a story is too long to fit in the frames provided, an overflow button appears below the last frame of the story when it is selected. This indicates that some of the story's text has not been set in type—or "paged" to use a term from desktop publishing.

This article has more text than will fit in the allotted frames

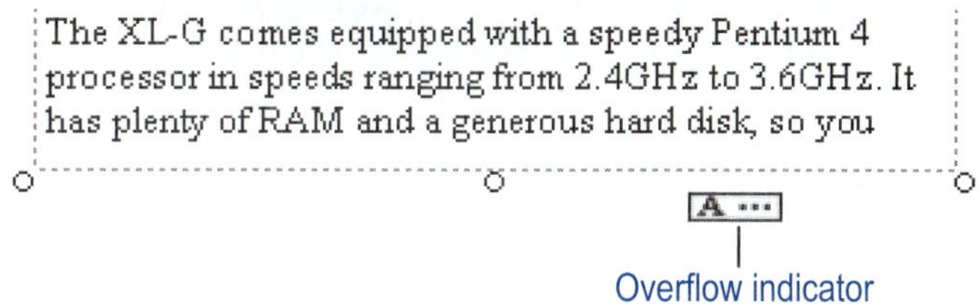

- You can make the text fit by lengthening the frame slightly. This works well if the article lacks just a few lines of fitting. Make sure that in a multicolumn layout, you lengthen each column the same amount, so it doesn't look unbalanced.
- You can also set the frames of the article to use the Shrink Text on Overflow AutoFit Text option, which means that the text of the article becomes small enough to fit in the frames. This can result in an unattractive newsletter, however, with inconsistent text size between articles.
- The final way to fix an overflow problem is to create additional frames in which to flow the article. They can be on the same page, or on a different page. Just create the new frames and then **link** them to the existing ones for that article.

Link Text Frames

- When you create a newsletter using one of Publisher's newsletter designs, certain frames are already linked. All the text boxes under a particular heading are linked, for example. You can enlarge these frames to help a story fit if needed.
- If the story needs to run longer, into additional text frames or onto other pages, you will need to manually link the additional frames to the others.
- To link frames, first create the new frame. Then select the last existing frame of the article, click the Create Text Box Link button 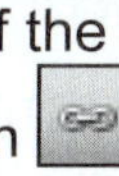, and click inside the newly created frame to flow the text into it.
- The mouse pointer becomes a pouring pitcher  when it is over a suitable frame.

Move Among Linked Frames

- When you select a frame that is part of a linked chain of frames, buttons appear above and/or below it offering to take you to the next or previous frame. Click one of these buttons to move to (and select) the next—or previous—linked frame in the article.

You may use these buttons for moving from frame to frame in a linked chain of frames

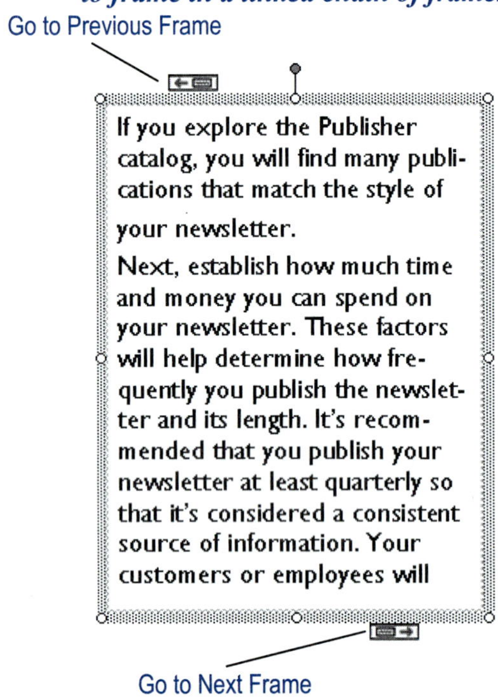

Break a Frame Link

- To break the links between frames, or **unlink** frames, select a linked frame and click the Break Forward Link button. This disconnects all the frames that come *after* the selected one in the chain. It does not affect backward links for that frame (that is, text that flows *into* that frame).
- When you break a link, the text that used to flow forward into other frames once again waits as overflow text for you to enlarge the selected text box or create other frames in which to flow.

Add a "Continued" Notation

- If an article continues from one page to another, you may want to add indicators to that effect. You can create text frames manually to do the job, but Publisher's automatic feature is much nicer. It keeps track of the page on which the next article falls and changes the page number reference as needed.

Publisher's "Continued" text places the correct page number automatically

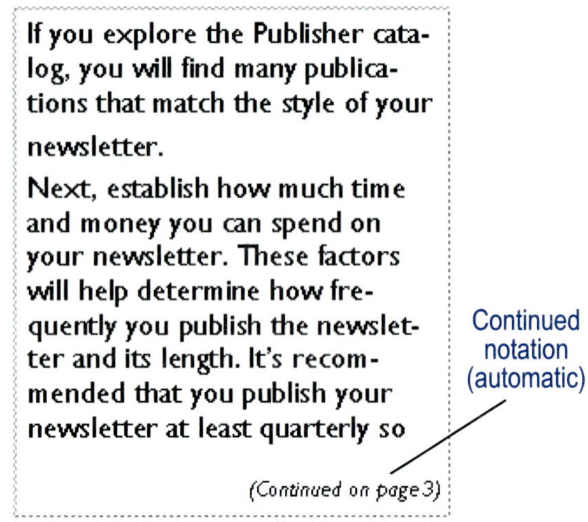

- You can add forward (Continued on page…) and backward (Continued from page…) notations.
- These notations do not appear unless the article is continued from or to another page, even when they are turned on.
- To turn on the Continued notations, select the text box and choose Format, Text Box. Then, on the Text Box tab, click the Include "Continued on page…" and/or Include "Continued from page…" check boxes.

Turn on the "Continued" notations in the text box's formatting properties

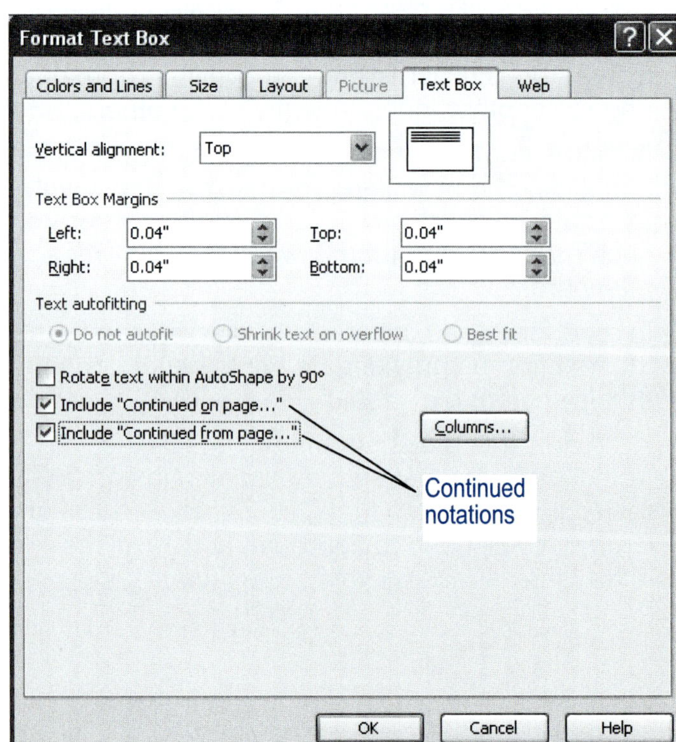

Procedures

Create a Newsletter

1. Start Publisher, if necessary.
2. Click **Newsletters** on the task pane.
3. Click the newsletter design you want.
4. Under One- or two-sided printing, click **1** or **2**.
5. Under Customer address, click **Include** or **None**.
6. Replace the sample text and graphics with your own text and graphics.

Change Number of Columns on a Page Layout

1. Display the page to change.
2. Display **Page Content** task pane, if needed.
3. If displaying a two-page layout:
   a. Open Select a page to modify list.
   b. Select **Right Inside Page** or **Left Inside Page**.
4. Under Columns, click **1**, **2**, **3**, or **Mixed**.

   ✓ *You can click the down arrow next to an option and choose **Apply to All Pages** to select the same setting for all pages at once.*

Change Content Layout for an Inside Page

1. Display the pages to change.

   ✓ *It must be an inside set of pages, not the first or last page.*
2. Display **Page Content** task pane, if needed.
3. Click content type for right page.
4. Open **Select a page to modify** list.
5. Select **Left Inside Page**.
6. Click content type for left page.

Link Text Frames

1. If needed, create the new text frame into which to flow the article.
2. Click the last current frame of the article.
3. Click the **Create Text Box Link** button.
4. Click in the new frame. The text flows into it.

Move Among Linked Frames

1. Click in a linked frame.
2. To move to the next frame in the chain, click the **Go to Next Text Box** button.

   OR

   To move to the previous frame in the chain, click the **Go to Previous Text Box** button.

Break a Text Box Link

1. Click in the frame from which you want to break forward links.
2. Click the **Break Forward Link** button.

Add a "Continued" Notation

1. Click in the text box for which you want a notation.
2. Click **Format** .... Alt+O
3. Click **Text Box** .... E

   ✓ *You can also right-click the text box and choose **Format Text Box** instead of doing steps 2–3.*
4. Click **Text Box** tab.
5. To add a forward notation, click the **Include "Continued on page..."** check box ..... Alt+O
6. To add a backward notation, click the **Include "Continued from page..."** check box .... Alt+F
7. Click **OK** .... Enter

Exercise Directions

1. Start Publisher, if necessary.
2. Create a new newsletter based on the Radial newsletter design.
3. Save the file as **42NEWS**.
4. Format the newsletter as follows:
   - Field color scheme
   - Galley font scheme
   - A placeholder for a customer address
5. Change all pages to two-column layouts.
6. On the inside right page, apply a Calendar content layout.
7. On the first page, change the newsletter title to **Art Update** and the business name to **Arts and Crafts Unlimited**, and replace the date placeholder with the current month and year.
8. Delete the following objects from page 1:
   - Special Points of Interest
   - Inside This Issue
   - Picture and caption
   - Secondary story headline and its text box, plus the text boxes for the secondary story body
   - Horizontal line separating lead story from secondary story
9. Change the lead story headline to **Come See What's New** and replace the sample text for the lead story with the text from **PUB42import.doc** (a Word document).

   ✓ *If you see a message asking whether you want to use Autoflow, click No.*
10. Turn off automatic hyphenation for the story (Tools, Language, Hyphenation).
11. Extend the text boxes for the lead story to the bottom of the page.
12. Turn on the Include "Continued on page" option for the last text box on page 1.
13. Delete the following objects from page 2:
    - Quote box
    - Figures and their captions
    - Second and third stories, including both heading and title text boxes
14. In the remaining headline text box, change the text to read **What's New**.
15. Delete the sample text and flow the story from page 1 into the text boxes on page 2. Lengthen the text boxes so they occupy the whole page.
16. Extend the text boxes on page 2 to the bottom of the page.
17. Turn on the Include "Continued from page" option for the first text box containing the story continuation on page 2.
18. Edit the story in Word, and change the story text to Arial. Then return to Publisher.

    ✓ *See Exercise 7 for help editing a story in Word.*
19. For both bulleted lists in the story, set the spacing after the paragraphs to 0 points (Format, Paragraph).
20. Place **42pastels.jpg** on page 1, as shown in Illustration A.
21. Place **42loom.jpg** on page 2, as shown in Illustration B. (You may need to shorten one or both of the text boxes to make it fit well.)
22. Print pages 1 and 2.
23. Save your work and exit Publisher.

On Your Own

1. Start Publisher, if necessary.
2. Using any of Publisher's Newsletter Wizard designs, create a newsletter devoted to your favorite subject. Save it as **42MYNEWS**.
3. Write a few articles, and make at least one of them wrap to a later page in the newsletter. Delete any placeholders for items you don't use.
4. Select and insert clip art and/or photos that complement your articles.
5. Experiment with different numbers of columns and one-sided versus two-sided layout.
6. Try changing to a different design and color scheme, to find the exact look you want.
7. Save your work and exit Publisher.

Illustration A

Volume 1, Issue 1 March 04

Art Update

Arts and Crafts Unlimited

Come See What's New

There's always something new and interesting in stock! Check out these new arrivals.

Derwent Watercolor Pencils, Special Edition Set

Celebrate 50 years of pure, consistent color from Derwent's Watercolor Pencils. This limited edition collection of 36 pencils in the original livery box design, celebrates Derwent's continuing commitment to produce the highest quality pencils. $21.88

Winsor & Newton Soft Pastel Sets.

Drawing on over 160 years of color-making experience, Winsor & Newton has developed a range of artists' soft pastels formulated to the very highest standards. They use only the purest, highest-grade pigments in high concentration to provide brighter, stronger, and cleaner colors. They have a supple, creamy consistency that minimizes dust and provides even texture throughout the pigment range, perfect for blending and layering. Each color is available in a range of five tints.

Each full stick is labeled with information about color, tint, and lightfastness. We carry the complete range of full sticks in open stock, so it's easy to maintain the value and completeness of your sets. Winsor & Newton Artists' Soft Pastels are non-toxic and permanent. Regular sticks measure 64× 10(2.5"× .375" in diameter), and are paper-wrapped. Half sticks measure 32× 10 (1.25"× .375"), and are unwrapped.

Winsor & Newton's quality and reputation make Artists' Soft Pastels an outstanding choice for gift giving. Sets are attractively packaged, and pastels are protectively encased in foam inserts to prevent damage or breakage.

- Set of 12, $18
- Set of 24, $36
- Set of 36, $55
- Set of 72, $109
- Set of 12 half-sticks, $9
- Set of 24 half-sticks, $18

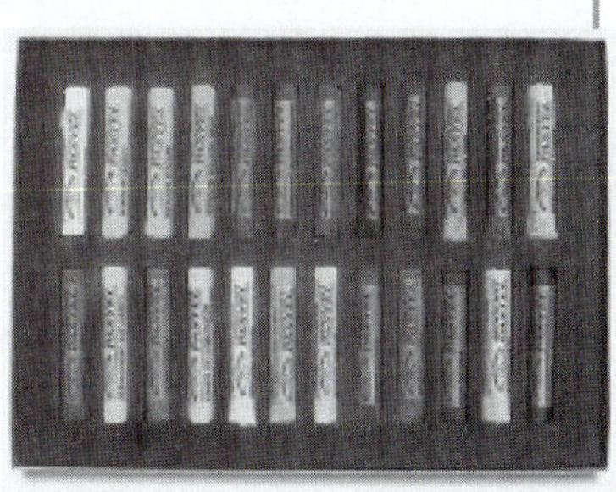

Riso Print Gocco B6 Hi Mesh Stamp Kit

Print Gocco is a small household screen printing kit, is extremely popular in Japan. It's an outstanding, low-cost way to set up and learn screen printing technology. Use it to create cards, invitations, posters, or even T-shirts.

The greeting card kit contains everything you need to make five

(Continued on page 2)

Illustration B

Art Update

Page 2

What's New

(Continued from page 1)

screen printing originals, and as many prints as you wish. Print size is 3½"× 5½" (9× 14cm), the perfect size for greeting cards, place cards, invitations, or announcements. The following materials are included:

- 5 screens
- flash lamp and 10 bulbs
- 7 colors of ink
- a fine-tip pen
- printing paper
- a 20 minute video "How to Use Print Gocco"
- batteries

An 18-page, full-color booklet with ideas and complete instructions

A selection of accessories is also available, so you can use your imagination to expand the creative possibilities. Overall, the kit measures 6¾"× 6"× 15" (17× 15× 38). $139

Spectra Treasure Chest of Paper Bag Puppets

Kids will love this on a rainy afternoon! Created to encourage young imaginations, this kit is truly a treasure chest. It contains the basic ingredients to create up to 175 paper bag puppets. Kids will have fun inventing characters, animals, monsters, or more as they develop skills with a variety of media. Adults can guide classes or groups of kids with the easy to follow project sheet and use the sturdy box to organize materials when not in use. $32

Leclerc Dorothy Table Loom

Ever wanted to create your own woven artwork but been held back by the large amount of space required for a loom? This loom weaves up to 15¾" (40), a practical size for schools, hobbyists, and occupational therapy. The four harness levers may be set on either the right or left side of the loom. The Leclerc Dorothy Table Loom is collapsible for storage. It includes 12-dent reed, 400 wire heddles, a shuttle, a reed hook, lease sticks, two beam slicks with cords, and instructions. The Dorothy is made of red birch with a colonial finish. $395.

Exercise 43

Skills Covered:

◆ **Create Mailing Labels** ◆ **Mail Merge Basics** ◆ **Create an Address List in Publisher** ◆ **Edit an Address List** ◆ **Set Up a Mail Merge with the Wizard** ◆ **Set Up a Mail Merge Manually**

On the Job

If you create publications to send to customers, such as newsletters, advertising flyers, and so on, chances are good that you also need to mail them. One way is to print customer mailing addresses directly on each copy of the publication. (You'll do that with postcards in Exercise 44.) Another is to create a sheet of mailing labels and paste a label on each copy, which is what you'll learn in this exercise.

Vanessa Bradley has been collecting people's names and addresses who would like to receive information about a sale she is managing, and now she wants to print some mailing labels. However, she doesn't have the addresses in any kind of computerized form; they're all on scraps of paper and in hard-copy address books. In this exercise, you will help her enter some of them into a Publisher address list and create a sheet of mail-merged labels.

Terms

Label sheet A page of peel-off labels designed to be printed on using a computer printer.

Mail merge The process of combining a list of names and addresses with a publication containing placeholder fields, so that a personalized copy of the publication is generated for each person on the list.

Record One complete collection of data in the data source for a single person, place, or thing. For example, all the information about a certain person in your address book is a record.

Mail and Catalog Merge The feature in Publisher that accomplishes a mail merge.

Publisher address list A simple database stored in a special Publisher format, containing contact information about people with whom you want to correspond.

Field One type of information from the data source. For example, First Name is a field.

Field code A code that indicates the spot in a publication where the Mail and Catalog Merge feature should insert a field from a record in the data source.

Notes

Create Mailing Labels

- The Label template creates a publication consisting of a single label. When you print a **label sheet** using this publication, it prints an entire sheet of the same label. This might be useful, for example, for creating your own return address labels.
- To create multiple labels each with a different name and address on it, you must do a merge, which is a separate activity discussed in the next section.

✓ *Besides the traditional mailing labels, Publisher can also print all kinds of special-purpose labels, such as jar/product labels, compact disc sleeves, bookplates, computer disk labels, and so on. Simply choose the label type you want from the list of designs in the task pane.*

Mail Merge Basics

- A **mail merge** combines the **records** from a database (usually names and addresses) with a publication template to produce custom versions of the publication for each record.
- The **Mail and Catalog Merge** feature in Publisher accomplishes the mail merge.

Mail vs. Catalog Merges

- The "catalog" portion of the name is new in Publisher 2003. As the first step of the wizard you are prompted to choose whether you will do a mail merge or a catalog merge.
- The main difference is that mail merge is used for publications where you will have one record per copy of the publication, whereas catalog merge is used where multiple records will appear per copy.
- For example, mail merge would be appropriate for letters, labels, post cards, and so on where each is addressed to a different person.
- Catalog merge would be appropriate for price lists, product inventories, and reports that list the items in a database one-by-one without placing each one on its own page.
- In this exercise we will be doing a mail merge, not a catalog merge.

Data Sources

- Every merge must have a data source. It must be one of these types:
  - An external file created in some other program (like Word, Excel, or Access)
  - A contact list from Outlook
  - An address list you create within Publisher.
- If you choose to create a Publisher address list, it is saved as a Microsoft Office Access file (.mdb format). You can reuse it in other publications, and you can open it in Access if you happen to have Access installed on your PC.

Create an Address List in Publisher

- Publisher's address list capability offers an easy way to create a database of names and addresses without having to rely on an external program.
- You can create multiple address lists in Publisher, and open the one you need for each project.

  ✓ *You cannot use a Publisher address list for a catalog merge; catalog merges must use external data sources only.*

- To start a new address list, choose Tools, Mail and Catalog Merge, Create Address List. Or, from the Mail and Catalog Merge Wizard, you can choose to type a new list.

Fill in these fields for each person; you can leave certain fields blank if they don't apply to that person, or if the information is currently unavailable

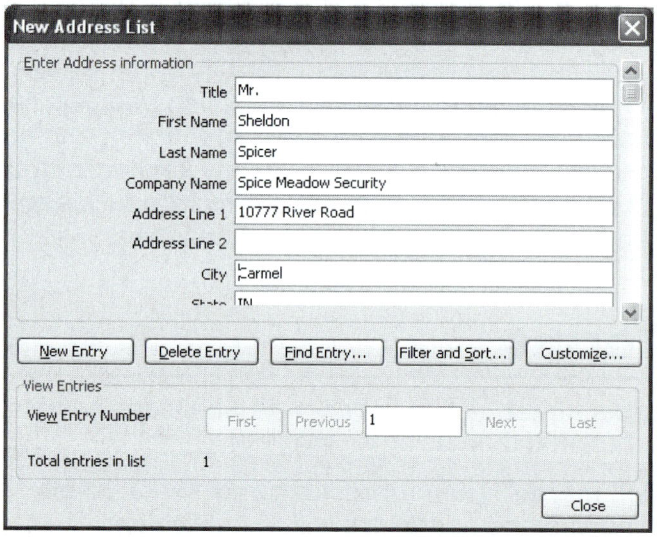

- Fill out the form and then click New Entry. Then fill it out again for the next person, and so on, until you have entered all the people for that list. Then click Close.
- When you click Close, a Save Address List dialog box opens, prompting you to save the list you just created. Give it a name and click Save. If you don't save it (that is, if you click Cancel), all the entries you typed are lost.
- Publisher saves data files by default in the My Data Sources folder, which is a subfolder in My Documents. You can save them anywhere you like, however.

  ✓ *It is optional to create the address list before running the Mail and Catalog Merge Wizard; there is an opportunity in the Wizard to create it on-the-spot. However, in this exercise we will create the address list beforehand.*

Edit an Address List

- To edit a saved address list, choose Tools, Mail and Catalog Merge, Edit Address List. Select the **address list** you want and click Open so you can resume data entry.

Set Up a Mail Merge with the Wizard

- After creating the publication that you want to use as the template (for example, the label, in this exercise), you can run the Mail and Catalog Merge Wizard to set up the merge **fields**.
- First you select a merge type: Mail merge or Catalog merge.
- Next you select the data source. At this point you can create a new address list in Publisher if you do not already have a data source.
- When you choose the data source file, a Mail Merge Recipients dialog box appears. All the records in the data source file are listed, with check marks beside them. Unmark the ones you don't want to include in this mail merge, if any.

Deselect any recipients that you don't want

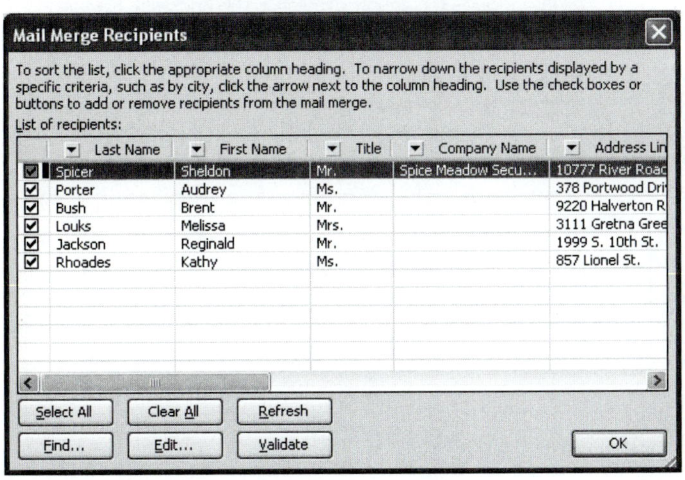

- The Mail Merge Recipients dialog box has some sophisticated sorting and filtering capabilities. To sort by a particular column, click the column heading.
- To filter by a particular field value, click the down arrow next to the column heading and choose the value from the drop-down menu that appears.

  ✓ *You'll learn more about sorting and filtering in Exercise 44.*

Select a particular value a record must have in the chosen field in order to display

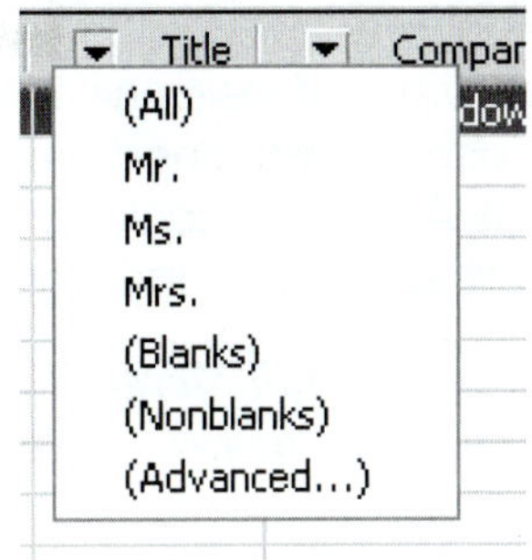

- Click OK when you are finished selecting the recipients. The data file's name then appears in the task pane, indicating a data source has been chosen.
- Then click the Next: Create your publication link at the bottom of the task pane to move to the next step of the wizard.

A data source has been selected

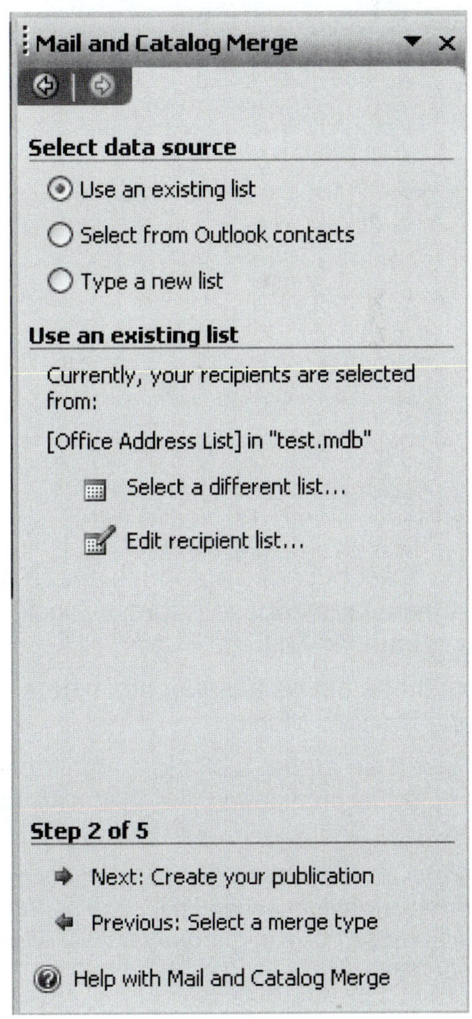

- After selecting the data source, you place codes in your publication that indicate where each field should go. These are called **field codes**.
- There are two ways of inserting the field codes. One is to choose a predefined collection of field codes, such as Address Block. The other is to manually insert each code individually.

Step 2 of the Mail Merge Wizard is to insert the field codes

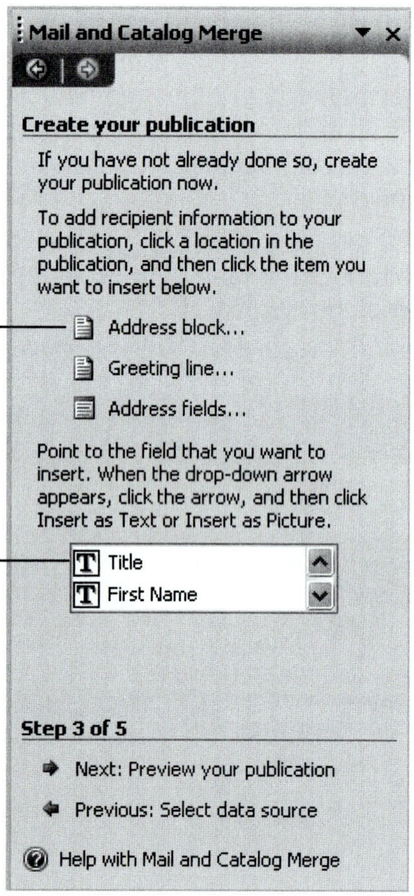

- To insert a set of codes automatically, in the Wizard task pane choose Address Block, Greeting Line, or Address Fields.
- Each of these opens a dialog box where you can fine-tune the field block.
- If you insert an address block, a single code appears in the publication like this: <<Address block>>.

✓ *You can format field codes using any of the normal formatting techniques, such as font, size, color, and so on. The merged text will have those attributes.*

- You can also insert individual fields by clicking their names on the list in the task pane (such as Title or First Name in the figure above). Doing this puts individual codes in the publication, such as <<Title>>.
- If you click in a text box before inserting a field code, it appears in that text box. Otherwise it appears in a new text box that Publisher creates for it automatically.

Specify how the address block should be constructed

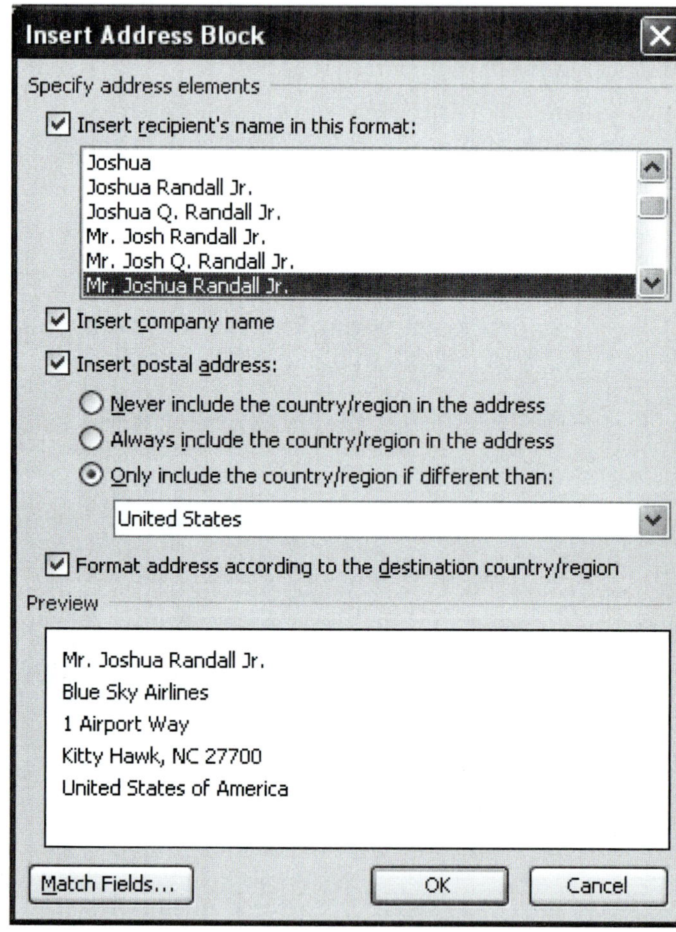

- Next the Wizard step enables you to preview your publication. The first record appears; you can scroll through the others with the right and left arrow buttons in the task pane.

Preview each copy of the merge

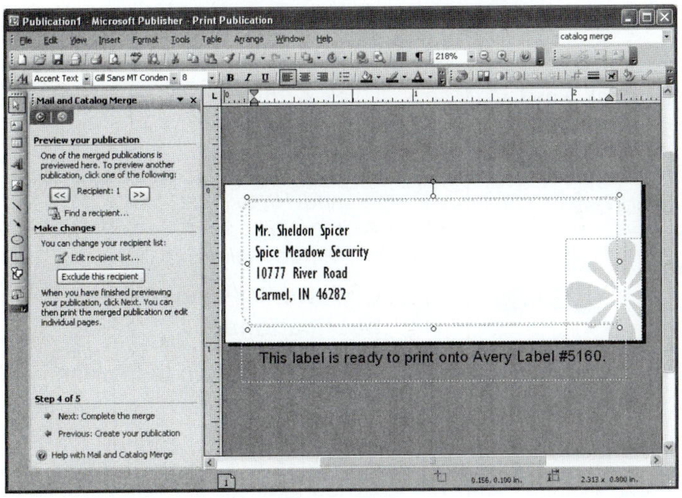

- If you encounter a record that you want to exclude from the merge, click Exclude this recipient.
- You can also click Edit recipient list to reopen the address list for editing, the same as earlier.
- As the final step of the wizard, you can print and/or save the publication.
- You can save it in one of two formats: you can add the merged pages to the end of the current publication, or you can save the merge results in a new publication.
- The Print Merge dialog box has a few special features not found in the normal Print dialog box, as shown below. You can choose a range of the entries (records) to print rather than specific page numbers, and you can exclude copies that contain empty fields.

Specify any print options

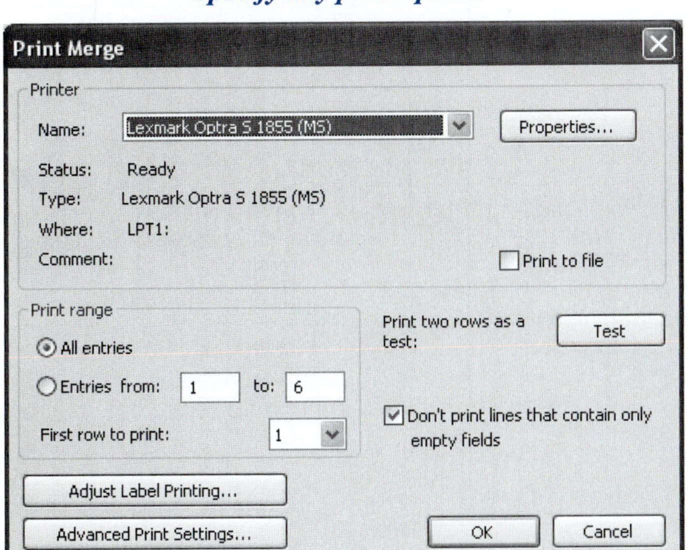

✓ *To run a test print of two rows, click the Test button. Then, if everything is okay, you can feed that same sheet back into the printer and begin the printing at row 3 by setting the First row to print setting to 3.*

Set Up a Mail Merge Manually

- You can merge without going through the Mail Merge Wizard. Experienced users might sometimes find this preferable and quicker.
- Start your publication, then choose Tools, Mail and Catalog Merge, Open Data source, and select the data source file. It can be an address list saved through Publisher or some other format (see Exercise 44).
- Next, insert the fields in your publication. Position the insertion point where you want a field, and then choose Tools, Mail and Catalog Merge, Insert Field. This opens the Mail and Catalog Merge Wizard task pane.
- Manually insert fields by clicking their names on the task pane.

Insert fields manually on the label if desired

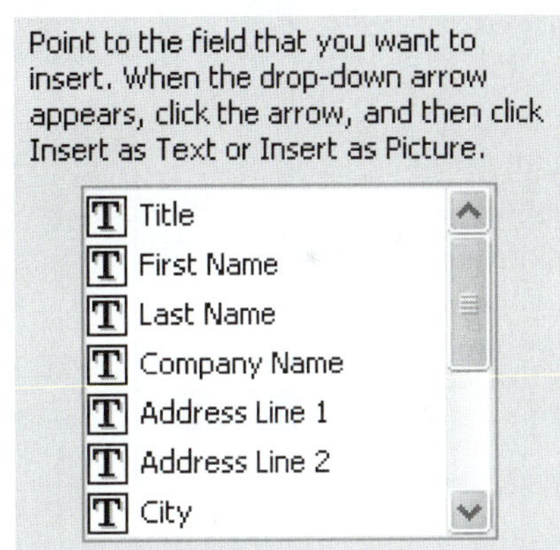

✓ *Normally you will want to insert them as text, so just click on them to insert them. Never mind the instructions above the list that imply you must open the drop-down list and choose Insert as Text every time.*

- The Insert as Picture option for a merge field is applicable only if your data source contains pictures. (Most don't.)
- To see a preview of the merge results, choose Tools, Mail and Catalog Merge, Show Merge Results.
- To print the merge, choose File, Print Merge.

Procedures

Create Labels (all the same text)

1. Start Publisher, if necessary.
2. Click **Labels** in the task pane.
3. Click the label design to use.
4. Replace the text on the label with your own text.
5. Print the publication normally.

Create Address List

1. Click **Tools**.................. Alt+T
2. Point to **Mail and Catalog Merge** .... G
3. Click **Create Address List** . C
4. Type the contact information for the first person into the fields provided.
   - ✓ *Scroll down in the box for additional fields.*
5. Click **New Entry**.......... Alt+N
6. Repeat steps 4-5 until you have entered all the contact information needed.
7. Click **Close**.
8. Type a file name for the address list in the **File name** box............ Alt+N
9. Click **Save**.................. Alt+S

Edit Address List

1. Click **Tools**.................. Alt+T
2. Point to **Mail and Catalog Merge** .... G
3. Click **Edit Address List**...... E
4. Click the list you want to open.
5. Click **Open**.................. Alt+O
6. Do any of the following:
   - To browse for a particular address, use **First**, **Previous**, **Next**, or **Last** buttons to browse through them.
   - To find an entry, click **Find Entry** and use the dialog box that appears..... Alt+F
   - To add a new address, click **New Entry** and then enter a new person............. Alt+N
   - To delete an entry, display it and then click **Delete Entry** .... Alt+D
7. When you are done editing the entries, click **Close**.

Create Labels with Mail Merge Wizard

✓ *These steps assume using an already-created Publisher address list as the data source.*

1. Create a new label publication.
2. Delete the sample text from the label.
3. Click **Tools** .... Alt+T
4. Point to **Mail and Catalog Merge** .... G
5. Click **Mail Merge Wizard** .... W
6. Click the **Mail Merge** option button.
7. Click **Next: Select Data Source**.
8. Click **Use an Existing List**.
9. Click Browse.
10. Select the data file.
11. Click **Open**...................... Enter
12. (Optional) Clear check boxes for address records to exclude from the merge.
    - ✓ *You can use the sorting and filtering capabilities in that dialog box to make it easier to locate the records you want to find and exclude. Sorting and filtering are covered in Exercise 44.*
13. Click **OK** .... Enter
14. Click **Next: Create your publication**.
15. Click **Address Block**.
16. Click **OK**.
    - ✓ *As an alternative to steps 15 and 16, to insert fields manually, see "Manually Insert Merge Fields."*
17. Click **Next: Preview your publications**.
18. Click [>>] button to browse label previews.
    - ✓ *If needed, click **Exclude this recipient** button to exclude currently displayed label.*
19. Click **Next: Complete the merge**.
20. Click **Print**.
21. Load label sheet(s) into printer.
22. Change any print settings if needed.
23. Click **OK** .... Enter

Manually Select a Data File

1. Click **Tools**.................. Alt+T
2. Point to **Mail and Catalog Merge**................................ G
3. Click **Open Data Source** .... O
4. Select the data file.
5. Click **Open** .... Enter

Manually Insert Merge Fields

1. Position insertion point where field should appear.
2. Click **Tools**.................. Alt+T
3. Point to **Mail and Catalog Merge**................................ G
4. Click **Insert Field** .... N
   - ✓ *Ctrl+Shift+I can be substitutes for steps 2-4.*
5. Click inside a text box.
6. Click the field to insert.
7. Type any spaces, line breaks, or punctuation needed.
8. Repeat steps 5-6 as needed.

Exercise Directions

1. Start Publisher, if necessary.
2. Create a new publication with the Large Mailing Address Label (Avery 5162) Wizard and save it as **43LABELS**.
3. Delete all the sample text from the label.
4. Create a new address list, and enter the following names and addresses:

   Thomas Reyes Kathy Carmichael
   115 W. 9th Street 3636 W. Bechdel
   Street
   Indianapolis, IN 46240 Carmel, IN
   46023

   Anna Beth Snyder John Amos
   76 Los Trancos Circle 1092 E.
   Haverstick Road
   New York, NY 10019 Macon, IL 62544

5. Save the new address list as **43MAIL**.
6. Insert an address block on the label that excludes the Company Name field.
7. Format the field code as 12-point Arial.
8. Exclude John Amos's record from the merge.
9. Print the labels.

   ✓ *For this exercise you can use regular paper; if you were creating the labels "for real," you would need special label paper.*

10. Save your work.
11. Create a new publication containing the label results and save it as **43RESULTS**.
12. Save your work and exit Publisher.

On Your Own

1. Start Publisher, if necessary.
2. Create a CD/DVD label for your favorite CD or DVD, and save it as **43CD**.
3. Create a new shipping label (any design).
4. Type your own name and address for the return address.
5. Change to a different color scheme and design for the label.
6. Select the data source file you created in this exercise (**43MAIL**) as the data source for a mail merge.
7. Place the needed fields on the label for a mail merge. Place them one-by-one; do not use an <<Address Block>>.
8. Format the field codes with Times New Roman font.
9. Save your publication as **43SHIP** and print the labels.
10. Save your work and exit Publisher.

Exercise 44

Skills Covered:

◆ **Use the Postcard Wizard** ◆ **Merge Addresses from Outlook**
◆ **Merge Addresses from an External File** ◆ **Filter and Sort a Merge**

On the Job

You can do a lot with mail merge. Besides printing mailing labels, you can merge letters, newsletters, postcards, and many other types of publications. In fact, you can mail merge any publication at all, simply by using the Catalog and Mail Merge feature that you saw in Exercise 43.

Dr. Tim Green needs to send out reminder postcards to some patients them that they are due for a check-up. In this exercise, you will create these postcards.

Terms

Tab-delimited text file A text file that contains database records in which fields are separated by tabs.

Comma-delimited text file A text file that contains database records in which fields are separated by commas.

Filter To exclude certain records from a merge based on a criterion you specify.

Notes

Use the Postcard Wizard

- The Postcard template helps you create any of a variety of postcard designs. It works just like any other template.
- You can print postcards on regular cardstock and cut them out by hand, or you can buy blank postcard paper and feed it into your printer as a custom paper size.
- Most postcard publications contain two pages: a front and a back. You will place your message on the front and the mailing address (or merge codes for a mailing address) on the back.

The Postcard template provides placeholders for addresses, promotional text, and more

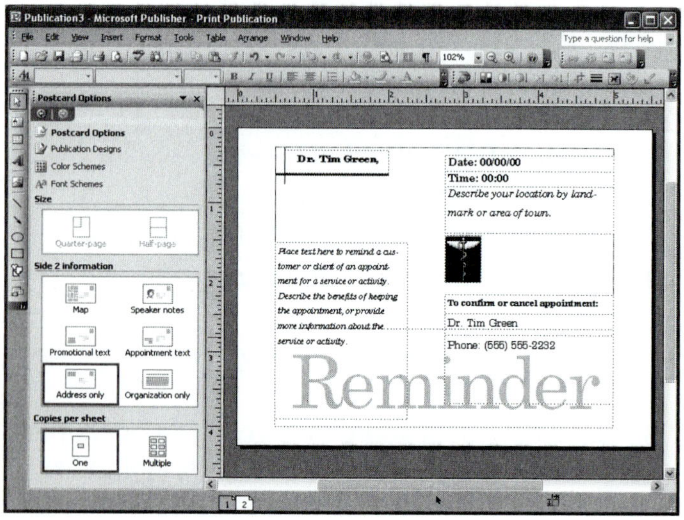

Merge Addresses from Outlook

- If you keep your contacts in Outlook, you can use that database of information for mail merges in Publisher.
- As you learned in Exercise 43, you can set up a merge with the Mail Merge Wizard or manually.
- If you are using the wizard method, in the task pane you'll click Select from Outlook Contacts, and then click Choose Contacts Folder.

  ✓ *This procedure works only if Outlook is your default mail client; it won't work if you have set up Outlook Express as the default. To set Outlook as your default, start Outlook. When asked whether you want to set it as the default mail client, click "Yes."*

- One or more dialog boxes might ask you to identify the Outlook profile and file to work with; then your Outlook contacts will appear in the Mail Merge Recipients dialog box, the same as with a Publisher address list (see Exercise 43).

These contacts are from my Outlook contact list

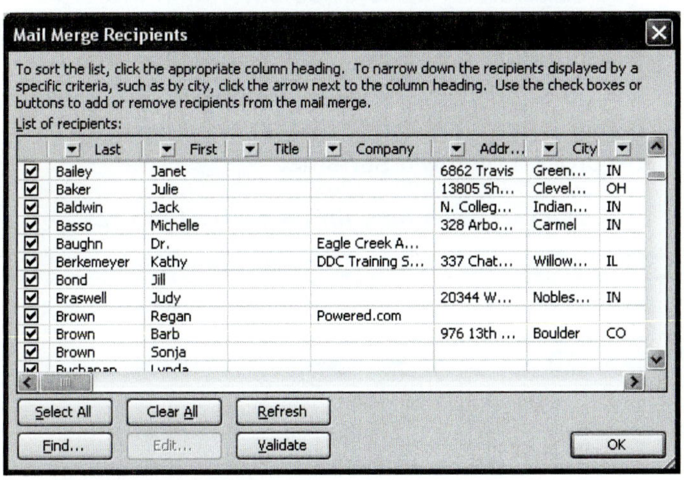

Merge Addresses from an External File

- Publisher can accept data from a variety of file types, including Excel, Word, Access, Works, Paradox, and dBase. It can also import from **tab-delimited** or **comma-delimited text files**.

  ✓ *If you are using data from a text file, a table, or spreadsheet, make sure that the first row contains your field names (such as First Name, Last Name, and so on). Edit the data file in its native program beforehand to ensure this.*

- To select one of the external data sources, click Use an existing list from the Mail Merge Wizard in the task pane, or choose Tools, Mail and Catalog Merge, Open Data Source. This is the same as if you were opening a Publisher-created address list (see Exercise 43).
- Then simply select a file in some other format. Depending on the data type chosen, you may see additional prompts.
- For example, if you choose an Excel workbook or an Access database, you will be asked to select the sheet or table that you want to use, and whether the first row contains column headers (for an Excel sheet).

Select the desired sheet from an Excel workbook

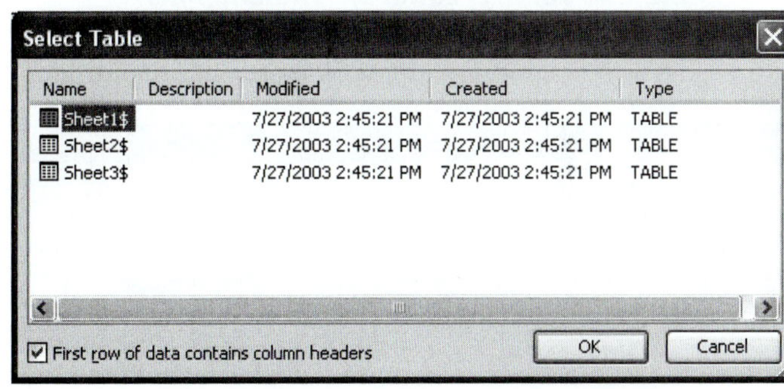

- If you use a text file as the data source, Publisher asks how the fields and records are delimited—that is, separated. The most common way is to separate columns (fields) with tabs or commas and to separate records with paragraph breaks.

Specify how the text file is delimited

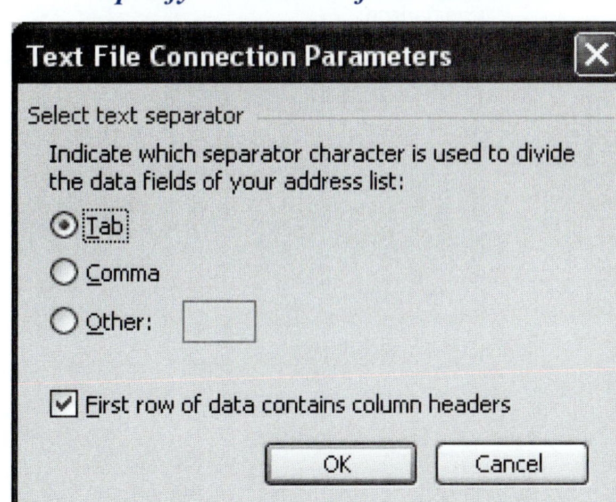

Filter and Sort a Merge

- After you specify the data source, you can open the Filter and Sort dialog box (Tools, Mail and Catalog Merge, Filter or Sort). It has two tabs—one for **filtering** and one for sorting.
- Use the Filter Records tab to set up a filter definition. This excludes some of the records, leaving only the ones you want. For example, you might exclude people whose last appointment was after a certain date, or people who live in a certain city.
- Each filter criterion has three parts: the field, the comparison, and the value to compare to.

This criterion chooses only records for which the City value is equal to "Indianapolis"

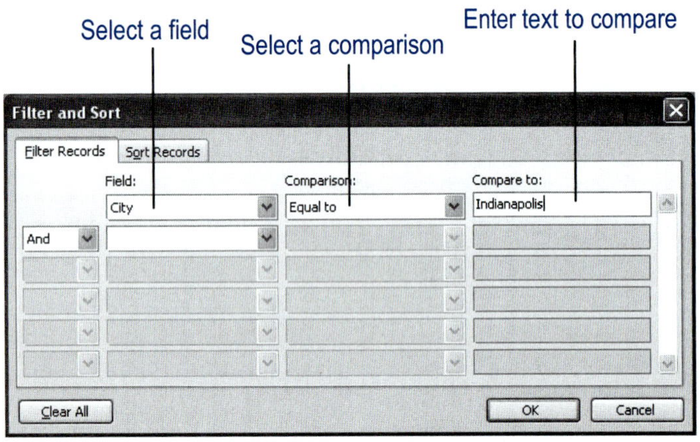

- For the comparison, choose one of values from the drop-down list:

Choose a value from the drop-down list

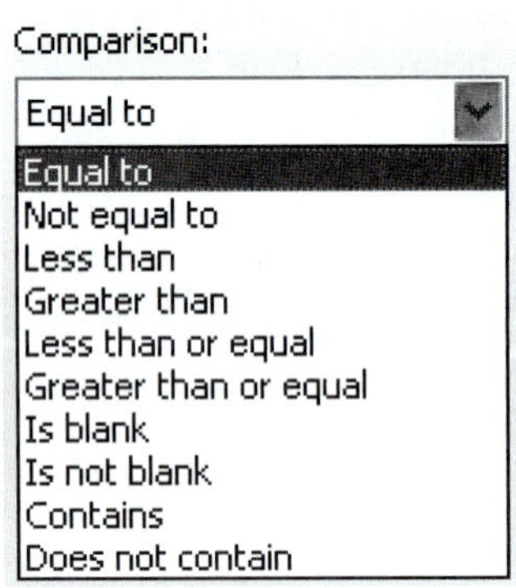

- If you use the Is greater than or Is less than comparison for text, they refer to alphabetic positioning. For example, if you set the Last Name field to greater than C, it will include only records in which the first letter in the Last Name field is D through Z.
- You can create multiple filters, and they can be inclusive or exclusive of one another by choosing And or Or from the leftmost drop-down list.
- For example, if you separate two filters with Or, records that match either of the criteria will be included. If you separate the same two filters with And, records must match both criteria to be included.
- The Sort Records tab in the Filter and Sort dialog box lets you arrange the merged records in a particular order for printing and on-screen viewing. For example, some bulk mailing companies require you to sort items by ZIP Code.
- You can sort by up to three criteria, in the order you specify. For example, you might first sort by Last, and then by First. That means that the list will be sorted by last name, and wherever two records have the same last name, the "tie" will be broken by the first name.

Set a sort order here for the merged records

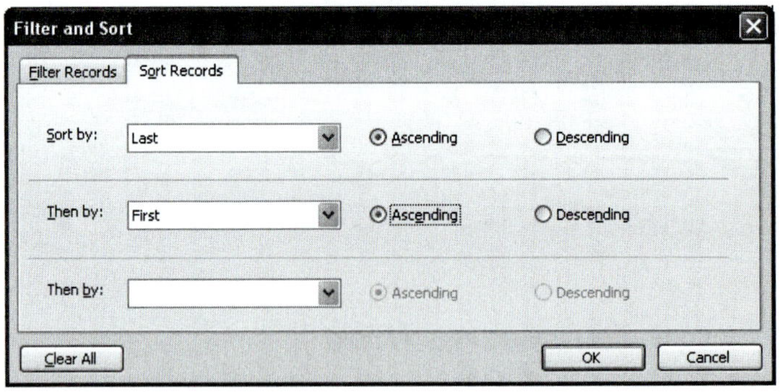

Procedures

Use the Postcard Template

1. Start Publisher, if necessary.
2. Click **Publications for Print** in the task pane.
3. Click **Postcards**.
4. Click desired postcard type.
5. Click desired postcard design.
6. Under Size (in task pane), click **Quarter-page** or **Half-page**.

   ✓ *Not all templates allow you to change the size.*

7. Under Side 2 information, click the type of placeholder to insert on page 2 of the publication.

   ✓ *For example, you could click Promotional Text.*

8. Under Copies per sheet, click **One** or **Multiple**.

   ✓ *Just like with business cards, you can specify a custom postcard size and number of cards to print per page in the Page Setup dialog box.*

9. Customize the text on both pages of the publication.
10. If desired, set up a mail merge, as described in Exercise 43 and the following procedures.

Merge Addresses from Outlook

1. Create the postcard or other publication.
2. Start a mail merge by doing the following:
   - Click **Tools** .... Alt+T
   - Point to **Mail and Catalog Merge** .... G
   - Click **Mail and Catalog Merge Wizard** .... W
3. Click **Next: Select data source**.
4. Click **Select from Outlook contacts**.
5. Click **Choose Contacts Folder**.
6. If prompted to select a profile, click a profile and click **OK**.
7. Select **Contacts** folder from list of folders.
8. Click **OK**.

   ✓ *The Mail Merge Recipients dialog box appears.*

9. Complete the mail merge normally. (See Exercise 43.)

Prepare an Excel File for a Mail Merge

1. Open the data file in Excel.
2. Make sure that:
   - The field names are in the first row.
   - There are no extra blank rows at the top.
3. Save your file and close Excel.

Prepare a Text File for a Mail Merge

1. Open the data file in a text editor (such as Notepad).
2. Make sure that:
   - The field names are in the first row.
   - There are no extra blank rows at the top.
   - Each record is in its own paragraph.
   - Fields are separated within each record in a consistent way (tabs or commas).
3. Save your file and close the text editor program.

Merge Addresses from an Excel Worksheet or Access Database

1. (Excel only) Prepare your data file. See "Prepare an Excel File for a Mail Merge."
2. Open Publisher and create the postcard or other publication.
3. Start a mail merge by doing the following:
   a. Click **Tools** .... Alt+T
   b. Point to **Mail and Catalog Merge** .... G
   c. Click **Open Data Source** .... O
4. Navigate to the folder containing the desired file.
5. Select the file.
6. Click **Open** .... Enter
7. Select table or sheet that contains the data.
8. (Excel only) Select or deselect the **First row of data contains column headers** check box ..... Alt+R
9. Click **OK** .... Enter

   ✓ *The Mail Merge Recipients dialog box opens.*

10. Complete the mail merge. (See Exercise 43.)

Merge Addresses from a Text File

1. Prepare your data file. See "Prepare a Text File for a Mail Merge."
2. Open Publisher and create the postcard or other publication.
3. Start a mail merge by doing the following:
   a. Click **Tools** .... Alt+T
   b. Point to **Mail and Catalog Merge** .... G
   c. Click **Open Data Source** .... O
4. Navigate to the folder containing the desired file.
5. Select the file.
6. Click **Open** .... Alt+O
7. Click a delimiter character (Tab, for example).
8. Click **OK** .... Enter

   ✓ *The Mail Merge Recipients dialog box opens.*

9. Complete the mail merge. (See Exercise 43.)

Filter a Merge

Prepare a mail merge normally, as described in Exercise 43. Then before printing, do the following:

1. Click **Tools** .... Alt+T
2. Point to **Mail and Catalog Merge** .... G

3. Click **Filter or Sort** .... S
4. Open the first **Field** drop-down list and choose a field to use as a filter.
5. Choose a comparison from the **Comparison** drop-down list.
6. Type a value in the **Compare to** text box.
7. (Optional) Set up additional criteria on the other two lines in the dialog box.
8. Click **OK** .... Enter

Sort a Merge

Prepare a mail merge normally, as described in Exercise 43. Then before printing, do the following:

1. Click **Tools** .... Alt+T
2. Point to **Mail and Catalog Merge** .... G
3. Click **Filter or Sort** .... S
4. Click **Sort Records** tab .... Alt+O
5. Open the **Sort by** drop-down list and choose a field .... Alt+S
6. Click **Ascending** .... Alt+A

   OR

   Click **Descending** .... Alt+D
7. (Optional) Select up to two other fields in the **Then by** boxes.
8. Click **OK** .... Enter

Exercise Directions

1. Start Publisher, if necessary.
2. Create a new publication based on the Connection Reminder Postcard Wizard:
   - Use all the default values in the template except choose Multiple copies per sheet.
   - Use the Primary Business contact information, and change it to the following information:

     Name: **Dr. Tim Green**
     Organization name: **Green Dental Practice**
     Address: **100 N Highway 47, Indianapolis, IN 46240**
     Phone: **317-555-9082**
     Fax: **317-555-9091**
     Email: **tim@timgreendds.com**
3. Save the file as **44REMIND**.
4. Delete the following objects from page 1:
   - Delete the Date, Time, and Describe your location text frames.
   - Delete the logo placeholder.
5. Change the text **To confirm or cancel appointment** to read **To make an appointment**:.
6. Delete the placeholder text in the **Place text here**... frame on page 1 and leave the insertion point in that text frame.
7. Enlarge the text frame to fit the width of the postcard, so that more text will fit in it.
8. Select the file **44DATA.xls** as a mail merge data file.
9. Using a combination of typing and inserting fields manually, place the following text in that frame:

   Dear <<First>>:
   Our records show you are due for a <<Service Due>> **on or after** <<Date Due>>.
   Please call us at your earliest convenience to schedule an appointment.
10. On page 2 of the card, delete the address placeholder text and insert an address block for the customer's address.

    ✓ *You can use the Mail and Catalog Merge Wizard to insert an address block, or you can construct an address block manually from individual fields.*
11. Format the address block in 12-point Arial font.
12. Preview the merge.
13. Sort the merge in ascending order by ZIP Code, and within ZIP Code, in descending order by last name.
14. Filter the data so that only people whose due dates are or before 5/1/2005 will receive postcards.
15. Print the postcards. The fronts (page 1's) should resemble Illustration A and the backs Illustration B.
16. Save your work and exit Publisher.

Illustration A

Green Dental Practice

Dear Sara:

Our records show you are due for a six-month checkup on or after 5/1/2005. Please call us at your earliest convenience to schedule an appointment.

Reminder

To make an appointment:

Phone: (317) 555-9082
Fax: (317) 555-9091
Email: tim@timgreendds.com

Illustration B

Green Dental Practice

100 N Highway 47
Indianapolis, IN 46240

PLEASE
PLACE
STAMP
HERE

Sara Kuester
Rt. 1 Box 79A
Indianapolis, IL 44118

On Your Own

1. Start Publisher, if necessary.
2. A friend has just moved into a new home. Here is her new address and phone number:

   Wendy Lee
   19874 Park Avenue
   New York, NY 10019
   (555) 977-8981

3. Create a change-of-address postcard for Wendy to send to her friends to let them know of her move. Save the file as **44CHANGE**.
4. Mail-merge the postcards with the names and addresses from the tab-delimited text file **44WENDY.txt**, sorted by ZIP Code and excluding all the blank records plus Loren Haddix.
5. Save your work and exit Publisher.

Exercise 45

Skills Covered:

◆ **Create a Brochure** ◆ **Choose a Color Model** ◆ **Use Specific Colors**
◆ **Use Trapping** ◆ **Link to External Graphics Files**
◆ **Embed Fonts** ◆ **Use Pack and Go**

On the Job

Many businesses use brochures as a marketing tool. The most common type of brochure is a single sheet, printed front and back and folded into thirds. You can create such brochures in Publisher and print copies on your office printer—or create a master for a commercial printing service instead.

Green Dental Practice, which you created a mail merge for in Exercise 44, now needs a brochure to hand out at the local health fair. In this exercise, you will create their brochure and prepare it for publication by a printing service.

Terms

Color model The method of color definition to be used for printing a publication. Choices are RGB, CMYK, and spot color.

RGB Stands for Red-Green-Blue, a type of color process, typically used for onscreen displays and low-end printing.

Spot color A color used for accent areas, rather than for blending into complex colors. This type of color printing is typically less expensive than other color printing because you can choose one or two colors besides black.

CMYK Stands for Cyan-Maroon-Yellow-Black, a type of color process, typically used for high-end printing.

Registration The proper alignment of the paper and ink in a multi-pass printing process such as CYMK.

Trapping In a color separation, the faint overlapping of two colors, done to prevent gaps in the printing in the event of a minor registration error.

Notes

Create a Brochure

- Create a new brochure with the Brochure template the same as you would any other type of document. There are several categories of brochures available, including Informational, Event, Price List, and Fund-raiser.
- For some brochure designs, you can choose between three and four panels. If you choose a four-panel layout, you will need to print on legal-size paper rather than letter.
- You can choose whether to include a customer address on some brochure designs. This makes the brochure into a mailer that can be bulk mailed.
- Just as with a flyer, you can choose to include an Order form, Response form, or Sign-up form on the brochure.

Sample brochure

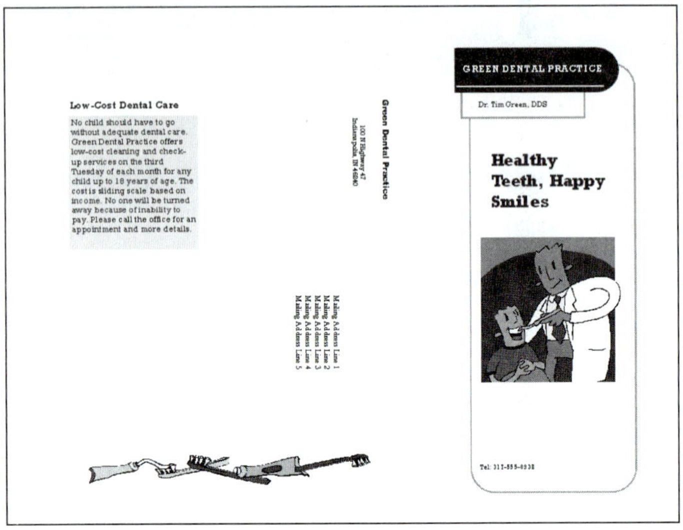

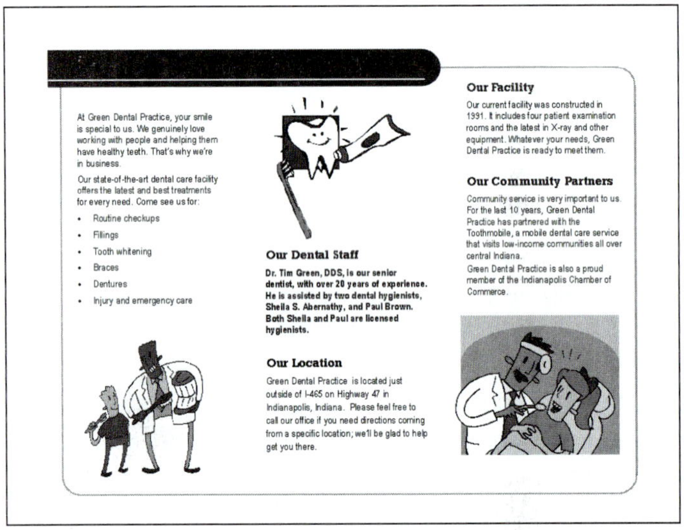

Choose a Color Model

- If you plan to print the brochure using a commercial printing service, contact the service and find out how you should prepare the file. Each service is different.
- If your brochure contains colors, you will want to set the **color model** for the kind the printing service recommends. You set the color model from Tools, Commercial Printing Tools, Color Printing.
- Single color converts the publication to monochrome (black, by default). If the printer uses some other ink than black, the publication will be printed in that color instead.

Select the way that colors should be represented

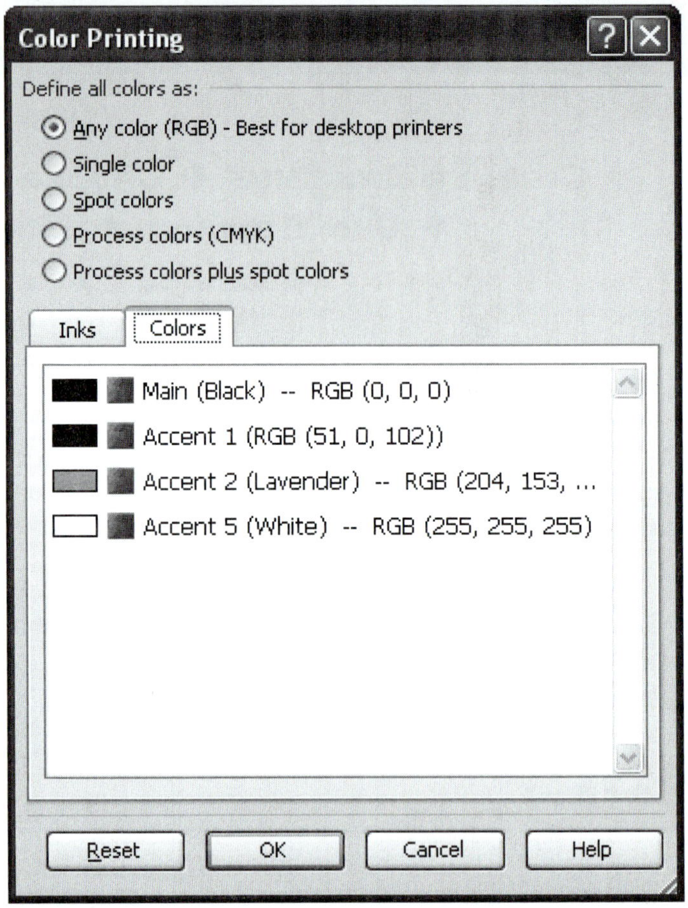

- Any color (**RGB**) is the best choice for desktop printing (that is, when you are printing it yourself on a single-pass color printer such as an inkjet).
  - ✓ *The main disadvantage of going with any other color model except RGB is the loss of transparency levels for fills that may be set up in Publisher.*
- **Spot color(s)** is a good choice when you are trying to economize on printing costs. When you buy spot printing, you pay by the ink color, and with spot color you can see and control how many ink colors you will need. Spot colors serve as an accent such as in headings, borders, or logos, but are not good for photos.
- Process colors **(CMYK)** sets up the publication for multipass process color printing, in which each color is printed separately.

- Process-color (CMYK) printing and spot-color printing differ in two ways: the range or number of colors each can reproduce, and the cost of printing. In process-color printing, a full range of colors is reproduced by combining four semitransparent inks. In spot-color printing, one or two colors are produced using semitransparent inks.
- The Process colors plus spot colors option lets you select Process colors as the primary color method, but also lets you add spot colors by clicking the Add button. For example, you might have normal colors plus a metallic or fluorescent color that can't be reproduced in CMYK.
- There are many advanced features available for working with the color models, including adding new ink colors for spot colors, but these are beyond the scope of this course.

Use Specific Colors

- Different PCs and different monitors and color models make colors look very different. You cannot rely on what you see onscreen as a gauge of what your publication will look like when professionally printed.
- One way to guarantee accurate color representation in a publication is to rely on a numeric definition of a certain color.
- There are four popular color models, and Publisher supports all four: RGB (Red, Green, Blue), HSL (Hue, Saturation, Lightness), CMYK (Cyan, Magenta, Yellow, Black), and PANTONE®.
- You can buy (or get for free) printed cards that show the colors in each of these color sets and their numeric values. Then you change the colors in your publication to match the numeric values of the colors you see on the cards.
- To change a color, edit the color scheme as you did in Exercise 10. When selecting the new color, choose More Colors from a New drop-down list and click the Custom tab.
- Choose a color model, and then enter the numeric value(s) for that color. Depending on the color model you choose, there may be either three (for RGB or HSL) or four numbers (for CMYK) to enter.

Specify a color by its numeric value

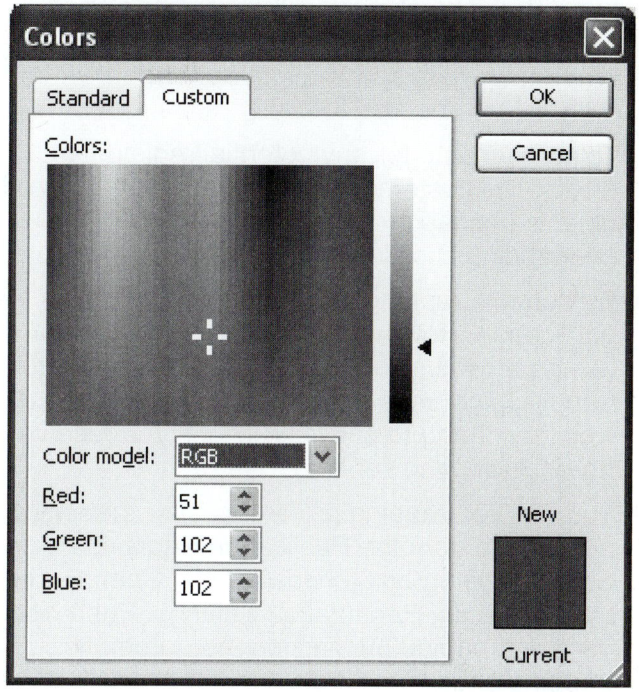

- PANTONE® is a special case. If you choose PANTONE®, a special dialog box appears in which you can select colors.

PANTONE® Colors have their own special dialog box for selection

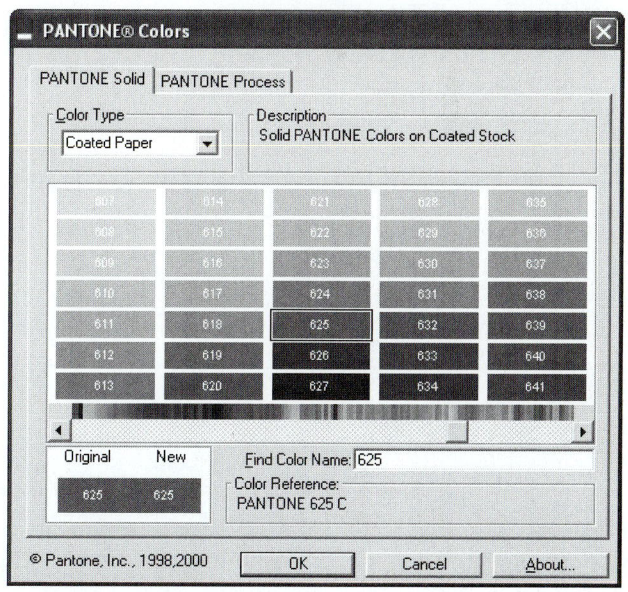

Use Trapping

- During multi-pass printing such as on a CMYK press, each color is laid down individually. Therefore the possibility exists for the paper to shift slightly between colors, resulting in **registration** errors.

- One typical registration error might occur when two colored blocks are adjacent to one another in the publication; if registration is off, a tiny amount of white space might appear between then.
- To compensate for any potential registration errors, it is customary to make adjacent colored objects overlap by about 1/3 of a point. This overlapping is called **trapping**.
- By default, trapping is turned off for a publication. However, if you are going to print using process colors (CMYK), you will want to turn trapping on, and possibly set its options as well (according to any instructions you receive from the printing service).
- You can set trapping preferences for the entire publication from the Publication Registration Settings dialog box (choose Tools, Commercial Printing Tools, Registration Settings, Publication. Turn on trapping by marking the Automatic trapping check box.

Turn on Automatic trapping

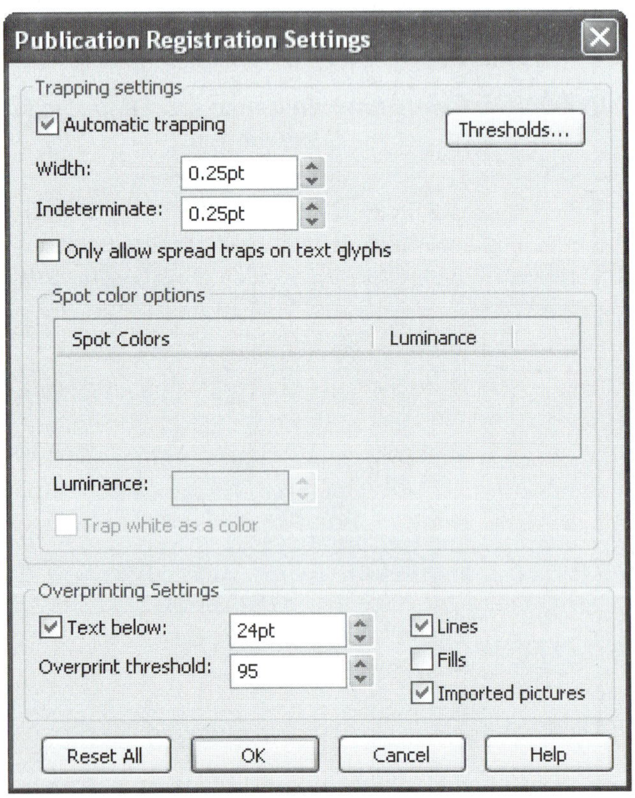

- You can also set individual trapping settings for each object. Choose Tools, Commercial Printing Tools, Registration Settings, Per Object). For each object you can set different trapping for the border, contents, and/or text.
- Your trapping options for an object include Overprint, Knockout, or Custom. These values override Publisher's default trap settings.

Set custom trapping for an individual object as needed

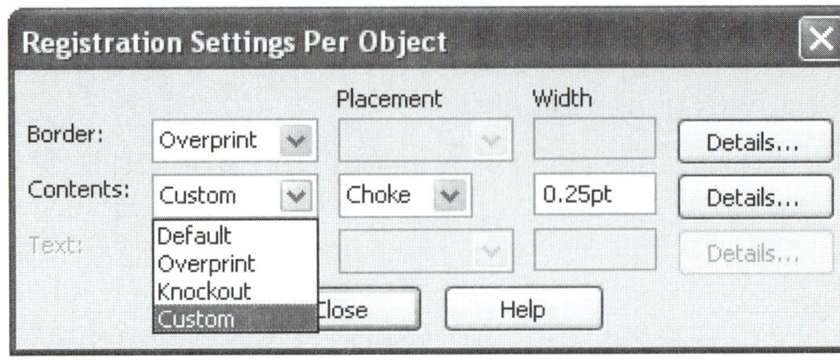

- Unless you are an experienced layout professional, or unless you have received specific instructions from your printing service, it is best to leave object trapping settings alone. Simply turn trapping on for the entire publication and let Publisher handle the rest with its defaults.

Link to External Graphic Files

- When you place clip art or other images in your publication, you usually embed them. That means the graphic is part of the publication, rather than separate from it. However, many printing services require you to submit separate graphic files along with your publication, with links to their positions in the layout.
- To solve this problem, you can create links for the graphics in your publication with the Graphics Manager (choose Tools, Graphics Manager).
- Open the drop-down menu for an embedded picture and click Save as Linked picture.

The Graphics Manager helps you separate embedded graphics from the publication

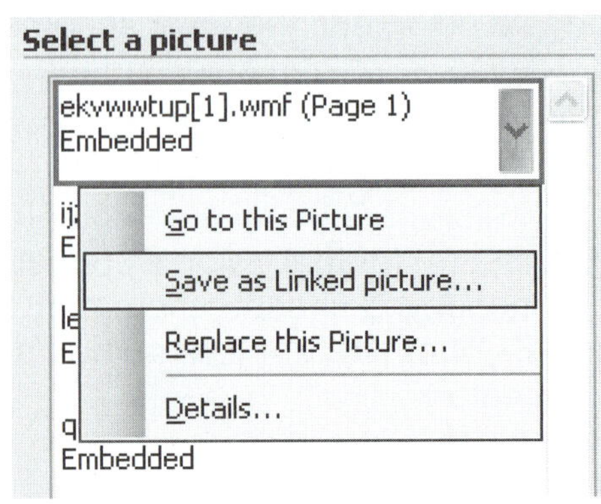

- This opens the Save As dialog box, where you can specify a file name and location.
- You can also specify a resolution for the picture, in dots per inch (dpi) by clicking the Change button.

Save a graphic externally and set a different resolution for the saved linked copy if desired

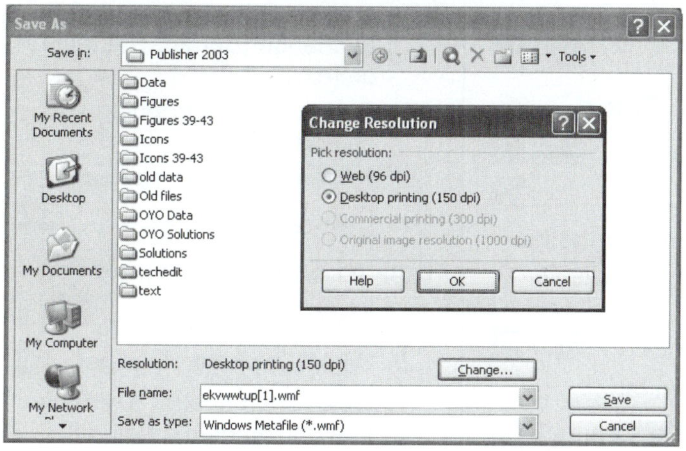

- You can decrease but not increase the resolution from the original setting. Your choices are Web (96 dpi), Desktop printing (150 dpi), Commercial printing (300 dpi), and Original image resolution.

Embed Fonts

- The printing service you use may not have the same fonts installed on its system as you do. If you use a font that it doesn't have, the publication won't look right, because it will have to substitute a different font for the one you had selected.
- A solution to this problem is to embed the needed fonts in your publication file. That way the fonts will be available, no matter what PC you use to open it. The tradeoff is that embedding fonts increases the file size.
- The Fonts dialog box (choose Tools, Commercial Printing Tools, Fonts) lists the fonts used in the publication and details the font type, the font source, and the license restrictions.
- The fonts Times New Roman, Arial, and Symbol may not be embedded by default. These are the default fonts in Windows, so everyone should have these. Some other fonts may not be embedded due to licensing restrictions.
- To embed fonts, mark the Embed TrueType fonts when saving publication check box.
- If you use the Pack and Go Wizard (refer to the next section), that wizard automatically turns font-embedding on for the packed file.
- You can select an individual font and choose not to embed it by clicking the Don't Embed button for it. That way you can exclude fonts that you know the printing service already has, to reduce the file size.

Select which fonts to embed in your publication

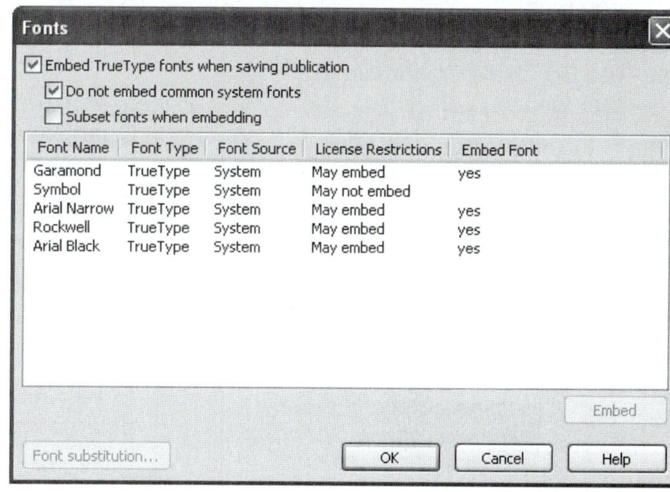

Use Pack and Go

- When you are ready to send your publication to a printing service, you will want to ensure that you send all the associated files along with the publication itself. These can include linked graphics, fonts, and so on.
- The Pack and Go Wizard enables you to pack the presentation, compressing and consolidating all needed files into one convenient package. It will also split large publications across multiple disks, if needed.
- When the printing service receives the packed file, it copies the file to its computer and then runs the Unpack program to decompress and separate the files.
- To run the Pack and Go Wizard, choose File, Pack and Go, Take to a Commercial Printing Service. Then just follow the prompts.

Procedures

Create a Brochure

1. Start Publisher, if necessary.
2. Click **Publications for Print** in the task pane.
3. Click **Brochures**.
4. Click the brochure type you want.
5. Click the brochure design you want.
6. Click the options you want in the Brochure Options in the task pane:
   - Under Page size, click **3-panel** or **4-panel**.
     - ✓ *If you choose 4-panel, you will need to print on legal-size paper.*
   - Under Customer address, click **Include** or **None**.
     - ✓ *If you choose Include, the second panel of the first page will contain mailing address placeholders.*
   - Under **Form**, click **None**, **Order form**, **Sign-up form**, or **Response form**.
     - ✓ *If you choose a form, it will appear in the last panel of the second page.*
7. Click **Color Schemes** and choose a different color scheme if desired.
8. Click **Font Schemes** and choose a different font scheme if desired.
9. Click **Publication Designs** and choose a different design if desired.
10. Customize the brochure with your own text and graphics.

Choose a Color Model

1. Click **Tools** .... Alt+T
2. Point to **Commercial Printing Tools** .... P
3. Click **Color Printing** C
4. Click the color model you want:
   - **Any color (RGB)** ... Alt+A
   - **Single color** .... Alt+I
   - **Spot colors** .... Alt+S
   - **Process colors (CMYK)** .... Alt+P
   - **Process colors plus spot colors** .... Alt+U

Choose a Specific Color

1. Click **Format** .... Alt+O
2. Click **Color Schemes** C
3. Click **Custom color scheme**.
4. Open New drop-down list for desired color.
5. Click **More Colors** .... Alt+M
6. Click the **Custom** tab.
7. Open **Color Model** list .... Alt+D
8. Select a color model.
9. Enter numeric value(s) for the desired color.
10. Click **OK** .... Enter
11. Repeat steps 4-10 for other colors if desired.
12. Click **OK** .... Enter

Turn On Automatic Trapping

1. Click **Tools** .... Alt+T
2. Point to **Commercial Printing Tools** .... P
3. Point to **Registration Settings** .... R
4. Click **Publication** .... P
5. Click the **Automatic trapping** check box ..... Alt+A
6. Set any other trapping settings desired.
7. Click **OK** .... Enter

Set Trapping for an Individual Object

1. Select the object.
2. Click **Tools** .... Alt+T
3. Point to **Commercial Printing Tools** .... P
4. Point to **Registration Settings** .... R
5. Click **Per Object** .... O
6. Open the drop-down list for the aspect of the object you want to change (Border, Contents, or Text).
7. Select the new trapping settings.
8. Repeat steps 6-7 as needed.
9. Click **Close** .... Enter

Link to External Graphic Files

1. Click **Tools** .... Alt+T
2. Click **Graphics Manager** .... N
3. Open the menu for a graphic that you want to create an external linked file for.
4. Click **Save as Linked picture** .... Alt+S
5. Enter a file name or accept the default name.
6. Change the location or accept the default location.
7. (Optional) Change the resolution:
   a. Click **Change** .... Alt+C
   b. Click different resolution.
   c. Click **OK** .... Enter
8. Click **Save** .... Enter

Embed Fonts

1. Click **Tools** .... Alt+T
2. Point to **Commercial Printing Tools** .... P
3. Click **Fonts** .... F
4. Click **Embed TrueType fonts when saving publication** .... Alt+T
5. To choose a font *not* to embed, do the following:
   a. Click the font name.
   b. Click **Don't Embed** ... Alt+D
6. Click **OK** .... Enter

Use Pack and Go

1. Click **File** .... Alt+F
2. Point to **Pack and Go** .... K
3. Click **Take to a Commercial Printing Service** .... P
4. If prompted to save your publication, click **OK** to do so.
5. When the Pack and Go Wizard resumes, click **Next** ..... Alt+N
6. Select the location to which you want to pack:
   - Click **A:**.

   OR

   - Click the button next to the unlabeled text box, and then type a location there (or browse for a location with the **Browse** button).
7. Click **Next** .... Alt+N
8. Clear the check box for any of these options you don't want:
   - **Embed TrueType fonts** .... Alt+E
   - **Include linked graphics** .... Alt+I
   - **Create links for embedded graphics** .... Alt+C
9. Click **Next** .... Alt+N
10. Click **Finish** .... Alt+F
11. Clear the check box for either of the printings that you don't want:
    - **Print a composite proof** ... Alt+C
    - **Print separations** .... Alt+S
12. Click **OK** .... Enter

Unpack a Packed Presentation

1. In Windows, open the folder containing the packed publication.

   ✓ *The folder name is the name of the publication plus PNG: For example,* JonesPNG.
2. Double-click the **Unpack** icon.
3. Enter the destination folder where you want to unpack the files (or browse for it with the **Browse** button).
4. Click **OK** .... Enter
5. If you see a warning that there may be files with the same name in the directory, click:
   - **Yes** to replace them .... Alt+Y

   OR

   - **No** to return to the previous box to select a different location. .... Alt+N
6. At the message that the publication was successfully unpacked, click **OK** .... Enter

Exercise Directions

1. Start Publisher, if necessary.
2. Open the file **PUB45**. Save it as **45BROCH**.

   ✓ *This brochure was created with the Brochure Wizard. Customized text and figures have been added for your convenience, so you do not have to spend a lot of time in this exercise typing text and practicing other skills you already know very well.*
3. In the Brochure Options, set the Customer address to None.
4. Set the brochure to use process colors (CMYK).
5. Turn on automatic trapping.
6. Using the Graphics Manager, save each of the embedded graphics as a new, linked graphic. (You can keep the same names for them as the originals.)
7. Embed all the embeddable fonts except Arial Narrow.
8. Use Pack and Go to pack the presentation to a floppy disk (or another location your teacher specifies) to take to a commercial printer. When prompted during Pack and Go, deselect the Print a composite and Print separations check boxes.
9. Save your work and exit Publisher.

On Your Own

1. Start Publisher, if necessary.
2. Create a brochure using the Ascent Event Brochure Wizard. Include a sign-up form and a customer address placeholder. Set the Personal Information to a fictitious business or charity organization.
3. Save the file as **45MYBRO**.
4. Customize the text and graphics, at least on the first page, to advertise a fictional charity event of your choosing. Illustration A shows one possible idea.
5. Set the presentation to print with spot colors.
6. Use Pack and Go to pack the presentation to take to another computer. Print a color separation when prompted at the end of the wizard.
7. Save your work and exit Publisher.

Illustration A

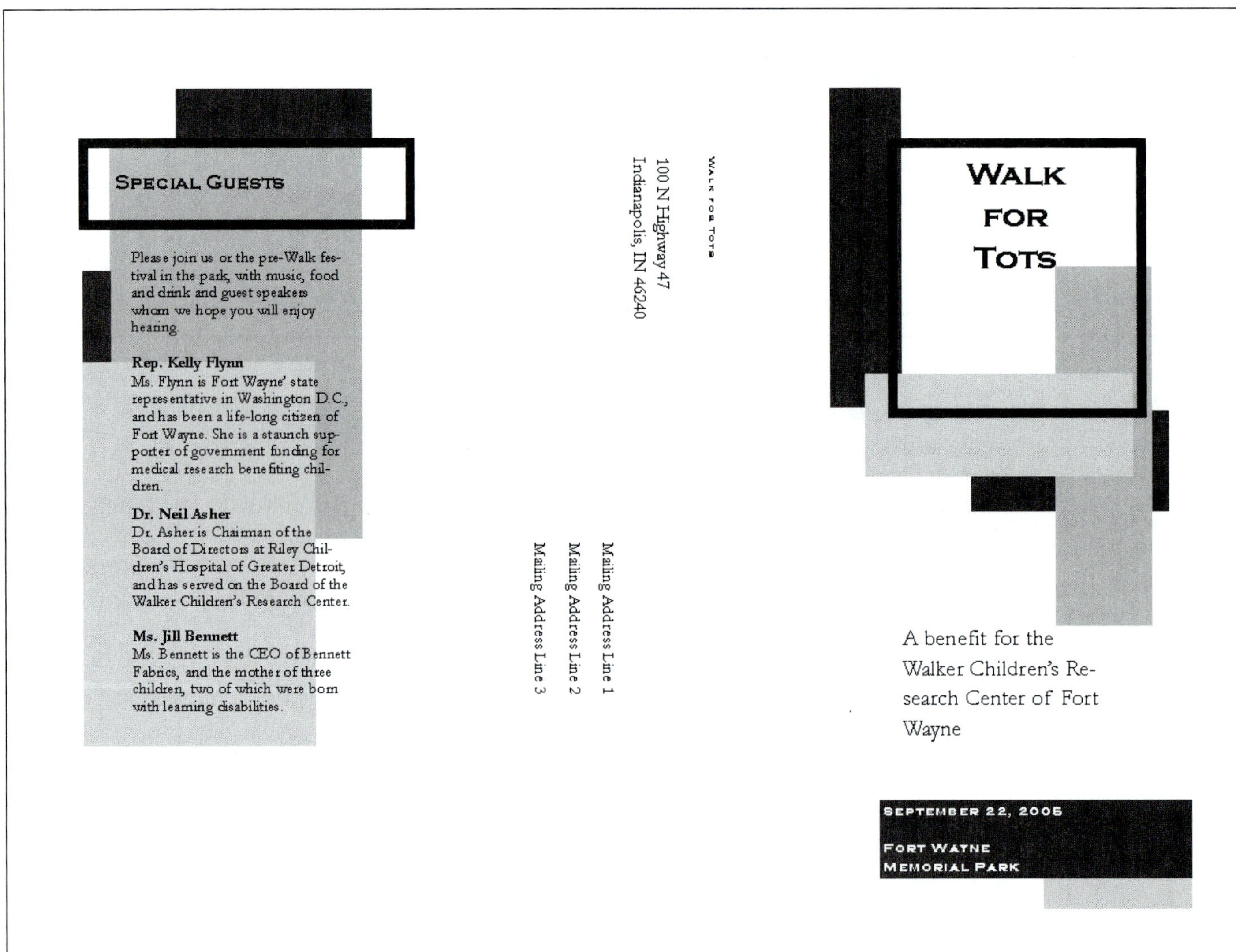

Exercise 46

◆ Critical Thinking

Benjamin Price, your favorite actor, is coming to town to appear in a theatre production. You are the president of the local chapter of his fan club, and you want to get the word out! In this exercise, you'll create a newsletter to send to all the members of your chapter and perform a mail merge to address the copies.

Exercise Directions

1. Start Publisher, if necessary.
2. Create a new newsletter using the Blends Newsletter Wizard. Include a placeholder for the customer address, and set it for single-sided printing. Save it as **46NEWS**.
3. Delete pages 2 and 3 (you won't need them).
4. Delete all the pictures on the remaining two pages.
5. Title your newsletter **The Price Report**.
6. Replace the lead story placeholder with the story from **46Story1.doc** (a Word document). Flow the text onto the back page of the newsletter, and add "Continued" indicators. (Do not flow the text into the boxes for the secondary article on the first page.)
7. Insert the picture **46BEN.jpg** on page 1 as shown in Illustration A.
8. Replace the article title placeholder with an appropriate story title, as shown in Illustration A.
9. Turn off automatic hyphenation for the story.
10. Create a secondary story at the bottom of page 1 from the file **46Story2.doc** and add its title: **Price Merchandise Swap Meet**.
11. Adjust the text box sizes on page 1 so that the secondary story fits. (The primary story can float to the second page.)
12. Add a **Dates to Remember** section as in Illustration A.
13. Place some clip art on the back page to fill the extra white space at the bottom.
14. Delete any page elements you don't need (such as the table of contents on page 1 and the Design Object placeholders on page 2).
15. Create a mail merge to address the newsletter to everyone on the mailing list found in **46ADDRESS.doc**, sorted by last name. Use an address block rather that inserting individual fields.
16. Save your work and close the file.
17. Now, suppose you decide to use mailing labels instead of merging the addresses directly onto the newsletter. Create a separate publication that creates the merged labels. Sort them by ZIP Code. Save the file as **46LABELS**.
18. Print the labels.
19. Save your work and exit Publisher.

Illustration A

BENJAMIN PRICE FAN CLUB

THE PRICE REPORT

Volume 1, Issue 1
March 04

BENJAMIN IN TOWN!

Exciting news, Price fans! Benjamin Price has just announced that he will be appearing in the play "Happiness" at the Phoenix Theatre in Indianapolis from May 30 through June 15 of this year. Tickets are available now by calling 317-555-0971.

"Happiness" is a comedy about growing up unpopular in a Midwestern high school in the 1970s. Benjamin will be playing the lead, Norman Neiderman, a much beleaguered "nice guy" who struggles for acceptance from the popular kids.

I spoke with Benjamin on the phone the other day, and he had this to say: "I am really looking forward to having fun with the role of Norman. Because I grew up in a small Midwestern town myself, many of the characters and situations are familiar to me. I even played in the band myself, just like Norman, although I played the drums instead of the tuba." When

(Continued on page 2)

Dates to Remember:

- May 30: Fan club trip to opening night of "Happiness" at the Phoenix Theatre
- October 2: Benjamin Price merchandise swap meet at the home of Nicole Bennett

PRICE MERCHANDISE SWAP MEET

Do you have any Benjamin Price merchandise to buy or sell? Lunchboxes? Posters? Autographed items?

In October, the fan club will be hosting a swap meet where you can buy and sell your merchandise, and maybe pick up that special item you have always wanted for your collection. It will be held at the home of Nicole Bennett, 123 S. Main St. in Indianapolis, starting at 7:00 p.m. and running until 10:00 p.m. So dig through that closet and find some Benjamin souvenirs to turn into cold hard cash!

Exercise 47

◆ **Critical Thinking**

You work for Sweet Treats, a local ice cream parlor, and you need create a flyer with a coupon that customers can redeem on their next visit. The owner plans to use a commercial printing service to print the flyers and wants to use spot color printing to hold down the costs. Design a flyer with a 2-for-1 banana split coupon, and prepare it for commercial printing.

Exercise Directions

1. Start Publisher, if necessary.
2. Create a new flyer using the Flyer Wizard (Mobile Special Offer design, Burgundy color scheme, no graphic, no customer address), and include a coupon on it.
3. Save the file as **47FLYER**.
4. Customize the flyer to resemble Illustration A:
   - Replace placeholder text with the text shown here.
   - Change the attention getter style with the Attention Getter Wizard.
   - Delete the unneeded text boxes and other objects.
   - Use the Coupon Wizard to modify the coupon.
   - Increase the size of the expiration date on the coupon to 9 points.
   - Turn off automatic hyphenation.
   - Set the spacing between lines for the body text to 1.25 sp.
5. Set the color model to Spot color(s).
6. Turn on automatic trapping for the whole publication.
7. Embed all fonts.
8. Print the publication and save it.
9. Use Pack and Go to save the publication onto a floppy (or other location your teacher specifies) for a commercial printing service.
10. Save your work and exit Publisher.

Illustration A

Sweet Treats
presents the...

Banana Split Extravaganza

2 for 1

March 22nd through
30th only!

You don't really want a small cone, do you? Nope, you want the big, sweet, sticky excess of a banana split, covered with toppings, nuts, whipped cream, and a cherry.

Well, now you and a friend can share this decadent pleasure together, because our Deluxe Banana Split is two-for-one. Just bring in the coupon below. That's right, your friend buys one and you get yours free! Or vice versa. We'll leave that up to you.

Sweet Treats is conveniently located at the corner of Brook Street and 10th Street in downtown Evansville.

2 for 1

Banana Split

SWEET TREATS

Buy one at regular price, get the second free

Expiration Date: 12/31/06

Lesson 6

Creating Web and E-mail Content

Exercise 48

- Create an E-mail Publication
- Insert an E-mail Hyperlink
- Send an E-mail Publication

Exercise 49

- Convert a Print Publication to Web Format
- Change the Page Width
- Change a Web Page Title
- Preview a Web Page
- Save a Publication as a Web Page

Exercise 50

- About Hyperlinks
- Place Hot Spots
- Simulate Hot Spots with AutoShapes

Exercise 51

- Create a 3-Page Web Site
- Use the Easy Web Site Builder
- Add Pages Manually
- Remove Pages
- Customize a Page Layout
- Customize the Navigation Bar

Exercise 52

- Create a Web Form
- Insert a Web Form from the Design Gallery
- Customize a Web Form
- Change a Form Control's Properties
- Set the Data Retrieval Method

Exercise 53

- Methods of Transferring Web Content to a Server
- Saving to a Web Location
- Saving to an FTP Location
- Other Transfer Methods

Exercise 54

- Critical Thinking

Exercise 48

Skills Covered:

- **Create an E-mail Publication**
- **Insert an E-mail Hyperlink**
- **Send an E-mail Publication**

On the Job

You probably get e-mails all the time that look almost like Web pages, with fancy graphics and formatting. There are many ways to accomplish such formatting, but one of the most common is to create and attach a special type of Web page to an e-mail message. Publisher 2003 comes with many templates for creating these.

The Greater Decatur PC Club is hosting an open house for prospective members, and they would like to send out an invitation via e-mail. In this exercise you will create the invitation using a Publisher template.

Terms

Hyperlink Text or a graphic object that does something when clicked such as opening a Web page or starting a new e-mail message.

Notes

Create an E-mail Publication

- Publisher provides many templates that you can use to create publications designed to be e-mailed to recipients.
- To create a new e-mail publication, begin from the New Publication task pane as usual, but choose Web Sites and E-mail instead of Publications for Print. Then choose either Web Sites or E-mail, and then a template.
- In many respects these are identical to their print counterparts. You can format them using all the same layout and formatting techniques you have learned in earlier lessons. The difference is that e-mail templates produce publications that are ideally sized and formatted to work well in e-mail format.

Choose an e-mail template

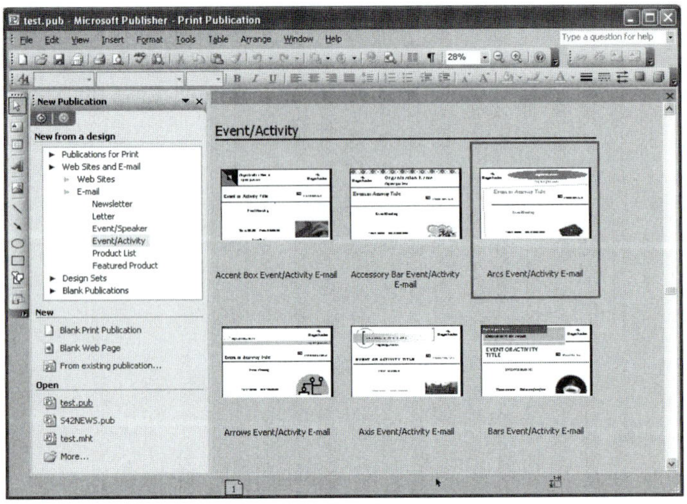

- The default page size for an e-mail is 5.818" wide by 11" high. The narrower-than-usual width is needed so that everyone can view the entire width of the publication onscreen even at a low Windows display resolution.

A publication constructed from an e-mail template

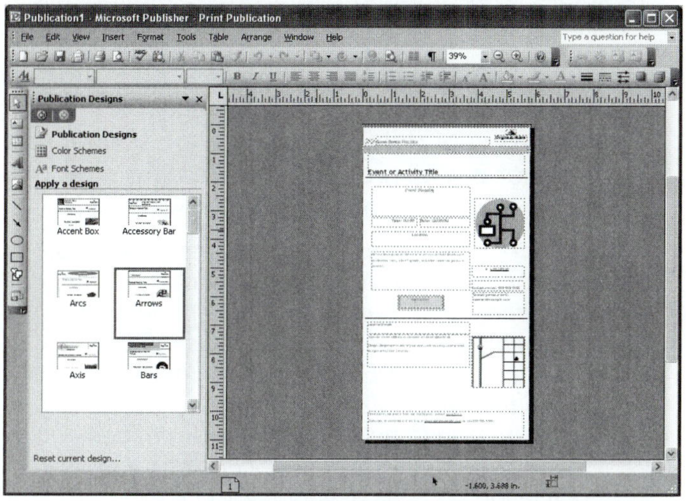

- The margins for e-mail pages are set to 0" on all sides. Since the publication will be displayed onscreen rather than printed, there does not need to be any extra white space at the edges.

Insert an E-mail Hyperlink

- A **hyperlink** is a bit of text or a graphic object that does something when clicked. Some of the possibilities include opening a Web page, starting a new e-mail message, or opening a document.
- A text hyperlink can show the actual address for the link like this:

E-mail us at **ben@decaturcomputerclub.org**

- Or it can show some other text, like this:

please **click here to e-mail us.**

- Select the text in the document that should be underlined as the hyperlink, and then choose Insert, Hyperlink (or click the Insert Hyperlink button 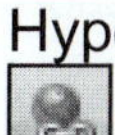 on the Standard toolbar).
- In the Insert Hyperlink dialog box, click E-mail Address. Then enter the desired address in the E-mail Address box.

Insert an e-mail hyperlink

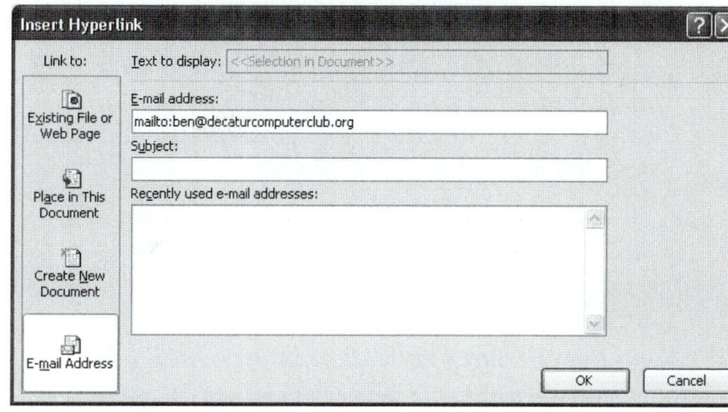

- You cannot type text in the Text to display box; as you can see above it is unavailable. The text that you selected prior to opening the dialog box will be the text to display. If you did not select any text, the word immediately before the insertion point will become the selected text.
- If you select a graphic before opening the dialog box, that graphic will become the object to be clicked to activate the hyperlink.
- If the insertion point is not in a text box, and no other object is selected, the Insert Hyperlink command will not be available.

Send an E-mail Publication

- An e-mail publication in Publisher is still a regular publication. When you save it, by default it saves in Publisher format (.pub), same as any print publication.
- There are two ways you can send the publication to other people via e-mail:
  - You can attach the Publisher file to an e-mail message. This sends the actual .pub file. Recipients must have Publisher in order to open it. The received copy is editable in Publisher.
  - You can send the file in the body of an e-mail. When the recipient opens the e-mail, they see the publication; Publisher is not required. The received copy is not editable.
- Both methods start the same way: File, Send E-Mail. Then choose either Send This Page as Message or Send This Publication as Attachment.
- Sending in an e-mail body works only with single-page publications. If you send a multi-page publication this way, only one page will be sent (whatever page was displayed when you issued the command).

- ✓ *An e-mail publication is just like a regular publication except for its page size and the fact that there is only one page. You can send regular publications via e-mail just like you can an e-mail publication. No special conversion is required. Keep in mind, however, that only one page will be included if there are multiple pages.*

- When you send the publication in the body of an e-mail, controls for sending the e-mail appear in Publisher as shown below.

Send the current publication in an e-mail body

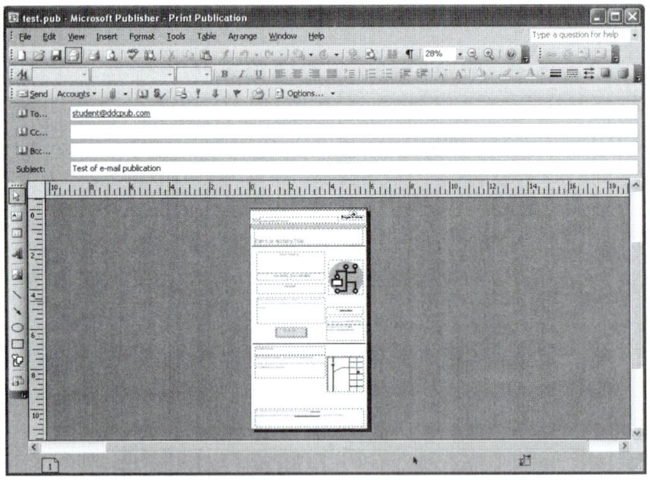

- If you change your mind about sending the publication, choose File, Send E-mail, Cancel E-Mail Message to turn off the e-mail controls in the Publisher window.
- The e-mail does not represent what the recipient will actually see. If you want to preview the recipient copy, choose File, Send E-Mail, E-Mail Preview.
- Sending a publication in the body of an e-mail works best if you use Outlook or Outlook Express as your default e-mail editor. If you use some other e-mail program, this feature may work differently or may not work at all.
  - ✓ *Some recipients with very old e-mail programs may not be able to read your publication when it is in the body of an e-mail. One way to get wider compatibility is to set Publisher to send the publication as a JPEG image with the e-mail. This makes the e-mail size much larger, though. To set up the mailing to be a JPEG image, choose Tools, Options and on the Web tab, choose Send entire publication page as a single JPEG image.*

Procedures

Create an E-mail Publication

1. Start Publisher, if necessary.
2. Click **Web Sites and E-mail** on the task pane.
3. Click **E-mail**.
4. (Optional) Click an e-mail category.
5. Click the design to use.
6. (Optional) Choose a different color scheme.
7. (Optional) Choose a different font scheme.
8. Edit the placeholder text and graphics with your own content.

Insert a E-mail Hyperlink

1. Select the text to be underlined as the hyperlink.
2. Click the **Insert Hyperlink** button .
   - ✓ *You can choose Insert, Hyperlink instead of step 2 if desired.*
3. Click **E-mail Address** .. Alt+M
4. Type the e-mail address for the hyperlink.
5. (Optional) Click in the **Subject** box and type a subject .... Alt+U
6. Click **OK** .... Enter

Send a Publication as an E-mail Attachment

1. Save the publication.
2. Click **File**...................... Alt+F
3. Point to **Send E-Mail** .... D
4. Click **Send Publication as Attachment**......................... A
5. In the **To** box, type the recipient's e-mail address.
6. In the **Subject** line, type a subject.
7. (Optional) In the message area, type a message.
8. Click **Send** .... Alt+S

Send a Publication in the Body of an E-mail

1. Save the publication.
2. Click **File** .... Alt+F
3. Point to **Send E-Mail**........... D
4. Click **Send This Page as Message** .... M
5. In the **To** box, type the recipient's e-mail address.
6. In the **Subject** line, type a subject.
7. Click **Send**.................. Alt+S

Preview an E-mail Message

1. Save the publication.
2. Click **File** .... Alt+F
3. Point to **Send E-mail** .... D
4. Click **E-mail Preview** .... P
5. Close the Web browser when finished viewing.

Exercise Directions

1. Start Publisher, if necessary.
2. Start a new e-mail publication based on the Bounce Event/Activity E-mail template and save it as **48EMAIL**.
3. Replace the picture with an appropriate piece of clip art from the Clip Organizer.
4. Change the text as shown in Illustration A.
5. Make the e-mail address at the bottom into a live hyperlink using the address ben@decaturcomputerclub.org.
6. Make the click here text at the bottom into a live hyperlink to the same e-mail address as in step 5.
7. Preview the publication as e-mail.
8. E-mail the publication to your instructor as an attachment.
9. E-mail the publication to your instructor in the body of the e-mail.
10. Exit Publisher.

On Your Own

1. Start Publisher, if necessary.
2. Create a new e-mail publication based on one of the e-mail letter templates. Save it as **48EMAIL**.
3. Write a letter to your friends and family telling them what you have been doing lately.
4. Include an e-mail hyperlink in the letter that people can use to send you an e-mail message.
5. Save the publication.
6. Preview the publication as e-mail.
7. (Optional) if you did not use the whole page length, decrease the height of the page in the Page Setup dialog box.
8. Send the publication to your instructor in the body of an e-mail message as a JPEG. (See the note at the end of the Notes section for how to do this.)
9. Exit Publisher.

Illustration A

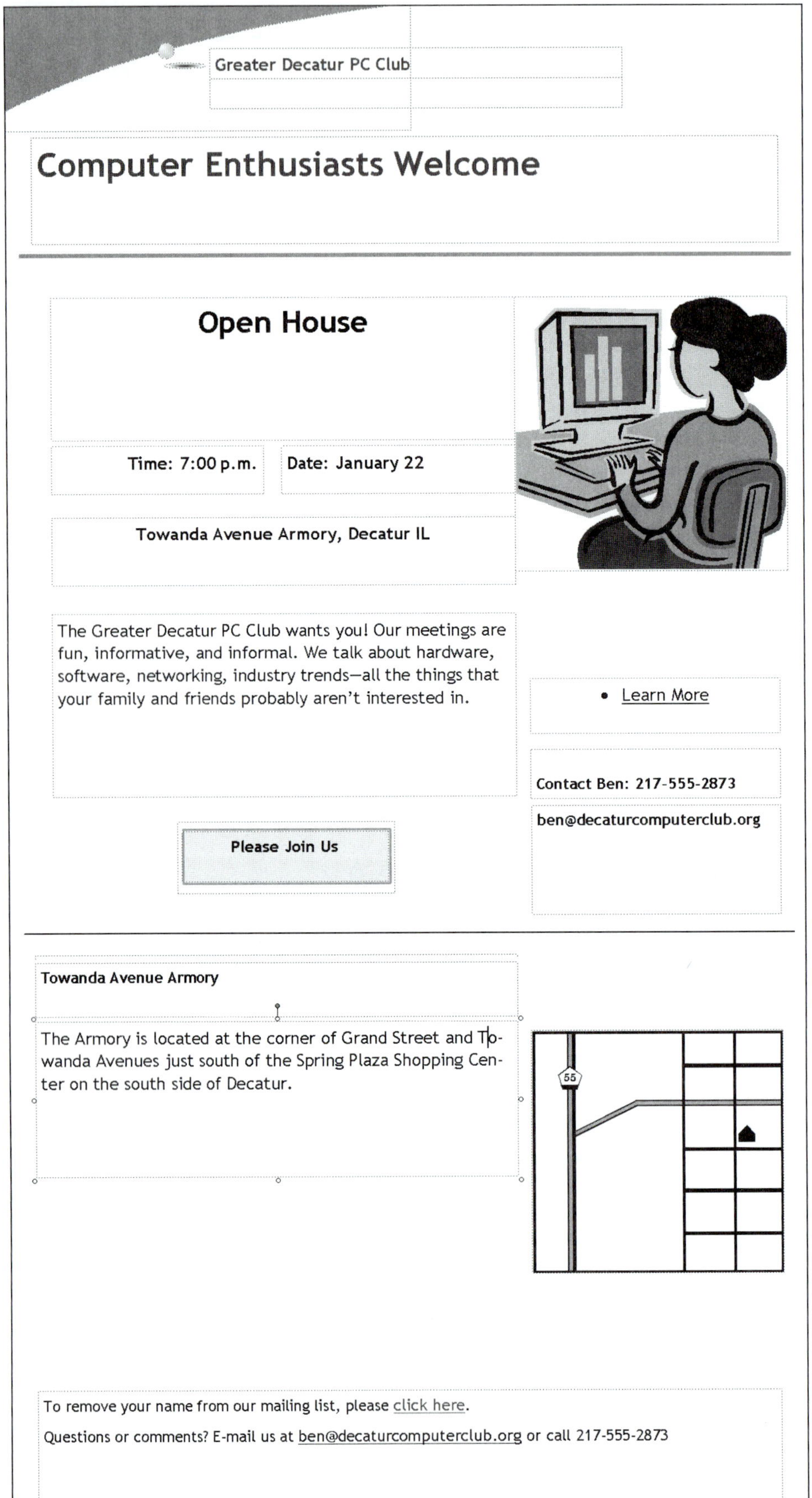

Exercise 49

Skills Covered:

- **Convert a Print Publication to Web Format**
- **Change the Page Width**
- **Change a Web Page Title**
- **Preview a Web Page**
- **Save a Publication as a Web Page**

On the Job

If you need to create a large, commercial Web site, Publisher is probably not the right tool for you. There are other programs, such as Microsoft Office FrontPage, that will give you better results. However, for creating personal and hobby Web sites, Publisher can serve quite effectively, allowing you to create Web pages and sites—or convert standard Publisher publications such as newsletters and brochures into Web documents.

The Greater Decatur Computer Club likes the e-mail you created in Exercise 48 for them, and would now like you to create a Web page that contains the same information that was contained in the e-mail.

Terms

Web page A document designed to be viewed in a Web browser.

Web site A related collection of Web pages with hyperlinks between them.

Navigation bar A collection of hyperlinks to other related pages in the same Web site, typically consistent across all pages in the Web site.

Pixel A dot in the grid of dots that comprises a computer's display. Each pixel can be a different color.

Web browser A program designed to display Web pages. Internet Explorer is the Web browser that comes with Microsoft Office 2003.

Display resolution The number of pixels that comprise the PC's display. A typical resolution is 800x600.

HTML Stands for HyperText Markup Language. The text encoding used to create Web pages.

Filtered HTML file An HTML file created in a Microsoft Office application (like Publisher) that contains only true HTML codes, with no codes for formatting in its original application.

Notes

Convert a Print Publication to Web Format

- One way to create a **Web page** (or multiple Web pages that work together as a **Web site**) is to convert an existing publication to Web format.
- If the existing publication has multiple pages, Publisher will create a separate Web page for each page. (In this exercise, however, we will keep it simple and work with a single page.)
- To convert a publication, open it in Publisher and choose File, Convert to Web Publication.

- As part of the conversion, Publisher asks whether you want a **navigation bar**. For a multi-page publication this can be helpful, but for a single page publication it is not needed. Navigation bars are covered in later exercises.
- After the conversion, you will notice some differences in the publication, such as:
  - The ruler uses **pixels** as the unit of measurement, rather than inches.
  - The New button on the Standard toolbar changes to a New Web Page button.
  - A few of the buttons on the Formatting toolbar are different.
  - The Web Tools toolbar opens.

A Web page in Publisher

Ruler shows pixels

✓ *Even though the publication is formatted for Web use, it is still a standard Publisher publication in .pub format; it is not a real Web page yet. It will not be until you save it in Web format. See "Save a Publication as a Web Page."*

Change the Page Width

- Notice that the Web page is very long (tall)—probably longer than you will need. This is not a problem, as when the page is displayed in a **Web browser** any extra length will be truncated.
- The page width is an important issue to consider, however, because if the page is greater (in pixels) than your audience's **display resolution**, they will have to scroll horizontally to see your page (which is annoying).
- Common display resolutions are 800x600 (that is, 800 pixels wide and 600 pixels tall) and 1024x768. However, some old computers use a lower resolution of 640x480.
- Choose File, Page Setup and click the Layout tab, and you will see that Publisher has the publication set up as a Web page with Standard width (for 800x600 screens). You can change this to Narrow (640x480 display) if you think that some people viewing your page might have that lower resolution.

Choose the appropriate page size for your Web publication

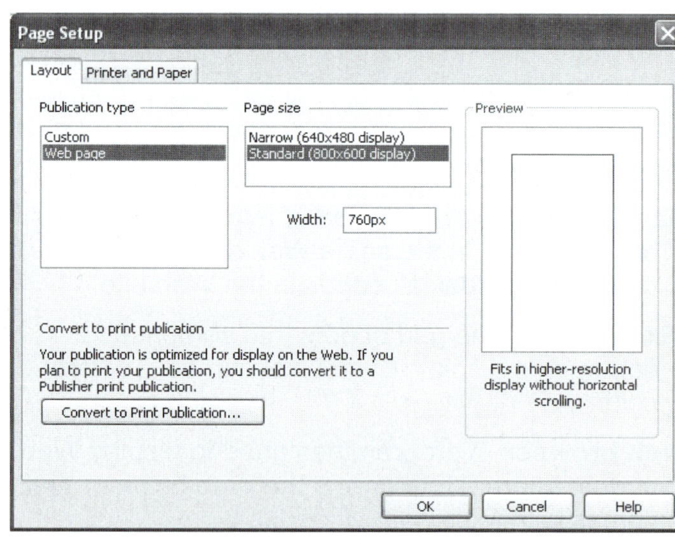

✓ *If you do not have a strong opinion about which width is better for your situation, go with Standard.*

Change a Web Page Title

- Each page has a title that appears in the title bar when the page is displayed in a Web browser. This is separate from the publication's file name.
- To change the page title, display the page, and then choose Tools, Web Page Options. In the Page title box, replace the default name with the title of your choosing.

The Page Title is the text that appears in the title bar of the Web browser program

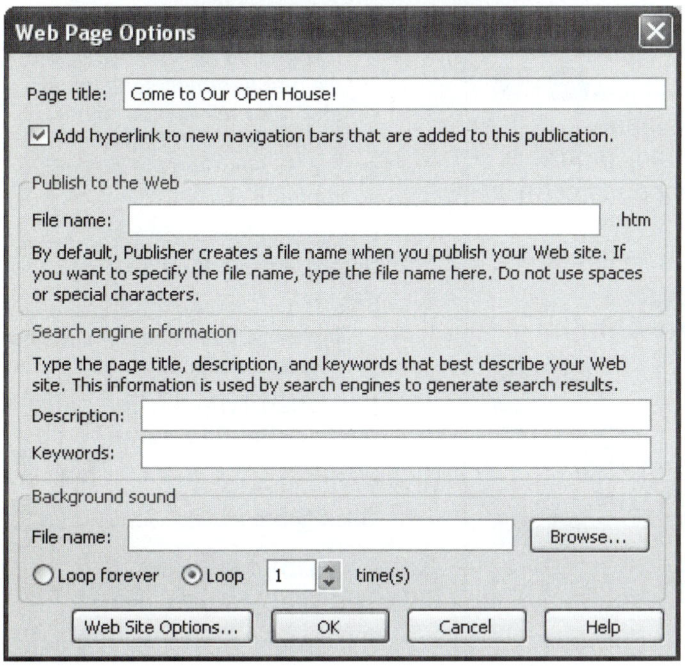

Preview a Web Page

- To preview the publication in a Web browser (your default one), choose File, Web Page Preview or press Ctrl+Shift+B.
- If you are working with a multi-page publication, a box appears asking whether you want to preview the entire Web site or the current page. You are not asked this question if you are working with a single page publication.
- When previewing, check to make sure that no text is cut off and that font usage is consistent. Evaluate the page width, the graphic placement, and anything else that you think your audience might find important.
- When you are done previewing the page, close the browser window and return to Publisher.

Save a Publication as a Web Page

- At this point, the Web page is still just an ordinary publication, in Publisher format. You must save it in Web format.
- There are three distinct Web formats you can save in through Publisher 2003:
  - Web page: This creates a version of the publication in **HTML** format that retains formatting codes for Publisher 2003. You can open this Web page in Publisher for editing later. However, because of the extra codes for Publisher, the file size is large. It also creates a folder containing the support files for the page, such as its graphics.
  - **Web page, Filtered:** This creates a version of the publication in HTML format that does not have any Publisher codes. It is a much smaller file than the above, but it cannot be reopened for editing in Publisher. It also creates a folder for support files.
  - Single File Web Page: This creates a version in a special format called MIME HTML (MHTML, often shortened as MHT) that contains the entire publication, including text and graphics, in a single file. No folder for support files is needed.
- To save in Web page or Single File Web Page format, you use the regular Save As dialog box but change the file format in the Save as Type drop-down list.
- To save in the Web page, Filtered format, you must use the File, Publish to the Web command (new in Publisher 2003).

  ✓ *Even though the command is called Publish to the Web, you can actually use it to publish (save) the file anywhere, including to your own hard disk. Saving directly to a server is covered in Exercise 53. Except for the name, and the type of file it creates, it is the same as an ordinary save.*

Procedures

Convert a Print Publication to a Web Page

1. Start Publisher, if needed.
2. Open the publication.
3. Click **File** .... Alt+F
4. Click **Convert to Web Publication** .... E
5. Click **Yes** or **No** to save the publication again or not.
   - ✓ *If you just opened it and have not made any changes there is no need to save it again.*
6. Click **Next** .... Enter
7. Click **Yes** or **No** to add a navigation bar or not.
   - ✓ *In a multi-page publication choose Yes; in a single-page publication choose No.*
8. Click **Finish**.................... Enter

Change the Web Page Width

1. Click **File** .... Alt+F
2. Click **Page Setup**.................... U
3. Click Layout tab.
4. Under Page Size, click **Narrow** or **Standard**.

   OR

   Type a custom page size in the **Width** box. .... Alt+W
5. Click **OK**.................... Enter

Change the Page Title

1. Click **Tools**.................... Alt+T
2. Click **Web Page Options** ... E
3. Type a new title in the **Page title** box.................... Alt+T
4. Click **OK**.................... Enter

Preview a Web Page

1. Click **File**.................... Alt+F
2. Click **Web Page Preview** .... B
3. (Multi-page sites only) Click one of the following:
   - **Web site** to view all pages..... Alt+S
   - **Current page** to view the current page only................ Alt+P
4. Proofread your page(s), making notes on any problems.
5. Return to Publisher and correct the problems.
6. Repeat steps 2–6 as needed.

Save a Publication as a Standard Web Page (.htm)

1. Click **File**.................... Alt+F
2. Click **Save As**.................... A
3. Click the down arrow ▼ to open the **Save as type** list.................... Alt+T
4. Click **Web Page**.
   - ✓ *Depending on your Windows file management settings, in step 4 it may appear either as Web Page or as Web Page (*.htm, *.html).*
5. (Optional) Navigate to a different save location if desired.
   - ✓ *If you want to save directly to a server, see Exercise 54.*
6. (Optional) Type a different file name in the **File name** box if desired.................... Alt+N
7. Click **Save** .... Enter

Save a Publication as a Single File Web Page (.mht)

1. Click **File** .... Alt+F
2. Click **Save As** .... A
3. Click the down arrow ▼ to open the **Save as type** list.................... Alt+T
4. Click **Single File Web Page**.
   - ✓ *Depending on your Windows file management settings, in step 4 it may appear either as Single File Web Page or as Single File Web Page (*.mht, *.mhtml).*
5. (Optional) Navigate to a different save location if desired.
   - ✓ *If you want to save directly to a server, see Exercise 53.*
6. (Optional) Type a different file name in the **File name** box if desired .... Alt+N
7. Click **Save** .... Enter

Save a Publication as a Filtered Web Page (.htm)

1. Click **File** .... Alt+F
2. Click **Publish to the Web** ... T
3. If a warning appears, click **OK**.................... Enter
4. (Optional) Navigate to a different save location if desired.
   - ✓ *If you want to save directly to a server, see Exercise 53.*
5. (Optional) Type a different file name in the **File name** box if desired .... Alt+N
6. Click **Save** .... Enter
   - ✓ *An information box may appear at this point describing the filtered format.*
7. If the information box appears, click **OK**.................... Enter

Exercise Directions

1. Start Publisher, if necessary.
2. Open the file PUB49. Save it as **49WEB**.
3. Convert it to a Web publication. Do not add a navigation bar.
4. Change the page width to the Narrow setting, and manually move the page content back onto the page if it hangs off.
   ✓ *An easy way: press Ctrl+A to select all object in the presentation and then move them as a group.*
5. Change the page title to **Greater Decatur Computer Club – Open House**.
6. Preview the Web page.
7. Save the Web page as a standard Web page called **49WEBSAVE1.HTM**.
8. Save the Web page as a filtered Web page called **49WEBSAVE2.HTM**.
9. Save the Web page as a Single File Web Page called **49WEBSAVE3.MHT**.
10. Exit Publisher.

Optional Exercise

1. Open a file management window (My Computer or Internet Explorer).
2. Navigate to the folder where you saved the files in steps 7-9 and note the following:
   - Which copy is the largest?
   - Which copy is the smallest?
   - Which ones(s) have support folders?
   - What is in those support folders?

On Your Own

1. Start Publisher, if necessary.
2. Open the file OPUB49. Save it as **O49WEB**.
3. Convert it to Web format, and allow Publisher to create a navigation bar.
4. For page 1, change the page title to **Art Update, Page 1**.
5. Change pages 2-4's page titles to the same as in step 4 except their own page numbers.
   ✓ *Notice that the navigation bar's page names do not automatically update.*
6. On each page, move the navigation bar so that it is in the same place on every page. (For now, don't worry if it covers up some content.)
7. Preview the Web page. While previewing, click the links in the navigation bar to move between pages.
8. Return to Publisher and save the Web site in Filtered Web Page format as **49MYWEB.HTM**.
9. Exit Publisher.

Optional Exercise

1. Open a file management window (My Computer or Internet Explorer).
2. Navigate to the folder where you saved the document, and double-click it to open it in Internet Explorer.
3. Notice the file name in the Address bar.
   ✓ *If the Address bar does not appear, choose View, Address Bar.*
4. Click the second link on the navigation bar (the second "Page 1") to go to the next page of the site.
5. Notice the file name in the Address bar again. It is a file in the support folder.
6. Close the Web browser.

Exercise 50

Skills Covered:

- ◆ **About Hyperlinks** ◆ **Place Hot Spots**
- ◆ **Simulate Hot Spots with AutoShapes**

On the Job

Hyperlinks are one of the defining features of Web pages. When you click a hyperlink, something happens. That "something" could be another Web page displaying, an e-mail window opening (as in Exercise 48), or some other action. A hyperlink can be either a text or a graphic, and using hot spots you can make different parts of a single image link to different locations.

One of the computer gurus at the Greater Decatur PC Club has been working a bit with the Web page you began in Exercise 49. He has included a map on the page, and he would like you to create some hot spot hyperlinks on it so users will see different Web pages based on where they click on the map. He would also like you to add a few regular text and graphic hyperlinks.

Terms

URL Stands for Uniform Resource Locator. The full path to a Web site, such as http://www.microsoft.com.

Notes

About Hyperlinks

- The most common type of hyperlink is a text one. A text hyperlink is typically underlined, as shown below. Clicking it displays whatever page or pointer is associated with the hyperlink.

An example of a text hyperlink

Text hyperlink

> Does it ever seem as if your dog or cat is reading your mind? Well, according to Annie Davis, animal psychic, that is exactly what's happening.

- A hyperlink can point to any of many different locations, including:
  - Other Web sites
  - Other pages within the same Web site
  - A specific spot on the current Web page
  - An e-mail address (as in Exercise 48)
  - A document (not necessarily HTML) on a hard disk (assuming that disk is accessible)
- A graphical hyperlink is functionally identical to a text hyperlink; the only difference is that instead of underlined text, it's a graphic.
- Not all graphics are necessarily hyperlinks. When the user moves the mouse pointer over a graphical hyperlink, the pointer changes to a hand.

An example of a graphical hyperlink

✓ *It may not be obvious to the readers of your Web page that a particular graphic is a hyperlink. Therefore you will usually want to include explanatory text either on the graphic or adjacent to it.*

- To begin a text or graphical hyperlink, select the text or graphic and then choose Insert, Hyperlink, or press Ctrl+K, or click the Insert Hyperlink button on the Standard toolbar. This opens the Insert Hyperlink dialog box.

Hyperlink to a Web Site

- Some hyperlinks point to Web addresses (**URL**s) outside of your own Web site. For addresses like that, you must enter the full address.
- In the Hyperlink dialog box, type the Web address (the URL) for the Web page in the Address box.

Create a hyperlink to a Web address

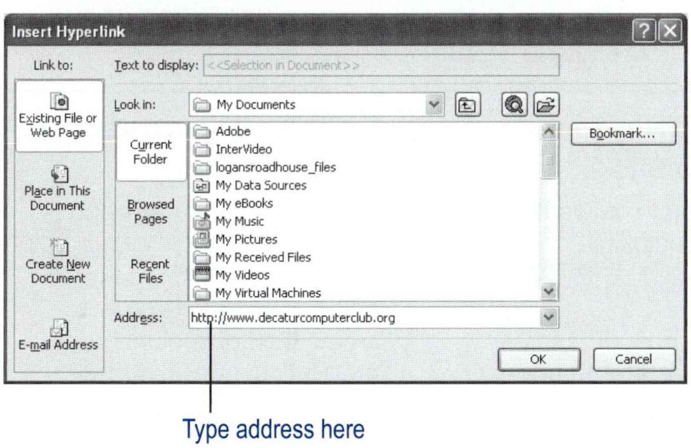

- If you don't know the exact address of the page, there are ways to look it up:
  - To select from pages you have recently viewed in Internet Explorer, click Browsed Pages and then select from the list.
  - To select a page by browsing to it from Internet Explorer, click the Browse the Web button. Internet Explorer will open. Navigate to the desired page, and then switch back to Publisher and that page's address will appear in the Address box.
  - To reuse an address you have previously created a hyperlink for, open the Address box's drop-down list and choose it from there.

Hyperlink to Another Page in Your Web Site

- A problem arises if you want to create a hyperlink that refers to another page in your Publisher publication. Eventually you will save to the Web and each page in your publication will become a Web page, but you haven't done that yet (perhaps) so there is no URL to which to refer.
- To overcome this problem, you can insert a Place in This Document hyperlink. It makes a note of the page to which you want to refer, and then when the publication is saved in Web format, it updates the link to the new name and location.

  ✓ *In Exercise 51 you will learn about using navigation bars as another way of linking between the pages in your Web publication.*

- Start out the same as usual, with the Insert, Hyperlink command. Then click Place in this document. This opens a list of all the pages in the current publication. Select the page you want the hyperlink to refer to.

Hyperlink to another page in the same publication

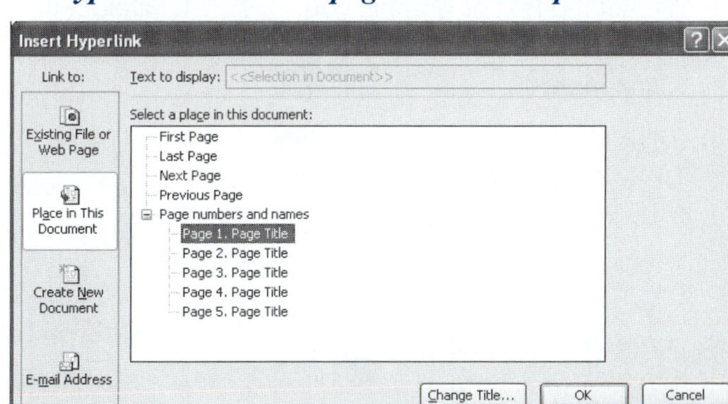

✓ *Notice above that all the pages have the generic title of Page Title in this example. You can rename them as you learned in Exercise 49, or you can click one and then click the Change Title button shown above to change its title.*

Place Hot Spots

- You might sometimes want different parts of a single graphic to have different hyperlinks. For example, on a map of your state, you might want different pages to appear when a user clicks on each city. You set this up by placing **hot spots** on the graphic.

A hot spot over the USA on a North America map

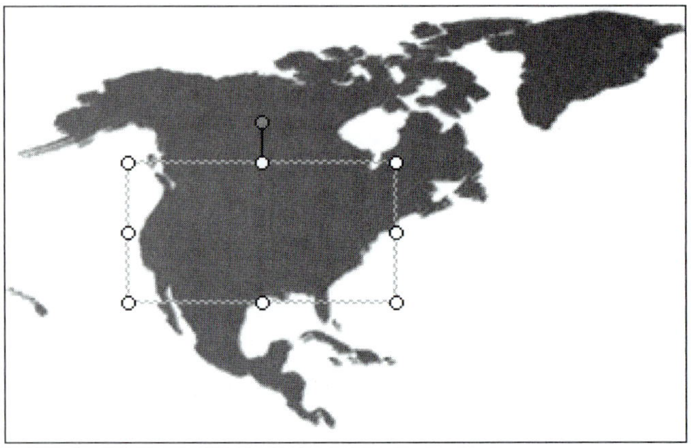

- Publisher has a Hot Spot button (on the Objects toolbar) you can use to create hot spots. This button appears only after you convert the publication to Web format. It also appears on the Web Tools toolbar.
- You can also create hot spots by placing borderless, unfilled AutoShapes over the picture.
- To use the Hot Spot feature, click the Hot Spot button and then drag to draw a rectangle over the desired area. When you release the mouse button, the Insert Hyperlink dialog box appears, and you specify the URL or page as you normally would.

Simulate Hot Spots with AutoShapes

- One drawback of the Hot Spot feature is that it creates only rectangles. Another is that you cannot apply a border or semi-transparent fill to a hot spot.
- If you need other shapes, or you want a border or fill on the hot spot, use this method instead.
- Draw an AutoShape (see Exercise 32) over the top of the graphic, and set its border and fill to None (see Exercise 33). Then select the AutoShape and set it up as a graphical hyperlink. When the page is displayed in a Web browser, the AutoShapes are invisible.

Procedures

Insert a Hyperlink to a Web Page

1. Select the text or graphic you want to make into a hyperlink.
2. Click **Insert** .... Alt+I
3. Click **Hyperlink** I

   ✓ *You can click the Insert Hyperlink button or press Ctrl+K instead of doing steps 2–3.*

4. Type the URL in the **Address** box .... Alt+E
5. Click **OK** .... Enter

Insert a Hyperlink to Another Page on Your Web Site

1. Select the text that you want to make into a hyperlink.
2. Click **Insert** .... Alt+I
3. Click **Hyperlink** I

   ✓ *You can click the Insert Hyperlink button or press Ctrl+K instead of doing steps 2–3.*

4. Click **Place in this document** .... Alt+A
5. Click the name of a page.
6. Click **OK** .... Enter

Create a Hot Spot with the Hot Spot Button

In a publication that has been converted to a Web page:

1. Place the graphic or other object over which you will create the hot spot in the publication
2. Click the **Hot Spot button** on the Objects toolbar.
3. Drag to create a hot spot over a section of the graphic.
4. The Insert Hyperlink dialog box appears when you release the mouse button.
5. Insert a hyperlink for the hot spot. (See the preceding sets of steps.)
6. Repeat steps 2-5 for other areas of the graphic.

Simulate a Hot Spot with an AutoShape

1. Place the graphic or other object in the publication over which you will create a hot spot.
2. Draw a shape (rectangle is most common) over a section of the graphic.
3. Click the down arrow next to the **Line Color** button.
4. Click **No Line**.
5. Add a hyperlink to the shape.
6. Repeat steps 2-5 for other areas of the graphic.
   - ✓ *To help your audience, add a text box near the graphic explaining that the hot spots are present.*

Remove a Hyperlink

1. Select the text that is hyperlinked (the underlined word or phrase).
2. Click **Insert** .... Alt+I
3. Click **Hyperlink** I
4. Click **Remove Link** ..... Alt+R

Exercise Directions

1. Start Publisher, if necessary.
2. Open the file **PUB50**. Save it as **50WEB**.
3. Convert it to a Web publication.
4. Remove the underlining from the **Learn More** text.
5. Make the **Learn More** text a hyperlink that points to page 6 of this publication.
6. Reopen the Insert Hyperlink dialog box, and change the titles of the pages to the following:
   - Page 1: **Main**
   - Page 2: **Northwest**
   - Page 3: **Northeast**
   - Page 4: **Southwest**
   - Page 5: **Southeast**
   - Page 6: **About the Club**
7. Make the e-mail address into an e-mail hyperlink that sends mail to ben@decaturcomputerclub.org.
   - ✓ *Refer to Exercise 48 if you don't remember how to create e-mail hyperlinks.*
8. Make the clip art picture a hyperlink that points to this URL: http://www.decaturcomputerclub.org.
9. Place four rectangular hot spots on the map using the AutoShape method, each covering one quadrant of it: northwest, northeast, southwest, and southeast.
   - ✓ *Use the AutoShape method, not the Hot Spot button. This is necessary because we are going to format them with shading, and you cannot do that to regular hot spots.*
10. Remove the border from each rectangle or hot spot, and apply a different color fill to each one with 85% transparency.
    - ✓ *Refer to Exercise 20 if you don't remember how to set up a semitransparent fill.*
11. Make the hyperlinks to the matching pages of the document. See Illustration A.
12. Preview the Web site and test all the hyperlinks, including all the hot spots. (Use the Back button to return to the main page after clicking a hyperlink.)
13. Exit Publisher.

On Your Own

1. Start Publisher, if necessary.
2. Open the file **OPUB50**. Save it as **50MYLINKS**.
3. Type a bulleted list of your top five favorite Web sites, along with a one-sentence explanation of what you like about each one. Make each Web site's name a working hyperlink.
4. At the bottom of the page, make the text **e-mail me** into a hyperlink that sends e-mail to your current e-mail address.
5. Save your work in Publisher, and then save again as a Single File Web Page (.mht) named **50MYLINKS.MHT.**
6. Preview the page in your Web browser and try all the links to make sure they work.
7. Return to Publisher, and exit Publisher.

Illustration A

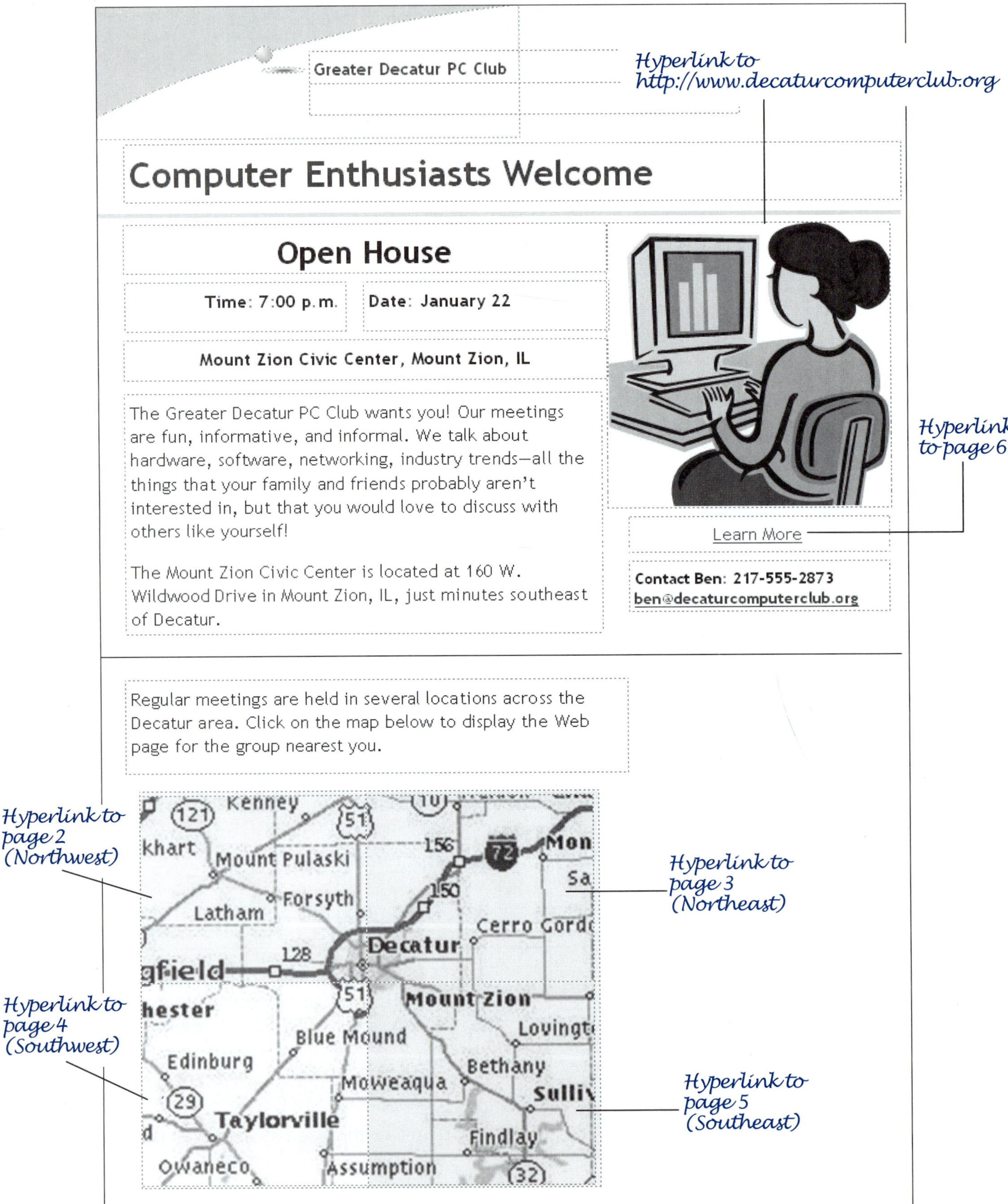

Exercise 51

Skills Covered:

◆ **Create a 3-Page Web Site** ◆ **Use the Easy Web Site Builder**
◆ **Add Pages Manually** ◆ **Remove Pages** ◆ **Customize a Page Layout**
◆ **Customize the Navigation Bar**

On the Job

Most Web sites consist of more than a single page. A typical Web site consists of several pages, each with a consistent navigation bar to help you move between them easily.

Under The Rainbow, one of your favorite local bands, needs a Web site. They would like a home page, a calendar page that lists their upcoming concert dates, a page containing contact information, and a set of pages that sell T-shirts, hats, and stickers with the band logo. In this exercise, you will start by creating the needed pages.

Terms

Home page The first or starting page in a Web site, from which most of the other pages branch off.

Navigation bar A list of hyperlinks to other pages in the same Web site.

Notes

Create a 3-Page Web Site

- Publisher has a special set of templates it calls 3-page Web sites. They are just what their name sounds like. They create publications that have three pages and are set up for Web use.
- To create a new 3-page Web site, start a new publication and choose Web Sites and E-mail, then choose Web sites, then choose 3-page Web Site. Then pick from one of the available designs, the same as with any other publication.

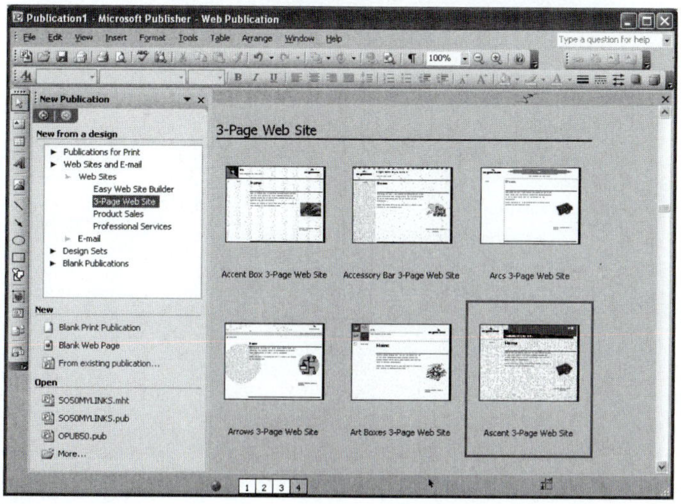

Select one of the 3-page Web site design templates

- The first page is the **home page.** The home page is the top-level page for the site. When you send people the URL for your Web site, you send them the address of this page.
- The other two pages can be anything you want them to be. Many templates are available. You can also add more pages, or delete one or more of the existing ones.

Use the Easy Web Site Builder

- The 3-Page Web Site template gives you no choice about the number or type of pages you wanted. When you need more control, the Easy Web Site Builder is a better way to go.
- To start a Web site based on the Easy Web Site Builder, choose one of the Easy Web Site templates.
- The Easy Web Site Builder displays a dialog box listing many types of Web page functionalities, like telling the customers about products or providing lists of hyperlinks.
- You place a checkmark next to each of the functionalities you want, and Publisher automatically creates the needed pages.
  - ✓ *There is usually a one-to-one relationship between the functionalities and the number of pages created. However, the Sell Products functionality creates multiple pages—a main page and multiple sub-pages branching off of it. These sub-pages do not appear by default in the navigation bar.*

Select the desired pages

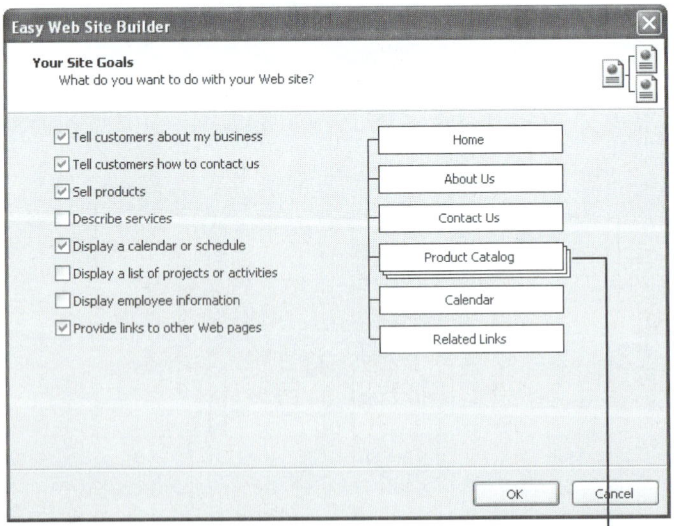

Multiple pages will be created here

- You can redisplay the Easy Web Site Builder at any time to add more pages by displaying the Web Site Options task pane and clicking the Add functionality hyperlink. This method only adds pages; it does not remove them. You can also add pages manually, as described next.

Add Pages Manually

- Publisher comes with page templates for several kinds of additional Web pages you might want for your Web site, such as forms, calendars, resumes, and special offers.
- To add a page, choose Insert a page from the Web Site Options task pane; choose Insert, Page; or press Ctrl+Shift+N. Any of these methods opens the Insert Web Page dialog box.

Use the Insert Web Page dialog box to place a new page in the publication

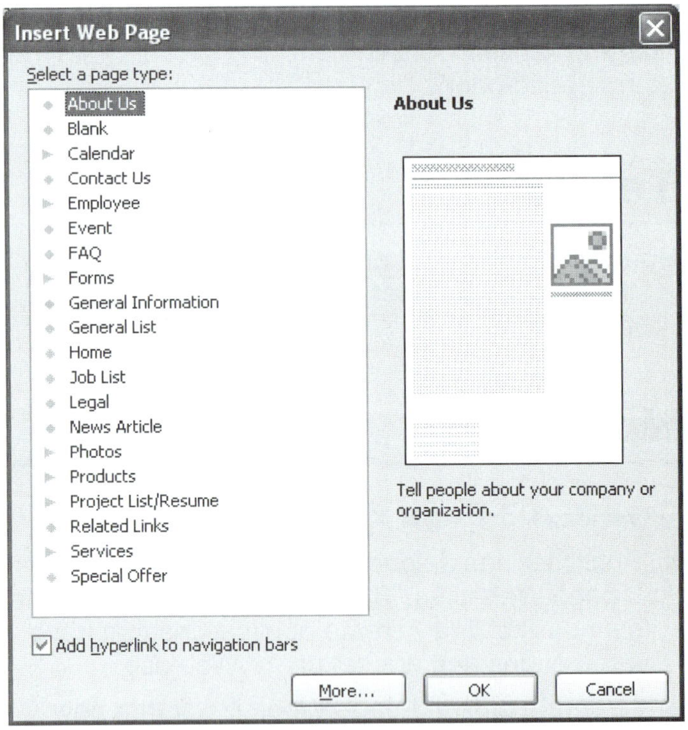

- To add the page to the Web navigation bar, make sure the Add hyperlink to navigation bars check box remains marked. (Usually this is good practice, but occasionally you may want a page that is not linked to every other page.)
- If you create a page that is not part of the navigation bar, you will need to insert a hyperlink to it somewhere so that people can access it. (See Exercise 50.)

Remove Pages

- Removing a page from a Web site is just like removing one from a regular document—choose Edit, Delete Page.
- Publisher removes the deleted page from the navigation bar automatically.

Customize a Page Layout

- Each page's layout can be separately chosen, like with a newsletter. Display the page and then choose a layout from the Page Content task pane.

Choose a layout for each page

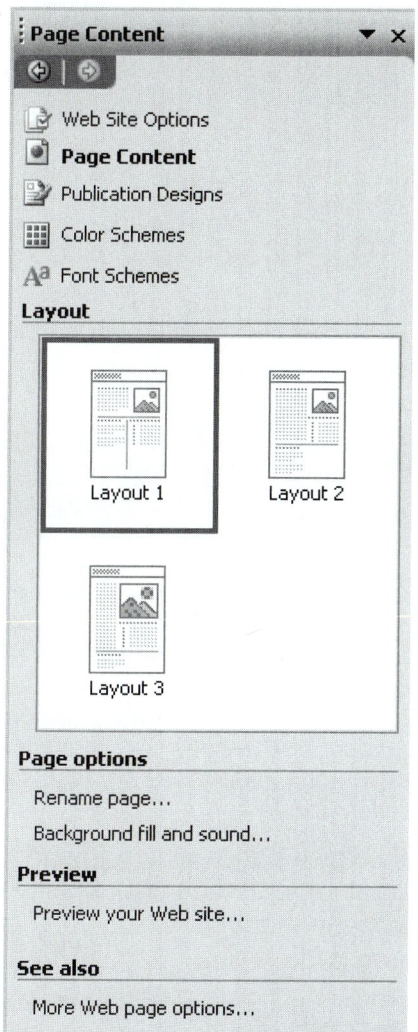

- Different types of pages have different layout choices. The default three pages in a 3-page Web site are fairly basic, but you can insert additional pages that have special elements on them and have more layout choices for such pages.

Customize the Navigation Bar

- The **navigation bar** contains hyperlinks to each of the pages, and is consistently placed on each page (usually).
- The navigation bar is an important part of a multi-page Web site because it enables the audience to move easily between the pages.
- There are many different placements available for the navigation bar. Choose among them from the Web Site Options task pane. Some of the choices involve having two different navigation bars—one at the top or side, and another at the bottom.

Configure navigation bar placement

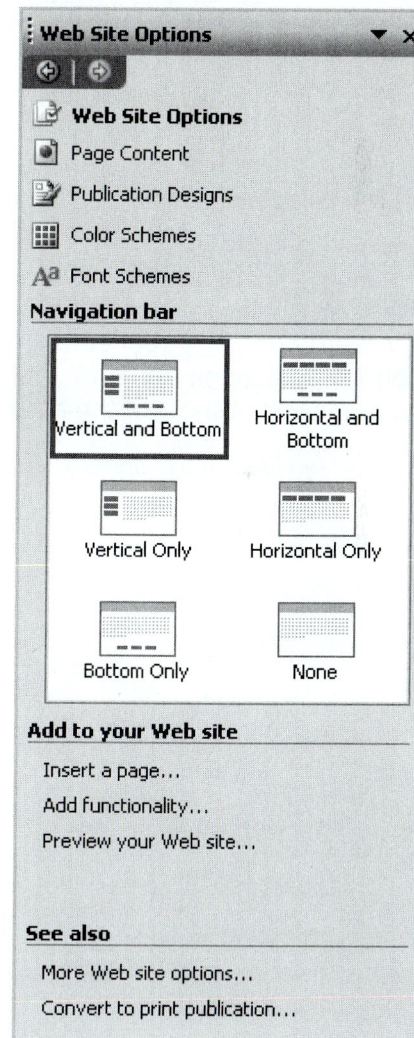

Example of a navigation bar at the bottom of a page

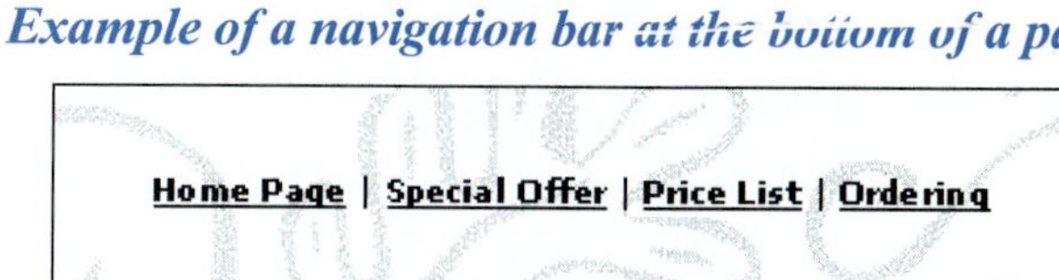

Example of a vertical navigation bar

- The navigation bar is a special design element like the ones in the Design Gallery. It has its own wizard you can activate to set its options.
- On any page, click the navigation bar and then click the Wizard button beneath it. The Navigation Bar task pane appears. In it you can change nearly every aspect of the navigation bar.

Set navigation bar options

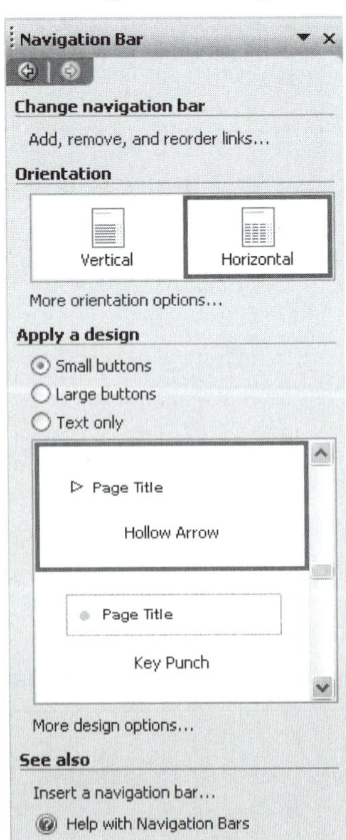

- To manually add or remove links, or reorder them, click the Add, remove and reorder links hyperlink near the top. This opens the General tab of the Navigation Bar Properties dialog box.

Reorder, add, or remove links here

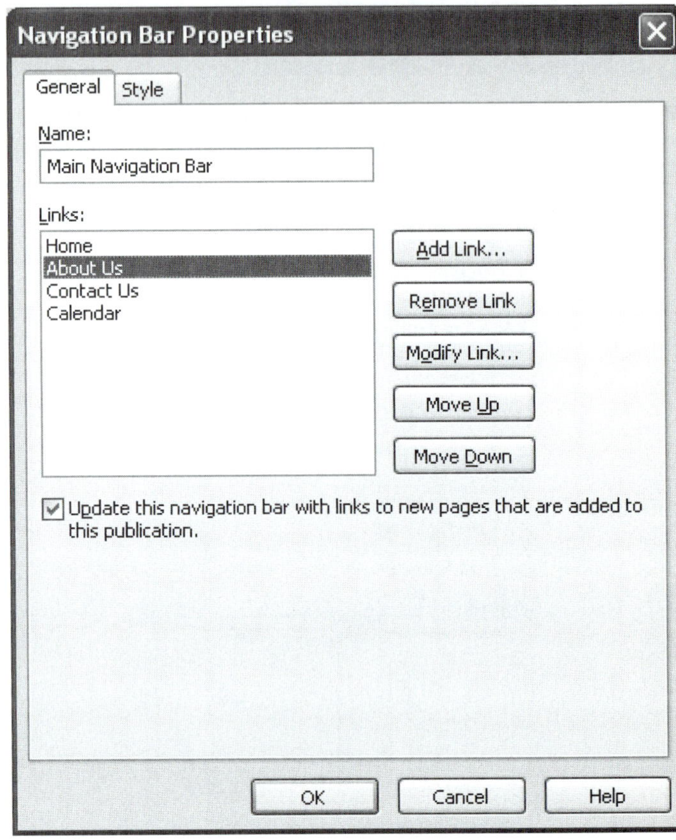

✓ *Typically you would not need to add or remove links from the navigation bar, as Publisher handles this automatically when you add and remove pages in your publication. However, you might occasionally want to include a page on your navigation bar that was not created in Publisher, or that you originally chose not to include in the navigation bar.*

- To modify which page a link refers to, select it on the General tab and then click Modify Link. A dialog box appears from which you can choose the desired page.
- From the Navigation Bar task pane you can also change the orientation (Vertical or Horizontal), or click More design options to open the Style tab of the Navigation Bar Properties dialog box.

Choose a button style for the navigation bar

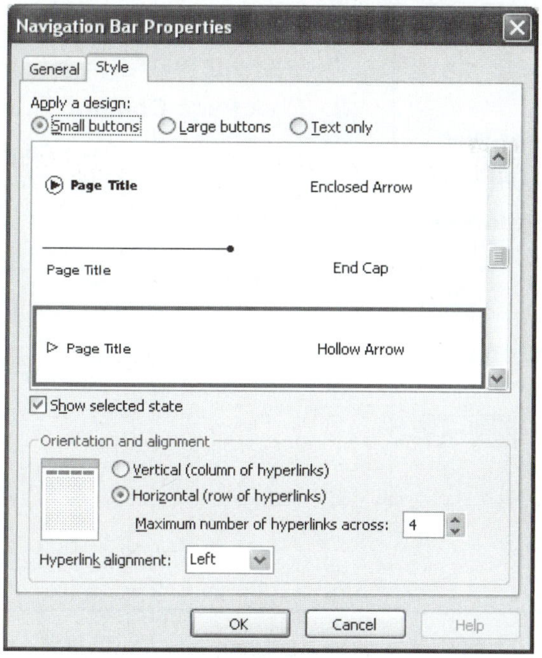

- The controls that appear in the above dialog box are similar to those in the Navigation Bar task pane (shown at left), but has some additional fine-tuning settings such as hyperlink alignment and maximum number of hyperlinks across.

Procedures

Create a 3-Page Web Site

1. Start Publisher, if necessary.
2. Click **Web Sites and E-mail** on the task pane.
3. Click **Web Sites**.
4. Click **3-Page Web Site**.
5. Click the design you want to use.
6. Click a navigation bar style in the task pane.
7. (Optional) Change any of these if desired:
   - Publication design
   - Color scheme
   - Font scheme

Create a Web Site with Easy Web Site Builder

1. Start Publisher, if necessary.
2. Click **Web Sites and E-mail** on the task pane.
3. Click **Web Sites**.
4. Click **Easy Web Site Builder.**
5. Click the design you want to use.
6. Click check boxes next to the pages you want.
7. Click **OK**.......................... Enter
8. Click a navigation bar style in the task pane.
9. (Optional) Change any of these if desired:
   - Publication design
   - Color scheme
   - Font scheme

Add Pages with Easy Web Site Builder

1. Display the Web Site Options task pane, if needed.
2. Click **Add Functionality**.
3. Click check boxes next to pages you want to add.
4. Click **OK** .... Enter

Add a New Web Page Manually

1. Display the page after which the new page should be inserted.
2. Click **Insert**................. Alt+I
3. Click **Page** .... G

   ✓ *You can press Ctrl+Shift+N instead of steps 2-3 if desired, or click Insert a Page from the Web Site Options task pane.*

4. Click a page type.
5. (Optional) Clear the **Add hyperlink to navigation bars** checkbox if needed.
6. Click **OK**.......................... Enter

Duplicate an Existing Page

1. Display the page to duplicate.
2. Click **Insert** .... Alt+I
3. Click **Duplicate Page** L

   ✓ *You can press Ctrl+Shift+U instead of steps 2-3 if desired.*

Delete a Web Page

1. Display the page to delete.
2. Click **Edit** .... Alt+E
3. Click **Delete Page**............... A
4. If a confirmation box appears, click **OK**.

Change the Navigation Bar Type and Position

1. Click **Format**.............. Alt+O
2. Click **Web Site Options** .. O
3. Click a different navigation bar style in the task pane.

Edit Navigation Bar

1. Click the navigation bar.
2. Click the **Wizard** button under it.
3. Click **Add, remove and reorder links**.
4. Do any of the following tasks.
5. When finished, click **OK** ... Enter

Reorder navigation bar:

1. Click a page on the list.
2. Click **Move Up** .... Alt+U

   OR

   Click **Move Down** .... Alt+D
3. Repeat steps 1-2 as needed.

Add link to navigation bar:

1. Click **Add Link** .... Alt+A
2. Click the page to link

   OR

   a. Click **Existing File or Web Page** .... Alt+E

   b. Type a URL in the **Address** box .... Alt+E
3. Click **OK** .... Enter

Remove link from navigation bar:

1. Click the link to delete.
2. Click **Remove Link** .... Alt+E

Change a Web Page Layout

1. Display the page to change.
2. Click **Format** .... Alt+O
3. Click **Page Content** .... G

   ✓ *You can click **Page Content** in the Web Site Options task pane instead of steps 2-3 if desired.*
4. Click a page layout.

Exercise Directions

1. Start Publisher, if necessary.
2. Create a new 3-Page Web Site using the Mobile 3-Page Web Site design.
3. Update the Other Organization personal information set so that both My Name and Organization Name are **Under the Rainbow**, and use that information set for this publication.
4. Change the color scheme to Wildflower.
5. Change the navigation bar to Horizontal and Bottom.
6. Delete the About Us page.
7. Insert a Calendar page after page 1. Do not include it in the navigation bar.
8. Change the calendar page's layout to Layout 3.
9. Add the calendar page to the navigation bar, in the second position.
10. Use Add functionality (Easy Web Site Builder) to add the Sell Products functionality to the site.

    ✓ *This will add seven pages to the publication: one for the product list and six for the individual products.*
11. Move the Sell Products button on the navigation bar to the third position and rename it **Stuff for Sale** (both on the navigation bar and in the page title).
12. Delete the Organization logo from the top of every page.
13. Preview the Web site and check that all links work.
14. Save the file as **51WEB** (in Publisher format).
15. Exit Publisher.

On Your Own

1. Start Publisher, if necessary.
2. Create a Web site using the Easy Web Site Builder that tells something about you. Include at least three pages.
   - Select a design and color scheme that reflects your personality.
3. Type text on the pages to customize them with your own information.
4. Change the page titles and the names in the navigation bar to be appropriate to the pages' content.
5. Add at least one more page manually, and make it not appear on the navigation bar. (Create a hyperlink from one of the other pages to it.)
6. Save your work as **51MYWEB**.
7. Exit Publisher.

Exercise 52

Skills Covered:

◆ **Create a Web Form** ◆ **Insert a Web Form from the Design Gallery**
◆ **Customize a Web Form** ◆ **Change a Form Control's Properties**
◆ **Set the Data Retrieval Method**

On the Job

In the past, including forms on Web pages was considered very difficult. It was best left to experienced programmers. However, Publisher makes it so easy to create forms that anyone can do it.

Your friends in the band Under the Rainbow have been hard at work on their Web site. They have decided not to sell logo merchandise on the Web, but they would like to have a form that people can use to sign up for their mailing list. You will create that form in this exercise.

Terms

Web form A series of fields that a Web site visitor can fill in and submit to the Web site owner.

Web server The computer that stores your Web site and provides it on the Internet. This may or may not be provided by the same company that provides your Internet connection.

Form control An individual field on a form, such as a check box, text box, or option button.

FrontPage Server Extensions Software that runs on the Web server that allows certain automated aspects of Microsoft Office FrontPage (and related programs like Publisher) to function.

Notes

Create a Web Form

- A **Web form** is a form that people can fill out online. The data they enter into the form is then either collected in a data file on the **Web server** or e-mailed to you, depending on your preference.
- The easiest way to create a form in Publisher is to add a page to the site that uses one of the form layouts. You learned how to add pages in Exercise 51.
- You can choose Order form, Response form, or Sign-up form, and then customize the resulting form any way you like.
- The forms created by Publisher do not include formulas for calculating totals, so users will need to fill in the appropriate totals manually for the order form. You may want a text note on your form explaining this.

Create a new page that has a form on it

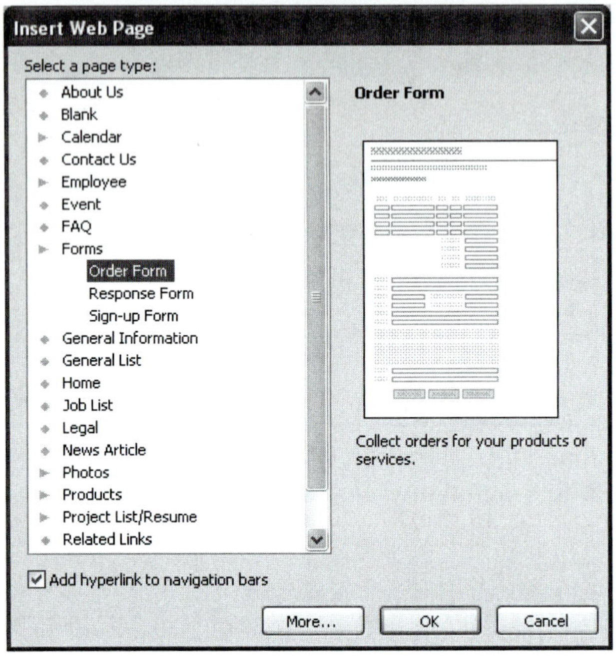

An order form, ready to be customized

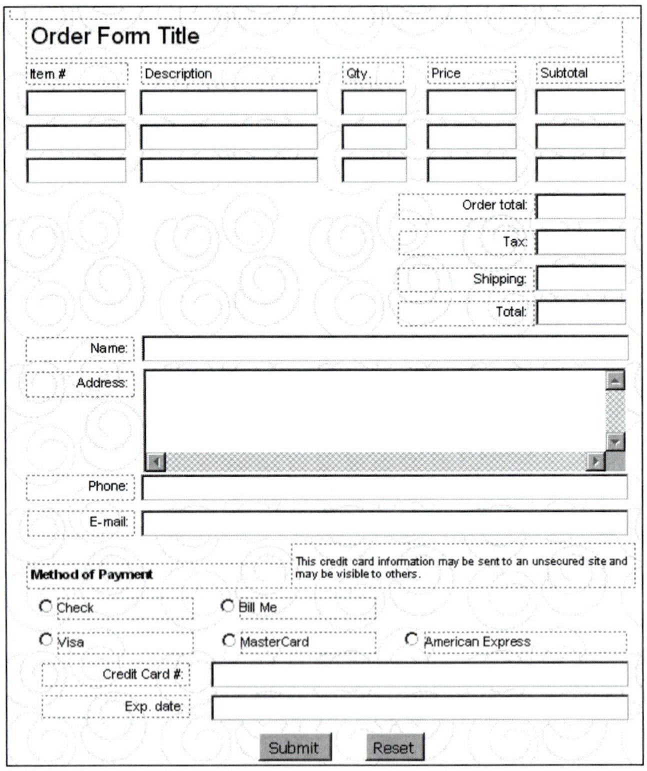

Insert a Web Form from the Design Gallery

- If you already have a page created on which you want to place a Web form, you can insert the form from the Design Gallery, just as you did in earlier exercises.

You can insert a Web form from the Design Gallery

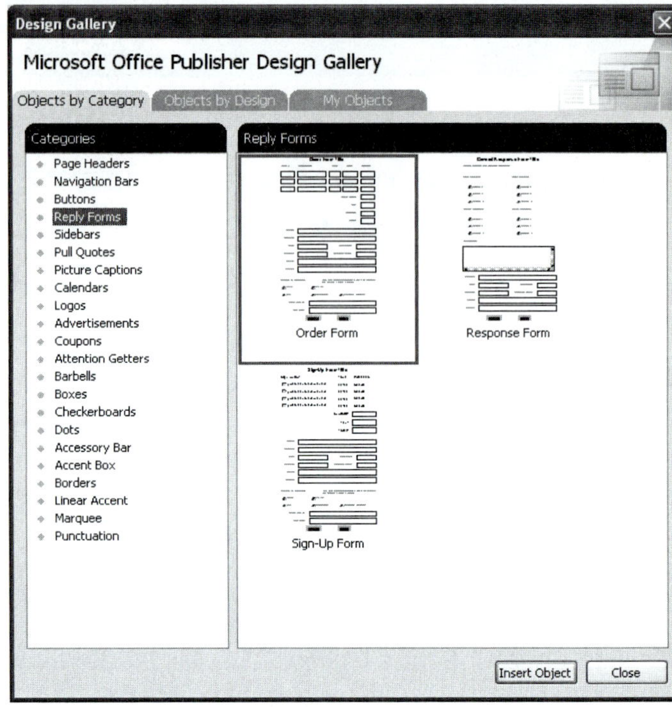

- You'll find the same forms available in the Web Reply Forms category in the Design Gallery that are available in the task pane for the template.

Customize a Web Form

- After placing a form in the publication, you can customize it by moving its frames around, deleting unwanted **form controls**, and adding new form controls.
- To delete a control, simply delete its frame as you would any frame.
- To add fields, click the Form Control button on the Objects toolbar, and then click the type of control you want. Then drag on the publication to create it.

Select a form control to add to the form

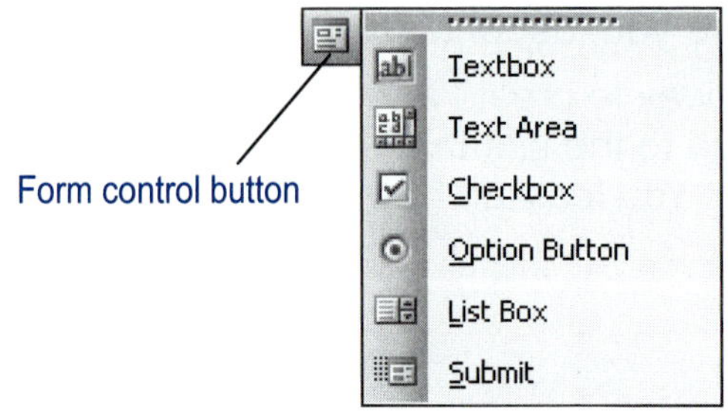

✓ *You also can display the control types by choosing Insert, Form Control.*

Change a Form Control's Properties

- To change the properties for a form control, right-click it and choose Format Form Properties.
- For text boxes, you can set default text (if any is desired) and the number of characters allowed, for example.
- You can also change the label to return with the data for the field, and specify whether the field is mandatory or not.

Set the properties for a text box form control

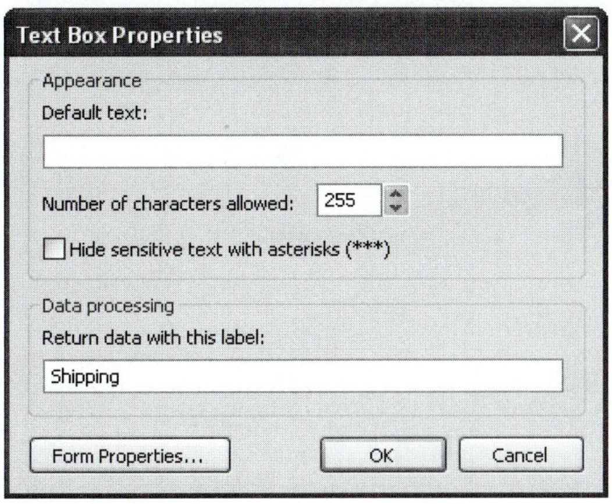

- For other control types, the properties are different. For example, for option buttons, you can set a default of Selected or Not Selected, and specify a button value and a label to return with the data.

Set the properties for an Option Button form control

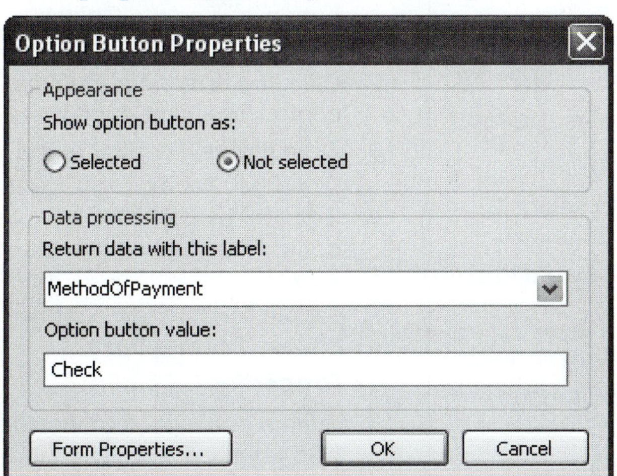

Set the Data Retrieval Method

- Every form must have a Submit button. You set the properties for that button to determine what happens to the form data when the user clicks Submit.
- Right-click the button (or any control on the form) and choose Format Form Properties to display the button's properties, and choose Submit or Reset as the button's action.
- You can also specify what text should appear on the button, or choose a graphic to appear there.

Specify the file name for data collection

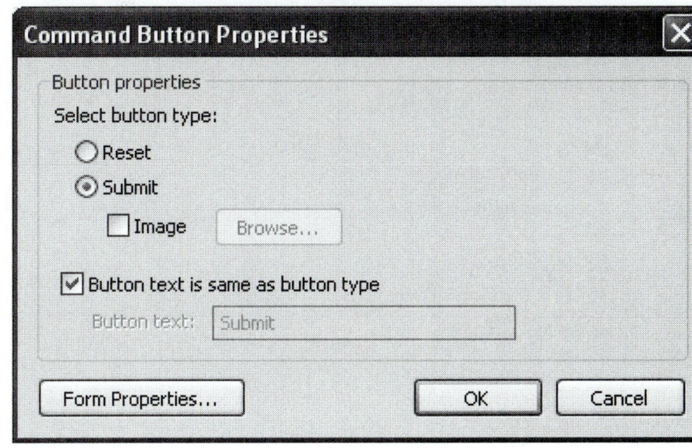

- Then click the Form Properties button to display the Form Properties dialog box, in which you specify the delivery method for the form data.

Specify how you will collect the form data

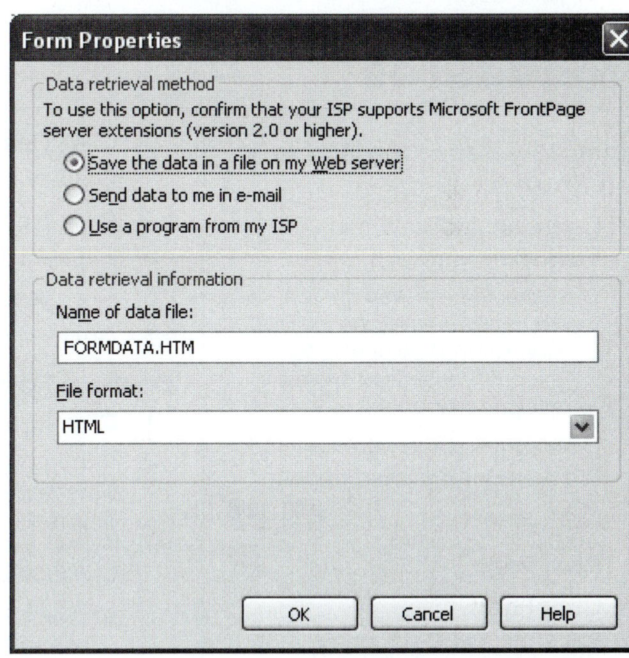

- The first option, Save the data in a file on my Web server, requires **FrontPage server extensions** 2.0 or higher on the server. The data is collected in a data file on the server in a file name you specify. (When you click that option, a text box appears in which you enter the file name.)

- The Send data to me in e-mail option requires FrontPage server extensions 3.0 or higher (that is, FrontPage 98 support or higher). This option sends e-mail to the address you specify, as shown below.

If you choose to receive data by e-mail, enter the address to which it should be delivered

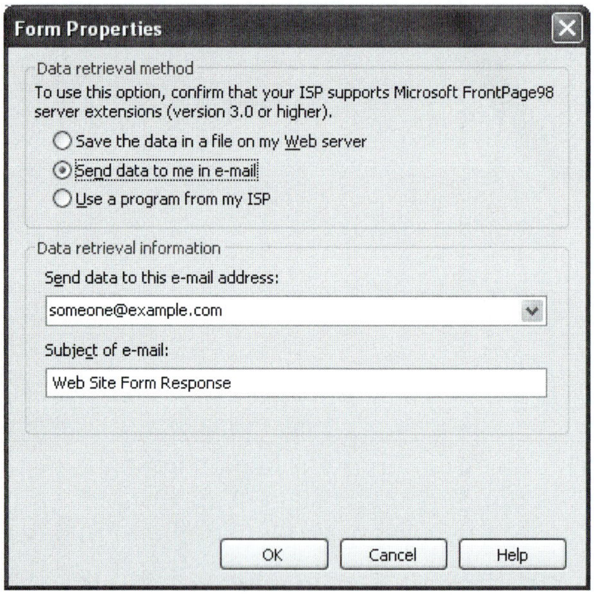

- The final option, Use a program from my ISP, does not require FrontPage server extensions, but does require your ISP to provide form results collection capability.

Use a program from your ISP

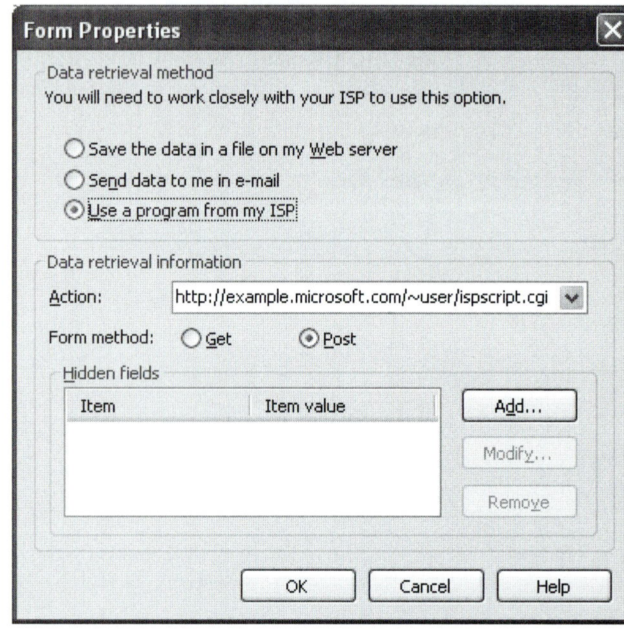

Procedures

Add a New Page Containing a Web Form

1. Open the publication in Publisher.
   ✓ *It should be a Web publication. You may need to choose File, Convert to Web publication if the publication was originally designed for print.*
2. Display the page after which the new page should appear.
3. Click **Insert** .... Alt + I
4. Click **Page**.......................... G
5. Click **Form**.
6. Click the desired form type.
7. Click **OK**.......................... Enter
8. Customize the form as desired.

Add a Web Form to an Existing Page

1. Display the page on which the form should go.
2. Click **Insert** .... Alt + I
3. Click **Design Gallery Object** .... D
4. Click **Reply Forms**.
5. Click the form you want.
6. Click **Insert Object**...... Alt + I
7. Customize the form as desired.

Delete a Form Control

1. Click form control to select it.
2. If the control is grouped with others that you don't want to delete:
   a. Click **Ungroup** button.
   b. Click away from group to deselect all.
   c. Click specific object to delete.
3. Click **Edit**..................... Alt + E
4. Click **Delete Object**............ D
   ✓ *You can press the Delete key instead of doing steps 3–4, or right-click and choose Delete Object.*

Add a Form Control

1. Click the **Form Control** button on the Objects toolbar.
2. Click the button for the type of control you want to add.
3. Drag the new control to the desired location.
4. Edit the text for the new control's text label, if it has one.
5. Right-click the new control and choose **Format Form Properties** I
6. Type a description to include with returned results in the **Return data with this label** box.............. Alt + L
7. Click **OK**.......................... Enter

Change a Form Control's Properties

1. Click the form to select it.
2. Click an individual control within the form to select it.

   ✓ *In a grouped form, gray circle-with-X selection handles appear around an individual control when selected.*

3. Right-click the form control.
4. Choose **Format Form Properties** I
5. Set the properties for that control.
6. Click **OK** .... Enter

Set the Data Retrieval Method

1. Click form to select it.
2. Click any control to select it.
3. Right-click that control.
4. Click **Format Form Properties** I
5. Click the **Form Properties** button .... Alt+P
6. Click a data retrieval method:
   - **Save the data in a file on my Web server** .... Alt+W
   - **Send data to me in e-mail** .... Alt+N
   - **Use a program from my ISP** .... Alt+U
7. Set the properties for the chosen method.
   - **For saving the data in a file**, specify the data file name and file format.
   - **For sending the data in e-mail**, specify an e-mail address and a subject line.
   - **For using a program**, specify a script in the Action box, and set up any hidden fields as directed by your ISP. For advanced users only.
8. Click **OK** .... Enter

Exercise Directions

1. Start Publisher, if necessary.
2. Open the file **PUB52**. Save it as **52WEB**.
3. Insert a new page after page 3 that contains a signup form. Name the new page Mailing List, both in the page title and in both of the navigation bars (top and bottom).
4. Delete the two text boxes above the form, and one of the red lines.
5. Delete the signup form from the page (from Signup Form Title all the way down to the Submit button).
6. Insert a response form from the Design Gallery to replace the deleted signup form. Size it to fit the available space.
7. Ungroup the form, and customize it to create the form shown in Illustration A. You will need to do the following:
   - Delete some fields.
   - Add some fields, and set the properties appropriately for the added fields.
   - Rearrange the fields.
   - Ungroup some text fields from their labels so you can move/resize them separately; then group them back together again.
   - Apply 10-point formatting to text labels.
8. Set the form properties for each control so it reports back understandable data.

   ✓ *For example, for the option buttons at the top, right-click a round button and choose Format Form Properties. Then in the Return data with this label field, type State, and for Option button value, type the name of the state that that button represents. The settings will be different for different field types.*

9. Set the form properties to send the data to yourself in an e-mail. Enter your own e-mail address for the address to use.

   ✓ *If you don't have an e-mail address, ask your instructor what address to use.*

10. Preview the form in your Web browser, and try out the form. (It will not work because it is not saved to a Web site that has FrontPage extensions, but that's okay.)

    ✓ *You might notice that the Tab key does not work very well in your Web browser to move you from field to field. Unfortunately Publisher lacks the ability to reset the tab order between the fields when you move them around.*

11. Save your work and exit Publisher.

Illustration A

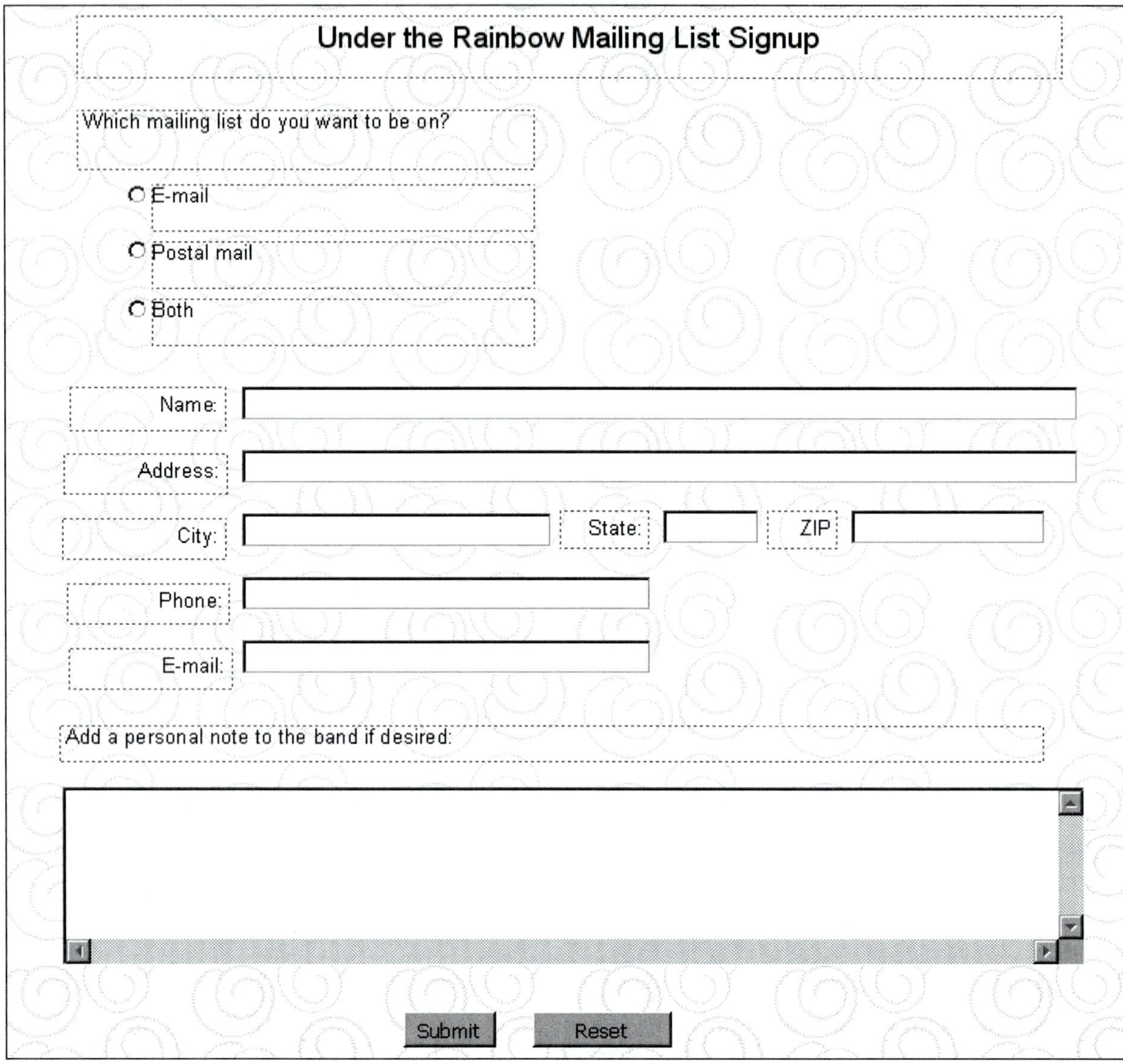

On Your Own

1. Start Publisher, if necessary.
2. Create a new, blank Web page. (Choose File, New and then click Blank Web Page.)
3. On the blank page, build a form "from scratch" that collects information from people. At the minimum, include two text boxes, a check box, and a set of option buttons.
   - ✓ *Manually insert each field; do not start with a form from the Design Gallery. Turning on Snap to Grid might be helpful. Use the Align command to make the fields line up neatly. Make sure every field has an identifying label.*
   - ✓ *For an option button group, set the same value for all buttons for the Return Data with This Label setting. Differentiate between the buttons by setting each one to a different Option Button Value setting.*
4. Set the form properties to save the results in a tab-delimited text file called **signup.txt**.
5. (Optional) Format the page in any way you like.
6. Save your work as **52MYFORM** and exit Publisher.

Exercise 53

Skills Covered:

- **Methods of Transferring Web Content to a Server**
- **Saving to a Web Location**
- **Saving to an FTP Location**
- **Other Transfer Methods**

On the Job

When your Web site is complete, you will want to publish it to a Web server so that the Internet public can visit it.

Your friends in the band Under the Rainbow would like you to post the prototype Web site a publicly available Web server so everyone can have a look at it. In this exercise, you will save it to a Web server.

Terms

FTP Stands for File Transfer Protocol, a non-Web method of transferring files between computers on the Internet.

My Network Places A feature that enables you to connect to a Web folder much like a drive or folder on a local area network.

Notes

Methods of Transferring Web Content to a Server

- To transfer files to a Web server, you can use any of the three save methods you learned in Exercise 49, and specify either a Web or **FTP** location for the storage.
- If possible, it is better to use a Web location because it's easier. However, not all Web servers allow you to upload to them directly. Some require you to save your Web files to an FTP address using the FTP protocol.

Saving to a Web Location

- To save to a Web location, click the **My Network Places** button in the Publish to the Web dialog box's Places bar. A list of the network shortcuts you have set up appears.
- If the desired Web location already appears there, double-click it to connect to it.
- The first time you save to a certain location, you will need to set it up.
- Type the URL of the Web site in the File name box and press Enter.

Save directly to the Web site address with My Network Places

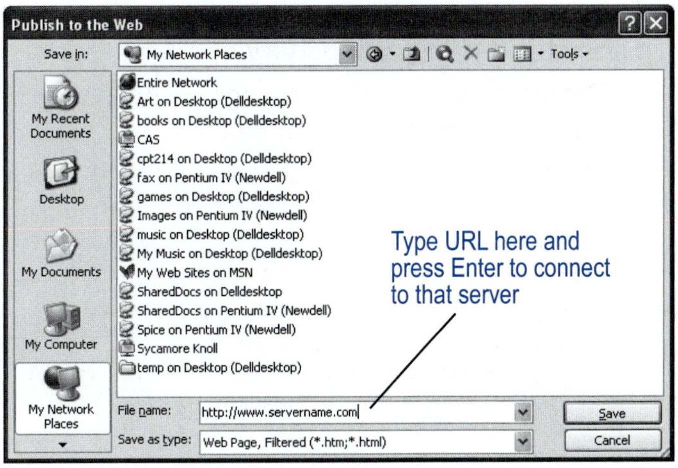

- You'll be prompted for a user name and password. Enter them and click OK to continue. You must have a valid user name and password for that server; see the system administrator if needed.

You will be prompted to log into the Web server

- The contents of the Web server appear in the window. Save normally, and the Web page(s) will be saved directly to the server.

Saving to an FTP Location

- Sometimes Web servers can be accessed by two different addresses: their Web address (http://) and their FTP address (ftp://). Some servers require that users upload their Web pages using the FTP address.
- To save with FTP, open the Look in drop-down list and choose an FTP location under FTP locations.
- The desired location does not appear, choose Add/Modify FTP Locations and set it up by filling in the dialog box that appears.

Choose Add/Modify FTP Locations

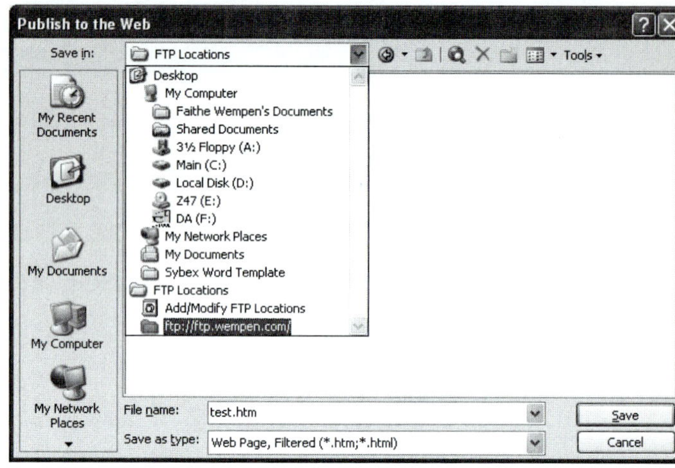

Set up an FTP location

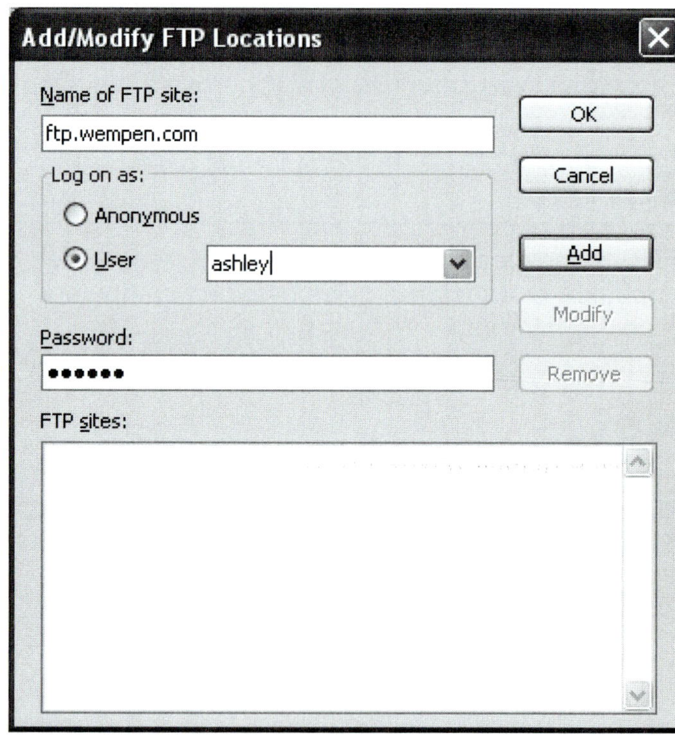

Other Transfer Methods

- Besides the file transfer methods from within Publisher, you can also transfer files to a Web server using a variety of other methods.
- Some versions of Windows include a Web Publishing Wizard. You can use it to transfer a single file or a single folder to a Web server.
- You can also download free or shareware FTP programs from most large file archives on the Internet, such as http://shareware.cnet.com.

Procedures

Save to a Web Address

1. Begin saving by doing one of the following:
   a. Click **File**................ Alt+F
   b. Click **Publish to the Web**................ T

   OR

   a. Click **File**................ Alt+F
   b. Click **Save As**................ A
2. Click **My Network Places**.
3. Double-click the Web location you want to save in.

   OR

   To set up a new Web location, do the following:
   - Type the Web address in the **File name** box......... Alt+N
   - Press **Enter**................ Enter
   - If prompted, enter user name and password and click **OK**.
4. Navigate to folder on Web server where you want to save.
5. Type file name to save under in the **File name** box .... Alt+N
6. Click **Save**................ Enter

Save to an FTP Server

1. Begin saving by doing one of the following:
   a. Click **File**................ Alt+F
   b. Click **Publish to the Web**................ T

   OR

   a. Click **File**................ Alt+F
   b. Click **Save As**................ A
2. Open the **Save in** drop-down list............. Alt+I
3. Click the FTP location you want to save to.

   OR

   - To set up an FTP location, do the following:
   - Click **Add/Modify FTP Locations**.
   - Type the FTP site name in the **Name of FTP site** box.......... Alt+N
   - Click the **User** option .... Alt+U
   - Enter your user name in the **User** text box.......... Alt+U
   - Enter your password in the **Password** text box................ Alt+P
   - Click **Add** .... Alt+A
   - Click **OK**................ Enter
   - Double-click the **FTP** location.
4. Navigate to the folder where you want to save.
5. Type file name to save under in the **File name** box....... Alt+N
6. Click **OK**................ Enter

Exercise Directions

1. Start Publisher, if necessary.
2. Open the file **PUB53**.
3. Use either FTP or Web folders to save the publication as a Web site directly to a Web server.
4. Use your Web browser to navigate to that location on the Web to make sure your pages are publicly accessible.
5. Send your instructor an e-mail message letting him or her know the URL of your site.
6. Exit Publisher.

On Your Own

1. Start Publisher, if necessary.
2. Open the file **OPUB53**.
3. Set the form properties to send an e-mail to your e-mail address when someone fills out the form.
4. Save your work as **53FORM**.
5. Use Publish to the Web but save to a location on your local hard disk.
6. Transfer the Web site to your Web server using a method that you did not use in the main exercise.
   - ✓ *For example, try the Web Publishing Wizard (which comes with some versions of Windows) or a third-party FTP program such as WS_FTP (available for free download from many file archives online). Or if you did not use FTP in the exercise, try it now.*
7. Using your Web browser, display the Web page on your server to confirm that it works there.
8. Try out the form by filling it out and submitting your data, to see if it will send you an e-mail of the form results.
   - ✓ *If it does not work (for example, if you get an error message when you click Submit), your Web server may not support FrontPage Server Extensions.*

Exercise 54

◆ **Critical Thinking**

Gardner's Garden Supply wants to have a Web site to showcase some of the plants and flowers it sells. Use text and graphics to build a Web site for the flower shop. Include an order form.

Exercise Directions

1. Start Publisher, if necessary.
2. Create a Web site based on the Summer design. Start it with the Easy Web Site Builder, but then do not choose any pages to add.
   ✓ *You will end up with a single page.*
3. Use the Primary Business personal information set, and set it up with the following information:
   - Name: **Jackie Gardner**
   - Address: **1644 West 206th St. Indianapolis, IN 46298**
   - Phone: **317-555-9871**
   - Email: **jackie@gardnergarden.com**
   - Organization name: **Gardner's Garden Supply**
   - Tagline or motto: **We help your garden grow**
   - Mist color scheme
4. Save the file as **54WEB**.
5. Make the following changes to the page:
   - Replace the sample text on page 1 with the text from the file **54TEXT.doc**.
   - Replace the clip art picture with a clip art or photo image of a flower from the Clip Organizer and delete the caption text box beneath it.
   - Tighten up the design where possible, eliminating extra vertical or horizontal blank space.
     ✓ *Illustration A shows one possibility.*
6. Add a new page, using the Product List page template.
7. Make the following changes to the page:
   - Name it Price List, both in the page title and in the navigation bar(s).
   - Change the phone number at the top of the page to 317-555-9871.
8. Modify the page to create a price list for at least four flowers. (Make up the prices as desired.) Use the pictures in the Datafiles folder to illustrate the various flowers. Or, use clip art and photos that you find on your own. The provided files are:
   - **54GOLDHOSTA.jpg**
   - **54BLACKEYEDSUSANS.jpg**
   - **54GREENHOSTA.jpg**
   - **54IMPATIENS.jpg**
   - **54SNAPDRAGONS.jpg**
   - **54MARIGOLDS.jpg**

   ✓ *Illustration B shows one possibility. It was done by deleting and combining some of the text boxes and making the pictures larger.*
9. Add another page, and use the Order Form page template. Name it Order Form, both in its title and in the navigation bar(s).
10. Customize the order form so that it can be used to order the flowers from step 10. Set the form's properties so that orders will be sent to **orders@gardnergarden.com**.
11. Add another page, and use the Special Offer page template. It should be the third page in the publication and the third item on the navigation bar.
12. On the new page, create a special 2 for 1 offer on one of the flower types. Make up the text, or use the sample text shown in Illustration C.
13. Delete the Organization logo from the top of each page.
14. Review the entire publication, making sure that a consistent font has been used and objects are placed attractively.

15. Preview the Web site and make any necessary changes.
16. Save your work.
17. Publish the Web site to a Web server specified by your instructor, or to a folder on your hard disk, in Filtered Web format.
18. Save your work and exit Publisher.

Illustration A

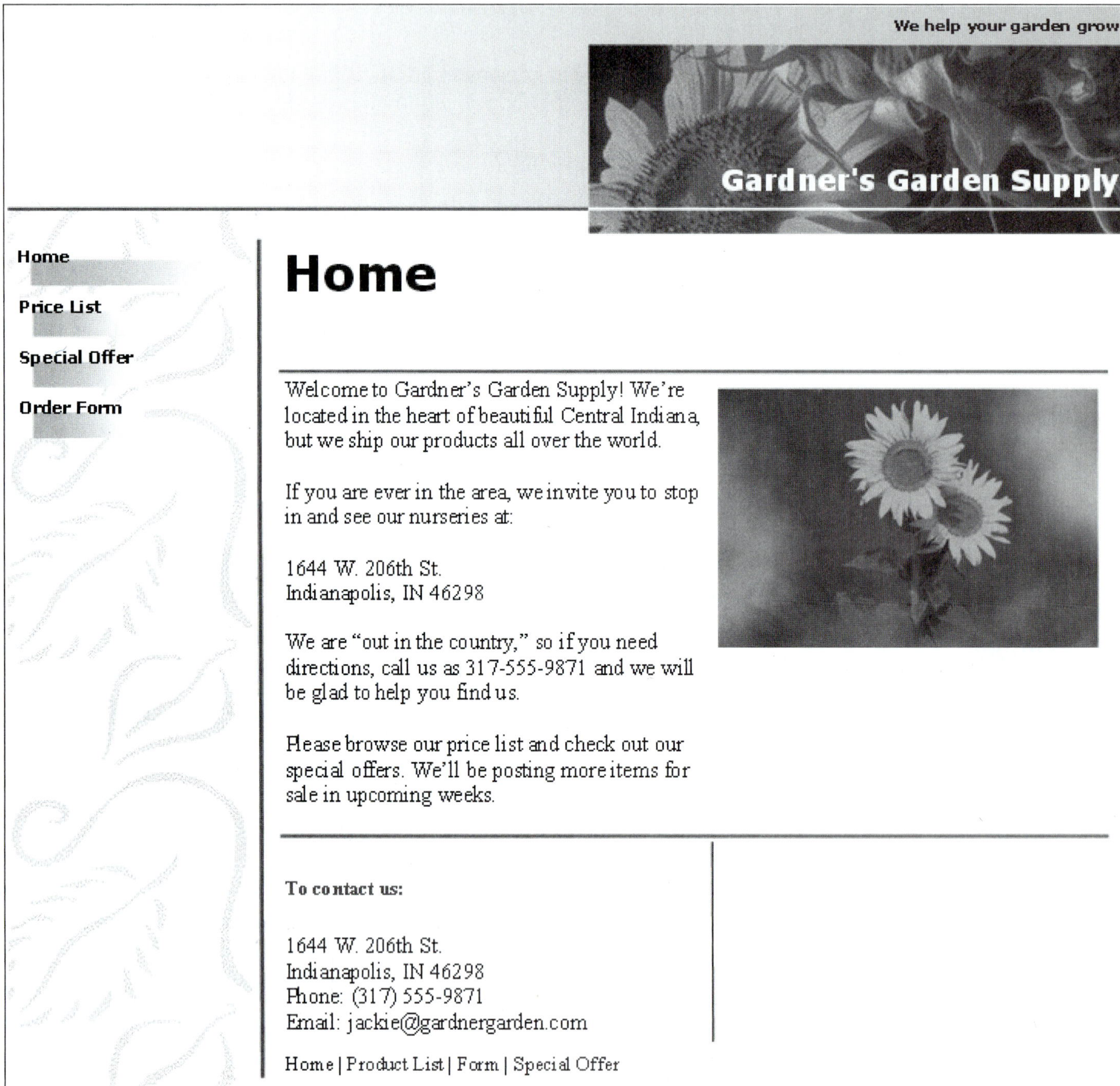

Illustration B

We help your garden grow

Home

Price List

Special Offer

Order Form

Price List

To contact us call:
317-555-9871

A few of our best-selling items appear here; visit our store for a larger selection.

Impatiens—Item #1001

Great for walkways and under trees. Prolific blooms in shady areas, many colors available including white, pink, peach, and red.

$1.99 per 6, $14 per flat

Gold Hosta—Item #1002

Thrives in the shade, and produces delicate white flowers on long spikes. Lush greenery for those hard-to-fill areas.

$4.99 per plant

Snapdragon—Item #1003

Cheerful sun-loving annuals that grow anywhere, even in rocky or sandy soil. Flowers grow up to 12" high.

$1.99 per 6, $14 per flat

Marigolds—Item #1004

Keep slugs and other pests away with these hardy buttons of color. Tolerates either sun or shade, but prefers sun.

$1.99 per 6, $14 per flat

Home | Product List | Form | Special Offer

Illustration C

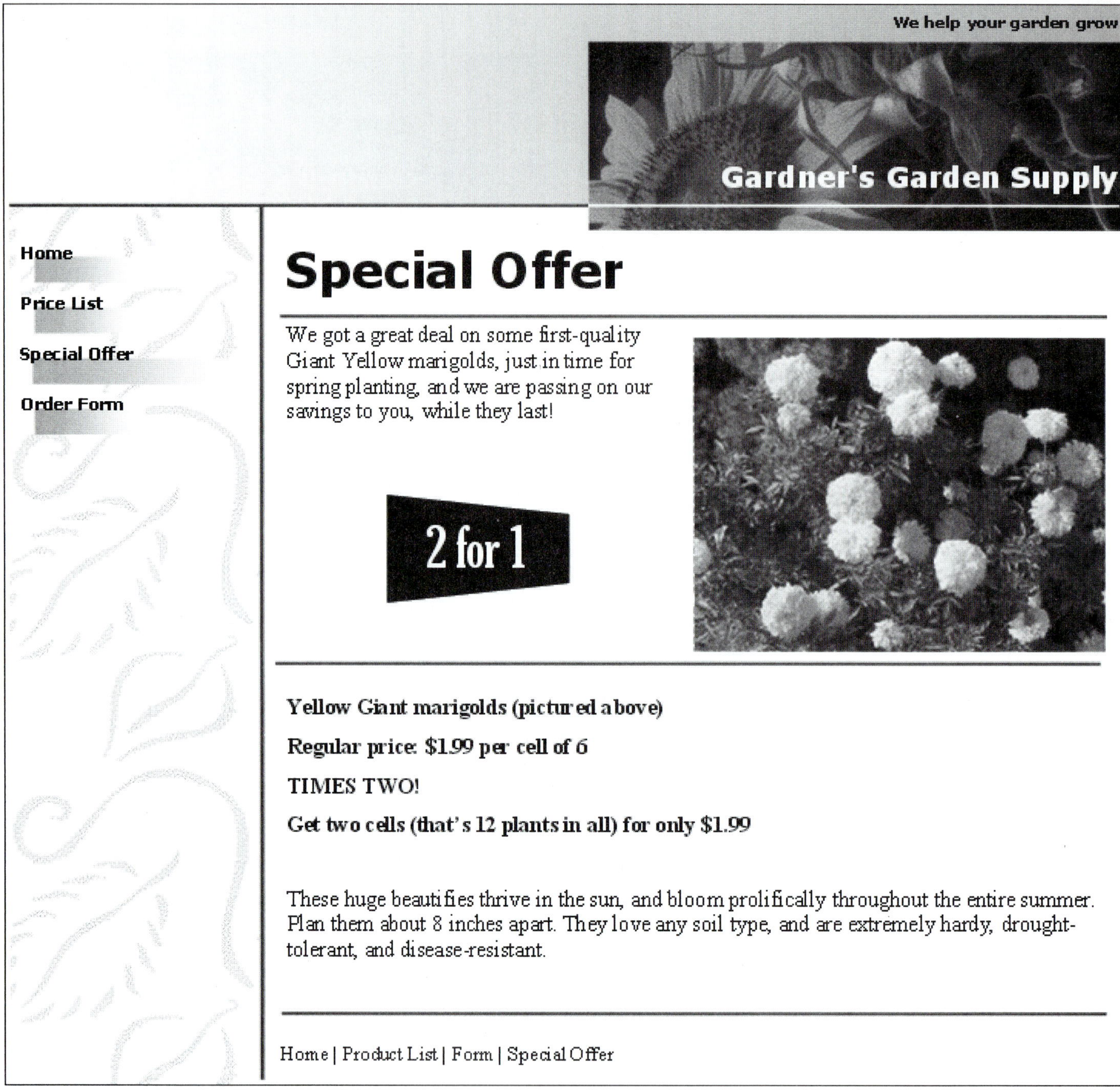

Index

D

E

F

Q

R

S

T

U

Notes

Notes

Notes

Notes

Notes

Notes

Notes

Notes

Notes

Notes

SINGLE PC LICENSE AGREEMENT AND LIMITED WARRANTY

READ THIS LICENSE CAREFULLY BEFORE OPENING THIS PACKAGE. BY OPENING THIS PACKAGE, YOU ARE AGREEING TO THE TERMS AND CONDITIONS OF THIS LICENSE. IF YOU DO NOT AGREE, DO NOT OPEN THE PACKAGE. PROMPTLY RETURN THE UNOPENED PACKAGE AND ALL ACCOMPANYING ITEMS TO THE PLACE YOU OBTAINED THEM. THESE TERMS APPLY TO ALL LICENSED SOFTWARE ON THE DISK EXCEPT THAT THE TERMS FOR USE OF ANY SHAREWARE OR FREEWARE ON THE DISKETTES ARE AS SET FORTH IN THE ELECTRONIC LICENSE LOCATED ON THE DISK:

1. GRANT OF LICENSE and OWNERSHIP: The enclosed computer programs and data ("Software") are licensed, not sold, to you by Pearson Education, Inc. ("We" or the "Company") and in consideration of your purchase or adoption of the accompanying Company textbooks and/or other materials, and your agreement to these terms. We reserve any rights not granted to you. You own only the disk(s) but we and/or our licensors own the Software itself. This license allows you to use and display your copy of the Software on a single computer (i.e., with a single CPU) at a single location for academic use only, so long as you comply with the terms of this Agreement.

2. RESTRICTIONS: You may not transfer or distribute the Software or documentation to anyone else. Except for backup, you may not copy the documentation or the Software. You may not network the Software or otherwise use it on more than one computer or computer terminal at the same time. You may not reverse engineer, disassemble, decompile, modify, adapt, translate, or create derivative works based on the Software or the Documentation. You may be held legally responsible for any copying or copyright infringement which is caused by your failure to abide by the terms of these restrictions.

3. TERMINATION: This license is effective until terminated. This license will terminate automatically without notice from the Company if you fail to comply with any provisions or limitations of this license. Upon termination, you shall destroy the Documentation and all copies of the Software. All provisions of this Agreement as to limitation and disclaimer of warranties, limitation of liability, remedies or damages, and our ownership rights shall survive termination.

4. LIMITED WARRANTY AND DISCLAIMER OF WARRANTY: Company warrants that for a period of 60 days from the date you purchase this SOFTWARE (or purchase or adopt the accompanying textbook), the Software, when properly installed and used in accordance with the Documentation, will operate in substantial conformity with the description of the Software set forth in the Documentation, and that for a period of 30 days the disk(s) on which the Software is delivered shall be free from defects in materials and workmanship under normal use. The Company does not warrant that the Software will meet your requirements or that the operation of the Software will be uninterrupted or error-free. Your only remedy and the Company's only obligation under these limited warranties is, at thc Company's option, rcturn of the disk for a refund of any amounts paid for it by you or replacement of the disk. THIS LIMITED WARRANTY IS THE ONLY WARRANTY PROVIDED BY THE COMPANY AND ITS LICENSORS, AND THE COMPANY AND ITS LICENSORS DISCLAIM ALL OTHER WARRANTIES, EXPRESS OR IMPLIED, INCLUDING WITHOUT LIMITATION, THE IMPLIED WARRANTIES OF MERCHANTABILITY AND FITNESS FOR A PARTICULAR PURPOSE. THE COMPANY DOES NOT WARRANT, GUARANTEE OR MAKE ANY REPRESENTATION REGARDING THE ACCURACY, RELIABILITY, CURRENTNESS, USE, OR RESULTS OF USE, OF THE SOFTWARE.

5. LIMITATION OF REMEDIES AND DAMAGES: IN NO EVENT, SHALL THE COMPANY OR ITS EMPLOYEES, AGENTS, LICENSORS, OR CONTRACTORS BE LIABLE FOR ANY INCIDENTAL, INDIRECT, SPECIAL, OR CONSEQUENTIAL DAMAGES ARISING OUT OF OR IN CONNECTION WITH THIS LICENSE OR THE SOFTWARE, INCLUDING FOR LOSS OF USE, LOSS OF DATA, LOSS OF INCOME OR PROFIT, OR OTHER LOSSES, SUSTAINED AS A RESULT OF INJURY TO ANY PERSON, OR LOSS OF OR DAMAGE TO PROPERTY, OR CLAIMS OF THIRD PARTIES, EVEN IF THE COMPANY OR AN AUTHORIZED REPRESENTATIVE OF THE COMPANY HAS BEEN ADVISED OF THE POSSIBILITY OF SUCH DAMAGES. IN NO EVENT SHALL THE LIABILITY OF THE COMPANY FOR DAMAGES WITH RESPECT TO THE SOFTWARE EXCEED THE AMOUNTS ACTUALLY PAID BY YOU, IF ANY, FOR THE SOFTWARE OR THE ACCOMPANYING TEXTBOOK. BECAUSE SOME JURISDICTIONS DO NOT ALLOW THE LIMITATION OF LIABILITY IN CERTAIN CIRCUMSTANCES, THE ABOVE LIMITATIONS MAY NOT ALWAYS APPLY TO YOU.

6. GENERAL: THIS AGREEMENT SHALL BE CONSTRUED IN ACCORDANCE WITH THE LAWS OF THE UNITED STATES OF AMERICA AND THE STATE OF NEW YORK, APPLICABLE TO CONTRACTS MADE IN NEW YORK, AND SHALL BENEFIT THE COMPANY, ITS AFFILIATES AND ASSIGNEES. HIS AGREEMENT IS THE COMPLETE AND EXCLUSIVE STATEMENT OF THE AGREEMENT BETWEEN YOU AND THE COMPANY AND SUPERSEDES ALL PROPOSALS OR PRIOR AGREEMENTS, ORAL, OR WRITTEN, AND ANY OTHER COMMUNICATIONS BETWEEN YOU AND THE COMPANY OR ANY REPRESENTATIVE OF THE COMPANY RELATING TO THE SUBJECT MATTER OF THIS AGREEMENT. If you are a U.S. Government user, this Software is licensed with "restricted rights" as set forth in subparagraphs (a)-(d) of the Commercial Computer-Restricted Rights clause at FAR 52.227-19 or in subparagraphs (c)(1)(ii) of the Rights in Technical Data and Computer Software clause at DFARS 252.227-7013, and similar clauses, as applicable.